"This book provides a 'fresh' look at co-occurring disorders with a consideration of the unification of all professionals to bridge a gap in the divide of treatment. It extends upon traditional treatment methods to include varied approaches to the rise in co-occurring disorders. A major feature includes the diverse list of contributors and the focus on the varied diagnoses in relation to SUDs via a cultural lens, taking into account the uniqueness of each client extending beyond a stereotypical DSM-5 checklist. Along with embedded assessment considerations, integrated care, and treatment protocol considerations, the breakdown of each section and the integrative treatments go beyond the typical protocols to expand the clinician's thinking."

Rosanne Nunnery, *PhD, LPC-S, NCC, BC-TMH, associate clinical professor of Counselor Education, Division of Education, MSU-Meridian*

"This text is a must read for counseling, social work, and psychology students as well as practicing clinicians. The content is presented in applied, rich, vivid detail, yet the authors are able to succinctly distill the main points of complicated issues (e.g., substance use disorder treatment) and theories into bite-sized nuggets which can be translated into clinical practice. The questions presented at the end of each chapter build off the content presented and challenge readers to think critically about the material. I highly recommend this book for mental health practitioners and students in training!"

Keith Klostermann, *PhD, LMHC, LMFT, NCC, CFT, core faculty, Walden University, fellow in Clinical Mental Health Counseling Education and Research, AMHCA*

"This is one of the few texts which conceptualizes the treatment of co-occurring disorders from an integrative counseling approach. The text reviews various evidence-based practices for application over multiple populations while addressing often overlooked aspects of treatment to support those living with co-occurring disorders. This text is appropriate for students obtaining their degrees in clinical mental health counseling programs, substance use programs, and future clinicians who will be working in the area of co-occurring disorders."

Samson Teklemariam, *LPC, CPTM, vice president, director of Clinical Services for Behavioral Health Group, LLC*

Co-occurring Mental Illness and Substance Use Disorders

This textbook details how mental health and addiction are interconnected through childhood trauma, how this affects neurobiology and neuropsychology, and the need for an integrated whole-person treatment for those of diverse backgrounds to enhance treatment outcomes.

Using an integrative pedagogy, the book helps readers broaden their understanding of co-occurring disorders through case studies, learning objectives, key terms, quiz questions, suggested resources, and references. By linking to previous knowledge and suggesting practical applications, each chapter provides clear direction for learning more about each treatment approach, diagnosis, and population discussed within the multicultural and biopsychosocial perspective.

Co-occurring Mental Illness and Substance Use Disorders will help graduate students in both substance use and mental health counseling make sense of integrative treatment with co-occurring disorders.

Tricia L. Chandler, PhD, MA, LPC, MAC, HomDI, began her clinical career in 1993 with adults, adolescents, and children with trauma, abuse, and co-occurring disorders in a variety of venues. She has been teaching in online and traditional university graduate counseling programs since 2010.

Fredrick Dombrowski, PhD, LMHC, LADC, has worked in behavioral health since 1999. He has won several awards for his work with marginalized populations. He is the president elect of the American Mental Health Counselors Association.

Tara G. Matthews, PhD, LPC, MAC, has worked in mental health and substance use treatment and prevention since 2004. She has been teaching in higher education since 2008.

Co-occurring Mental Illness and Substance Use Disorders

Evidence-based Integrative Treatment and Multicultural Application

Edited by Tricia L. Chandler, Fredrick Dombrowski, and Tara G. Matthews

NEW YORK AND LONDON

Cover image: © Getty Images

First published 2022
by Routledge
605 Third Avenue, New York, NY 10158

and by Routledge
4 Park Square, Milton Park, Abingdon, Oxon, OX14 4RN

Routledge is an imprint of the Taylor & Francis Group, an informa business

Library of Congress Cataloging-in-Publication Data
Names: Chandler, Tricia L., editor. | Dombrowski, Fredrick, editor. | Matthews, Tara G., editor.
Title: Co-occurring mental illness and substance use disorders : evidence-based integrative treatment and multicultural application / edited by Tricia L. Chandler, Fredrick Dombrowski, Tara G. Matthews.
Description: New York, NY : Routledge, 2022. | Includes bibliographical references and index.
Identifiers: LCCN 2021047452 (print) | LCCN 2021047453 (ebook) | ISBN 9781032116525 (hardback) | ISBN 9781032116518 (paperback) | ISBN 9781003220916 (ebook)
Subjects: LCSH: Mental illness—Treatment—Textbooks. | Substance abuse—Treatment—Textbooks. | Psychotherapy—Textbooks.
Classification: LCC RC480 .C565 2022 (print) | LCC RC480 (ebook) | DDC 616.89/18—dc23/eng/20211220
LC record available at https://lccn.loc.gov/2021047452
LC ebook record available at https://lccn.loc.gov/2021047453

ISBN: 978-1-032-11652-5 (hbk)
ISBN: 978-1-032-11651-8 (pbk)
ISBN: 978-1-003-22091-6 (ebk)

DOI: 10.4324/9781003220916

Typeset in Times New Roman
by Apex CoVantage, LLC

Contents

About the Editors   x
About the Contributors   xii
Editor's Note   xv
Acknowledgements   xvi
TRICIA L. CHANDLER, TARA G. MATTHEWS, AND FREDRICK DOMBROWSKI

SECTION I
Disorders of Mental Health and Addiction   1
FREDRICK DOMBROWSKI

1   **Trauma, PTSD, Substance Use, and Neuroscience**   3
TOM ALEXANDER, MARY C. HOKE, KARLENE BARRETT, AND TRICIA L. CHANDLER

2   **Mood and Anxiety Disorders**   17
TRICIA L. CHANDLER AND FREDRICK DOMBROWSKI

3   **Psychotic Disorders and Co-occurring Substance Use Disorders**   29
TRICIA L. CHANDLER AND FREDRICK DOMBROWSKI

4   **Co-occurring Personality and Substance Use Disorders**   43
FREDRICK DOMBROWSKI

5   **Attention Deficit Hyperactive Disorder**   58
FREDRICK DOMBROWSKI, NATASHA CHUNG, AND ROBERT YATES III

6   **Process Use Disorders**   72
FREDRICK DOMBROWSKI AND TARA G. MATTHEWS

SECTION II
Populations   85
TARA G. MATTHEWS

7   **Women With Co-occurring Disorders**   87
TRICIA L. CHANDLER, TARA G. MATTHEWS, AND FREDRICK DOMBROWSKI

8 **Men With Co-occurring Disorders**   98
TARA G. MATTHEWS AND TOM ALEXANDER

9 **Adolescents With Co-occurring Disorders**   112
TRICIA L. CHANDLER AND FREDRICK DOMBROWSKI

10 **Co-occurring Disorders Among the Older Adult Population**   123
KARLENE BARRETT AND TRICIA L. CHANDLER

11 **LGBTQIA+ and Co-occurring Disorders**   133
FREDRICK DOMBROWSKI

12 **Multicultural Perspectives in Co-occurring Treatment**   143
NATASHA CHUNG, KARLENE BARRETT, AND TARA G. MATTHEWS

SECTION III
Integrative Treatment Approaches for Those With Co-occurring
Disorders   157
TRICIA L. CHANDLER

13 **Assessment of Co-occurring Disorders, Levels of Care, and**
    ASAM Requirements   159
ELIZABETH REYES-FOURNIER, TARA G. MATTHEWS, AND TOM ALEXANDER

14 **Recovery Programming: 12 Steps, Cognitive Behavioral Therapy,**
    and Motivational Interviewing   177
FREDRICK DOMBROWSKI, TOM ALEXANDER, AND TRICIA L. CHANDLER

15 **Biological Approaches: Pharmacotherapy, MAT, Orthomolecular**
    Psychiatry, and Nutrition   196
TRICIA L. CHANDLER, MARY C. HOKE, TARA G. MATTHEWS, AND
ELIZABETH REYES-FOURNIER

16 **Consciousness: Spirituality, Mindfulness, Meditation, and**
    Mindfulness-Based Therapies   210
TRICIA L. CHANDLER, TARA G. MATTHEWS, KARLENE BARRETT, AND
M. A. LAWLESS COKER

17 **Creative Arts and Somatic Therapies: Psychodrama, Eye Movement**
    Desensitization Regulation, and Body/Mind Therapies   226
TRICIA L. CHANDLER, ROBERTA SHOEMAKER-BEAL, AND
M. A. LAWLESS COKER

**18 How East Met West: The Emergence of Energy Psychology as a
Body/Mind Treatment Approach** 241

TRICIA L. CHANDLER

19 Animal-Assisted Therapies 254

TARA G. MATTHEWS AND DAWN YELVINGTON

Conclusion 266

Index 267

About the Editors

Tricia L. Chandler, PhD, MA, LPC, MAC, HomD, Art therapist

Clinical background dates from 1993 working with adults, adolescents, children, and families with trauma, abuse, and co-occurring disorders in a variety of venues including day treatment programs, inpatient hospital and residential programs, day treatment school programs, outpatient programs, Child Protective Services, and Victims' Assistant programs, providing supervision for both interns and paraprofessionals. She has taught for the past 11 years at both online and traditional university graduate programs for Professional Counseling, Marriage Family Counseling, and Addiction Counseling Programs. In 2018-2020 as the liaison for revisions to the Addiction Counseling Program for Purdue University Global as the Subject Matter Expert to assist course lead instructors in revising the program leading to the recertification of the program with NCC AP. She has presented for NAADAC, ISSSEEM, as well as published in peer-reviewed journals and the History of Psychology encyclopedia published by Springer (2011). As a holistic therapist that has bridged allopathic and complementary treatment approaches throughout her clinical career, she has pursued education in trauma-informed care, energy healing, somatic expressive, and mindfulness-based therapies for improved integrative and thorough approaches for client care.

Fredrick Dombrowski, PhD, LMHC, CASAC, LPC, LADC, NCC, CCMHC, MAC, ACS, BC-TMH, HS-BCP, ICADC, DCMHS

He is the president elect of the American Mental Health Counselors Association. He is also a department chair and full-time professor with the University of Bridgeport. His clinical work started in 1999 with children, adolescents, adults, and older adults living with co-occurring disorders in various treatment settings. He has been a supervisor and director at outpatient substance use and mental health programs, inpatient treatment programs, and maximum security forensic hospitals. His work in higher education began in 2010, providing face-to-face and online education with mental health counseling programs, substance use programs, and post-graduate MD psychiatry programs. His commitment to teaching and supervision has contributed to receiving multiple awards as Teacher of the Year from the Westchester Medical College. He specializes in transgender treatment and has won multiple awards for work and advocacy for marginalized populations. He has multiple conference presentations over the past several years, including the ACA, AMHCA, NAADAC, and ACES. He currently serves on the AMHCA diplomate committee as well as a joint committee between AMHCA and NAADAC to enhance mental health and substance use counselor skills to treating those living with co-occurring disorders.

Tara G. Matthews, PhD, MA, LPC, MAC, INHC

Clinical background began in 2004 working with teenage girls and adults living with co-occurring disorders. This experience led to a passion for treatment and prevention and a strong desire to educate those living with co-occurring disorders. Background includes work with adolescents and young adults in the field of prevention and early intervention education as well as providing substance abuse education to adult probationers. There have been more than 15 years' experience facilitating clinical outpatient treatment groups with adults, specializing in single-gender groups and individualized treatment for co-occurring disorders. Higher education career began in 2009, which led to developing an online substance abuse certificate program in 2017. Since 2016, teaching graduate psychology courses in an addiction counseling program and maintaining a small private practice have been her focus. In 2018, Dr. Matthews earned a certificate as an integrative nutrition health coach and has applied that knowledge to help her clients clinically. Additionally, there is an extensive presentation background, including presenting at the National Conference on Addiction Disorders, NAADAC, the Tompkins Institute, and Virginia Summer Institute for Addiction Studies, as well as developing training programs for the Alcohol Safety Action Program.

About the Contributors

Tom Alexander, PhD, LPC, serves as a full-time adjunct faculty member in the graduate psychology department at Purdue University Global. He is passionate about teaching and leading others to better understand and engage in effective treatment practices within the field of addiction counseling. His clinical work and research interests are centered around the intersection of trauma and addiction.

Karlene Barrett, PhD, is a clinical psychologist and Credentialed Alcohol and Substance Abuse Counselor Master (CASAC Master) practicing in New York. Her experience as a clinician for over 20 years includes work as an internship supervisor, director of an outpatient SUD treatment program, and director of the department of counseling at a local church. Her specialization in working with diverse populations includes ethnic minorities and immigrant groups, geriatrics, people of faith, and people in recovery from substance use disorders. She is an adjunct faculty in the graduate psychology program at Purdue University Global, where she is also a thesis reader. Dr. Barrett currently maintains a private practice, and her research and clinical interests include trauma, cultural diversity, substance use disorders, and faith and spirituality.

Natasha Chung, PhD, is a clinical psychologist with 26 years of experience working with clients across the lifespan. She has specialized in the early diagnosis of childhood mental health and developmental/learning disorders, the behavioral treatment of inpatient children, and the multisystemic treatment of juvenile offenders with dual diagnosis issues. Dr. Chung has worked extensively with parents and families, adults with developmental disabilities who have comorbid mental health disorders, adults with dual diagnosis chronic mental health and substance abuse diagnoses, and sex offenders. Dr. Chung has appreciated the opportunity to work with a diverse clientele and with traditional and nontraditional students in the classroom, in addition to students completing practicums and internships. Dr. Chung is an associate professor at Baker College, an adjunct professor at Purdue University Global, and a faculty instructor at the University of Phoenix. She has worked with both graduate and undergraduate students for 13 years, teaching a wide variety of classes, including Cultural Psychology and Cross-cultural Psychology. Dr. Chung holds a second master's degree in instructional design and technology, specializes in online courses, and has participated in the design of several cross-cultural psychology courses. Dr. Chung also presents trainings on cultural competence and diversity within the workplace.

Mary C. Hoke, PhD, is associate faculty in the department of behavioral sciences at the University of Arizona Global Campus. She holds a doctorate in psychology and is licensed in both Arizona and Missouri. She is certified in mediation, holds the Master Addiction Counselor (MAC) credential and the Board-Certified TeleMental Health Provider (BC-TMH) credential. Dr. Hoke has experience as the chief operating officer and chief program officer of a clinical organization, with media (TV/radio/print/podcast), and with prevention programs, as well as experience in the direct delivery of clinical and addiction services, including diagnostic and developmental testing. Dr. Hoke is actively involved in teaching and developing curricula at the graduate level. She is published in the areas of group therapy with children, program evaluation, and nonprofit compensation strategy. Dr. Hoke's current research interest is in the area of the intersection between trauma and addiction.

Melinda A. (M. A.) Lawless Coker, PsyD, LMFT, CAP, TEP, has been a licensed marriage and family therapist for about 30 years and became a licensed psychologist 16 years ago. In addition, she's been an addictions professional for more than 25 years and became a psychodramatist trainer 8 years ago. She works with individuals, couples, families, and groups using action methods to confront trauma, enhance healthier communication, and support positive changes in people's lives. She's been a graduate educator for several years at Purdue University and was at Florida Atlantic University in the past. Regarding her philosophy, Melinda (or M. A.) compassionately orients herself to the unique needs of her diverse clients, establishing strong working alliances. This is a spiritual journey that brings groundedness in self-perceptions with others. Melinda believes it's essential to be gentle with others and to learn how practical it is to be in the here and now.

Elizabeth Reyes-Fournier, PhD, MA, is an instructor in the College of Social and Behavioral Sciences in the graduate psychology department in the general and addiction programs of Purdue University Global. She holds a PhD in psychology and a master's in counseling. When not teaching, she is focused on research in the areas of interpersonal relationships, lifelong learning, and education. Prior to academia, she worked as a psychotherapist, working primarily with use disorders. She has worked as the clinical director and program director for nonprofits, working with the Bureau of Prisons and the Department of Juvenile Justice to create programs for substance-dependent inmates and youth with co-occurring disorders. She is certified as a clinical hypnotherapist, NLP practitioner, and NLP life coach.

Roberta Shoemaker-Beal, MFA, ATR-BC, DTh (hon), is a pioneering art therapist, first as a clinician, then as an art therapy educator, researcher of arts-based assessments, and creativity consultant for 50 years, Shoemaker-Beal has been intrigued by our creativity dynamics and a creativity paradox: Creativity is ubiquitous in a healthy society, yet the personal creative process is unique to every person. During training and work at the Sheppard and Enoch Pratt Hospital, founded by two Quakers, she was able to develop a holistic art therapy approach during the early years of neurological research in the 70s in Baltimore. She developed a whole brain map for the creative arts therapies, first called the CONED: A continuum of neurological and evolutionary development for the preverbal therapies. In a desire to develop an accurate assessment of the complexity of challenging 'people puzzles', she worked on addictions units for 10 years in New Orleans. In a city with bars open 24-7, many addicted people were undiscovered 'preverbal perceivers, processors and producers', who were blocked in expressing themselves due to early developmental trauma, and who were detoured from developing healthy life designs. Recognized for her pioneering work, she was awarded an honorary Doctorate of Theology.

Robert Yates III, PhD, LP, LCAC, is a licensed clinical psychologist and licensed clinical addiction counselor. Dr. Yates is an adjunct instructor in the College of Social and Behavioral Sciences in the graduate general psychology program at Purdue University Global. Dr. Yates also teaches as an adjunct instructor at Fort Hays State University in the undergraduate psychology program. In addition to teaching, Dr. Yates is the owner and CEO of Serenity Psychological Services and Consulting LLC, a group mental health practice, in Hays, Kansas. Dr. Yates's clinical interests include working with individuals and families experiencing substance use problems, mood disorders, and anxiety disorder. He is involved in providing individual and family therapy services as well as a variety of psychological evaluations. Dr. Yates's research interests include neurocognitive issues related to alcohol and other drug use.

Dawn Yelvington, PhD, LMFT, qualified supervisor, Equine-Assisted Growth and Learning Association (EAGALA) Certified Professional MH and ES, EAGALA Military Certified individual and program designation. She is the clinical director of Healing Hearts Therapies & Equine, LLC where her organization provides equine-assisted therapy services to short-term co-occurring residential facilities treating both civilian and military populations. Dr. Yelvington's equine-assisted psychotherapy practices help clients struggling with PTSD, trauma, grief, co-occurring conditions, and many other challenges and diagnoses.

Editor's Note

Mental health counselors and substance use counselors, respectively, work primarily within their discipline at treatment programs that focus on either substance use or mental health. While this approach may have worked when mental health disorders and substance use disorders were considered separate issues, the literature and expansion of neurobiological understanding of brain functioning has expanded the knowledge of these disorders as being co-occurring and often having a correlation to early childhood trauma. Graduate courses in co-occurring disorders are a relatively new development in both addiction counseling and mental health counseling, and many of the textbooks created to assist with the conceptualization of working with individuals living with co-occurring disorders comes from medical doctors who are primarily trained in the administration of medicine to treat various diagnoses. The various contributions of countless medical doctors to the fields of mental health and substance use counseling are invaluable and have helped these fields grow and enhance personalized treatment. With that said, the vast majority of front-line workers providing treatment to those living with co-occurring disorders are not medical doctors and may vary in their education with primary focuses on substance use counseling, clinical mental health counseling, family therapy, and social work. Many co-occurring textbooks are not written from the perspective of counselors who provide treatment to individuals living with co-occurring mental health and substance use disorders. Thus, this text seeks to fill this void to enhance the services provided by both mental health counselors and substance use counselors. This text contains a compilation of mental health disorders and substance use issues that counselors will encounter in treating individuals and the specific treatment needs of a variety of populations that may have these co-occurring disorders, along with both traditional and newer evidence-based modalities while also providing foundational knowledge regarding different treatment options. The text has been written by practicing clinical counselors who are also working in academic settings teaching this course.

Acknowledgements

We would first like to acknowledge the family and friends who supported each of us throughout the development of this textbook. Without their support, we could not have found the courage, endurance, patience, or energy to complete this project. We would like to thank our mentors, our clients, and our students, who inspired our desire to create this textbook. We acknowledge that many voices are stronger than one and hope that our commitment to lifelong learning inspires your own.

We would like to acknowledge and thank the contributors to this textbook. Our scholar-practitioner colleagues with years of clinical practice in the counseling field, as well as years of teaching graduate counseling students, who contributed their valuable expertise to the text include Tom Alexander, Karlene Barrett, Mary C. Hoke, Natasha Chung, Elizabeth Reyes-Fournier, M. A. Lawless-Coker, and Robert Yates; thank you for all your work on this text.

A special thank you to the two experts in art therapy and equine-assisted therapy who collaborated on those chapters with their writing expertise and also for allowing us to use their artwork: Roberta Shoemaker-Beal, who contributed her original art on the Rainbow Brain, and Dawn Yelvington, who contributed a photograph of an adolescent with a horse in therapy.

There are others who gave their permission to use their illustrations that we would like to thank as well:

The CDC for the use of the ACEs Pyramid of Trauma.

Ratts, M. J., Singh, A. A., Nassar- McMillan, S., Butler, S. K., & McCullough, J. R. (2015), who allowed us to use the Multicultural and Social Justice Counseling Competencies illustration.

Richard P. Wilkes for the tapping diagram for emotional freedom technique (EFT) and thought field therapy (TFT).

Last but not least, thank you to our graphic designer at ELEMENTO PRO LLC for providing all the design work to professionally develop our art and illustrations into useable graphics for the text.

ELEMENTO PRO LLC
Printing – Web Design – Graphic Design Services
www.elementopro.com

We appreciate the collaboration and the creative work that has come forth to contribute to this text. We thank Grace McDonnell and Routledge Publishing for their assistance in so many ways in making this text a reality.

We would like to thank all the clinicians from various helping backgrounds who daily work to assist the lives of those living with co-occurring disorders. We thank the researchers who have come before us willing to conceptualize the need to treat mental health and substance use diagnoses concurrently while identifying the limitations of a one-track-at-a-time approach. We thank all the agencies that have worked tirelessly to promote community health via equity and advocacy. We thank those from various mental health and substance use organizations, specifically the American Mental Health Counselors Association and the Association for Addictions Professionals (NAADAC), which have remained committed to enhancing the skills needed by counselors to work with those living with co-occurring disorders.

We thank the friends and family members of those living with co-occurring mental health and substance use diagnoses as your support truly makes a difference even when things seem hopeless. The authors and editors of this text sincerely hope that this publication provides an opportunity to improve treatment, enhancing the lives of all clients, improving their relationships with their families, and promoting community and global change through an approach based on respect, cultural humility, equity, inclusion, and ongoing research enhancing the helping professions.

Most importantly, we thank the countless individuals who are enduring various diagnoses as they attempt to engage in meaningful life activities. We thank you for making your voices heard, allowing us clinicians to research and improve treatment. We are in awe of your resilience and would like to remind you that you are NOT a diagnosis but rather an entire person who can make the world a better place! Together we will make a difference!

Tricia L. Chandler
Tara G. Matthews
Fredrick Dombrowski

Section I

Disorders of Mental Health and Addiction

Fredrick Dombrowski

Those seeking treatment for mental health or substance use disorders often live with various diagnoses and face multiple stressors that impact their recovery. The divergent treatment modalities of substance use and mental health diagnoses have caused individuals who are living with co-occurring disorders to have incomplete treatment as their primary provider may treat only mental health or only substance use. Mental health counselors and substance use counselors are siloed and often approach treatment from their primary discipline, although it is rare that they will work with a client who only lives with a substance use or mental health diagnosis. It is more the expectation than the exception that an individual living with mental health disorders will also live with some form of substance use disorder. The helping professions have advocated for treatment options that allow an individual to work on mental health and substance use at the same time. However, many substance use counselors may feel unprepared to address mental health needs as they may feel this is out of their scope of practice. Additionally, mental health providers may lack the sufficient understanding of substance use treatment models and can confuse the behaviors associated with active substance use with mental health diagnoses. Both mental health counselors and substance use counselors can feel overwhelmed when working with an individual living with co-occurring disorders. The following section is designed to educate the reader about common mental health diagnoses that may present when treating an individual with a substance use disorder. This section will identify how personal experiences of trauma have long-lasting impacts on the lives of the individual and how this creates a pathway for various mental health diagnoses and the use of illicit substances to cope. This section will review how symptoms of various diagnoses may be misinterpreted if an individual is under the influence of substances. This section also reviews how individuals living with certain mental health diagnoses will have reactions to specific illicit substances and how this can exacerbate mental health symptoms. The purpose of this first section is to provide both substance use and mental health counselors with foundational information regarding the presentation of various mental health diagnoses with co-occurring substance use while also considering the role of trauma in the development of such disorders. By providing this information, the counselor can accurately assess their client's needs and link with appropriate treatment to allow an individualized and effective treatment plan to meet each client's unique needs.

DOI: 10.4324/9781003220916-1

1 Trauma, PTSD, Substance Use, and Neuroscience

Tom Alexander, Mary C. Hoke, Karlene Barrett, and Tricia L. Chandler

Introduction

Traumatic experiences can play a significant role in the development of substance use disorders throughout the lifespan. The overall impact of trauma on an individual is unique from person to person, but there are trends throughout epidemiological data and within scholarly literature that point to specific ways that trauma and substance use interact. The following chapter section will explore both the prevalence of co-occurring trauma and substance use and some of the underlying mechanisms by which past trauma influences substance use behavior through the mechanisms of trauma-related cuing and substance use craving response.

Learning Objectives

- Understand the impact of early brain development and childhood adversity on long-term mental and physical health outcomes
- Recognize the complex nature of co-occurring trauma and substance use disorders (SUD) in the lived experience of individuals
- Understand the importance of integrated care for both trauma and SUD
- Identify best practices treatment approaches for co-occurring trauma and SUD
- Understand the public health impact of trauma and SUD

Key Terms

Adverse Childhood Experiences (ACE): Trauma that occurs in childhood that affects an individual throughout the lifespan and increases the likelihood of developing other mental health and substance use disorders.

Co-occurring Disorder: A definition used when an individual has mental health disorders and substance and/or process use disorders.

Concurrent Treatment: Treatment that occurs simultaneously for all disorders.

Integrated Care: A team approach to treating those with co-occurring disorders that occurs in the same facility and can include multiple approaches to working with the individual from a biopsychosocial perspective.

Hope: A state of optimism that provides the individual with a brighter outlook on life despite adverse events that is one of the aspects noted in resiliency.

Neuroscience: The study of the brain.

Lifespan Perspective: A qualitative approach to including the perspective from the client of how different aspects of life have impacted their development and coping styles.

Posttraumatic Stress Disorder (PTSD): A severe anxiety disorder that develops from unresolved trauma events that adversely affect the individual on a biological, mental, emotional, and spiritual level.

DOI: 10.4324/9781003220916-2

Public Health: Includes all agencies, from schools, interfaith communities, the CDC, and mental health and medical professionals, who contribute to prevention and treatment programming.

Resilience: The ability to thrive despite adversity in one's life. It incorporates such aspects as hope, optimism, faith, well-being, wisdom, creativity, self-control, morality, gratitude, and forgiveness.

Overview of Trauma and SUD

Does trauma lead to substance abuse, or does substance abuse lead to trauma? This is a question often posed by students and clients, and the answer requires an understanding of the nature of substance dependence, trauma, and human development. The short answer is that trauma can lead to substance abuse, and substance abuse can lead to trauma, but how that happens can be complicated by many variables. Genetics and neuronal wiring present important insights into how this may occur.

Genetics and Neuroscience in Trauma and SUD

Substance use disorders (SUDs), as described in the American Psychiatric Association's *Diagnostic and Statistical Manual of Mental Disorders*, Fifth Edition (DSM-5) (2013), are primary, progressive, chronic, relapsing, and – most importantly – treatable diseases with evidence-based treatment principles and protocols. Neuroscience is defined as the study of how the nervous system develops, its structure, and what it does. It focuses on the brain and its impact on behavior and cognitive functions. From the perspective of neuroscience and considering the brain's plasticity, SUDs can be described as a remolding of the brain's circuitry, which can occur through both the introduction of psychoactive substances and the experience of early trauma (Fenster et al., 2018). In 2004, the World Health Organization (WHO) published a report entitled *Neuroscience of Psychoactive Substance Use and Dependence*. The report summary enumerated several points, including:

- A need to increase awareness of the complex nature and biological processes underlying drug dependence.
- Recent advances in neuroscience that demonstrate substance dependence is a disorder of the brain similar to other neurological illnesses.
- Substance dependence is a disorder with both a biological and genetic basis.
- The 'silo' mentality, which fragments mental health and SUD services, is a barrier to integrated treatment.

Research Studies

In the surgeon general's 2016 report, *Facing Addiction in America*, a number of options available currently, given the newest research studies, were not discussed. One of the newer treatments is medication-assisted treatment (MAT). Because addiction and the recovery process are often marked by cravings following successful completion of detox and treatment, MAT has been shown to be an effective adjunct to other treatment interventions. These cravings, which are of frequent occurrence, can impact treatment and increase the risk of relapse. The newer medications have proven to be successful in managing cravings and promoting abstinence.

Prevention

As with other behavioral health issues, the Mental Health Association (2016) continues to emphasize the need for effective prevention and the 2016 surgeon general's report supports that position.

Prevention is of particular importance in avoiding the effects of early substance use on the developing brain. During the transition from adolescence to adulthood, significant changes occur in the body, including rapid hormone alterations and the formation of new networks in the brain. Psychoactive drugs have been shown to produce an intoxicating effect by acting on one or more chemical messenger systems in the brain with potentially lasting consequences (Blum et al., 1995).

Recent Research in Genetics and Neuroscience

The most recent research suggests that SUDs can be treated by identifying individual differences in the addiction recovery process (Modestino et al., 2015). By exploring the molecular neurobiological basis of each step of a specific individual's recovery, the impact on the Reward Deficiency Syndrome (RDS) can be determined regardless of any genetic addiction risk (Blum et al., 2000).

The Reward Deficiency Syndrome (RDS)

RDS portrays behaviors found to have gene-based association with hypodopaminergic function. RDS is a useful concept to increase the understanding of SUDs, addictions, and other obsessive, compulsive, and impulsive behaviors (Comings & Blum, 2000). In personalizing each individual's recovery process, the Genetic Addiction Risk Score (GARS®) can play a major role (Blum et al., 2014).

The Genetic Addiction Risk Score (GARS)

The GARS has been found to be useful in the following ways:

*   Providing evidence genetically and biologically to predict risk for SUD
*   Guiding MAT dosing by considering certain genetic variations tested by GARS
*   Providing an exact mirror of the individual's brain's chemical messenger function (both receptor number and chemical production)

The GARS is a simple cheek swab that can identify an individual's genetic predisposition toward addictive, compulsive, and impulsive behaviors and personality disorders. These behaviors have been shown to share a common physiological root – an altered chemical balance in the brain, or RDS (Archer et al., 2011). There is extensive research on the neurogenetics of brain reward systems with reference to the genes related to dopaminergic function in particular. The RDS concept was developed based on animal and human research that explored the molecular biology of neurotransmission and behavioral genetics. The primary driver of RDS has been found to be a hypodopaminergic trait (genes) as well as epigenetic states (methylation and deacetylation on chromatin structure). This new era in addiction medicine embraces the neuroscience of addiction and RDS as a pathological condition in brain reward circuitry that calls for appropriate evidence-based therapy and early genetic diagnosis (Blum et al., 2018).

Customized Treatment Utilizing Genetics

Research demonstrates that 33% of the US population carries genetic mutations that result in a predisposition to certain addictions. If a person understands their addictive predisposition, there is more of an opportunity to minimize exposure. The GARS can provide insight into a patient's genetic predisposition to addictive behaviors and offers health care providers an opportunity to customize patient care. For example, if a health-care provider decides to prescribe a narcotic to a patient, GARS will identify whether or not that patient has a high predisposition to opioid addictive behavior. This will guide the best way to manage the patient's treatment medications. Thus, if a patient shows a high predisposition to opioids, a provider may want to prescribe a non-opioid medication. If there are no other alternatives and the patient must be prescribed an opioid, then use of the GARS can alert the prescribing professional that this patient needs to be prescribed a lower-grade opioid for a shorter amount of time with more monitoring, to help prevent addiction.

Lifespan Perspectives of Trauma and SUD

In addition to genetics, our understanding of trauma has further been expanded with the findings of research into childhood adversity and its long-term impact on adult health outcomes. Trauma can occur throughout the lifespan. Trauma can be a contributing factor for substance use disorders. Life-threatening situations associated with ongoing substance use can also cause trauma. Trauma will have a lasting impact on the individual if no interventions are provided.

Childhood Trauma

An important aspect of treating trauma is understanding the destabilizing nature of childhood adversity on emotional, cognitive, and physical development. The adverse childhood experiences (ACE) study conducted by Felitti et al. (1998) was a benchmark research into the impact of negative experiences during childhood on later adult life. Since then, research into the impact of childhood trauma has exploded, as has the understanding of risk and protective factors. Intervention strategies have also been developed that include preventing and addressing trauma within families and developing treatments to help both children who experience trauma and adult survivors of childhood trauma.

According to the Centers for Disease Control and Prevention (CDC, 2019) a child in the context of the research on ACE is 17 years or younger. The experiences of trauma may be directly and personally experienced by the child or involve family dysfunction. Direct traumatic experiences include physical abuse or neglect, emotional neglect, or verbal or sexual abuse. Those involving the family may include parental divorce or abandonment, parental substance abuse or incarceration, domestic violence, or serious illness of a family member. Risk factors include experiencing one or more ACE during childhood, and the risk increases as the number of adverse experiences increase. A recent study of ACE in 23 states (N=214,157) indicated that over 61% of adults 18 or older who participated had experienced at least one ACE, and almost 25% reported more than three ACE (Merrick et al., 2018).

Persons with a history of ACE are more likely to engage in behaviors that lead to chronic health conditions in adulthood; they have a lower life potential and may die earlier than others who do not have such a history (CDC, 2019). Also linked to ACE outcomes are socioeconomic issues such as unemployment and low educational achievement. Merrick et al. (2018) found the top three ACE were emotional abuse, parental divorce or separation, and substance abuse in the home. In the benchmark Felitti et al. (1998) study 20 years earlier, the most common risk-factor ACE were physical neglect, substance abuse in the home, and having criminally involved family members. Substance abuse in the home continues to be a significant causative factor of adversity during childhood.

For obvious reasons, the original research by Felitti et al. (1998) did not include other possible experiences of childhood trauma, such as those occurring in a social context outside the home. The impact of poverty, ethnic identity, socioeconomic status, and demographic challenges also factors into how children experience trauma and their access to quality treatment and support. This emphasizes the need to expand our understanding and definition of childhood trauma. One framework is complex trauma, which begins in childhood and, like ACE, has a potentially lifelong impact on physical and mental health as well as the individual's trajectory for social, educational, and economic well-being (Felitti et al., 1998). McLaughlin (2017) has expanded the framework for evaluating trauma and its effects with a model that consolidates research and identifies high/low threat and deprivation factors. This approach differentiates the functions of deprivation (neglect, abandonment) and threat (violence, abuse) and addresses the role of poverty and other social variables. The high frequency of childhood trauma combined with the potential lifelong negative mental and physical health outcomes create a significant public health problem. The need to address childhood trauma is urgent.

Approaches to Addressing Childhood Trauma and ACE

The generally accepted approach to addressing the drug epidemic in the US includes a three-pronged approach: prevention, treatment, and recovery. The National Drug Control Policy update (2005) indicated that prevention, treatment, and destabilizing the drug trade would be key strategies to addressing the drug epidemic in the US. Prevention is the most effective approach to addressing all disorders, including those that arise from childhood traumatic experiences. A key aspect of prevention focuses on educating parents about the dangers of substance abuse and prevention strategies with their children of different ages.

Primary prevention provides public education and the involvement of other health and social disciplines in addressing at-risk populations. For example, enabling medical professionals to screen for family substance use and educate families on risk factors is a preemptive step. With the raising of

> ACE Pyramid from the CDC website aligns with the research published on the correlation of childhood trauma with subsequent co-occurring mental health and substance use disorders from (Felitti et al., 1998). This research was a coordinated study supported by the CDC and Kaiser Permanente, and the study can be seen in the public domain of www.cdc.org.

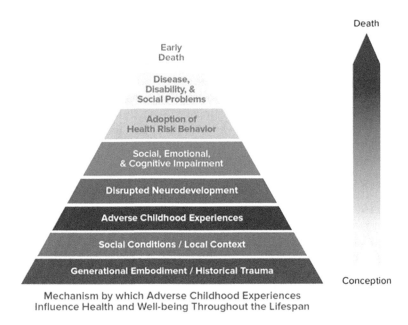

Mechanism by which Adverse Childhood Experiences
Influence Health and Well-being Throughout the Lifespan

Figure 1.1 ACE Pyramid Displays Mechanism by Which Adverse Childhood Experiences Influence Health and Well-Being throughout the Lifespan

Source: With clear indication that the use of CDC illustrations does not mean CDC endorsement, this is free art.

the level of awareness in communities, the vision is to facilitate positive attitudes and behaviors that prevent the onset of drug use. Secondary prevention utilizes early intervention strategies. In terms of ACE, strategies include educating parents, health-care providers, and communities regarding the impact of adversity on children and providing supportive resources to improve parenting and caregiving. Tertiary prevention involves treatment and rehabilitation of family members who are abusing substances, as well as children who are exposed to or have experienced these adversities.

Research indicates that intervention can ameliorate negative outcomes and capitalize on resilience factors (McLaughlin, 2017). There are different approaches to intervention, but all include the role of family and community supports, education, and resource access. One evidence-based approach is the Strengthening Families Program (SFP), which incorporates education and group-based interventions for both parents and children. It focuses on bringing families together to address problem behaviors, improve intergenerational communication, and develop life and social skills and has been utilized internationally and among different ethnic groups (Kumpfer et al., 1989).

Integrative Treatment Approaches

Impact of Complexity in Trauma Diagnosis

Trauma is prevalent in our society and often co-occurs with other mental or physical disorders (Felitti et al., 1998; Giordano, 2016). There are differences in how trauma is perceived within society and its clinical definition by the American Psychiatric Association (APA). The APA (2013) identifies four trauma- and stressor-related disorders among children and adults. However, much of the current research focuses on posttraumatic stress disorder (PTSD). To meet diagnostic criteria for PTSD, an individual has to have been exposed to a traumatic experience, either personally or indirectly: threat of death, witnessing someone dying, serious injury, or sexual violence. In addition, they will have experienced related intrusive symptoms, persistently avoided related stimuli, and experienced negative changes in thinking or mood and increases in arousal and reactivity for more than a month (APA, 2013). Some researchers and clinicians believe the definition begs for expansion to capture the lived experience of other kinds of trauma victims or survivors. Briere and Scott (2014) indicate that the current diagnostic criteria approach discounts events that may be traumatic but not life threatening and so does not fully capture the actual experience of everyone who experiences trauma. These authors take the perspective that traumatic experiences are those that are distressing, exhaust an individual's coping resources, and cause lasting psychological effects (Briere & Scott, 2014, p. 10). In summary, the literature generally agrees that trauma is pervasive within our society and involves significant distress and/or impairment in functioning.

Some types or sources of trauma exposure include:

* Interpersonal violence (e.g., domestic/partner violence, harassment, racism, bullying, etc.)
* Sexual violence (e.g., abuse, rape, sex trafficking)
* Military combat
* Gang-related behaviors
* Sudden and unexpected events (e.g., explosions, accidents, acts of terror)
* Medical procedures and health-related issues
* Consequences of drug use (e.g., homelessness, involuntary prostitution, serious health problems)
* Genocide (e.g., ethnic cleansing, persecution, political oppression)
* Natural disasters

Persons who experience trauma may face significant and long-lasting effects that include emotional, cognitive, and behavioral dysregulation along with physical health problems. Traumatic experiences can impact individuals, families, communities, and nations, and there are significant public health implications. For example, the Department of Defense spent almost $300 million in 2012 to treat veterans diagnosed with primary or secondary PTSD, and the individual cost was higher for those with co-occurring disorders (Institute of Medicine, 2014).

Importance of Treating Mental Health and SUDs Concurrently

There is a substantial relationship between mental health and substance use disorders. The analysis of the National Epidemiological Survey on Alcohol and Related Conditions (NESARC) (2017) demonstrated that of adults reporting a substance use disorder, 54% had experienced an anxiety disorder in their lifetime, and 34% had experienced a personality disorder in their lifetime. According to the 2016 surgeon general's report on substance use disorders, of the 20.8 million people aged 12 or older who had a substance use disorder during the past year, about 2.7 million (13%) had both an alcohol and an illicit drug use disorder, and 41.2% also had a mental illness. Particularly striking is the high prevalence of co-existing alcohol use disorder in those meeting the criteria for PTSD. It is estimated that between 30% and 60% of patients seeking treatment for alcohol use disorder meet the criteria for PTSD, and approximately one-third of individuals who have experienced PTSD have also experienced alcohol dependence at some point in their lives. According to SAMHSA's 2014 National Survey on Drug Use and Health (NSDUH), approximately 7.9 million adults had co-occurring disorders in 2014.

Mental Health America (MHA) advocates integration of the treatment of substance use and mental health disorders. MHA also recommends that early identification of both substance use and mental health disorders should be followed by early treatment. Prevention of disorders and promotion of health and wellness also should be fully integrated. Throughout this position statement, MHA seeks to raise the issue of parity of treatment for the substance use and mental health aspects of each issue addressed, even when the preceding literature has emphasized one or the other.

Prevalence in Current Research

To begin understanding the interaction of trauma and substance use behavior, one must consider the overall prevalence. Multiple research studies have found a significant link between trauma and the development of substance use disorders. Schäfer et al. (2014) conducted a study of over 3,500 participants with an opioid use disorder. The researchers reviewed data related to the experience of sexual violence by the participants; 65.6% of the female participants reported surviving sexual violence in the past, compared to 10.9% of the male respondents in the study. Keep in mind that the Schäfer et al. (2014) study specifically examined the presence of sexual violence and did not include the overall experience of other types of traumas. Additional research confirms high rates of various types of traumas experienced by persons with substance use disorders.

Giordano et al. (2016) conducted a study of 121 individuals in outpatient treatment for substance use disorder. Over 85% of the participants indicated surviving at least one traumatic event in their lifetime. Moreover, of the individuals who had experienced trauma, over 80% stated that they had survived more than one type of traumatic experience. Overall, Giordano et al. found that on average, those with a history of trauma had typically survived more than three traumatic experiences throughout their life. What the research by Giordano et al. (2016) confirms is that traumatic events are very common and complex among those in treatment for substance use, often including multiple experiences by those who have a history of surviving trauma. Along with Schäfer et al. (2014) and Giordano et al. (2016), a recent meta-analysis provides even more insight into the link between trauma and the development of a substance use disorder.

Halpern et al. (2018) conducted a meta-analysis review of ten research studies regarding the role of trauma and its effect on the development of a substance use disorder. The review focused on studies that specifically looked at the impact of childhood maltreatment, including physical abuse and sexual abuse. Concerning physical abuse, Halpern et al. (2018) found that survivors are 74% more likely to develop a substance use condition. Survivors of childhood sexual abuse were 73% more likely to have a substance use condition. Again, the preponderance of research evidence points to a high prevalence of trauma history among persons with a substance use condition. Though it is critically important to understand the considerable prevalence of trauma and co-occurring SUD, it is perhaps even more important to conceptualize the mechanisms by which past experiences can influence present behavior: namely, substance use behavior.

Exploring the Interface of Trauma and SUD

Lived Experience

When considering how early life trauma affects present-day substance use, it is important to consider data directly from the voice of persons who have survived trauma and are currently or have been in the treatment and recovery process for substance use disorder trauma. To effectively find such data, one must consider the rich knowledge that can be gleaned from qualitative research on the interaction of trauma and SUD. Gielen et al. (2016) conducted an impactful qualitative analysis related to the way in which persons who use substances experience the connection between their past trauma, craving, and recurrence of substance use.

To begin, Gielen et al. (2016) report that a significant connection was found within the interaction of PTSD, craving, and relapse. Regarding craving, the researchers discuss that the mechanism of craving regarding substance use can be triggered by symptoms related to traumatic experiences. Specifically, traumatic memories and even nightmares were discussed by one of the participants as triggers for substance use craving. Moreover, another participant described that substance use temporarily removed thoughts related to traumatic memories but led to increased depression when the effects of the substance wore off. Overall, Gielen et al. (2016) report that each of the participants in the study supported the hypothesis that traumatic intrusive thinking was correlated with craving and ultimately self-medicating behaviors. Prior to the study by Gielen and colleagues, additional qualitative analyses pointed to the link between substance use to cope with the effects of traumatic experiences.

Rothman et al. (2010) conducted a qualitative analysis that examined the link between adverse childhood experiences and underage drinking among young persons in the US. In total, 22 participants who reported experiencing more than two adverse childhood experiences and had initiated substance use prior to age 18 were given an in-depth, structured interview about their use of substances. Several themes emerged from the study that provide a glimpse into the etiology of substance use among youth, but the role of trauma stood out. The researchers highlight that youth who engage in heavy drinking on a daily basis typically use this behavior as a coping mechanism for living with challenging family situations, stress, and trauma (Rothman et al., 2010).

For youth who had lived through more than two adverse childhood experiences, the role of trauma in substance use behavior seemed to be significant. One can assume that the traumatic memories and nightmares discussed in the Gielen et al. (2016) study might have contributed to the daily/heavy substance use by the participants in the Rothman et al. (2010) article. Ultimately, we know directly from the voices of those who have survived trauma and use substances that the effects of trauma appear to be very direct upon substance use behavior. Looking beyond the substance use behavior alone, we find that there are some biological contributors to the impact of trauma on substance use and recurrence of use.

Neurobiological Implications

One of the keys to understanding the interface of trauma and substance use is found beneath the surface of the behavior alone and in the limbic system of the brain. Van Dam et al. (2014) conducted a highly impactful study related to the impact of child maltreatment upon the gray matter volume in the limbic system of the brain. The researchers discovered that persons who had survived childhood maltreatment had significantly less gray matter volume in the limbic regions of the brain, including the hippocampus. Van Dam et al. (2014) discuss that the lessened gray matter volume in the limbic system was found to be associated with greater risk for substance use relapse, along with the overall severity of relapse as well. Principally, Van Dam and colleagues highlight the underlying neurological mechanisms that impact substance use behavior among persons with co-occurring SUD and lived trauma experiences. Combining lived experience from qualitative research along with biological understanding from neurological study allows for a holistic view of the complex mechanisms that underpin substance use behavior among persons who have survived trauma. Conceptualizing the interface mechanism between trauma and substance use is only the beginning of what is needed to accurately diagnose and treat persons with SUD and trauma. The following section explores the vital roles of screening, assessment, and integrated care.

Screening, Assessment, and Integrated Care

Screening and Assessment

Due to the high prevalence of trauma among persons with substance use disorders, it is imperative to focus on best practices that can ensure early treatment response and intervention for co-occurring concerns. Van den Brink (2015) reviewed the literature focused on co-occurring trauma and substance use and recommended a more robust screening process. Specifically, Van den Brink (2015) recommends conducting a screening for trauma among those who are seeking substance use treatment and screening for substance use among persons seeking help for past trauma. A robust screening process would allow for increased awareness and subsequent monitoring of the interface between trauma and substance use throughout a person's treatment and recovery.

Evidence-Based Screening and Assessment Tools

When treating persons with co-occurring disorders it is important, as Van den Brink (2015) suggests, to thoroughly screen and assess for trauma history among all clientele. The Substance Abuse and Mental Health Services Administration (SAMHSA) (2014a) provides direct guidance on evidence-based screening and assessment tools aimed at identifying clients who may need further treatment and support for trauma-related sequelae. Some of the recommended screening and assessment tools provided by SAMHSA (2014a) include the PC-PTSD screen, the SPAN, and the PTSD Checklist (pp. 108–109). The PC-PTSD and the SPAN are very brief screening tools, aimed at determining whether or not further, more in-depth assessment is warranted for a client (SAMHSA, 2014b). The PTSD Checklist is a 17-item questionnaire that provides a bit more in-depth information about symptomatology that might be consistent with trauma response and, potentially, a diagnosis of PTSD.

Ultimately, evidence-based screening tools can be very effective in determining the potential need for assessment and subsequent treatment for trauma-related conditions. However, client self-report during the treatment process is vital as well, especially in the context of an effective therapist-client treatment alliance. Essentially, if the client trusts the health professional, the client may choose to disclose information about significant trauma that has been experienced.

Overall, when using client self-report and evidence-based assessments, a focus on establishing an environment of safety and trust with the client is key.

Integrated Care

Van den Brink (2015) also suggests that providing integrated treatment for trauma and SUD is best practice. Specifically, instead of utilizing one professional to treat trauma and another to treat SUD, Van den Brink suggests utilizing one professional who can treat both conditions simultaneously. From a clinical standpoint, integrated treatment allows the client to address both trauma and substance use behavior in the same context. In essence, integrated treatment allows the person in recovery to connect the impact of trauma on substance use in a cohesive and comprehensive manner. Treatment that is not integrated may pose barriers to progress and recovery due to the disjointed communication and lack of one overarching treatment plan between multiple providers and the person in recovery.

Treatment Protocols

As stated, best practice in treating co-occurring trauma and SUD disorders is to treat both concurrently and in an integrated manner (Burke & Carruth, 2012; Harris, 1998; Najavits, 2001). Evidence-based trauma and SUD treatment utilize different approaches. One approach is primarily education and skills based and teaches persons who have experienced trauma to develop healthy cognitive, behavioral, and emotional strategies to address the symptoms and after-effects of trauma and substance use. Building skills that address cognitive, behavioral, and emotional after-effects of traumatic experiences (such as flashbacks, dissociation, anxiety, fear, shame, guilt, and substance abuse) can help persons move forward, regain control of their lives, and implement safe behaviors for both substance use and trauma symptoms. This approach focuses on empowerment and safety and is usually group based. Some methods in this approach allow for sharing trauma experiences after developing safety skills (Covington, 2016; Najavits, 2001). The sharing is through a guided process that is nonintrusive and may include creative expressions such as art, dance, music, or storytelling.

Another approach involves enabling persons to talk more specifically about what happened through a process that prepares them emotionally and cognitively to do so. This method may incorporate cognitive, behavioral, and psychodynamic strategies and typically requires clinicians to be trained in specific techniques. Examples include exposure therapy and eye movement desensitizing and reprocessing (EMDR), as well as emotional freedom technique (EFT) (Argen et al., 2012; Nicosia et al., 2019; Shapiro, 2017). While these methods focus primarily on trauma treatment, there are benefits to those in recovery from SUD as they are also gaining skills that apply to other areas of coping.

Conclusion

Traumatic experiences have been shown through substantial research to play a significant role in the development of substance use disorders throughout the lifespan, as well as leading to other mental health disorders. The overall impact of trauma on an individual is unique from person to person, but the scholarly literature and neurological understanding of the limbic and reward systems of the brain have pointed to specific ways that trauma, mental health disorders, and substance use interact. The prevalence of co-occurring trauma and substance use, along with some of the underlying mechanisms by which past trauma influences substance use behavior through the mechanisms of trauma-related cuing and substance use craving response, demonstrates the need for increased prevention measures in society, along with integrative treatment for all these issues simultaneously for the best options for treatment and recovery.

Questions for Consideration

1.   What are the possible consequences of not identifying and treating underlying trauma?
2.   Not only does stigma play a role in the secrecy of trauma, but the skill level of the counselor to identify and address the trauma is also key to effective treatment. What steps can you take to ensure that your clients are treated holistically, and appropriate referrals are made?
3.   Addressing trauma takes specialized training, supervision, and experience. What trauma training have you had, and are you willing to engage in ongoing trauma training? Why or why not?

Case Study

Sally is a 34-year-old woman who is a successful professional emergency room nurse in a local hospital who has come into treatment for depression, suicidal ideation, and increased anxiety. She states that she does not understand why she has had this surge in depressive symptoms over the past few months, and she is very concerned with her emotional dysregulation and increased anxiety, along with poor sleep. She started drinking wine every night to try to help her fall asleep, but that has not helped her function better, and the level of drinking has increased from a couple of glasses to finishing a bottle of wine by herself daily. Her poor coping behaviors are beginning to impact her ability to work, and she is calling in to say she is sick almost every week for one or more shifts. When asked if there have been any changes in work or home environment that might have contributed to her increased anxiety and depressive symptoms she thinks for a few minutes before relating an incident that happened about three months ago. A child came into the ER who had been removed from the home by Child Protective Services for abuse. The child was a 6-year-old girl who had been physically beaten to the point of broken bones and bruises all over her body, and when examined thoroughly, there was evidence she had also been sexually abused. Sally stated that it broke her heart to see the awful treatment this child had endured, and once she had treated the child, she became visibly anxious and weepy, resulting in her leaving her shift early. Since that occurrence, she has felt increasingly despondent, depressed, and anxious to the point of feeling unsafe, being hypervigilant, and, in the past few days, having feelings of wanting to end her life. Sally states that she had a happy childhood to the best of her memory, and she does not understand why these feelings are occurring.

Questions

1.   If you were the counselor in this situation what would be the red flags in this case study?
2.   What would you want to know more about to help you formulate a case conceptualization of the client?
3.   What assessments might help you develop a thorough understanding of the trauma issues that Sally has experienced in her early childhood?
4.   How would you develop an understanding of the level of care Sally needs?
5.   What would your diagnosis and treatment recommendations be for her, based on reported symptoms? What is the evidence to support this diagnosis?

Case Study

Marcia is a 24-year-old Hispanic female who has been referred to you by a social worker in the emergency room. You are working as the emergency counselor at the local social services office and have been called to access her need for ongoing treatment. Marcia was left at the hospital after being beaten and losing consciousness. Marcia's roommate, Beth, brings Marcia to your office straight from the hospital and tells you they were separated last night during a party and that Marcia 'seemed really out of it' when she last saw her. Neither of them knows what happened or how she ended up in the emergency room. The social worker's report indicated that Marcia had been sexually assaulted and had a high level of opioids and alcohol in her system at the time of admission. Since Marcia has no recollection of what happened the previous night, Marcia has invited Beth to add as much clarity as possible. Before Beth leaves, she tells you that she noticed that her pain medicine was missing, and she believes that Marcia took several pills before they went to the party.

Questions

1. What clinical concerns do you have for Marcia?
2. Since she does not remember the sexual assault, how important do you think that will be in her treatment plan?
3. What background or history would you like to collect from Marcia before making a diagnosis or treatment recommendation?

Recommended Reading

Working with individuals who have experienced a recent traumatic incident (natural disaster, accident, terrorist attack) can be difficult for front-line staff. It is recommended that counselors become aware of the application of psychological first aid to help enhance recovery of the individual while preventing long-term symptoms of PTSD. The World Health Organization provides free information about psychological first aid. This can be found at the following link:

www.who.int/publications/i/item/psychological-first-aid

As many counselors will use CBT-based approaches to work with individuals living with trauma, a specific trauma-focused CBT program has been created. Counselors interested in becoming certified in trauma-focused CBT can visit the following website:

www.tfcbt.org/

References

American Psychiatric Association. (2013). *Diagnostic and statistical manual of mental disorders* (5th ed.). Author.

Archer, T., Oscar-Berman, M., & Blum, K. (2011). Epigenetics in developmental disorder: ADHD and endophenotypes. *Journal of Genetics Syndromes and Gene Therapy, 2*(104), 1–17.

Argen, T., Engman, J., Frick, A., Bjorkstrand, J., Larsen, E., Fumark, T., & Fredrikson, M. (2012). Disruption of reconsolidation erases a fear memory trace in the human amygdala. *Science, 337*, 1550–1552.

Blum, K., Braverman, E., Holder, J., Lubar, J., Monastra, V., Miller, D., . . . Comings, D. (2000). Reward deficiency syndrome: A biogenetic model for the diagnosis and treatment of impulsive, addictive and compulsive behaviors. *Journal of Psychoactive Drugs, 32*(1), 112.

Blum, K., Madigan, M., Fried, L., Braverman, E., Giordano, J., & Badgaiyan, R. (2018). Coupling Genetic Addiction Risk Score (GARS) and pro dopamine regulation (KB220) to combat Substance Use Disorder (SUD). *Global Journal of Addiction and Rehabilitation Medicine, 1*(2). doi:10.19080/GJARM.2017.01.555556

Blum, K., Oscar-Berman, M., Demetrovics, Z., Barh, D., & Gold, M. (2014). Genetic Addiction Risk Score (GARS): Molecular neurogenetic evidence for predisposition to Reward Deficiency Syndrome (RDS). *Molecular Neurobiology, 50*(3), 765–796.

Blum, K., Wood, R., Braverman, E., Chen, T., & Sheridan, P. (1995). The D2 dopamine receptor gene as a predictor of compulsive disease: Bayes' theorem. *Functional Neurology, 10*(1), 37–44.

Briere, J. N., & Scott, C. (2014). *Principles of trauma therapy: A guide to symptoms, evaluation, and treatment* (2nd ed). Sage.

Burke, P. A., & Carruth, B. (2012). Addiction and psychological trauma: Implications for counseling strategies. In L. L. Levers (Ed.), *Trauma counseling: Theories and interventions* (pp. 214–230). Springer.

Centers for Disease Control and Prevention. (2019, April). *Violence prevention: About adverse childhood experiences*. US Department of Health and Human Services.

Comings, D., & Blum, K. (2000). Reward deficiency syndrome: Genetic aspects of behavioral disorders. *Journal of Progressive Brain Research, 126,* 325–341.

Covington, S. (2016). *Beyond trauma: A healing journey for women* (2nd ed.). Hazelden.

Felitti, V. J., Anda, R. F., Nordenberg, D., Williamson, D. F., Spitz, A. M., Edwards, V., . . . Marks, J. S. (1998). Relationship of childhood abuse and household dysfunction to many of the leading causes of death in adults: The Adverse Childhood Experiences (ACE) study. *American Journal of Preventive Medicine, 14*(4), 245–258.

Fenster, R., Lebois, L., Ressler, K., & Suh, J. (2018). Brain circuit dysfunction in post-traumatic stress disorder: From mouse to man. *Nature Reviews Neuroscience, 19*(9), 535–551.

Gielen, N., Krumeich, A., Tekelenburg, M., Nederkoorn, C., & Havermans, R. C. (2016). How patients perceive the relationship between trauma, substance abuse, craving, and relapse: A qualitative study. *Journal of Substance Use, 21*(5), 466–470. doi:0.3109/14659891.2015.1063717

Giordano, A. L., Prosek, E. A., Stammman, J., Callahan, M. M., Loseu, S., Bevly, C. M., . . . Chadwell, K. (2016). Addressing trauma in substance abuse treatment. *Journal of Alcohol and Drug Education, 60*(2), 55–71.

Halpern, S. C., Schuch, F. B., Scherer, J. N., Sordi, A. O., Pachado, M., Dalbosco, C., . . . Von Diemen, L. (2018). Child maltreatment and illicit substance abuse: A systematic review and meta-analysis of longitudinal studies. *Child Abuse Review, 27*(5), 344–360. https://doi.org/10.1002/car.2534

Harris, M. (1998). *Trauma recovery and empowerment: A clinician's guide for working with women in groups.* The Free Press.

Institute of Medicine. (2014). *Treatment for posttraumatic stress disorder in military and veteran populations: Final assessment.* The National Academies Press.

Kumpfer, K. L., DeMarsh, J. P., & Child, W. (1989). *Strengthening families program: Children's skills training curriculum manual, parenting training manual, children's skill training manual, and family skills training manual (Prevention services to children of substance abusing parents).* University of Utah, Social Research Institute, Graduate School of Social Work.

McLaughlin, K. (2017). The long shadow of adverse childhood experiences. *Psychological Science Agenda.* Retrieved from www.apa.org/science/about/psa/2017/04/adverse-childhood

Mental Health Association. (2016). Retrieved from www.mhanational.org/

Merrick, M. T., Ford, D. C., Ports, K. A., & Guinn, A. S. (2018). Prevalence of adverse childhood experiences from the 2011–2014 behavioral risk factor surveillance system in 23 states. *JAMA Pediatrics, 172*(11), 1038–1044.

Modestino, E., Blum, K., Oscar-Berman, M., Gold, M., Duane, D., . . . Auerbach, S. (2015). Reward deficiency syndrome: Attentional/arousal subtypes, limitations of current diagnostic nosology, and future research. *Journal of Reward Deficiency Syndrome (Journal of Addiction Science), 1*(1), 6–9.

Najavits, L. M. (2001). *Seeking safety: A treatment manual for PTSD and substance abuse.* Guilford.

National Epidemiological Survey on Alcohol and Related Conditions (NESARC). (2017). Retrieved from www.niaaa.nih.gov/

Nicosia, G., Minewiser, L., & Freger, A. (2019). World trade center: A longitudinal case study for treating post traumatic stress disorder with emotional freedom technique and eye movement desensitization regulation. *Work, 63*(2), 199–204.

Office of National Drug Control Policy. (2005). *National drug control strategy update.* The White House. Retrieved from www.ncjrs.gov/pdffiles1/ondcp/208669.pdf

Rothman, E. F., Bernstein, J., & Strunin, L. (2010). Why might adverse childhood experiences lead to underage drinking among US youth? Findings from an emergency department based qualitative pilot study. *Substance Use & Misuse, 45*(13), 2281–2290. https://doi.org/10.3109/10826084.2010.482369

Schäfer, I., Gromus, L., Atabaki, A., Pawils, S., Verthein, U., & Reimer, J. (2014). Are experiences of sexual violence related to special needs in patients with substance use disorders? A study in opioid-dependent patients. *Addictive Behaviors, 39,* 1691–1694. Retrieved from www.ncbi.nlm.nih.gov/pubmed/25117843

Shapiro, F. (2017). *Eye Movement Desensitizing and Reprocessing (EMDR) therapy: Basic principles, protocols, and procedures* (3rd ed.). Guilford.

Substance Abuse and Mental Health Services Administration. (2014a). *National survey on drug use and health*. US Department of Health and Human Services.

Substance Abuse and Mental Health Services Administration. (2014b). *Trauma-informed care in behavioral health services*. Treatment Improvement Protocol (TIP) Series 57. HHS Publication No. (SMA) 13–4801.

Substance Abuse and Mental Health Services Administration (US), & Office of the Surgeon General (US). (2016). *Facing addiction in America: The surgeon general's report on alcohol, drugs, and health*. US Department of Health and Human Services.

Van Dam, N. T., Rando, K., Potenza, M. N., Tuit, K., & Sinha, R. (2014). Childhood maltreatment, altered limbic neurobiology, and substance use relapse severity via trauma specific reductions in limbic gray matter volume. *JAMA Psychiatry*, *71*(8), 917–925. https://doi.org/10.1001/jamapsychiatry.2014.680

Van den Brink, W. (2015). Substance use disorders, trauma, and PTSD. *European Journal of Psychotraumatology*, *6*. doi:10.3402/ejpt.v6.27632

World Health Organization. (2004). Retrieved from www.who.int/

2 Mood and Anxiety Disorders

Tricia L. Chandler and Fredrick Dombrowski

Introduction

Mood and anxiety disorders are commonly diagnosed concurrently. Substance use disorders can be triggered by ineffective coping skills to gain relief from untreated mood and anxiety disorders or develop simultaneously. In those who have co-occurring disorders, it has been noted that depression rarely is seen in an individual without a significant amount of anxiety as well (Watson, 2005; Kessler et al., 2007). Thus, it seems relevant to combine the two types of disorders in the same chapter. This chapter will discuss how these underlying disorders can develop, causal issues that contribute to the development of these disorders, and how these disorders often lead to self-medicating with substance use and process use disorders.

Within the depressive or uni-polar disorders, both major depressive disorder and persistent depressive disorder are common. Depression can be seasonal, connected to the menses cycle, and post-partum after having a baby, as well as being brought on by trauma, grief, loss, and deficiencies in serotonin and norepinephrine in transmitters. Long-term or diathesis stress is also a contributor (Schildkraut, 1965; Garlow & Nemeroff, 2003; Southwick et al., 2005; Thase, 2009a; Pinel & Barnes, 2018). Bipolar I and bipolar II disorders represent the mood disorders that contain elements of both mania or hypomania and depressive symptoms. Anxiety has been separated into three different chapters in the *DSM-5* (American Psychiatric Association, 2013) due to the different reasons the disorders manifest from a developmental perspective. The first classification of anxiety disorders includes those induced by fear and avoidance due to persistent anticipation of negative experiences in the future, such as separation anxiety, panic, and social or generalized anxiety disorders (American Psychiatric Association, 2013). The second section focuses on obsessive-compulsive disorders, which include OCD, body dysmorphic disorder, and hoarding disorders that are characterized by the creation of rituals that are excessive and persistent to manage anxiety around intrusive thoughts (American Psychiatric Association, 2013). The third classification of anxiety disorders includes trauma and acute stress disorders, of which posttraumatic stress disorder and acute stress disorder are discussed (American Psychiatric Association, 2013). With the prevalence of mood and anxiety disorders contributing to maladaptive coping methods in those who have no or minimal access to appropriate treatment, this chapter will discuss the disorders – prevalence, age of onset, and gender differences in developing these disorders – and the reasons that people of all ages, cultures, and socioeconomic status may self-medicate to numb their symptoms.

Learning Objectives

- Examine the overlapping issues between mood and anxiety disorders
- Understand the correlation between mood and anxiety disorders and substance use disorders
- Learn about the neurotransmitters that are affected by mood and anxiety disorders

DOI: 10.4324/9781003220916-3

Key Terms

Affect: The physical display of an emotional response. For example, if an individual hears a funny joke, they will laugh.

Anxiety: A combination of worry, unease, and nervousness often associated with danger or an uncertain outcome. Anxiety is an appropriate human emotion that helps signal the individual to act.

Anxiety Disorder: A set of diagnoses that occur when the feelings associated with anxiety have a detrimental impact on various aspects of the individual's life.

Depressive Disorder: A set of diagnoses related to feelings of sadness in which the symptoms have impacted various aspects of the individual's life, limiting optimal functioning.

Manic Depression: A term previously used to describe symptoms associated with bipolar disorder.

Mood Disorder: A set of diagnoses related to the elevation or lowered aspects of an individual's mood. These symptoms are observed in such diagnoses as major depressive disorder and bipolar disorder.

Psychological Decompensation: When an individual's symptoms become so severe that they are unable to take immediate steps on goals or desired outcomes, often indicating a higher level of care. Such instances can be associated with psychosis or suicidality.

Sadness: A combination of unhappiness associated with disappointment and sorrow. Sadness is an appropriate human emotion that allows the individual to respond to an unperceived and undesired outcome.

DSM-5 **Criteria for Mood Disorders**

Depressive Disorders

Depression is characterized as a disorder that adversely affects emotional regulation, with varying levels of intense feelings of sadness, emptiness, and hopelessness; decreased or increased appetite; sleep disturbances daily; fatigue and loss of energy leading to lower motivation; diminished ability to think and concentrate; and feelings of worthlessness and, for some, suicidal ideation in adolescents and adults (American Psychiatric Association, 2013). The way that these symptoms manifest and the reasons for developing depression are as diverse as the individuals who have the disorders.

Major Depressive Disorder (American Psychiatric Association, 2013, pp. 160–168)

In major depressive disorder, the individual needs to meet criteria for five or more of the symptoms of those noted here with persistent disturbance for two weeks to receive the diagnosis with either depressed mood or loss of interest and pleasure being one of the criteria. The main feature of major depressive disorder is that the symptoms have been persistently present every day for at least two weeks, and these symptoms are significantly interfering with the individual's ability to function (American Psychiatric Association, 2013, pp. 160–168). While major depressive episodes can go into remission for weeks, months, or years, research has indicated the reoccurrence occurs frequently, and when diathesis stress is extreme, the symptoms can become progressively worse over time.

Persistent Depressive Disorder (American Psychiatric Association, 2013, pp. 168–171)

Persistent depressive disorder (PDD) is the name given to what used to be called dysthymic disorder prior to the latest edition of the *Diagnostic and Statistical Manual of Mental Disorders*

(*DSM-5*). PDD is a chronic but less severe form of depression that requires at least two of the depressive criteria and symptoms that happen for most of the day, for more days than not, over a two-year period for adults and a one-year period for children and adolescents, which also may include irritable mood in children (American Psychiatric Association, 2013, p. 168). Research has indicated that between 10% and 20% of people who have major depressive disorder (MDD) will still have symptoms after two years, and PDD will be the diagnosis (Boland & Keller, 2009; Gilmer et al., 2005). PDD can remit over some years or go on for decades, and chronic or diathesis stress can increase the severity of symptoms over time (Dougherty et al., 2004).

Prevalence, Age of Onset, and Gender Differences

While children, adolescents, and adults can develop depression, major depressive disorder has been thought to occur more often as a first episode in adolescents, with 15% to 20% of teens developing MDD, and 10% to 20% of adolescents will additionally develop lower levels of depressive symptoms, even if these are not clinically identified (Avenevoli et al., 2008; Lewinsohn & Essau, 2002). PDD often begins in adolescence as well, with 50% of those beginning prior to age 21 (Klein et al., 2006; Klein, 2010). PDD is quite common, with statistics suggesting between 2.5% and 6% of the population has the disorder (Kessler et al., 2005c). Due to its chronic nature, PDD can lead to poor outcomes for recovery (Klein, 2010). The lifetime prevalence of developing MDD is 17% of the population (Kessler et al., 2003, 2005c, 2007). Females are twice as likely as males to develop depressive symptoms, and these disorders seem to be the most prevalent from adolescence to elder years (Hasin et al., 2005; Nolan-Hoeksema & Hilt, 2009; Nolen-Hoeksema, 2012).

Genetics and Neurobiological Factors

Mood disorders have a genetic connection that suggests if there is familial history of individuals with the disorders, then there is an increased propensity for first-degree relatives to have a two-to-four-times higher risk for developing one of the mood disorders, with heritability considered to be at 49% of those who develop MDD or PDD, especially if there is also neuroticism as a personality trait in the individual (American Psychiatric Association, 2013, p. 166). Brain regions implicated in PDD include the prefrontal cortex, anterior cingulate, amygdala, and hippocampus (p. 170). Neurotransmitters serotonin and norepinephrine began being studied for the correlation between potential vitamin, amino acids and mineral deficiencies leading to depression due to the catecholamine hypothesis of affective disorders (Schildkraut, 1965; Thase, 2009b). While this direction of research has not been followed by allopathic medicine initially, it is known that these particular neurotransmitters are involved in the regulation of behaviors and activities, stress levels, emotional expression, and physiological activities like appetite, sleep, and arousal to stimuli, and all of these correspond to symptoms found in mood disorders (Garlow & Nemeroff, 2003; Southwick, 2005; Thase, 2009b). Additionally, abnormal hormone regulation and immune systems have been studied with the correlation to the hypothalamic – pituitary adrenal – hormone cortisol (HPA) and adrenal glands, as human stress response elevated activity of the HPA axis, which is partially controlled by norepinephrine and serotonin (Thase, 2009b). Elevated cortisol levels are adaptive when one is faced with life-threatening situations that involve the fight, flight, freeze response in the limbic brain but become maladaptive if the levels stay elevated long term and can lead to obesity, hypertension, and/or heart disease.

Bipolar Disorders

Bipolar I and bipolar II disorders are characterized as having two distinct poles of mania or hypermania, along with depressive episodes, while cyclothymic disorder can be diagnosed in adults if they have experienced two years of hypomania and depressive episodes that do not meet clinical criteria for either BDI or BDII (American Psychiatric Association, 2013, p. 123).

Bipolar I Disorder (American Psychiatric Association, 2013, pp. 123–168)

To be diagnosed with bipolar I disorder (BDI), a manic episode must either precede or follow a major depressive or hypomanic episode. The manic episode includes a period of abnormal and persistently elevated, expansive, or irritable mood with persistently increased goal-directed activity or energy for at least a week with symptoms most of the day, nearly every day. During the manic episode, three of the following issues are experienced: inflated self-esteem or grandiosity, decreased need for sleep, more talkative with pressured speech, easily distracted, increase in goal-directed activity, and/or excessive involvement with activities that are risks for high-potential consequences, such as unrestrained shopping, sexual indiscretions, or unwise investments (p. 124). Additionally, the mood disturbance is sufficient to cause marked impairment in social or occupational settings and, if severe enough, can lead to hospitalization, especially if symptoms lead to psychotic features. In the case of hypomania, the same criteria apply, but the symptoms and impairment are not severe enough to result in hospitalization. The major depressive episode has the same features as the uni-polar MDD criteria (American Psychiatric Association, 2013).

Those who have BDI can have long-term major depression that abates for a few weeks of mania periodically, more manic episodes than depressive episodes, or rapid cycling of the extremes in moods. Those with mixed episodes have worse long-term outcomes than those with either depressive or manic episodes (Baldessarini et al., 2010; Dodd et al., 2010). Psychotic features can occur during the manic stage due to sleep deprivation, lack of nutrition during the mania, and/or using illicit substances.

Bipolar II Disorder (American Psychiatric Association, 2013, pp. 132–139)

A major distinction between bipolar I and bipolar II disorders is that someone with BDII will not have manic episodes that result in euphoria but will have evidence of hypomanic episodes that are less extreme than mania but often include increased energy and persistently elevated, expansive, or irritable moods consistently for at least four days and can have many of the same types of criteria as those with BDI, along with five criteria for major depressive episodes (p. 132).

Cyclothymic Disorder (American Psychiatric Association, 2013, pp. 139–141)

Cyclothymic disorder is a less severe form of bipolar disorder in that neither the hypomania nor the depressive symptoms have met the criteria for being labeled bipolar, but disturbance of mood has occurred for at least a year in children and adolescents or two years for adults with symptoms of both poles of mood disorders for at least half that time and symptoms for more than two months at a time during that period. Cyclothymic disorder often develops in adolescence or early adulthood and is less prevalent than BDI or BDII (p. 140). Symptoms of depression in cyclothymia will often be expressed as a dejected mood, low energy, and loss of pleasure in activities, which are similar to those of persistent depressive disorder. The hypomanic stage brings increased energy with increased creativity and productivity (Goodwin & Jamison, 2007).

Prevalence, Age of Onset, and Gender Differences

The prevalence of BDI in the US has been noted as 0.6% and internationally is anywhere from 0.0 to 0.6%, with the male-to-female ratio being 1.1:1 and is found to be more evident in industrialized countries, with 1.4% to 0.7% difference in higher socioeconomic to lower socioeconomic countries (p. 130). There is evidence of genetic propensity, with 10 times more likelihood of developing the disorder if one's blood relatives have the disorder. Females tend to get rapid cycling bipolar I disorder more than males do and appear to have more depressive episodes than males, and the comorbidity for eating disorders and alcohol use disorders increases in females as well. The other concerning factor in bipolar I disorder is the risk of suicide being so high during the manic phase: it is estimated to be 15 times higher than in the general population (p. 141).

The average age of onset for BPDII is in the mid-20s although adolescents and adults can develop the disorder. The overall prevalence of the disorder is 0.8% in the US and 0.3% internationally. Interestingly females tend to have the rapid cycling episodes and mixed depressive episodes, with childbirth being indicated as a trigger for developing a hypomanic episode in as high as 10% to 20% of that population (p. 137). Suicide risks are as high as one-third of those with the disorder at least attempting suicide. Both BPDI and II have high comorbidity with co-occurring mental health issues, with anxiety disorders reaching up to 75% of those with BDII and 37% having an additional substance use disorder, along with roughly 14% of those having some form of eating disorder (p. 139). Merikangas et al. (2003) suggested that these rates of prevalence are fairly stable across many different countries and cultures, with anxiety disorders being the most prevalent comorbid disorder with co-occurring bipolar disorder.

Cyclothymic disorder is found in 0.4% to 1% of the population, with onset usually occurring in adolescence or early adulthood, and those who have the disorder are considered to have a cyclothymic temperament (Goodwin & Jamison, 2007); 15% to 50% of those with cyclothymic disorder are at risk of it turning into BDI or BDII over time. (American Psychiatric Association, 2013, p. 140). Children who develop the disorder have more likelihood of having a diagnosis of attention-deficit hyperactivity disorder (ADHD).

Genetics and Neurobiological Factors

Research has suggested that there is a greater genetic propensity involved in bipolar I disorder than there is a uni-polar depressive disorder, with 8% to 10% of those with a first-degree blood relative with bipolar I disorder developing it (Plomin et al., 2008; Willcutt & McQueen, 2010). The monoamine hypothesis for bipolar disorder suggests that if deficiencies in serotonin and norepinephrine contribute to the development of depressive disorders, then increased norepinephrine contributes to the manic phase of bipolar disorder (Goodwin & Jamison, 2007), while increased dopamine affects symptoms of hyperactivity, grandiosity, and euphoria (Goodwin & Jamison, 2007). These same symptoms can be seen in those who use drugs like cocaine and amphetamines and demonstrate manic symptoms. Elevated cortisol levels are found in those with bipolar disorder and have been also found in the HPA axis due to abnormalities in thyroid functioning in those clients (Goodwin & Jamison, 2007).

Anxiety Disorders (American Psychiatric Association, 2013, pp. 189–234)

As noted, the *DSM-5* separated the anxiety disorders into three distinct chapters based on the developmental considerations of how fear and anxiety manifest and persist (2013). Anxiety disorders that often have transient fear and are stress induced and persistent in duration include separation anxiety disorder, selective mutism, phobias, panic disorder, agoraphobia and, most commonly, social anxiety and generalized anxiety disorder (p. 231). The common theme in all these forms of anxiety disorders is excessive worry as an anticipatory issue that has gone on for at least six months and can be around events or activities like work or school performance that can lead to restlessness, being easily fatigued, difficulty concentrating, irritability, muscle tension, and/or sleep disturbances. Social anxiety is a fear of social gatherings and essentially the fear of being humiliated, embarrassed, or rejected by others in school, work, or social activities (p. 203). Phobias, agoraphobia, and panic disorders tend to have specific targets like a fear of spiders, extensive debilitating fear of stepping outside one's own home, or panic in enclosed spaces. While insecure attachment issues can lead to separation anxiety, in which there is a fear of separating from those one is highly attached to, there may be unreasonable fears the individual will be lost due to some accident or event happening while out of the sight of the client (p. 191).

Prevalence, Age of Onset, and Gender Differences

The prevalence of generalized anxiety disorder (GAD) is 0.9% in adolescents and 2.9% in adults in the US. Internationally, the rate of prevalence is between 0.4% and 3.6%, with a lifetime morbid risk of 9.0%. Females tend to be twice as likely to develop GAD, and usually it is diagnosed and peaks in middle age and tends to go into remission more often as the individual ages (p. 224).

Social anxiety disorder presents at 7% in the US, and median prevalence in Europe is 2.3%, with higher rates of the disorder identified in females than in males. It is much more prevalent in adolescent females, and there appears to be a strong indication of genetic propensity being involved with the disorder (p. 205), which includes high drop-out-of-school rates and decreased well-being, employment, workplace productivity, socioeconomic status, and quality of life.

Panic and phobia disorders are not as prevalent as these other categories, with the US and European countries having a prevalence of 2% to 3% in adults and adolescents (p. 210). The average age of onset is early 20s, but it can still be diagnosed in one's 40s. If left untreated, the disorder will become chronic, with a prevalence in females to males of 2:1 (p. 213).

Obsessive-Compulsive and Related Disorders (American Psychiatric Association, 2013, pp. 235–264)

The obsessive-compulsive and related disorders include OCD, body dysmorphic disorder, and hoarding disorder, along with trichotillomania and excoriation disorders (hair pulling and skin picking (American Psychiatric Association, 2013). Obsessive-compulsive disorder (OCD) is the most common of these disorders, and criteria include obsessions that are reoccurring and persistent thoughts, urges, and/or images that are intrusive, unwanted, and lead to extreme stress. The individual attempts to control the intrusive thoughts through repetitive actions that develop into the compulsive behaviors, such as hand washing, or mental acts like counting that are done in an increasingly obsessive manner to prevent worry or anxiety, although the ritualistic behaviors and thoughts are not rationally going to alter the obsessive thoughts and urges (p. 237). Body dysmorphic disorder has the same type of obsessing over perceived body flaws or defects and repetitive behaviors, and preoccupation with body image creates clinically significant distress and impairment of functioning (pp. 242–243). Over time, the individual could develop an eating disorder in conjunction with the body dysmorphic disorder; this can also lead to hair-pulling and skin-picking disorders in some people with body dysmorphic disorder (p. 243). The behaviors of skin picking and hair pulling are done so extensively that there can be bald spots and scars from continually picking at the skin until self-harm has been done. Hoarding disorder is characterized by difficulty parting with possessions to the point of potential harm. The perceived need to hold on to anything despite its apparent worth creates incredible stress and anxiety in those individuals and impairs functioning substantially (p. 247).

Prevalence, Age of Onset, and Gender Differences

The average age of onset for OCD is 19.5 years in the US, with 25% of cases starting by age 14 (p. 239). Males have been noted to develop OCD earlier than females, with nearly 25% of them developing the disorder prior to age 10. Left untreated, OCD becomes a chronic disorder, and remission rates are low in adults, with up to 20% of those with the disorder still having symptoms 40 years later. Risk factors include high internalizing of symptoms, greater negative emotionality, and behavioral inhibition in childhood (239). Childhood physical and sexual abuse has been associated with an increased risk of developing OCD.

The prevalence of body dysmorphic disorder has an average age of onset of 16 to 17 years of age, with early onset in 12- to 13-year-old adolescents; two-thirds of those who will develop the disorder do so prior to age 18. This disorder is associated with depression, high levels of anxiety, social anxiety, social avoidance, neuroticism, low self-esteem, and perfectionism (p. 244). In the US, the prevalence in adults is 2.4%, with the prevalence in females at 2.5% and in males 2.2%. Internationally, Germany has prevalence of 1.7% to 1.8% in adults, with a similar gender distribution as the US. The prevalence of this disorder can be found to be much higher in those individuals who engage in dermatology procedures (9%–15%, cosmetic surgery 7%–8% in the US, 3%–16% internationally), along with 8% among adult orthodontia patients and 10% of those presenting for oral or maxillofacial surgery (p. 244).

Genetics and Neurobiological Factors

The most consistent finding in the anticipatory anxiety disorders suggests a temperament of behavioral inhibition with both neurotic tendencies and introversion is associated with developing these disorders (Bienvenu et al., 2007). When infants display avoidance and fear and are easily distressed by unfamiliar stimuli, it has been found that they are at greater risk for developing fear-based anxiety and have an increased likelihood of developing social phobias (Hayward et al., 1998). There have been twin studies that show a small genetic influence (Hettema et al., 2005; Smoller et al., 2008), but there is also speculation that these are learned behaviors from socially traumatic experiences (Hackmann et al., 2000).

Trauma and Stress-Related Disorders (American Psychiatric Association, 2013, pp. 265–290)

This text is based in research around how trauma can lead to additional psychiatric and substance use disorders. Posttraumatic stress disorder (PTSD) and acute stress disorder are the two most common anxiety disorders in this section. Reactive attachment disorder in young children is due to trauma, abuse, and changes in caregivers. Posttraumatic stress disorder is characterized by directly experiencing, witnessing, learning about, or experiencing extreme exposure to traumatic and life-threatening events (American Psychiatric Association, 2013). These experiences lead to intrusive symptoms of involuntary and recurring distressing memories of the event(s), recurring dreams and nightmares about the event(s), dissociative reactions, intense and prolonged psychological distress at both external and internal triggers that resemble an aspect of the traumatic event being activated, with marked physiological reactions to those cues. The individual persistently avoids external reminders and distressing memories with increasing negative alterations in cognition and mood, along with marked alterations in arousal and reactivity associated with the traumatic event. Symptoms have lasted longer than a month (pp. 271–275). Acute stress disorder is similar to PTSD but is diagnosed if the symptoms occur three days to one month after the trauma occurred (pp. 280–281).

Prevalence, Age of Onset, and Gender Differences

PTSD can occur at any age after the first year of life, and symptoms typically develop within three months of the traumatic event, with statistics suggesting that in the US, the prevalence for adults is around 3.5% of the population, and it's between 0.5% and 1.0% internationally (American Psychiatric Association, 2013, pp. 276–277). Childhood sexual abuse, physical abuse, and other trauma events predispose females to have a higher prevalence of PTSD, and in males, active service in military deployment is associated with higher levels of symptoms.

Neurological Considerations

Trauma activates the limbic brain (survival mechanism) of fight, flight, freeze, which thwarts the executive cognitive functioning of the prefrontal cortex from effectively being in control of brain functioning, and human beings tend to repress memories of trauma rather than engaging in activities that would reset the brain in the way animals do when they have experienced trauma (Levine, 1997, 2010). It has been determined that the hippocampus, which is part of the limbic brain and the brain's reward center, is smaller in people who have PTSD; however, this phenomenon also exists in those with major depression (Gilbertson et al., 2002).

Differential Diagnosis

All the anxiety disorders are found to be highly correlated with mood disorders. A common theme in the *DSM-5* is that one rules out determining if a medical condition or a substance use disorder could be directly causing the symptoms noted prior to a diagnosis for a psychiatric condition (American Psychiatric Association, 2013). Yet most often, these disorders are comorbid when one has a substance use disorder and is detoxed, and due to lack of access to treatment or trust in the treatment approaches available, these same individuals are at higher risk of self-medicating with alcohol and drugs, along with behavioral or process use disorders.

Barriers to Treatment

There are any number of barriers to receiving treatment for mood and anxiety disorders that can lead to self-medicating behaviors in those with these issues. Among these barriers are not realizing help might be available for the mood and anxiety issues when they are first manifesting, lack of availability and access to effective treatment, multicultural considerations, and shame in admitting one has these problems, and in many cultures, there is a lack of trust in allopathic approaches to treating these issues due to intergenerational trauma, bias within the system toward minority cultures, and practices that are intrusive.

Treatment barriers can be related to concerns about the stigma of seeing a counselor (Brewer et al., 2010). Many individuals living with mood disorders may feel a sense of shame struggling with such symptoms as these symptoms are associated with traditional emotions such as anxiety and sadness. The individual can feel shame in not being able to manage these feelings, and considering the possibility of a diagnosis can make the individual feel worse, preventing them from seeking treatment (Kessler et al., 2003). Additional factors such as finances, transportation, wait times, and availability of services can also serve as treatment barriers.

Best Practices

Since pharmaceutical companies turned their attention to the development of psychotropic medications, it has been common for mood disorders to be treated with medications. These medications can be helpful in the short term but lead to their own problems, including long-term dependence, and often, the client has to have medications changed as their efficacy is compromised over time, and the client needs more of the same substance to mask and manage symptoms. The issue of medications is that they alter brain chemistry over time in much the same way as an illicit substance does, with dependency on the substance, which creates adverse health effects (Breggin, 2011). Used short term for symptom relief, these medications can help a client while other therapy approaches are developed. Optimally, a psychiatrist is involved with determining proper medications and doses that will be of assistance to the client.

In some people, there is an adverse reaction to medications and, in some, an allergic reaction that creates a need for other options for these clients. With the understanding that brain chemistry maintains a healthy balance in the neurotransmitters through mega doses of vitamins, amino acids, and minerals, it would seem that nutritional and orthomolecular medicine approaches may be the most individualized way to treat chemical imbalance in a healthy and non-intrusive way (Hoffer & Saul, 2008; Pauling, 1968, 1986; Procyk, 2016; Walsh, 2014). A holistic doctor, a naturopathic doctor, or an informed nutritionist are among the professionals who work with those who choose a holistic approach to improving mood and anxiety.

Psychotherapeutic approaches to treating mood and anxiety disorders include, traditionally, cognitive behavioral therapy (CBT), along with interpersonal therapy, creative arts therapies, and other theoretical approaches to working with personal issues. Additionally, there has been research into mindfulness-based behavioral therapies, such as dialectic behavioral therapy (DBT) and acceptance and commitment therapy (ACT) (A-Tjak et al., 2015; Azkhosh et al., 2016; Brewer et al., 2010; Chapman, 2006; Forman et al., 2007); somatic expressive therapies (Dayton, 2003; Kiepe et al., 2012; Mala et al., 2012; Matto et al., 2003; Pelletier, 2004); and emotional freedom technique (EFT) or eye movement desensitization regulation (EMDR) for emotional regulation of anxiety, depression, and trauma (Nicosia et al., 2019). These different therapeutic approaches are discussed in the treatment section of the text in more depth, and these therapy approaches are also showing efficacy for co-occurring substance use disorder in clients.

Conclusion

As mood and anxiety disorders are so commonly linked together and, in many cases, are underlying issues that contribute to individuals self-medicating with drugs and alcohol, it is relevant for counselors to assess for co-occurring disorders whether the client seeks help for the SUD or for the mental health issue initially. There are multiple aspects to the broad terms of mood or anxiety disorders with different sequels of symptoms, which are often outcomes of trauma as well. The complexity of these disorders, along with additional issues of substance use, can be difficult to assess and diagnose initially and will take clinical care to address with integrative and individualized care. The combination of biological support in the form of psychopharmacology and cognitive treatment may help some, but it has been found that alternative treatments that include nutrition and somatic and creative therapies, along with energy approaches like EMDR or EFT, show efficacy for beginning the healing process (van der Kolk, 2014).

Questions for Consideration

1. Mood and anxiety disorders are prevalent, and substances (alcohol or other drugs) are often used to self-medicate. While this may be a short-term solution, in the long term, unmediated mood and anxiety disorders and continued use of substances may cause significant issues in a client's life. What issues do you think may surface?
2. How would you know if the client you are working with has an underlying mood or anxiety disorder?
3. What differentiates mood and anxiety disorders from several identified short- and longer-term withdrawal symptoms of various substances?

Case Study

Pria is a 22-year-old unmarried female who recently moved into her first apartment. She has always lived with roommates, but now she is on her own due to her high-paying sales job earned right after graduating college. Her friends had always called her moody, and she joked about how her productivity is high sometimes, and at other times, she needs to be left alone for several days. Her family thought of her moods as hormonal, but over the past two years, her lows have seemed to last several days, and they have grown concerned. Pria has always been proud of her productivity on her up days and reports that she likes the creativity. Pria's new job has introduced her to many people who live at a fast pace and require her to be 'up' all the time. Pria is not seeking treatment; rather, she has been brought to the emergency room due to a car accident. Her system was flooded with cocaine and alcohol. Her blood alcohol content was .29. Prior to her discharge, you have been asked to assess her for possible treatment needs.

Questions

1. What are your primary clinical concerns for Pria?
2. Based on your understanding of mood and anxiety disorders, does Pria have co-occurring disorders, or have her drinking and cocaine use caused the mood swings? How could you determine this?
3. What recommendations for discharge planning would be suggested for Pria?

References

American Psychiatric Association. (2013). *Diagnostic and statistical manual of mental disorders* (5th ed.). American Psychiatric Association.
A-Tjak, J. G. L., Davis, M. L., Morina, N., Powers, M. B., Smits, J. A. J., & Emmelkamp, P. M. G. (2015). A meta-analysis of the efficacy of acceptance and commitment therapy for clinically relevant mental and physical health problems. *Psychotherapy & Psychosomatics, 84*(1), 30–36.
Avenevoli, S., Knight, E., Kessler, R. C., & Merikangas, K. R. (2008). Epidemiology of depression in children and adolescents. In J. R. Z. Abela & B. L. Hankin (Eds.), *Handbook of depression in children and adolescents* (pp. 6–32). Guilford Press.
Azkhosh, M., Farhoudianm, A., Saadati, H., Shoaee, F., & Lashani, L. (2016). Comparing acceptance and commitment group therapy and 12-steps narcotics anonymous in addict's rehabilitation process: A randomized controlled trial. *Iranian Journal of Psychiatry, 11*(4), 244–249.
Baldessarini, R. J., Salvatore, P., Khalsa, H. M. K., & Tohen, M. (2010). Dissimilar morbidity following initial mania versus mixed-states in type-I bipolar disorder. *Journal of Affective Disorders, 126*(1–2), 299–302.
Bienvenu, O. J., Hettema, J. M., Neale, M. C., Prescott, C. A., & Kendler, K. S. (2007). Low extraversion and high neuroticism as indices of genetic and environmental risk for social phobia, agoraphobia, and animal phobia. *American Journal of Psychiatry, 164*(11), 1714–1721.
Boland, R. J., & Keller, M. B. (2009). Course and outcome of depression. In I. H. Gotlib & C. L. Hammen (Eds.), *Handbook of depression* (2nd ed., pp. 23–43). Guilford Press.
Breggin, P. R. (2011). Psychiatric drug-induced Chronic Brain Impairment (CBI): Implications for long-term treatment with psychiatric medication. *Journal of Risk & Safety in Medicine, 23*(4), 193–200.
Brewer, J. A., Bowen, S., Smith, J. T., Marlatt, G. A., & Potenza, M. N. (2010). Mindfulness-based treatments for co-occurring depression and substance use disorders: What can we learn from the brain? *Addiction, 105*(10), 1698–1706.
Chapman, A. L. (2006). Dialectical behavior therapy: Current indications and unique elements. *Psychiatry, 3*(9), 62–68.
Dayton, T. (2003). Addictions and women. In J. Gershoni (Ed.), *Psychodrama in the 21st century: Clinical and educational applications.* Springer.
Dodd, S., Kulkarni, J., Berk, L., Ng, F., Fitzgerald, P. B., de Castella, A. R., Filia, S., Filia, K., Montgomery, W., Kelin, K., Smith, M., Brnabic, A., & Berk, M. (2010). A prospective study of the impact of subthreshold mixed states on the 24-month clinical outcomes of bipolar I disorder or schizoaffective disorder. *Journal of Affective Disorders, 124*(1–2), 22–28.
Dougherty, L. R., Klein, D. N., & Davila, J. (2004). A growth curve analysis of the course of dysthymic disorder: The effects of chronic stress and moderation by adverse parent-child relationships and family history. *Journal of Consulting and Clinical Psychology, 72*(6), 1012–1021.

Forman, E. M., Herbert, J. D., Moltra, E., Yeomans, P. D., & Geller, P. A. (2007). A randomized controlled effectiveness trial of acceptance and commitment therapy and cognitive therapy for anxiety and depression. *Behavior Modification, 31*(6), 772–799.

Garlow, S. J., & Nemeroff, C. B. (2003). Neurobiology of depressive disorders. In R. J. Davidson, K. R. Scherer, & H. H. Goldsmith (Eds.), *Handbook of affective sciences* (pp. 1021–1043). Oxford University Press.

Gilbertson, M. W., Shenton, M. E., Ciszewski, A., Kasai, K., Lasko, N. B., Orr, S. P., & Pitman, R. (2002). Smaller hippocampal volume predicts pathologic vulnerability to psychological trauma. *Nature Neuroscience, 5*, 1242–1247.

Gilmer, W. S., Trivedi, M. H., Rush, A. J., Wisniewski, S. R., Luther, J., Howland, R. H., Yohanna, D., Khan, A., & Alpert, J. (2005). Factors associated with chronic depressive episodes: A preliminary report from the STAR-D project. *Acta Pyschiatrica Scandinavica, 112*(6), 425–433.

Goodwin, F. K., & Jamison, K. R. (2007). *Manic depressive illness: Bipolar disorders and recurrent depression* (2nd ed.). Oxford University Press.

Hackmann, A., Clark, D. M., & McManus, F. (2000). Recurrent images and early memories of social phobia. *Behavior, Research, and Theory, 38*, 601–610.

Hasin, D. S., Goodwin, R. D., Stinson, F. S., & Grant, B. F. (2005). Epidemiology of major depression disorder: Results from the national epidemiologic survey on alcoholism and related conditions. *Archival of General Psychiatry, 62*(10), 1097–1106.

Hayward, C., Killen, J. D., Kraemer, H. C., & Taylor, C. B. (1998). Linking self-reported childhood behavioral inhibition to adolescent social phobia. *Journal of American Academic Child and Adolescent Psychiatry, 37*, 1308–1316.

Hettema, J. M., Prescott, C. A., Meyers, J. M., Neale, M. C., & Kendler, K. S. (2005). The structure of genetic and environmental risk factors for anxiety disorders in men and women. *Archives of General Psychiatry, 62*(2), 182–189.

Hoffer, A., & Saul, A. W. (2008). *Orthomolecular medicine for everyone: Megavitamin therapeutics for families and physicians.* Basic Health Publications, Inc.

Kessler, R. C., Berglund, P., Demler, O., Jin, R., Koretz, D., Merikangas, K. R., Rush, J., Walters, E., & Wang, P. (2003). The epidemiology of major depressive disorder: Results from the National Comorbidity Survey Replication. *JAMA, 289*(23), 3095–3105.

Kessler, R. C., Birnbaum, H., Bromet, E., Hwang, I., Sampson, N., & Shahly, V. (2010). Age differences in major depressive disorder: Results from the National Comorbidity Survey Replication (NCS-R). *Psychological Medicine, 40*(2), 225–237.

Kessler, R. C., Chiu, W. T., Demler, O., & Walters, E. E. (2005c). Prevalence, severity and comorbidity of 12-month DSM-IV disorders in the National Comorbidity Survey Replication. *Archives of General Psychiatry, 62*, 617–627.

Kessler, R. C., Merikangas, K. R., & Yang, P. S. (2007). Prevalence, comorbidity, and service utilization for mood disorders in the United States at the beginning of the twenty-first century. *Annual Review of Clinical Psychology, 3*, 137–158.

Kiepe, M., Stockgit, B., & Keil, T. (2012). Effects of dance therapy and ballroom dances on physical and mental illnesses: A systematic review. *The Arts in Psychotherapy, 39*(5), 404–411.

Klein, D. N. (2010). Chronic depression: Diagnosis and classification. *Current Directions in Psychological Science, 19*(2), 96–100.

Klein, D. N., Shankman, S. A., & Rose, S. (2006). Ten-year prospective follow-up study of the naturalistic course of dysthymic disorder and double depression. *American Journal of Psychiatry, 163*(5), 872–880.

Levine, P. A. (1997). *Waking the tiger: Healing trauma.* North Atlantic Books.

Levine, P. A. (2010). *In an unspoken voice: How the body releases trauma and restores goodness.* North Atlantic Press.

Lewinsohn, P. M., & Essau, C. A. (2002). Depression in adolescents. In I. H. Gotlib & C. L. Hammen (Eds.), *Handbook of depression* (pp. 541–555). Guilford Press.

Mala, A., Karkou, V., & Meekums, B. (2012). Dance/Movement Therapy (DMT) for depression: A scoping review. *The Arts in Psychotherapy, 39*, 287–295.

Matto, H., Cocoran, J., & Fassler, A. (2003). Integrating solution-focused and art therapies for substance abuse treatment: Guidelines for practice. *The Arts in Psychotherapy, 30*(1), 265–272. doi:10.1016/j.aip.2003.08.003

Merikangas, K. R., Zhang, H., Avenevoli, S., Acharya, S., Neuenschwander, M., & Angst, J. (2003). Longitudinal trajectories of depression and anxiety in a prospective community study. *Archives of General Psychiatry*, *60*(10), 993–1000.

Nicosia, G., Minewiser, L., & Freger, A. (2019). World Trade Center: A longitudinal case study for treating post traumatic stress disorder with emotional freedom technique and eye movement desensitization regulation. *Work*, *63*(2), 199–204.

Nolan-Hoeksema, S. (2012). Emotion regulation and psychopathology: The role of gender. *Annual Review of Clinical Psychology*, *8*, 161–187.

Nolan-Hoeksema, S., & Hilt, L. (2009). Gender differences in depression. In I. H. Gotlib & C. L. Hammen (Eds.), *Handbook of depression* (2nd ed.). Guilford Press.

Pauling, L. (1968). Orthomolecular psychiatry. *Science*, *160*, 265–271.

Pauling, L. (1986). *How to live longer and feel better*. W. H. Freeman.

Pelletier, C. L. (2004). The effect of music on decreasing arousal due to stress: A meta-analysis. *Journal of Music Therapy*, *41*, 192–214.

Pinel, J. P. J., & Barnes, S. J. (2018). *Biopsychology* (10th ed.). Pearson Education.

Plomin, R., DeFries, J. C., McClearn, G. E., & McGuffin, P. (2008). *Behavioral genetics* (5th ed.). Worth Publishers.

Procyk, A. (2016). *Nutritional and integrative interventions for mental health disorders*. CMI Education Institute, Inc.

Schildkraut, J. J. (1965). The catecholamine hypothesis of affective disorders: A review of supporting evidence. *American Journal of Psychiatry*, *122*, 509–522.

Smoller, J. W., Gardner-Schuster, E., & Misiaszek, M. (2008). Genetics of anxiety: Would the genome recognize the DSM? *Depression and Anxiety*, *25*(4), 368–377.

Southwick, S. M., Vythilingam, M., & Charney, D. S. (2005). The psychobiology of depression and resilience to stress: Implications for prevention and treatment. *Annual Review of Clinical Psychology*, *1*(1), 255–191.

Thase, M. E. (2009a). Neurobiological aspects of depression. In I. H. Gotlib & C. L. Hammen (Eds.), *Handbook of depression*. Guilford Press.

Thase, M. E. (2009b). Selective serotonin-norepinephrine reuptake inhibitors. In B. J. Sadock, A. A. Sadock, & P. Ruiz (Eds.), *Kaplan and Sadock's comprehensive textbook of psychiatry* (9th ed., pp. 3184–3190). Williams & Wilkins.

van der Kolk, B. (2014). *The body keeps score: Brain, mind, and body in the healing of trauma*. Penguin Books.

Walsh, W. J. (2014). *Nutrient power: Heal your biochemistry and heal your brain*. Skyhorse Publishing, Inc.

Watson, D. (2005). Rethinking the mood and anxiety disorders: A quantitative hierarchical model for DSM-V. *Journal of Abnormal Psychology*, *114*(4), 522–536.

Willcutt, E., & McQueen, M. (2010). Genetic and environmental vulnerability to bipolar spectrum disorders. In D. J. Miklowitz & D. Cicchetti (Eds.), *Understanding bipolar disorder: A developmental psychopathology perspective* (pp. 225–258). Guilford Press.

3   Psychotic Disorders and Co-occurring Substance Use Disorders

Tricia L. Chandler and Fredrick Dombrowski

Introduction

'Psychosis' is a term that infers that someone is experiencing a different form of reality or consciousness that may include hearing, seeing, and in other ways sensing stimuli that others do not experience. These forms of altered senses of reality can have a variety of etiologies as to why they exist, and to consider these symptoms from a multicultural approach is to examine when these are symptoms of mental illness, when these might be symptoms caused by substances, and when these might be symptoms of increased spiritual consciousness, called 'spiritual emergence' (American Psychiatric Association [APA], 2013; Grof & Groff, 1989; Podvoll, 1990). Psychotic disorders can be especially difficult to treat in individuals living with co-occurring substance use disorders as many symptoms of various substances can mimic such disorders (Destoop et al., 2021). From the perspective of the *DSM-5*, psychosis is not a definable disorder but a symptom of another disorder (APA, 2013). This chapter will discuss the three forms of disturbance that might contribute to psychotic symptoms, how to determine the etiology of the symptoms, and best practices for treatment.

Learning Objectives

- Students will list features to differentiate between various psychotic disorders.
- Students will identify how to differentiate between psychotic disorders and substance intoxication.
- Students will identify appropriate treatment options for those living with co-occurring substance use and psychotic disorders.

Key Terms

Audio Hallucinations: When an individual hears sounds without an external source of the sound. These sounds can be in the form of voices, direct language, and music.

Delusions: Notions or ideas that are believed by the patient but are generally unsupported by others and lack evidence.

Negative Symptoms: Symptoms that take away a certain aspect of functioning. For example, an individual with negative experiences will show a lack of self-care (showering or bathing) or experience a blunt affect (in which their emotions do not match the experience) or a deficit in speech.

Paranoia: Intense belief of potential threat, persecution, and hazard in the absence of evidence.

Positive Symptoms: Symptoms that add to the experience of an individual. Audio and visual hallucinations are positive symptoms as the hallucination is in addition to what is actually present. Delusions and paranoia are also positive symptoms.

DOI: 10.4324/9781003220916-4

Schizophasia: Often referred to as 'word salad', it is the mixture of seemingly random words and phrases often exhibited by people experiencing psychosis.

Spiritual Emergence: An aspect of human development seeking meaning through spirituality in which an individual feels a deeper connection to a sense of spirituality, to others, to a higher power, and to the environment.

Tardive Dyskinesia: Involuntary movements of the mouth, jaw, and tongue that are often a side effect of anti-psychotic medications.

Visual Hallucinations: The experience of seeing something that is not actually there. An individual may perceive movement when there is no movement or see people and objects that are not actually present.

DSM-5 Criteria

Schizophrenia is a severe and disabling psychiatric disorder characterized by persistent delusions, hallucinations, disorganized speech, disorganized behavior, and negative symptoms such as the absence of emotional expression or a lack of motivation or initiative (APA, 2013). Of the disorders labeled as having psychotic symptoms, schizophrenia is the most common diagnosis; however, brief psychotic disorder, schizoaffective disorder, and schizophreniform disorder are also represented. There are also personality disorders that have features of psychosis in the Cluster A personality disorders (APA, 2013).

Schizophrenia and psychotic spectrum disorders have two distinct sets of symptoms, which include the positive symptoms of delusions, hallucinations, disorganized thinking, abnormal motor behavior, and paranoia, along with the negative symptoms of diminished emotional expression; decreased motivation for self-directed activities and interests; and diminished speech, ability to experience pleasure, and interest in social interactions (APA, 2013, pp. 87–88). Anti-psychotic medications attempt to mask the positive symptoms of the disorder while anti-depressants might be needed to reduce symptoms of depression. The type of diagnosis will depend on the length of time the symptoms have been noted and whether there are overlapping mood issues involved.

Despite overlap in symptoms, there are various psychotic disorders, and how these disorders manifest are unique (Hunt et al., 2018). The type of illness an individual is living with when appropriately diagnosed helps create an effective treatment plan to meet the individual's needs. Assessment of individuals living with psychotic disorders can be difficult as many individuals may not adhere to treatment as prescribed and may be brought to a psychiatric emergency room at the behest of their family or brought by the police for a public disturbance (Hunt et al., 2018). During psychiatric assessment, positive symptoms such as hallucinations and deficits in speech can be present. However, the severity of the symptoms may make it difficult to assess unique variances between disorders, and individuals may experience an inaccurate diagnosis. It is recommended that those working in such settings become aware of the diagnostic criteria for various psychotic disorders. Among the disorders are:

Schizophrenia Disorder 295. 90 Criteria From the DSM-5 (APA, 2013)

1. Two or more of the following, present for a significant amount of time during a one-month period.

    a. Delusions, hallucinations, disorganized speech (one of these)
    b. Grossly disorganized or catatonic behaviors
    c. Negative symptoms

2. Level of functioning for a significant period of time is affected by the symptoms; work, interpersonal relationships, or self-care has markedly decreased from what was achieved prior to the onset of symptoms. If the onset is in childhood or adolescence, there is marked failure to achieve expected level of interpersonal, academic, or occupational functioning.
3. Continuous signs of the disturbance for at least six months with negative symptoms being demonstrated and at least one of the three main positive symptoms.
4. Schizoaffective, depressive, and bipolar disorder with psychotic features have been ruled out.
5. The disturbance is not attributable to the physiological effects of a substance or another medical condition.
6. If there is a history of autism spectrum disorder or a communication disorder in childhood, the additional diagnosis of schizophrenia is made only if prominent delusions or hallucinations are present for at least a month (p. 99).

Schizophreniform Disorder (295.40) Criteria From the DSM-5 (APA, 2013)

As with schizophrenia disorder, the main characteristics of positive symptoms and negative symptoms are present in those living with schizophreniform disorders. The frequency and duration of symptoms varies between these disorders. Those living with schizophreniform disorder show symptoms that have been present for a total duration of more than one month and less than six months. The time limit associated with this diagnosis indicates the expectance that symptoms would resolve within six months of their onset. In situations where symptoms remain after six months, the diagnosis is changed to schizophrenia disorder (pp. 96–97). This condition can be misdiagnosed if a patient is experiencing difficulty with memory recollection and may be a poor historian. The lack of information available to the assessing counselor may cause them to assume that the symptoms observed are relatively acute, although connection with collateral contacts and reading information about previous episodes of care may provide further clarity on differentiating between schizophrenia and schizophreniform disorders.

Brief Psychotic Disorder (298.8) Criteria From the DSM-5

The symptoms associated with brief psychotic disorder may seem self-explanatory. The observation of positive and negative symptoms associated with schizophrenia are present. However, the symptoms have lasted one day but have often lasted less than a month (pp. 94–95). Those living with brief psychotic disorder can be misdiagnosed in the presence of substance use as many symptoms associated with substance use intoxication may look like psychosis (Steeds et al., 2015). When the effects of the substance dissipate within a day to a few weeks, this can be interpreted as the individual recovering from the effects of substances. Appropriately diagnosing this disorder is needed in the absence of substance use. See Figure 3.1 for the Psychotic Disorder Matrix. This matrix breaks down the difference between brief psychotic disorder, schizophreniform disorder, and schizophrenia. While the positive symptoms and negative symptoms remain similar across diagnoses, the diagnoses differ in presentation time and duration of symptoms.

Schizoaffective Disorder

1. An uninterrupted period of illness during which there is a major mood episode (depressive or manic) concurrent with criteria 1 for schizophrenia.
2. Delusions or hallucinations for two or more weeks in the absence of a major mood episode during the lifetime duration of the illness.

Psychotic Disorder Matrix		
Brief Psychotic Disorder	*Schizophreniform Disorder*	*Schizophrenia Disorder*
Positive Symptoms: Hallucinations Delusions Confused Trouble Concentrating	**Positive Symptoms:** Hallucinations Delusions Confused Trouble Concentrating	Positive Symptoms: Hallucinations Delusions Confused Trouble Concentrating
Negative Symptoms: Lack of Pleasure Disorganized Speech Flat Affect Withdrawal Loss of Self-Care	**Negative Symptoms:** Lack of Pleasure Disorganized Speech Flat Affect Withdrawal Loss of Self-Care	**Negative Symptoms:** Lack of Pleasure Disorganized Speech Flat Affect Withdrawal Loss of Self-Care
Time Frame: One day to one month	**Time Frame:** Resolves in six months	**Time Frame:** Longer than six months, can span a lifetime

Figure 3.1 Psychotic Disorder Matrix: Listing the positive and negative symptoms in addition to time frames of the psychotic illnesses.

3. Symptoms that meet criteria for a major mood episode are present for the majority of the duration of the active and residual portions of the illness.
4. The disturbance is not attributable to the effects of a substance or another medical condition.
5. When diagnosing this disorder, the type of mood issue must be identified:

Bipolar Type: 295.70 (F25.0)
Depressive Type: 295.70 (F25.1) (pp. 105–106).

Those living with schizoaffective disorder may often be misdiagnosed with schizophrenia based on the report of delusions and hallucinations (Hartman et al., 2019). When an individual is brought to an emergency psychiatric assessment, it can be difficult for the counselor to fully assess affective aspects such as symptoms of depression or decreases in interpersonal functioning. Focusing only on psychotic symptoms without addressing emotional experiences and interpersonal experiences can impact treatment adherence and outcomes (Archibald et al., 2019). As many individuals living with psychotic disorders are also living with comorbid substance use disorders, it is also important for evaluating counselors to obtain urinalysis and collateral contact when available to assess how substance use is impacting current symptoms.

See Figure 3.2, which identifies the difference between schizoaffective disorder and other psychotic disorders, including a dimension focused on affective symptoms.

Substance Use

The Epidemiologic Catchment Area (ECA) study found that 33.7% of people with a diagnosis of schizophrenia or schizophreniform disorder also met criteria for alcohol use disorder, and 47%

```
┌─────────────────────────────────────────────────┐
│ Schizoaffective Disorder                          │
├─────────────────────────────────────────────────┤
│ Positive Symptoms:                                │
│                                                   │
│ Hallucinations                                    │
│ Delusions                                         │
│ Confused thoughts                                 │
│ Disorganized speech                               │
│ Trouble concentrating                             │
├─────────────────────────────────────────────────┤
│ Negative Symptoms:                                │
│                                                   │
│ Lack of enjoyment in activities                   │
│ Trouble with speech                               │
│ Flat affect                                       │
│ Withdrawal                                        │
│ Lack of self-care                                 │
│ Lack of follow through                            │
├─────────────────────────────────────────────────┤
│ Affective Symptoms:                               │
│                                                   │
│ Depression                                        │
│ Anxiety                                           │
│ Interpersonal difficulties                        │
│ Increased mood lability                           │
├─────────────────────────────────────────────────┤
│ Time Frame:                                       │
│                                                   │
│ Lifelong                                          │
│ Chronic                                           │
│ Controlled through medication                     │
└─────────────────────────────────────────────────┘
```

Figure 3.2 Schizoaffective Disorder

met criteria for other substance use disorders (Regier et al., 1990). The Composite International Diagnostic Interview (CIDI) reported by Robins et al. (1988) found a lifetime 51.4% of those with SUDs also had at least one other psychiatric disorder, and 50.9% of those with a history of mental health disorders also had a lifetime history of having at least one SUD, with SAMHSA reporting co-occurring disorders as being more prevalent in males (4.1% of the adult population) while women's prevalence rated at 3.1% (Morisano et al., 2017). Alcohol may be one of the more common substances abused by this population, but nicotine is by far most prevalent abused substance by those with a schizophrenia diagnoses (Cuffel, 1996). Rates of substance use disorders seem to have higher association with males of all ages (Drake & Mueser, 2002). While people with schizophrenia may use substances for a number of reasons, there has been research that suggests there is a high level of use attempting to alleviate the general symptoms of the mental illness and self-medicating to alleviate the adverse side effects of psychotropic medication, but poverty; limited opportunities for vocational, recreational, and social interaction; and living with the stigma of mental illness may contribute to use of substances (Dixon et al., 1990; Lamb & Bachrach, 2001).

Substances or Psychosis?

There are various disorders that can be diagnosed based on the consumption of substances (Steeds et al., 2015). The qualifier 'substance induced' is placed on these diagnoses to indicate that the symptoms observed are a result of specific substance use, and when the individual is not using substances, these symptoms most likely will not be present (Brown et al., 2019). Substance-induced psychotic disorder can occur if an individual is using a variety of substances. An individual using phencyclidine (also known as PCP or angel dust) may experience symptoms of euphoria, hallucinations, and distortions of self and reality. Those using phencyclidine may be perceived as having delusions or paranoia as the substance can cause an impending feeling of doom (Steeds et al., 2015). More common substances such as THC can cause instances when individuals experience distortions in reality and some audio or visual hallucinations. Those who have used cocaine for several days may show symptoms of paranoia and altered reality, which is worsened by a lack of sleep associated with the use of the drug. It is also not uncommon for those experiencing withdrawal to report incidents of hallucinations or altered perception (Massoud et al., 2018). With substance-induced disorders, the time frame for symptoms is acute and related to substance use, with most symptoms dissipating within a few days of taking the substance, although they can last up to two weeks. Urinalysis and speaking with collateral contacts are recommended during assessments to help differentiate between psychotic disorders and mood-induced disorders.

There are several substances that can mimic symptoms associated with psychotic disorders. The main class of substances that would induce such symptoms fall within the field of hallucinogenic drugs. When people use hallucinogenic substances, they can experience such symptoms as auditory and visual hallucinations, feelings of paranoia, intensified senses, loss of perception of time, and memory loss (NIDA, 2019). The following is a brief list of substances that include symptoms during intoxication that may present as psychotic disorders: Cocaine, THC, LSD, DMT, PCP, ketamine, and salvia. When assessing for diagnoses, it is important for the counselor to identify whether the psychotic symptoms began before the use of substances as well as whether the psychotic symptoms persist when substances are no longer used. The importance of differentiating between symptoms during sobriety and during intoxication can help shape treatment options.

Developmental Factors

Those who have been exposed to adverse childhood experiences (such as abuse, neglect, or trauma) are at greater risk of developing substance use disorders and mental health diagnoses than their peers (Vallejos et al., 2017). There are various factors associated with adverse childhood experiences that make it difficult to effectively predict how an individual may respond later in life. With that said, children who have experienced trauma and abuse are more likely to report symptoms of psychotic disorders than their peers who have been spared these negative experiences (Trotta et al., 2016). As many children who experience adverse childhood experiences may be taught to not share such experiences with those outside the family, concerns arise regarding paranoia symptoms being misinterpreted, especially if the individual or family members (such as parents) have experienced justice involvement (DeRosse et al., 2014). A lack of trust in providers from an early age can also impact those attempting to cope with and live with psychotic disorders as they may stop the use of prescribed medications, miss treatment sessions, and become justice involved themselves if their symptoms create a public disturbance (Trotta et al., 2016). These experiences may impact the development of global coping strategies that can increase the likelihood of success in treatment.

People living with psychotic disorders experience ongoing stress and stigma when compared to their counterparts without diagnoses (Karpov et al., 2017). There remains an assumption that those living with psychotic disorders are more likely to cause physical harm to others than those free from such symptoms. Various news outlets may highlight stories associated with an individual who is experiencing psychotic symptoms and engaging in lawless behavior. The concern regarding command hallucinations and interpersonal conflict makes sense when news agencies focus on stories of an individual who claims to have engaged in harm to others as a result of hallucinations that encouraged such harm. Despite public opinion and the focus on such stories, those living with psychotic disorders are far more likely to be victims of crimes than to engage in criminal activities (Harenski et al., 2017). The stigma associated with psychotic disorders can impact those living with such diagnoses as they worry about how others will perceive them and therefore isolate and even avoid treatment.

Biological and Neurological Factors

The causes of schizophrenia used to be considered a genetic issue, but gene studies have indicated that individual genes increase the risk of developing schizophrenia to less than two times that of the average population (Gilmore, 2010). Pre- and perinatal complications, along with environmental exposures, appear to be more relevant to developing the disorder, with maternal depression during the pregnancy increasing the risk in offspring up to 9% if a parent also had a psychotic disorder and environmental exposure, increasing the risk even more (Gilmore, 2010). Stressors or infections during pregnancy may contribute to neurological changes in the fetus, but these are not a sure outcome for the development of schizophrenia, and the genetic propensity does not ensure that schizophrenia will necessarily develop. Biological and neurological factors that have been considered in the development of schizophrenia, and the additional substance use disorders include the dysregulation of the brain chemical dopamine, although there are a number of neurotransmitters affected by the development of schizophrenia (Chambers et al., 2001). Psychotropic medications for the treatment of schizophrenia have significant adverse side effects that also affect brain chemistry. Considering the severity of the side effects of prescribed medications, many people may turn to illicit substances to cope with symptoms.

Psychological Factors

People with schizophrenia syndromes have poor impulse control, impaired thinking, and impairment in social judgments that may also contribute to those with the disorder being more inclined to use substances (Mueser et al., 1998; Drake & Mueser, 2002). Prior to the deinstitutionalization of psychiatric hospitals, often people with severe schizophrenia were maintained in long-term hospitals where daily hygiene, nutritional needs, and medication needs were provided by medical professionals, with psychotherapy and socialization part of daily life. With federal policy changes that occurred in the 1980s under then-President Reagan, communities were expected to improve support for these individuals. Many communities were underprepared for such deinstitutionalization as access to various services was limited. Even communities that had more access to services experienced a lack of vocational, recreational, and social opportunities and housing that is affordable for this adult population. The lack in resources contributed to an increase in homelessness and lack of compliance or even access to treatment, including psychotropic medication, along with being vulnerable to being victimized.

Despite ongoing attempts to create community programs to meet the needs of these populations, lack of resources and supports contributes to more than half of individuals living with psychotic disorders adhering to treatment at six-month follow-ups after inpatient stays (Vega et al., 2021). A lack of trust in services providers (exacerbated by public stigma) and the unpleasant side effects of medications are ongoing factors that must be considered for individuals living with psychotic disorders (Williams et al., 2019).

Prevalence, Age of Onset, and Gender Differences

Psychotic features of schizophrenia tend to develop during the late teens to early 20s for males and is more prevalent in males than females. Those females who develop schizophrenia tend to do so in the late 20s or 30s. Development of symptoms may begin with depressive symptoms, and earlier onset is predictive of a worse prognosis, and cognitive impairments may emerge prior to full psychotic episodes (APA, 2013). Psychopathology increases the risk of substance use, abuse, dependence, and withdrawal, and in some cases, the use of certain substances that mimic psychotic features may speed up the onset of schizophrenia and other psychotic disorders if there is a genetic propensity for the disorder. Some of these substances include cannabis, methamphetamines, crack cocaine, and alcohol, which, under certain conditions, can contribute to the disorder manifesting sooner than it would have. Considering the changes in many state laws that allow for the use of recreational cannabis, treatment providers must be aware of how continued use within the young populations can impact the development of mental health diagnoses. Although the public perception of cannabis is that it is a harmless substance, there is an association between the use of high-potency THC and the development of mental health diagnoses (Hines et al., 2020).

Other Socio-cultural Considerations

As mentioned earlier in the chapter, spiritual emergence and seeking altered states of consciousness may be issues to consider, especially when working with indigenous cultures and those who are having a spiritual awakening, rather than assuming that a psychotic episode is actually a disorder (Grof & Grof, 1989). There are times when a radical personality transformation occurs that creates, for a time, a psychospiritual crisis in which one's senses are hypersensitive and visions, voices, and other phenomena may occur temporarily. These types of phenomena can be found in mystical literature, as well as in stories of the lives of shamans, mystics, and spiritual teachers while the medical model and Western psychiatrists do not differentiate psychospiritual crisis from mental health disorders. When a psychospiritual crisis is treated as such, with supportive family and expert assistance, often this episode will improve psychosomatic health, increase enthusiasm for life with a more rewarding life view and increased consciousness that includes higher existential values (Grof & Grof, 1989). When a psychospiritual crisis is treated by Western medicine, the client will be diagnosed with a psychotic disorder and may be started on anti-psychotic medications that will interfere with a natural resolution of the temporary psychosis. A psychospiritual crisis is not a pathological breakdown of brain chemistry but can be brought on by episodes of unitive consciousness, a crisis of psychic opening, past-life experiences, communication with spirit guides, near-death experiences, and some substance use experiences (Grof & Grof, 1989). Native Americans and a number of indigenous cultures use hallucinogens, such as peyote, psilocybin, and ayahuasca, to raise spiritual consciousness, and, in fact, these substances are currently being researched for treating PTSD, mood disorders, and some substance use disorders. Grof suggests that, for those with substance use disorders, combining 12-step programs with transpersonal psychology approaches is most likely the best way to treat those issues (Grof, 2008).

Those living with low socioeconomic status are at greater risk for diagnoses of various mental health and substance use disorders (Hunt et al., 2018). Living with the ongoing stress related to financial and resource insecurities can exacerbate mental health–related symptoms and contribute to those in these groups using illicit substances in an attempt to cope with such stress (Trotta et al., 2016). A lack of resources such as transportation and access to pharmacies can make it difficult for those living with psychotic disorders to follow up with treatment outside an inpatient stay (Williams et al., 2019). Adherence to treatment can be especially difficult for those of low socioeconomic status as they may lack the ability to attend treatment as prescribed while also living with ongoing feelings of fear of or discrimination by treatment providers.

Ongoing homelessness and financial struggles are major concerns for those living with co-occurring substance use and psychotic disorders (Moulin et al., 2018). The symptoms associated with psychotic disorders can impact long-term planning and money management for those living with such disorders. Additionally, the negative symptoms such as lack of follow through make it difficult for those who are diagnosed with a psychotic disorder to complete reauthorization paperwork for disability and insurance. Those who are living with such illnesses may struggle to maintain their benefits, thus losing any assistance they have to maintain housing, food, and basic needs (Elbogen et al., 2021). As the individual experiences a lapse in financial assistance, they will also experience a lapse in insurance coverage, thus impacting their ability to attend scheduled sessions and take medications as prescribed. In these instances, open community centers such as libraries can become hubs for those living with such disorders to obtain daily water, have an opportunity to wash in the bathroom, and seek shelter and warmth. Despite the use of these services, the staff working at such agencies are not trained clinicians and may struggle to assist those who may be using the amenities of a public forum (Pressley, 2017). As these open areas allow homeless individuals living with co-occurring disorders to congregate, staff at such agencies are more likely to call 911 when members of the public show disorganized and hallucinatory symptoms. These individuals are then taken to psychiatric emergency rooms, where they are assessed and often admitted. Despite admission, many individuals, upon discharge, may lack appropriate services and housing, impacting their ability to follow up with aftercare and maintaining a cycle of symptoms that impacts public and personal health (Elbogen et al., 2021).

Best Treatment Practices

Considering the multidimensional needs of those living with co-occurring psychotic disorders and substance use disorders, an integrated treatment module with access to various services is recommended (Moulin et al., 2018). Integrated treatment at an all-in-one facility will include multidisciplinary approaches with various team members of different backgrounds. When conceptualizing the needs of the client, the severity of symptoms may dictate which level of care they meet the criteria for. Those who are brought into treatment after several weeks of not medicating may need inpatient hospitalization to stabilize symptoms and to help reconnect the individual to medications. At the inpatient level, the team must consist of a psychiatrist to manage medications, a counselor to help enhance motivation to commit to outpatient treatment, potential family therapy to help connect the client back with their family supports, and a social worker to help re-establish benefits and to connect the individual with housing after their inpatient stay. In many cases, follow-up with a medical doctor is also needed as the individual may have neglected their physical health while in the throes of exacerbated symptoms. When considering discharge from an inpatient stay, the severity of symptoms and co-occurring disorders will create a plan for discharge based on the client's unique needs. If the client met criteria for substance use disorder, it is best that they be discharged to a dual-diagnosis facility treating both mental health and substance use disorders.

When referring those with co-occurring psychotic disorders and substance use disorders to outpatient treatment, it is recommended that treatment be inclusive to work on mental health needs and substance use needs concurrently. The client will still benefit from a social worker to help maintain appropriate needed benefits to help secure medications and financial assistance. While the individual may complete the outpatient substance use portion of their treatment, it is essential to identify the need for ongoing clinical mental health treatment to help maintain gains through pharmacotherapy and counseling support. Some individuals have been so impacted by their symptoms that they meet criteria for residential treatment, which provides room and board, shared living spaces, food, medication management, and money management skills to help prevent the individual from returning to inpatient treatment. Within any treatment module, it is recommended that the individual maintain a full team of providers including a psychiatrist, counselor, and social worker to maintain benefits (Drake & Mueser, 2002).

Barriers to Treatment

Multiple barriers to treatment exist for those living with co-occurring psychotic disorders and substance use disorders. The main focus in regards to barriers is access to services due to lapsed coverage (Moulin, 2018). When an individual loses their insurance coverage, they no longer have access to medications, mental health treatment, medical treatment, and even transportation. It is important that counselors have contingency management plans to assist this population in the form of family supports, social workers, and friends to help assist the individual with maintaining their benefits (Destoop et al., 2021). When an individual loses their insurance coverage, they will experience struggles with treatment, causing worsening symptoms. These symptoms make follow through with obligations very difficult, which can cause the individual to eventually become homeless (Moulin et al., 2018). In many instances, primary counselors may not be aware of services that are available to this population. They also may not feel comfortable assisting clients with completing the paperwork to secure services to help pay for treatment. With that said, it is recommended that counselors become familiar with local services in their areas, including residential services, to assist this population. Counselors must be versed in current Medicaid, Medicare, and Social Security disability applications as the difficulty of these applications can be a barrier to clients obtaining needed care (Vega et al., 2021).

Medication side effects can also be a barrier to treatment. While the medications used to treat psychotic disorders can decrease positive symptoms and allow the individual to have energy to respond to negative symptoms, the side effects of such medications can have an impact on various aspects of the individual's life, including weight gain, sexual functioning, and ability to sleep (Khokhar et al., 2018). An additional side effect of anti-psychotic medications is an involuntary movement of the mouth, jaw, or tongue commonly known as tardive dyskinesia (Pardis et al., 2019). This side effect is quite visible to others and can make the individual feel disconnected or judged as these movements are involuntary and hard to control. While counselors may discuss with their clients the benefits of adhering to medication management, some clients may have various reasons for struggling to medicate as prescribed.

When conceptualizing an individual's experience living with a psychotic disorder, the counselor may not be aware of the unintended consequences of treatment. For example, in her book *The Quiet Room* (1994), Lori Schiller discusses her experience living with schizoaffective disorder. She identifies her struggles to connect with treatment providers as well as identified instances in which she felt discriminated against based on her diagnoses. While she reviews her use of alcohol and substances to manage her symptoms, she also discusses various failed attempts at prescribed medications to alleviate her symptoms. With that said, when Lori documents her experience with finding the right medication, she identifies how she missed the hallucinations she experienced. Lori describes her hallucinations as being primarily auditory and persecutory, often saying bad things about herself and others. However, when appropriate medications were used and the voices became muted, Lori describes missing the hallucinations as she felt they kept her company even in difficult times, despite how negative these experiences were. It is recommended that counselors work to build a therapeutic rapport based on unconditional positive regard to allow the individual to speak about such experiences without feeling judged. A lack of connection to treatment providers can be an ongoing limit to treatment (Williams et al., 2019).

Conclusion

Psychotic disorders can be very difficult to treat as many of the symptoms presented can be very similar to substance use intoxication (Brown et al., 2019). It is essential for intake counselors to include urine toxicology and collateral contacts in their assessment to identify if psychotic symptoms existed prior to substance use and/or in the absence of substance use (Harenski et al., 2017). Those living with co-occurring psychotic disorders face vast barriers to treatment as symptoms of psychosis make it extremely difficult for these individuals to follow up with work, school, or extracurricular activities. As those living with these disorders experience negative symptoms such as a lack of follow through, they are constantly at risk for losing their benefits, stopping medication usage, becoming homeless, and being brought into psychiatric emergency rooms to receive emergency treatment (Moulin et al., 2018). While it can be disturbing to observe someone respond to audio and visual hallucinations, the stigma regarding those living with psychotic disorders is not supported as these individuals are much more likely to be victims of violent crime than to complete violent crimes (Villatoro et al., 2018).

For those working in various clinical settings with these populations, it is important to provide the individual with a treatment team of various specialties to help meet their needs and to improve treatment outcomes (Moulin et al., 2018). For counselors working in individual therapy with those living with co-occurring psychotic disorders and substance use diagnoses, it is important to be aware of the link between adverse childhood experiences and the manifestation of psychotic features (DeRosse et al., 2014). Additionally, the socioeconomic impact on those living with these disorders requires the counselor to be aware of various services to assist these clients with their long-term goals (Villatorro et al., 2018). Ongoing barriers associated with low socioeconomic status will potentially prevent clients from following up with services.

When an individual does follow up with treatment, the severity of their symptoms and adherence to medications (as well as status of substance use) will dictate treatment options. A full team of clinicians is required to work with these populations. Counselors should consider the benefits of residential placement for those who experience chronic homelessness, lapses in medication adherence, a loss of benefits, and/or frequent emergency room visits and hospitalizations (Karpov et al., 2017). In some cases, ongoing use of substances may be a triggering factor in the onset of psychotic disorders (Hines et al., 2020). Treatment must consider both the mental health aspects and the substance use aspects to be effective. When treatment becomes effective, counselors must also consider how a change in symptomology can be difficult for the client, even if they experience command or unpleasant hallucinations. Ongoing supervision is recommended for all counselors working with clients living with co-occurring substance use disorders and psychotic disorders.

Questions

1. How could you differentiate between a primary substance use diagnosis and a primary mental health diagnosis?
2. What substances can mimic the symptoms of psychosis?
3. What are special considerations a counselor should have when working with someone living with substance use and co-occurring psychosis diagnoses?

Case Study

Alex is a 47-year-old, single white male brought into the psychiatric emergency room by the local police as the staff of a local library called emergency services as Alex appeared to be arguing with people who did not exist. Upon Alex's arrival at the emergency room, his intake counselor sees that Alex has been admitted to inpatient mental health treatment five times in the last 12 months. Upon the intake assessment, Alex is unable to maintain a conversation and continues to argue with audio and visual hallucinations. Toxicology reports indicate that Alex is positive for THC and cocaine. According to reports, he was last seen in outpatient treatment four weeks ago but did fill his medication prescriptions. Alex is admitted into inpatient treatment and immediately placed on medication management. As Alex shows an improvement in mental health symptoms, he indicates that he was evicted from his home four weeks ago as he had no money to pay for rent. His disability benefits have lapsed, and Alex receives no monthly income. Throughout the ten days of treatment, Alex appears to struggle with understanding what is being said to him as he asks 'What?' when staff or other clients attempt to talk to him. On the ninth day of his inpatient hospitalization, Alex was seen by the hospital audiologist to assess for hearing loss. Alex was found to have obstructions in his ear canals of cigarette butts, dirt, and toilet paper. When these items were removed, Alex was asked to describe how they were placed in his ears. Alex reported, 'I wanted to stop the voices, but it didn't work'.

Questions

1.   What are some unique circumstances that contributed to Alex's increased symptoms?
2.   How can the symptoms Alex is presenting with slow down treatment?
3.   What treatment options would be appropriate for Alex?

References

American Psychiatric Association. (2013). *Diagnostic and statistical manual of mental disorders* (5th ed.). American Psychiatric Association.

Archibald, L., Brunette, M. F., Wallin, D. J., & Green, A. I. (2019). Alcohol use disorder and schizophrenia or schizoaffective disorder. *Alcohol Research: Current Reviews*, *40*(1), arcr.v40.1.06. https://doi.org/10.35946/arcr.v40.1.06

Boland, J. K., & Rosenfeld, B. (2018). The role of controlled substance use in diversion outcomes among mentally ill offenders: A pilot study. *International Journal of Offender Therapy and Comparative Criminology*, *62*(9), 2709–2725. https://doi.org/10.1177/0306624X17735093

Brown, H. E., Kaneko, Y., & Donovan, A. L. (2019). Substance-induced psychosis and co-occurring psychotic disorders. In A. Donovan & S. Bird (Eds.), *Substance use and the acute psychiatric patient: Current clinical psychiatry*. Humana. https://doi.org/10.1007/978-3-319-23961-3_7

Chambers, A., Krystal, J. H., & Self, D. W. (2001). A neurobiological basis for substance abuse comorbidity in schizophrenia. *Biological Psychiatry*, *50*, 71–83.

Cuffel, B. J. (1996). Comorbid substance use disorder: Prevalence, patterns of use, and course. In R. E. Drake & K. T. Mueser (Eds.), *Dual diagnosis of major mental illness and substance disorder: Recent research and clinical implications*. Jossey-Bass.

DeRosse, P., Nitzburg, G., Kompancaril, B., & Malhotra, A. (2014). The relation between childhood maltreatment and psychosis in patients with schizophrenia and non-psychiatric controls. *Schizophrenia Research*, *155*(1–3), 66–71. https://doi.org/10.1016/j.schres.2014.03.009

Destoop, M., Docx, L., Morrens, M., & Dom, G. (2021). Meta-analysis on the effect of contingency management for patients with both psychotic disorders and substance use disorders. *Journal of Clinical Medicine*, *10*(4), 616. https://doi.org/10.3390/jcm10040616

Dixon, L., Haas, G., Weiden, P., Sweeney, J., & Frances, A. (1990). Acute effects of drug abuse in schizophrenia patients: Clinical observations and patients' self-reports. *Schizophrenia Bulletin*, *16*, 69–79.

Drake, R. E., & Mueser, K. T. (2002). Co-occurring alcohol use disorder and schizophrenia. *Alcohol Research & Health*, *26*(2), 99–102.

Elbogen, E., Lanier, M., Wagner, H., & Tsai, J. (2021). Financial strain, mental illness, and homelessness. *Medical Care*, *59*, 132–138. doi:10.1097/MLR.0000000000001453

Gilmore, J. H. (2010). Understanding what causes schizophrenia: A developmental perspective. *The American Journal of Psychiatry*, *167*(1), 8–10.

Grof, S. (2008). *Spiritual emergencies: Understanding and treatment of psychospiritual crisis*. Retrieved from https://realitysandwich.com/spiritual_emergencies/

Grof, S., & Grof, C. (Eds.). (1989). *Spiritual emergency: When personal transformation becomes a crisis*. J. P. Tarcher.

Harenski, C., Brook, M., Kosson, D., Bustillo, J., Harenski, K., Caldwell, M., . . . Kiehl, D. (2017). Socio-neuro risk factors for suicidal behavior in criminal offenders with psychotic disorders. *Social Cognitive and Affective Neuroscience, 12*(1), 70–80. https://doi.org/10.1093/scan/nsw164

Hartman, L., Heinrichs, W., & Marshhadi, F. (2019). The continuing story of schizophrenia and schizoaffective disorder: One condition or two? *Schizophrenia Research: Cognition, 16*, 36–42.

Hines, L., Freeman, T., Gage, H., Zammit, S., Hickman, M., Cannon, M., . . . Herod, J. (2020). Association of high-potency cannabis use with mental health and substance use in adolescence. *JAMA Psychiatry, 77*(10), 1044–1051. doi:10.1001/jamapsychiatry.2020.1035

Hunt, G., Large, M., Cleary, M., Xiong Lang, H., & Saunders, J. (2018). Prevalence of comorbid substance use in schizophrenia spectrum disorders in community and clinical settings, 1990–2017: Systematic review and meta-analysis. *Drug and Alcohol Dependence, 191*, 234–258.

Karpov, B., Joffe, G., Aaltonen, K., Suvisaari, J., Baryshnikov, I., Koivisto, M., . . . Isometsä, E. (2017). Psychoactive substance use in specialized psychiatric care patients. *The International Journal of Psychiatry in Medicine, 52*(4–6), 399–415. https://doi.org/10.1177/0091217417738937

Khokhar, J. Y., Dwiel, L. L., Henricks, A. M., Doucette, W. T., & Green, A. I. (2018). The link between schizophrenia and substance use disorder: A unifying hypothesis. *Schizophrenia Research, 194*, 78–85. https://doi.org/10.1016/j.schres.2017.04.016

Lamb, H. R., & Bachrach, L. (2001). Some perspectives on deinstitutionalization. *Psychiatric Services, 52*, 1039–1045.

Massoud, S., Arnaout, B., & Yoon, G. (2018). Alcohol withdrawal hallucinations in the general population, an epidemiological study. *Psychiatry Research, 262*, 129–134.

Morisano, D., Babor, T. F., & Robaina, K. A. (2017). Co-occurrence of substance use disorders with other psychiatric disorders: Implications for treatment services. *Nordic Studies on Alcohol and Drugs, 31*, 5–25.

Moulin, A., Evans, E. J., Xing, G., & Melnikow, J. (2018). Substance use, homelessness, mental illness and Medicaid coverage: A set-up for high emergency department utilization. *The Western Journal of Emergency Medicine, 19*(6), 902–906. https://doi.org/10.5811/westjem.2018.9.38954

Mueser, K. T., Drake, R. E., & Wallach, M. A. (1998). Dual diagnosis: A review of etiological theories. *Addiction Behaviors, 23*, 717–723.

NIDA. (2019, April 22). *Hallucinogens drug facts.* Retrieved April 21, 2021, from www.drugabuse.gov/publications/drugfacts/hallucinogens

Pardis, P., Remington, G., Panda, R., Lemez, M., & Agid, O. (2019). Clozapine and tardive dyskinesia in patients with schizophrenia: A systematic review. *Journal of Psychopharmacology, 33*(10), 1187–1198. https://doi.org/10.1177/0269881119862535

Podvoll, M. E. (1990). *Recovering sanity: A compassionate approach to understanding and treating psychosis.* Shambhala Publications, Inc.

Pressley, T. (2017). Public libraries, serious mental illness, and homelessness: A survey of public librarians. *Public Library Quarterly, 36*(1), 61–76. doi:10.1080/01616846.2017.1275772

Regier, D. A., Farmer, M. E., Rae, D. S., Locke, B., Keith, S., Judd, L., & Goodwin, F. (1990). Comorbidity of mental disorders with alcohol and other drug abuse: Results from the Epidemiologic Catchment Area (ECA) study. *JAMA: Journal of the American Medical Association, 264*, 2511–2518.

Robins, L. N., Wing, J., Wittchen, H., Helzer, J., Babor, T., Burke, J., Farmer, A., Jablenski, A., Pickens, R., Regier, D., Sartorious, N., & Towle, L., (1988). The composite international diagnostic interview: An epidemiologic instrument suitable for use in conjunction with different systems and in different cultures. *Archives of General Psychiatry, 45*, 1069–1077.

Schiller, L., & Bennett, A. (1994). *The quiet room.* Warner Books.

Steeds, H., Carhart-Harris, R. L., & Stone, J. M. (2015). Drug models of schizophrenia. *Therapeutic Advances in Psychopharmacology, 5*(1), 43–58. https://doi.org/10.1177/2045125314557797

Trotta, A., Murray, R., David, A., Kolliakou, A., O'Connor, J., Di Forti, M., . . . Fisher, H. (2016). Impact of different childhood adversities on 1-year outcomes of psychotic disorder in the genetics and psychosis study. *Schizophrenia Bulletin, 42*(2), 464–475. https://doi.org/10.1093/schbul/sbv131

Vallejos, M., Cesoni, O. M., Farinola, R., Bertone, M., & Prokopez, C. (2017). Adverse childhood experiences among men with schizophrenia. *Psychiatry Quarterly, 88*, 665–673. https://doi.org/10.1007/s11126-016-9487-2

Vega, D., Acosta, F., & Saavedra, P. (2021). Nonadherence after hospital discharge in patients with schizo-phrenia or schizoaffective disorder: A six-month naturalistic follow-up study. *Comprehensive Psychiatry, 108*. https://doi.org/10.1016/j.comppsych.2021.152240

Villatoro, A., Mays, V., Ponce, N., & Aneshensel, C. (2018). Perceived need for mental health care: The intersection of race, ethnicity, gender, and socioeconomic status. *Society and Mental Health, 8*(1), 1–24. doi:10.1177/2156869317718889

Williams, S., Agapoff, J., IV, Lu, B., Hishinuma, E., & Lee, M. (2019). The frequency of hospitalizations and length of stay differences between schizophrenic and schizoaffective disorder inpatients who use cannabis. *Journal of Substance Use, 24*(1), 21–28. doi:10.1080/14659891.2018.1489013

4 Co-occurring Personality and Substance Use Disorders

Fredrick Dombrowski

Introduction

Personality disorders (PDs) are unlike other mental health diagnoses, given the unique character-istics that accompany these disorders (Bennet & Johnson, 2017). Unlike other illnesses such as depression, anxiety, schizophrenia, and mania, PDs largely focus on difficulties with interpersonal functioning and interaction (Hasin et al., 2011). People living with PDs may use illicit substances to cope with these symptoms, although substance use will only further exacerbate interpersonal problems (Hasin & Kilcoyne, 2012). In many cases, people with PDs will attempt to engage in functional, gainful life activities. As the symptoms associated with PDs are not as overt as those of other mental health diagnoses, people interacting with those living with PDs may respond with increased judgment, frustration, and isolation from those with PDs (Jauk & Dieterich, 2019).

This chapter will review the unique experiences of those living with co-occurring PDs and SUD. Providing an in-depth analysis regarding the different types of PDs and discussing co-occurring substance use will allow for discussions about treatment options. Evidenced-based treatments will be reviewed for those living with PDs and SUDs. This chapter concludes with resources to access skills and treatment specifically related to the treatment of PDs.

Learning Objectives

- Identify the unique experiences of those living with personality disorders and co-occurring substance use disorders
- Identify the main diagnostic criteria of each personality disorder
- Identify the risks for countertransference when working with those living with co-occurring substance use and personality disorders
- Identify evidenced-based treatment modalities for personality disorders
- Obtain information about several national organizations dedicated to the treatment of personality disorders

Key Terms

Countertransference: When a clinician observes behaviors in the client that remind them of their past experiences, often transferring these past feelings onto the present client.

Non-suicidal Self-injury: A form of self-harm an individual will engage in with the intent of providing emotional relief as opposed to completing suicide.

Personality Clusters: Current classification criteria used in the *DSM-5* (APA, 2013) to differentiate between personality disorders with shared components and those without shared components.

Personality Disorder: Interpersonal cognitive, emotional experiences and behaviors deviating from cultural norms, causing ongoing distress and impairment in functioning.

DOI: 10.4324/9781003220916-5

Therapeutic Boundaries: A set of clear-cut rules and expectations within the clinical environment guiding acceptable behaviors of the patient and the treatment team.

Transference: When a client connects their clinician with past negative experiences and responds to the clinician as if they are a perpetrator of or a participant in these past negative experiences.

History of Personality Disorders and the *DSM*

Personality disorders (PDs) have been conceptualized in varying ways throughout the twentieth century. The mental health community has identified PDs as primarily treatable disorders in the *DSM-5* (APA, 2013). The previous version of the *DSM* placed PDs on the Axis II level, indicating a difference between PDs and other mental health diagnoses (APA, 2000). This distinction of Axis II diagnoses indicates disorders that are usually observable in childhood and have ongoing impact throughout the span of the individual's life. More traditional mental health disorders such as bipolar disorder, anxiety disorder, and substance use disorders were placed on Axis I, indicating the need for treatment of a primary mental health condition, usually with an onset of early adulthood. Additional axes were provided in the *DSM-IV*, such as Axis III, indicating pertinent patient medical information; Axis IV, identifying environmental and psychosocial factors; and Axis V, giving an individual a score between 1 and 100, indicating the client's overall level of functioning. Oftentimes, insurance carriers would not reimburse for treatment of Axis II disorders, despite the severity of symptoms experienced by the client (Doweiko, 2009). While clinicians during this time were able to recognize the need for treatment of personality disorders, the lack of reimbursement served to slow the development of evidence-based practices for these disorders.

The research on PDs is rather limited, as the majority of the research focuses on borderline personality disorder. Additional research has attempted to identify how gender correlates to personality disorders as it is believed that men are much more likely to be diagnosed with narcissistic personality disorder, whereas women are more likely to be diagnosed with borderline personality disorder (APA, 2013). There are critiques about the research on sex differences as concerns build that personality disorders may present themselves differently between men and women (Schulte Holthausen & Habel, 2018). Continued research on various personality disorders remains in demand as the symptoms associated with these disorders have global impact on the client.

Research has uncovered early childhood factors that can be predictors of the development of personality disorders (Neumann, 2017). Childhood abuse and maltreatment have been associated with an increased likelihood of the development of narcissistic personality disorder, antisocial personality disorder, and borderline personality disorder (Johnson et al., 1999). There are concerns that those parents living with personality disorders may model such behaviors to their children (Dittrich et al., 2018). As children grow and develop, they may take on such characteristics, which then, in turn, cause additional interpersonal difficulties with supports and with work. The individual will then experience additional interpersonal problems with their relationships and can struggle to create effective boundaries (Neumann, 2017). Difficulties with romantic and interpersonal interactions serve to enhance the distorted view of reality that an individual living with a personality disorder experiences.

The ongoing struggles with interpersonal interactions, coupled with extreme emotional distress, makes those living with PDs prime targets for substance use disorders (Walker & Druss, 2017). The interpersonal difficulties experienced by those with PDs contribute to client isolation and struggles to complete goals. Turning to the use of substances can seem like an option as interpersonal relationships (although toxic or unhelpful) can be maintained through the mutual use of illicit substances (Trull et al., 2018).

Primary Symptomology

Those living with PDs may struggle in traditional group and individual treatment. Their inter-personal difficulties can alienate other clients and contribute to a breakdown of the therapeutic alliance (Tanzilli et al., 2017). The type of PD experienced by the client is indicative of varying potential for interpersonal problems. To help counselors further understand the impact of these interpersonal difficulties, the varying PDs were separated into three categories that use basic core features to distinguish diagnoses. The personality disorders associated with Cluster A are defined by interpersonal behavior that may seem odd or eccentric. Those experiencing Cluster A personality disorders may seem somewhat distant and disconnected in their relationships with others. Those with Cluster A PDs can have interests or a focus that is not shared by many others and seem more content with less social contact. Additionally, those with Cluster A personality disorders generally lack trust in others and may be guarded interpersonally and in treatment (APA, 2013). The diagnoses linked with Cluster A personality disorders are paranoid personality disorder, schizoid personality disorder, and schizotypal personality disorder.

Those living with Cluster B PDs experience exaggerated and unpredictable interpersonal behavior (Raynol & Chabrol, 2016). Clients living with Cluster B PDs will experience very intense emotions and have impulsive reactions to triggers. Substance use and illegal and potentially harmful behaviors are conducted by the client toward others and toward themselves (Oldham, 2018). Their interpersonal difficulties make long-term friendships highly unlikely, thus supporting negative core beliefs about the world, themselves, and others (Linehan, 1993). Many behaviors associated with active substance use often look like symptoms of Cluster B PDs. For example, if an individual is living with a severe substance use disorder, their willingness to take money and resources from family members or engage in dangerous illegal activity (such as armed robbery) can make it seem as if the individual lacks empathy and shows a disregard for the rights of others (Doweiko, 2009). In other instances, those living with severe substance use disorders may engage in illicit sexual activity to help cover the costs of obtaining substances. These actions may be viewed as a sense of self-harm on behalf of the individual as they are placing themselves at risk. At other times, an individual living with severe substance use disorder may experience rigidity and irritability in cognition, causing others to interpret these reactions as signs that the patient expects preferential treatment over others (Howard et al., 2020). The disorders associated with Cluster B are histrionic personality disorder, borderline personality disorder, antisocial personality disorder, and narcissistic personality disorder (APA, 2013).

Symptoms of anxiety, fearfulness, and difficulties with interpersonal connections are the primary factors associated with Cluster C PDs (Gustavo & Grant, 2018). Those with Cluster C disorders may find themselves in abusive relationships, unable to leave as they feel dependent on their abuser. Those within this cluster can have trouble with changes in their lives and their settings that cause intense symptoms of fear as they lack control (Knapek et al., 2017). Finally, those with Cluster C disorders may avoid interpersonal relationships in an attempt to prevent potential harm caused by interpersonal interactions. The diagnoses associated with Cluster C disorders are dependent personality disorder, obsessive-compulsive personality disorder, and avoidant personality disorder (APA, 2013).

Cluster A Personality Disorders

The primary feature of odd or eccentric behavior may cause those living with Cluster A personality disorders to feel on the fringes of society and disconnected from potential supports (Fonseca-Pedrero et al., 2018). The three diagnoses in Cluster A personality disorders focus on interpretations of the world in which others are not to be trusted for concerns of the safety of the individual. Those living with Cluster A personality disorders may show symptoms that are akin to schizophrenia, such as negative symptoms (decreased hygiene, flat affect, etc.) and may share beliefs of the world that may be viewed as paranoid. Although these symptoms share overlap with other illnesses, the positive symptoms associated with schizophrenia, such as audio or visual hallucinations, are not present (Berichon et al., 2019). Men are more likely to live with Cluster A personality disorders than women (Rosell et al., 2014).

Paranoid personality disorder is classified in the *DSM-5* (APA, 2013) as code 301.0. Those living with paranoid personality disorder (PPD) experience symptoms that can make treatment difficult. The very nature of PPD and substance use disorders leads to unique challenges, such as the belief that others will harm, deceive, or manipulate them without sufficient evidence. Those living with PPD question the loyalty of their friends and family and are hypervigilant toward signs of betrayal from their supports (Fryd Birkeland, 2017). The individual will struggle to disclose concerns, even to treatment providers, as they worry this information will be used against them. Even in benign or objective-based statements, those living with PPD will interpret hidden meanings of personal invalidation. Romantic relationships are impacted by these symptoms as those living with PPD often assume their significant other is unfaithful. Those living with PPD will hold on to grudges associated with instances of invalidation and will interpret interpersonal responses to be attacks on their character or reputation (APA, 2013).

Those living with PPD will struggle to build successful connections at work, in their personal lives, and even with health-care professionals (Lee, 2017). The assumption that others will attempt to harm the individual makes co-occurring treatment difficult as it is viewed from the perspective that the professional cannot be trusted. The nature of the disorder can make treatment particularly challenging from the standpoint of the counselor. Counselors working with those living with PPD can become frustrated as the client may struggle to connect and be open with the counselor. Those living with PPD are at higher risk of substance use and illegal activities than those not living with personality disorders (Nijdam-Jones et al., 2018). Their connection to treatment may be through court mandates, which require counselors to disclose the clients' progress to legal authorities, thus strengthening the belief that the professional cannot be trusted (Berichon et al., 2019). The lack of trust in the counselor can make the counselor feel as if the client is being 'resistant', whereas they are responding to the symptoms associated with the disorder they are living with.

Schizoid personality disorder is classified in the DSM-5 (APA, 2013) as code 301.2. The characteristics associated with schizoid personality disorder (SPD) allow for others to describe the individual as a curmudgeon based on the negative symptoms, such as indifference to praise, support, and interpersonal connection (Coolidge et al., 2013). The individual living with SPD can also seem detached from reality and preoccupied with fantasy and appear to not consider social norms (Danzer, 2015). Those with SPD will struggle in Alcoholics Anonymous or treatment that includes group counseling as they will often seem disinterested in connecting with others, contributing to greater incidence of isolation. The symptoms associated with SPD can be confusing to clinicians as the individual living with this disorder will have little interest in connecting with other clients and counselors alike, impacting the therapeutic alliance (Ward, 2018). Those living with SPD are indifferent to activities that would be considered fun and may seem indifferent to sexual interactions. The interpersonal struggles to build connections are not as overt as symptoms experienced with other personality disorders, and those with SPD may be successful in isolated work activities.

Counselors can be at risk of misinterpreting the symptoms associated with SPD as a lack of motivation to change. Such inaccurate interpretations of symptoms can cause an inappropriate treatment plan in which the counselor attempts to enhance the client's motivation to change, although the client has little interest in adjusting aspects of their lives (such as isolation), which may be viewed as problematic by the counselor (Coolidge et al., 2013). Treatment of those living with this disorder will usually be prompted by concerned family members as opposed to intrinsic motivation on the part of the individual.

Schizotypal personality disorder is classified in the *DSM-5* (APA, 2013) as code 301.22. Symptoms associated with schizotypal personality disorder (STPD) are similar to those of other diagnoses within Cluster A of personality disorders. The individual can experience odd or eccentric beliefs and struggle to connect with others. The individual can also have unusual patterns of speech and show pervasive misinterpretation of events (APA, 2013). Those living with STPD may have distorted perceptions of events, odd speech, and a flat affect, putting them at risk for misdiagnosis of schizophrenia. Those living with STPD do not have the positive symptoms associated with schizophrenia, such as auditory or visual hallucinations (Danzer, 2015).

Counselors can experience challenges to treatment of those living with co-occurring substance use and STPD as an individual may express inaccurate interpretations of events during group counseling (Rosell et al., 2014). The research regarding treatment of STPD has highlighted some benefits for psychiatric intervention. However, the research has been limited to small sample sizes, making it difficult for generalizable application (Kirchner et al., 2018). Counselors will need to be patient when working with those living with STPD as they will need to take time to understand the client's unique rate and pattern of speech, coupled with how the client makes sense of their life and personal situations (Cicero et al., 2020).

Cluster B Personality Disorders

Cluster B personality disorders comprise borderline personality disorder, histrionic personality disorder, antisocial personality disorder, and narcissistic personality disorder (APA, 2013). Those living with these disorders experience intense emotional mood swings and struggle to have empathy for others. In many instances, the lawless behaviors associated specifically with this group of personality disorders can include illegal substance use, stalking or harassment, and even inflicting cruelty or harm on self and others (Trull et al., 2010).

Borderline personality disorder is classified in the *DSM-5* (APA, 2013) as code 301.83. Borderline personality disorder (BPD) is one of the most widely treated Cluster B personality disorders (Shaw & Zanarini, 2018). Those living with BPD experience intense emotional distress, which is often triggered by misinterpreted social cues. Those living with BPD have a fear of abandonment and may misinterpret benign actions (such as a friend not returning a text immediately) as evidence to support the belief they are being abandoned (Chanen et al., 2020). The misinterpreted social cues flood the individual with intense emotions of anxiety, panic, and frustration. The individual will experience unstable relationships as they react to others in ways that are combative, hurtful, or irritating, causing their supports and even family members to avoid them. Upon realizing that their actions toward others may have been based on misunderstood information, the individual then experiences an increased rush of negative thoughts toward themselves and extreme negative feelings. The intense emotional distress is a trigger for self-injurious behaviors, specifically cutting and increased suicidal ideation (APA, 2013).

Those living with BPD have higher rates of self-harm and are at greater risk of suicide than those not living with a personality disorder (Carpenter et al., 2015). Self-harm experienced by this population manifests in various ways, such as scratching, cutting, and even burning. A common misinterpretation of self-harm occurs when counselors assume that the individual is engaging in self-harm as an attempt for attention or a cry for help. On the contrary, those living with BPD engage in self-harm as a result of severe emotional dysregulation and to sublimate psychic pain. In other words, the sense of fear and anxiety that occur as the individual perceives potential abandonment is so overwhelming that the act of engaging in self-harm moves the focus toward the physical pain and away from the overwhelming emotions (Terzi et al., 2017).

Those living with BPD have higher rates of comorbid substance use disorders and other mental health diagnoses (Trull et al., 2018). The interpersonal difficulties associated with BPD often leave the individual feeling isolated and alone, fostering the development of major depressive disorder. As mood swings are very intense, alcohol and substance use become options to manage these intense mood swings (Howard et al., 2020). Vocational and career goals are often blocked as misinterpreted interpersonal cues contribute to problems in the workplace (Carpenter et al., 2015).

The intense emotional mood swings experienced by those living with BPD require the counselor to develop appropriate therapeutic boundaries. It is not uncommon for clients with BPD to make several calls to their counselors per day asking for help (Cristea et al., 2017). When a counselor is unable to respond relatively quickly, the client will misinterpret the lack of response as evidence that the counselor is abandoning them. This misinterpretation contributes to the client being aggravated at the counselor, and they may be rude or disrespectful to the counselor and even file complaints and grievances against them (Howard et al., 2020). Many counselors work in the helping professions with the goal of helping others and may struggle initially to maintain appropriate therapeutic boundaries, which can encourage a client to call several times per day (Mehr et al., 2010). Because of this, counselors must have easily identifiable objective boundaries with clients that inform them of the role of the counselor, options to respond to the patient, and information regarding crisis services or services when the office is not open.

Within our society, individuals such as rock stars, politicians, and movie stars may experience being the center of national attention at varying times and intensities. In these instances, being the center of attention may be a side effect of their work or vocation. However, the need to be the center of attention becomes diagnosable as the need causes individuals to lie, exaggerate, or purposefully harm themselves or others to obtain this attention. Histrionic personality disorder (HPD) is mainly defined as this need to be the center of attention at a cost of social supports and successful interpersonal functioning (APA, 2013). HPD is classified in the *DSM-5* (APA, 2013) as code 301.50. When those living with HPD are not the center of attention, they will feel uncomfortable, often making the necessary changes to become the center of attention (Hughes et al., 2020). Those living with HPD may wear provocative clothing or engage in sexually inappropriate behavior. With the need to be the center of attention, culturally appropriate behaviors and interactions will be more dramatic than necessary, and extreme language will be used. Those with HPD will then misinterpret the depth and strength of their relationships as they may feel they have intense bonds with others, but these beliefs are not shared by those with whom they supposedly have the bonds (Albein-Urios et al., 2019). The desire to be the center of attention allows those with HPD to be easily suggestible, often engaging in activities that they may personally not agree with so as to obtain or maintain being the center of attention.

Antisocial personality disorder is classified in the *DSM-5* (APA, 2013) as code 301.7. When thinking of antisocial personality disorder (ASPD), individuals such as Ted Bundy and Jeffrey Dahmer may come to mind as these two men specifically lacked the ability to have empathy for others. The lack of empathy and mutual human connection is paramount for those living with ASPD (Bennet & Johnson, 2017). Whereas most humans will express empathy toward others and attempt to understand the lived experience of another, this appears to be missing in those with ASPD, and as a result, the experiences of others are not as important to the individual as their own experience (Brook et al., 2016). Just as most people would not feel bad crumpling up and throwing out a napkin, those with ASPD experience a similar disregard but for the rights of others. Many people may view their interactions with others as being a reflection on their own character. This is not shared by those living with ASPD as lying, cheating, manipulating, and stealing are acceptable coping strategies necessary for obtaining goals (DeLisi et al., 2019). Many of those living in active addiction often show signs of this personality disorder as their need for their substance of choice propels them to harm others. However, in the absence of substance use, these behaviors may have never been an option for the individual. Treating SUDs for those living with ASPD is especially difficult as rules and laws seem almost optional, and the consequence of engaging in lawless behavior remains the only deterrent to engaging in these behaviors, whereas others may feel morally conflicted when they engage in lawless behavior (Kolla & Mishra, 2018).

As those living with ASPD may engage in behaviors that encroach the safety and well-being of others, it is not uncommon for counselors to experience countertransference and feelings of fear toward those living with ASPD (Dunbar et al., 2020). Those living with ASPD may not view their predatory behaviors toward others as being unethical or illegal. Populations living with ASPD will not independently seek treatment but are mandated through forensic treatment and justice-linked diversion (Di Virgilio et al., 2021). With this said, counselors in various levels of care will still most likely work with this population and must work to manage team countertransference while also protecting other clients from being victims of predatory behavior. Those living with ASPD will also most likely experience greater rates of withdrawal from services as treatment may be imposed as opposed to intrinsically sought (Thylstrup, & Hesse, 2016).

Cluster B personality disorders also include narcissistic personality disorder (NPD). NPD is classified in the *DSM-5* (APA, 2013) as code 301.81. Characterized by a grandiose sense of self-importance, those living with NPD struggle in social relationships as their own needs will supersede the needs of others (Crisp & Gabbard, 2020). In many ways, this lack of recognition of the needs for others can be viewed as a lack of empathy as those with NPD struggle to identify how others are suffering, and they generally have no interest in attempting to do so. Those living with NPD will have an expectation of admiration from others and a distorted view of self-importance (APA, 2013). Those living with NPD will experience higher rates of substance use disorders and depression as symptoms cause interpersonal difficulties and increased isolation (Tanzilli et al., 2017). There is an ongoing dissonance between the individual's sense of being and their interactions with others who are not affirming of a grandiose sense of self-importance. Many people living with NPD will feel sad and lonely, causing them to turn specifically to the use of substances. Additionally, as those with NPD age, they also experience increased rates of depression as they become physically limited and are unable to engage in actions they used to do with ease, increasing internal conflict within their sense of self.

Those living with NPD are not prone to seek counseling on their own as they typically do not believe they have a problem and often are referred by their work employee assistance program (EAP) to seek help to maintain their jobs. Treating those living with NPD can be difficult in various treatment settings. As those with NPD primarily focus on themselves and their own needs while expecting admiration from others, this can make group treatment especially difficult (Weinberg & Ronningstam, 2020). The expectation of praise from others can also cause counselors to experience countertransference with this population as treatment providers may become frustrated that the client lacks insight into the experiences of others.

Key indicators of Cluster C personality disorders are ongoing fear and anxiety related to interpersonal functioning and lack of control. Within this subset, counselors will encounter dependent personality disorder (DPD) (*DSM-5* Code 301.6). Those living with DPD have a fear of being alone and may lack faith in their most basic decision making, often leaning on others to take control of their lives (APA, 2013). Anxiety associated with loneliness will often cause an individual to maintain relationships that can be detrimental to them (Rashn et al., 2018). Such relationships can contain physical, sexual, or emotional abuse and coercion. Those living with DPD may struggle to attend treatment as their primary focus is on their significant other. Although those living with DPD may want to pursue different life options, they maintain these relationships due to fears of being alone. Thus, those living with DPD will engage in substance use to cope with internal conflict (Furnham, 2018). As those living with DPD often rely on others to make decisions for them, this can cause counselors to experience countertransference as there may be a desire for the client to be self-determined (Sachse & Kramer, 2019). Treatment barriers can become insurmountable, especially if the significant other of an individual living with DPD is not supportive of treatment. Ongoing agreeableness and lack of self-assertion can contribute to an individual with DPD maintaining substance use if their significant other is still using substances (Furnham, 2018).

Obsessive-compulsive personality disorder is classified in the *DSM-5* (APA, 2013) as code 301.4. Those living with obsessive-compulsive personality disorder (OCDPD) have rigid expectations of cleanliness, order, and control (APA, 2013). The rigid expectations cause the individual to struggle with flexibility in layouts of home and other personal spaces. Making adjustments to schedules, moving objects, or making quick responses to unexpected stressors are hard for those living with OCDPD (Gurok et al., 2019). As the need for control is paramount, those living with OCDPD experience interpersonal difficulties with friendships and with vocational interactions, causing interpersonal friction. Due to such concerns, those living with ODCPD may choose to isolate from others, making treatment for substance use and OCDPD difficult for those living with this illness (Atroszko et al., 2020).

Avoidant personality disorder is classified in the *DSM-5* (APA, 2013) as code 301.82. Ongoing isolation and a lack of trust of others are major symptoms associated with avoidant personality disorder (AvPD). Those living with AvPD may lack trust in others and have a belief that they will experience ridicule or harsh criticism in social situations (Lampe & Malhi, 2018). Those living with AvPD often have low self-esteem and conceptualize the world in a framework of fear. To avoid potential criticism, those living with AvPD tend to be isolated and limit their interactions with others (Simonsen et al., 2019). Increased anxiety in mandatory interpersonal situation can cause those living with AvPD to seek illicit substances to manage overwhelming feelings of uneasiness (Havranek et al., 2017). The euphoria experienced with some substances can minimize potential interpersonal concerns, and therefore, those living with AvPD may rely on substances for all interpersonal interactions (Maillard et al., 2019).

Many counselors in busy outpatient clinics may not work with many clients living with AvPD as the volume of people attending treatment can exacerbate symptoms. As a result, those who seek treatment choose to do so in a private practice with fewer clientele (Lampe & Malhi, 2018). This can be difficult for treating those living with co-occurring AvPD and substance use disorder as concerns about being judged may prevent them from seeking an enhanced treatment program as groups in which interaction with other patients is necessary (Maillard et al., 2019). Some counselors may misinterpret the patient's disconnection from others as being a sign that the individual may not be serious about treatment or recovery. Given the recommendation for group counseling and social support through AA and NA, those living with AvPD may find steps to recovery to exacerbate symptoms associated with their co-occurring personality disorder (Gurok et al., 2019).

Countertransference Experienced by Counselors

While the previous descriptions touched on difficulties experienced by counselors working with those with co-occurring substance use disorders and personality disorders, there are some global experiences of countertransference that counselors may share regarding these populations. As many personality disorders may cause the client to withdraw from others, some counselors may misinterpret this as being evidence that counseling is not working or even challenge the client's commitment to treatment (Di Virgilio et al., 2021). Concerns regarding countertransference are heightened for counselors who are currently early in their careers or working in their internships as they are less likely to discuss such concerns with supervisors (Mehr et al., 2010). Those living with co-occurring personality disorders and substance use disorders have often been viewed as problematic and more difficult to treat by those in the helping professions (Yakeley, 2019). The interpersonal difficulties associated with these disorders can make counselors feel unprepared and overwhelmed when working with these groups (Michaud et al., 2020).

Some living with personality disorders may be at ongoing risk of self-harm, whereas others may struggle to have empathy for others (Howard et al., 2020). Counselors in observation of these behaviors can become frustrated as such behaviors may be a direct contradiction of their own values and beliefs (Tanzilli et al., 2017). The counselor can feel frustrated and angry at the client as they may believe that the client is attempting to manipulate them or other clients (Kolla & Mishra, 2018).

Those living with Cluster B personality disorders will struggle with interpersonal boundaries (Howard et al., 2020). Such interpersonal boundaries may cause the counselor to over-identify with the client, especially as those living with personality disorders may make such statements as 'You are the only counselor who has ever helped me'. In these instances, staff may be pitted against each other as the individual living with a personality disorder may tend to view one staff member as 'all good' or 'all bad' (Linehan, 1993). Inconsistencies in how the client reacts to staff cause a lack of clarity regarding treatment trajectory and can even pose concerns as to how counselors may respond to the patient (Green, 2018).

In some instances, counselors may become frustrated and resort to arguing with their clients. When this occurs, change is most likely not going to happen as the counselor has deviated from their clinical skill set (Weinberg & Ronningstam, 2020). Counselors can become frustrated when working with those who struggle interpersonally as this can cause problems in group sessions (Di Virgilio et al., 2021). For less structured groups, it would not be uncommon for an individual living with a personality disorder to monopolize the group, have strong responses to other group members, or isolate from participating altogether (Michaud et al., 2020). To assist with managing instances of countertransference, counselors working with those living with comorbid substance use and personality disorders must have regular supervision to create appropriate treatment plans, assess for countertransference, maintain boundaries, and consider any potential changes needed in the level of care (Dunbar et al., 2020).

Evidence-Based Treatment

Using manualized and structured evidence-based theories can help in navigating some of the pitfalls associated with treating those living with co-occurring personality and substance use disorders (Grenyer et al., 2018). One of the most widely used and researched evidence-based practices is dialectic behavioral therapy (DBT). Created by Marsha Linehan, DBT was modified from cognitive behavioral therapy (CBT), utilizing Eastern-based philosophies such as mindfulness to help patients become aware of and modify their emotional states (Reyes-Ortega et al., 2020). When clients engage in DBT, they are linked with a rigid structure of individual and group psychotherapy where they engage in the four basic modules of treatment: mindfulness, emotional regulation, interpersonal effectiveness, and distress tolerance (Linehan, 1993). The rigidity of the program requires clients to engage in a succession of sessions that follow the skills associated with each module. Clients are required to complete regular target-based activities such as diary cards indicating which skills they used and worksheets. The client is expected to attend all sessions, which can include multiple group sessions and an individual session throughout the week for the duration of the program, which can be between six months and two years, depending on the setting of the clinic. Roughly 25% of clients drop out of DBT, although this number is not significantly different from other treatment modules (Dixon & Linardon, 2020). Evidence has been found to support the use of DBT for both adults and adolescents living with co-occurring substance use and personality disorders (McCauley et al., 2018).

Mentalization-based therapy (MBT) is another evidence-based modality that also uses time-limited and structured sessions to assist those living with co-occurring personality disorders and substance use. Within an MBT framework, traditional psychodynamic considerations are connected with current research regarding attachment and social cognition (Batemen et al., 2018). The issues associated with personality disorders can be connected to how an individual builds and views attachment to caregivers throughout their lives (Fonagy & Allison, 2014). If a child is ignored or abused or struggles to develop relationships with primary caregivers, they may develop personality disorders later in life (Rossouw & Fonagy, 2012). The client will then interpret ongoing interpersonal interactions through these lenses, which may be distorted or inaccurate with the current evidence. Clients engaging in MBT will work to become aware of their internal responses by actively attempting to pause their internal experiences for assessment and re-evaluation. This can be done through the use of worksheets and even games (Grimes & Williams, 2020). MBT has been found to be helpful in treating adults and adolescents living with co-occurring substance use and mental health diagnoses (Beck et al., 2020).

As it can be difficult to treat those living with personality disorders as they struggle with interpersonal interactions, it is important for counselors to remain abreast of ongoing research and connecting with institutions committed to the treatment of such disorders. As there are various personality disorders, so, too, are there various groups and organizations committed to ongoing research and treatment. The list of groups in the Recommended Reading section include their current website addresses to enhance the readers' information about personality disorders.

Conclusion

Those living with co-occurring personality disorders and substance use disorders often struggle with traditional treatment as interpersonal relationships and the therapeutic alliance are strained. The interpersonal difficulties present as barriers to many living with personality disorders attending treatment as they will lack trust in treatment providers or other patients. Many patients living with personality disorders will use substances to manage interpersonal anxiety or to cope with severe emotional dysregulation. The issue of countertransference remains ongoing for those working with patients living with personality disorders as the patient may isolate from others, become frustrated with treatment, or engage in manipulative tactics with other patients. Ongoing supervision is mandatory for those working with patients living with co-occurring personality disorders and substance use disorders. Treatment outcomes are improved when clinics use structured, evidence-based practices that help mitigate interpersonal difficulties. Ongoing research on behalf of the counselor is needed to remain abreast of changes in treatment modalities. Being linked with national organizations can help the counselor improve their skill set for these various populations.

Questions for Consideration

1. Personality disorders can be challenging to work with. Which PD do you believe would be the most challenging for you and why?
2. What do you think the greatest obstacles are to effective treatment for persons living with personality disorders and substance use disorders?
3. Which therapeutic skills do you believe are most important when working with co-occurring personality and substance use disorders?

Case Study

Janet is a 27-year-old single Caucasian female living with her mother. Janet was hospitalized for six days following an episode of suicidal ideation in which she described her intent to run into traffic. During her outpatient intake assessment, she indicates that she has engaged in the practice of non-suicidal self-injury (specifically cutting) since the age of 13, during which time she also began experimenting with alcohol and marijuana. She reports her belief that she is unable to trust people as she feels that she has loved people only to have them betray her. Janet reports that she struggles to make and maintain friends as she will become angry with them when they do not return her calls. When her friends do not respond to her, she feels overwhelmed with emotion and assumes that others have abandoned her. She reports her main source of social support to be people she has connected with at a local bar. While Janet reports that her mother is her strongest support, she reports that their relationship is strained due to ongoing arguments.

Questions to Consider

1. Which personality disorder do you think Janet may be living with?
2. What symptomology is present that leads to your diagnosis?
3. As Janet's counselor, how can you best help her reach her treatment goals?

Recommended Reading

The National Education Alliance for Borderline Personality Disorder. www.borderlinepersonalitydisorder.org/
New England Personality Disorder Association. www.nepda.org/
International Society for the Study of Personality Disorders. www.isspd.com/
Treatment and Research Advocacy for Borderline Personality Disorder. www.tara4bpd.org/

References

Albein-Urios, N., Martinez-Gonzalez, J., Lozano-Rojas, O., & Verdejo-Garcia, A. (2019). Dysfunctional personality beliefs linked to emotion recognition deficits in individuals with cocaine addiction and personality disorders. *Frontiers in Psychiatry*, *18*. https://doi.org/10.3389/fpsyt.2019.00431

Alcorn, J. L., 3rd, Gowin, J. L., Green, C. E., Swann, A. C., Moeller, F. G., & Lane, S. D. (2013). Aggression, impulsivity, and psychopathic traits in combined antisocial personality disorder and substance use disorder. *Journal of Neuropsychiatry and Clinical Neurosciences*, *25*(3), 229–232. doi:10.1176/appi.neuropsych.12030060

American Counseling Association. (2014). *ACA code of ethics*. Author.

American Psychiatric Association. (2000). *Diagnostic and statistical manual of mental disorders* (4thed., 5th ed.). Author.

American Psychiatric Association. (2013). *Diagnostic and statistical manual of mental disorders* (5th ed., text rev.). Author.

Atroszko, P. A., Demetrovics, Z., & Griffiths, M. D. (2020). Work addiction, obsessive-compulsive personality disorder, burn-out, and global burden of disease: Implications from the ICD-11. *International Journal of Environmental Research and Public Health*, *17*(2). http://dx.doi.org/10.3390/ijerph17020660

Batemen, A., Campbell, C., Luyten, P., & Fonagy, P. (2018). A mentalization-based approach to common factors in the treatment of borderline personality disorder. *Current Opinion in Psychology*, *21*, 44–49.

Beck, E., Bo, S., Jørgensen, M. S., Gondan, M., Poulsen, S., Storebø, O. J., . . . Simonsen, E. (2020). Mentalization-based treatment in groups for adolescents with borderline personality disorder: A randomized controlled trial. *Journal of Child Psychology and Psychiatry*, *61*, 594–604. https://doi.org/10.1111/jcpp.13152

Bennet, A., & Johnson, D. (2017). Co-morbidity of personality disorder and clinical syndrome in high-risk incarcerated offenders. *The Journal of Forensic Practice*, *19*(3), 207–216.

Berichon, M., Birgy, T., Konrath, C., & Abraham, S. (2019). Challenges of treatment and living with the stigma related to paranoid personality disorder. *Human Journals*, *12*(3), 51–64.

Boog, M., Van Hest, K., Drescher, T., Verschuur, M., & Franken, I. (2018). Schema modes and personality disorder symptoms in alcohol dependent and cocaine dependent patients. *European Addiction Research*, *24*(5), 226–233.

Brook, J., Zhang, C., Rubenstone, E., Primack, B., & Brook, D. (2016). Comorbid trajectories of substance use as predictors of antisocial personality disorder, major depressive episode, and generalized anxiety disorder. *Addictive Behaviors*, *62*, 114–121.

Carpenter, R., Wood, P., & Trull, T. (2015). Comorbidity of borderline personality disorder and lifetime substance use disorders in a nationally representative sample. *Journal of Personality Disorders*, *30*(3), 336–350. https://doi.org/10.1521/pedi_2015_29_197

Chanen, A., Nicol, K., Betts, J., & Thompson, K. (2020). Diagnosis and treatment of borderline personality disorder in young people. *Current Psychiatry Reports, 22*(5). https://doi.org/10.1007/s11920-020-01144-5

Cicero, D., Gawęda, Ł., & Nelson, B. (2020). The placement of anomalous self-experiences within schizotypal personality in a nonclinical sample. *Schizophrenia Research, 218*, 219–225.

Coolidge, F., Estey, A., Segal, D., & Marle, P. (2013). Are alexithymia and schizoid personality disorder synonymous diagnoses? *Comprehensive Psychiatry, 54*(2), 141–148.

Corey, G. (2018). *Theory and practice of counseling and psychotherapy* (10th ed.). Cengage Learning. ISBN: 978-1305263727

Crisp, H., & Gabbard, G. (2020). Principles of psychodynamic treatment for patients with narcissistic personality disorder. *Journal of Personality Disorders, 34*. https://doi.org/10.1521/pedi.2020.34.supp.143

Cristea, I., Gentili, C., Cotet, C., Palomba, D., Barbui, C., & Cuijpers, P. (2017). Efficacy of psychotherapies for borderline personality disorder: A systematic review and meta-analysis. *JAMA Psychiatry, 74*(4), 319–328. doi:10.1001/jamapsychiatry.2016.4287

Danzer, G. (2015). Integrating object relations and alcoholics anonymous principles in the treatment schizoid personality disorder and co-occurring alcohol dependence. *Journal of Theory Construction & Testing, 19*(2), 55–64.

DeLisi, M., Drury, A., & Elbert, M. (2019). The etiology of antisocial personality disorder: The differential roles of adverse childhood experiences and childhood psychopathology. *Comprehensive Psychiatry, 92*, 1–6.

Dittrich, K., Boedeker, K., Kluczniok, D., Jaite, C., Hindi Attar, C., Fuehrer, D., . . . Bermpohl, F. (2018). Child abuse potential in mothers with early life maltreatment, borderline personality disorder and depression. *The British Journal of Psychiatry, 213*(1), 412–418. doi:10.1192/bjp.2018.74

Di Virgilio, P., De Page, L., & Titeca, P. (2021). Countertransference in forensic patients with psychosis: Associations with symptomatology, inpatient violence, and psychopathic personality traits. *Journal of Forensic Psychology Research and Practice*. doi:10.1080/24732850.2021.1874975

Dixon, L., & Linardon, J. (2020). A systematic review and meta-analysis of dropout rates from dialectical behaviour therapy in randomized controlled trials. *Cognitive Behaviour Therapy, 49*(3), 181–196.

Doweiko, H. (2009). *Concepts of chemical dependency* (7th ed.). Pearson Publishing.

Dunbar, E. T., Koltz, R. L., Elliott, A., & Hurt-Avila, K. M. (2020). The role of clinical supervision in treating clients with antisocial personality disorder. *The Journal of Counselor Preparation and Supervision, 13*(3).

Fonagy, P., & Allison, E. (2014). The role of mentalizing and epistemic trust in the therapeutic relationship. *Psychotherapy, 51*, 372–380.

Fonseca-Pedrero, E., Debbané, M., Ortuño-Sierra, J., Chan, R. C. K., Cicero, D. C., Zhang, L. C., . . . Jablensky, A. (2018). The structure of schizotypal personality traits: A cross-national study. *Psychological Medicine, 48*(3), 451–462.

Fryd Birkeland, S. (2017). Paranoigenic extremes: A reappraisal concerning paranoid personality disorder. *Current Psychiatry Reviews, 13*(1), 23–34.

Furnham, A. (2018). A big five facet analysis of sub-clinical dependent personality disorder (Dutifulness). *Psychiatry Research, 270*, 622–626.

Gillespie, N. A., Aggen, S. H., Neale, M. C., Knudsen, G. P., Krueger, R. F., South, S. C., . . . Reichborn-Kjennerud, T. (2018). Associations between personality disorders and cannabis use and cannabis use disorder: A population-based twin study. *Addiction, 113*, 1488–1498. https://doi.org/10.1111/add.14209

Green, H. (2018). Team splitting and the "borderline personality": A relational reframe. *Psychoanalytic Psychotherapy, 32*(3), 249–266.

Grenyer, B., Lewis, K., Fanaian, M., & Kotze, B. (2018). Treatment of personality disorder using a whole of service stepped care approach: A cluster randomized controlled trial. *PLoS One, 13*(11), e0206472. https://doi.org/10.1371/journal.pone.0206472

Grimes, C. W., & Williams, L. L. (2020). Mentalization-based treatment activities, games, and intersession activities. In L. Williams & O. Muir (Eds.), *Adolescent suicide and self-injury*. Springer. https://doi.org/10.1007/978-3-030-42875-4_4

Gurok, M., Korucu, T., Kilic, M., Yildirim, H., & Atmaca, M. (2019). Hippocampus and amygdalar volumes in patients with obsessive-compulsive personality disorder. *Journal of Clinical Neuroscience, 64*, 259–263.

Gustavo, M., & Grant, J. (2018). Gambling disorder and obsessive: Compulsive personality disorder: A frequent but understudied comorbidity. *Journal of Behavioral Addictions, 7*(2), 366–374.

Hasin, D. S., Fenton, M. C., Skodol, A., Krueger, R., Keyes, K., Geier, T., & Grant, B. (2011). Personality disorders and the 3-year course of alcohol, drug, and nicotine use disorders. *Archives of General Psychiatry, 68*(11), 1158–1167. doi:10.1001/archgenpsychiatry.2011.78

Hasin, D. S., & Grant, B. F. (2015). The National Epidemiologic Survey on Alcohol and Related Conditions (NESARC) waves 1 and 2: Review and summary of findings. *Social Psychiatry and Psychiatric Epidemiology, 50*(11), 1609–1640. doi:10.1007/s00127-015-1088-0

Hasin, D. S., & Kilcoyne, B. (2012). Comorbidity of psychiatric and substance use disorders in the United States: Current issues and findings from the NESARC. *Current Opinion in Psychiatry, 25*(3), 165–171. doi:10.1097/YCO.0b013e3283523dcc

Havranek, M. M., Volkart, F., Bolliger, B., Roos, S., Buschner, M., Mansour, R., . . . Ruch, W. (2017). The fear of being laughed at as additional diagnostic criterion in social anxiety disorder and avoidant personality disorder? *PLoS One, 12*(11), e0188024. https://doi.org/10.1371/journal.pone.0188024

Heintz, H. L., Freedberg, A. L., & Harper, D. G. (2020). Dependent personality in depressed older adults: A case report and systematic review. *Journal of Geriatric Psychiatry and Neurology.* https://doi.org/10.1177/0891988720933361

Hiebler-Ragger, M., Unterrainer, H., Rinner, A., & Kapfhammer, H. (2016). Insecure attachment styles and increased borderline personality organization in substance use disorders. *Psychopathology, 49*, 341–344. https://doi.org/10.1159/000448177

Hjorthøj, C., Albert, N., & Nordentoft, M. (2018). Association of substance use disorders with conversion from schizotypal disorder to schizophrenia. *JAMA Psychiatry, 75*(7), 733–739. doi:10.1001/jamapsychiatry.2018.0568

Howard, R., Hasin, D., & Stohl, M. (2020). Substance use disorders and criminal justice contact among those with co-occurring antisocial and borderline personality disorders: Findings from a nationally representative sample. *Personality and Mental Health.* https://doi.org/10.1002/pmh.1491

Hughes, A., Brewer, G., & Khan, R. (2020). Sexual coercion by women: The influence of pornography and narcissistic and histrionic personality disorder traits. *Archives of Sexual Behavior, 49*, 885–894. https://doi.org/10.1007/s10508-019-01538-4

Jauk, E., & Dieterich, R. (2019). Addiction and the dark triad of personality. *Frontiers in Psychiatry, 10*, 662. https://doi.org/10.3389/fpsyt.2019.00662

Johnson, J., Cohen, P., Brown, J., Smailes, E., & Bernstein, D. (1999). Childhood maltreatment increases risk for personality disorders during early adulthood. *Archives of General Psychiatry, 56*(7), 600–606.

Kirchner, S., Roeh, A., Nolden, J., & Hasan, A. (2018). Diagnosis and treatment of schizotypal personality disorder: Evidence from a systematic review. *Schizophrenia, 4*(1). https://doi.org/10.1038/s41537-018-0062-8

Knapek, E., Balázs, K., & Szabó, I. (2017). The substance abuser's partner: Do codependent individuals have borderline and dependent personality disorder? *Heroin Addict Related Clinical Problems, 19*(5), 55–62.

Köck, P., & Walter, M. (2018). Personality disorder and substance use disorder: An update. *Mental Health & Prevention, 12*, 82–89.

Kolla, N., & Mishra, A. (2018). The endocannabinoid system, aggression, and the violence of synthetic cannabinoid use, borderline personality disorder, antisocial personality disorder, and other psychiatric disorders. *Frontiers in Behavioral Neuroscience, 12.* https://doi.org/10.3389/fnbeh.2018.00041

Lampe, L., & Malhi, G. S. (2018). Avoidant personality disorder: Current insights. *Psychology Research and Behavior Management, 11*, 55–66. https://doi.org/10.2147/PRBM.S121073

Lee, R. (2017). Mistrustful and misunderstood: A review of paranoid personality disorder. *Current Behavioral Neuroscience Reports, 4*, 151–165.

Linehan, M. (1993). *Cognitive-behavioral treatment of borderline personality disorder.* Guilford Press.

Liu, G., Fusunyan, M., Bornstein, R., Unruh, B., & Mischoulon, D. (2020). Needing too much: Managing crisis in a patient with dependent personality traits. *Harvard Review of Psychiatry, 28*(6), 412–420.

Maccaferri, G., Dunker-Scheuner, D., De Roten, Y., Despland, J., Sachse, R., & Kramer, U. (2019). Psychotherapy of dependent personality disorder: The relationship of patient-therapist interactions to outcomes. *Psychiatry, 83*(2), 179–194.

Maillard, P., Pellaton, J., & Kramer, U. (2019). Treating comorbid depression and avoidant personality disorder: The case of Andy. *Journal of Clinical Psychology, 75*, 886–897. https://doi.org/10.1002/jclp.22764

McCauley, E., Berk, M., Asarnow, J., Adrian, M., Cohen, J., Korslund, K., . . . Linehan, M. (2018). Efficacy of dialectical behavior therapy for adolescents at high risk for suicide: A randomized clinical trial. *JAMA Psychiatry, 75*(8), 777–785. doi:10.1001/jamapsychiatry.2018.1109

Mehr, K., LaDany, N., & Caskie, G. (2010). Trainee nondisclosure in supervision: What are they not telling you? *Counseling and Psychotherapy Research, 10*(2), 103–113.

Michaud, L., Ligier, F., Bourquin, C., Corbeil, S., Saraga, M., Stiefel, F., . . . Turecki, G. (2020). Differences and similarities in instant countertransference towards patients with suicidal ideation and personality disorders. *Journal of Affective Disorders, 265*, 669–678.

Neumann, E. (2017). Emotional abuse in childhood and attachment anxiety in adult romantic relationships as predictors of personality disorders. *Journal of Aggression, Maltreatment, and Trauma, 26*(4), 430–443.

Nijdam-Jones, A., Rosenfeld, B., Gerbrandij, J., Quick, E., & Galietta, M. (2018). Psychopathology of stalking offenders: Examining the clinical, demographic, and stalking characteristics of a community based sample. *Criminal Justice and Behavior, 45*(5), 712–731.

Oldham, J. (2018). DSM models of personality disorders. *Current Opinion in Psychology, 21*, 86–88.

Paris, J. (2014). After DSM-5: Where does personality disorder research go from here? *Harvard Review of Psychiatry, 22*(4), 216–221. doi:10.1097/HRP.0000000000000041

Pinto, A., Ansell, E., Wheaton, M. G., Krueger, R. F., Morey, L., Skodol, A. E., & Clark, L. A. (2018). Obsessive: Compulsive personality disorder and component personality traits. In W. J. Livesley & R. Larstone (Eds.), *Handbook of personality disorders: Theory, research, and treatment* (pp. 459–479). The Guilford Press.

Rashn, S., Makvand-Hosseini, S., Rezaei, A., & Tabatabaee, S. (2018). The effect of long-term dynamic psychotherapy on the personality structure of patients with dependent personality disorder. *Journal of Clinical Psychology, 9*(4), 1–12. doi:10.22075/jcp.2018.13685.1343

Raynol, P., & Chabrol, H. (2016). Association between schizotypal and borderline personality disorder traits, and cannabis use in young adults. *Addictive Behaviors, 60*, 144–147. https://doi.org/10.1016/j.addbeh.2016.04.018

Reyes-Ortega, M. A., Miranda, E. M., Fresán, A., Vargas, A. N., Barragán, S. C., Robles García, R., & Arango, I. (2020). Clinical efficacy of a combined acceptance and commitment therapy, dialectical behavioural therapy, and functional analytic psychotherapy intervention in patients with borderline personality disorder. *Psychology and Psychotherapy: Theory, Research, and Practice, 93*, 474–489. https://doi.org/10.1111/papt.12240

Rosell, D., Futterman, S., McMaster, A., & Siever, L. (2014). Schizotypal personality disorder: A current review. *Current Psychiatry Reports, 16*(7). https://doi.org/10.1007/s11920-014-0452-1

Rossouw, T., & Fonagy, P. (2012). Mentalization-based treatment for self-harm in adolescents: A randomized controlled trial. *Journal of American Academic Child and Adolescent Psychiatry, 51*, 1304–1313.

Sachse, R., & Kramer, U. (2019). Clarification-oriented psychotherapy of dependent personality disorder. *Journal of Contemporary Psychotherapy, 49*, 15–25. https://doi.org/10.1007/s10879-018-9397-8

Savci, M., Turan, M. E., Griffiths, M. D., & Ercengiz, M. (2019). Histrionic personality, narcissistic personality, and problematic social media use: Testing of a new hypothetical model. *International Journal of Mental Health and Addiction*. https://doi.org/10.1007/s11469-019-00139-5

Schulte Holthausen, B., & Habel, U. (2018). Sex differences in personality disorders. *Current Psychiatry Reports*. https://doi.org/10.1007/s11920-018-0975-y

Shaw, R., & Zanarini, M. (2018). Comorbidity of borderline personality disorder: Current status and future directions. *The Psychiatric Clinics of North America, 41*(4), 583–593. doi:10.1016/j.psc.2018.07.009

Simonsen, S., Eikenæs, I., Nørgaard, N., Normann-Eide, E., Juul, S., & Wilberg, T. (2019). Specialized treatment for patients with severe avoidant personality disorder: Experiences from Scandinavia. *Journal of Contemporary Psychotherapy, 49*(1), 27–38.

Smith, N., & Cottler, L. (2020). What's old is new again: Updated findings on personality disorders and substance use disorders. *Current Opinion in Psychiatry, 33*(1), 51–56.

Sørensen, K. D., Råbu, M., Wilberg, T., & Berthelsen, E. (2019). Struggling to be a person: Lived experience of avoidant personality disorder. *Journal of Clinical Psychology, 75*, 664–680. https://doi.org/10.1002/jclp.22740

Stenason, L., & Vernon, P. (2016). The dark triad, reinforcement sensitivity and substance use. *Personality and Individual Differences, 94*, 59–63.

Tanzilli, A., Muzi, L., Ronningstam, E., & Lingiardi, V. (2017). Countertransference when working with narcissistic personality disorder: An empirical investigation. *Psychotherapy, 54*(2), 184–194. https://doi.org/10.1037/pst0000111

Terzi, L., Martino, F., Berardi, D., Bortolotti, B., Sasdelli, A., & Menchetti, M. (2017). Aggressive behavior and self-harm in borderline personality disorder: The role of impulsivity and emotion dysregulation in a sample of outpatients. *Psychiatry Research, 249*, 321–326.

Thylstrup, B., & Hesse, M. (2016). Impulsive lifestyle counseling to prevent dropout from treatment for substance use disorders in people with antisocial personality disorder: A randomized study. *Addictive Behaviors, 57*, 48–54.

Trull, T. J., Freeman, L. K., Vebares, T. J., Choate, A. M., Helle, A. C., & Wycoff, A. M. (2018). Borderline personality disorder and substance use disorders: An updated review. *Borderline Personality Disorder and Emotion Dysregulation, 5*, 15. doi:10.1186/s40479-018-0093-9

Trull, T. J., Jahng, S., Tomko, R. L., Wood, P. K., & Sher, K. J. (2010). Revised NESARC personality disorder diagnoses: Gender, prevalence, and comorbidity with substance dependence disorders. *Journal of Personality Disorders, 24*(4), 412–426. doi:10.1521/pedi.2010.24.4.412

Volkert, J., Gablonski, T., & Rabung, A. (2018). Prevalence of personality disorders in the general adult population in Western countries: Systematic review and meta-analysis. *The British Journal of Psychiatry, 213*(6), 709–715.

Walker, E., & Druss, B. (2017). Cumulative burden of comorbid mental disorders, substance use disorders, chronic medical conditions, and poverty on health among adults in the U.S.A. *Psychology, Health, & Medicine, 22*(6), 727–735.

Walsh, J. (2017). Schizotypal personality disorder: A clinical social work perspective. *Journal of Social Work Practice, 31*(1), 67–78.

Ward, S. (2018). The black hole: Exploring the schizoid personality disorder, dysfunction, deprivation with their roots in the prenatal and perinatal period. *Journal of Prenatal & Perinatal Psychology & Health, 33*(1), 51–66.

Weinberg, I., & Ronningstam, E. (2020). Dos and don'ts in treatments of patients with narcissistic personality disorder. *Journal of Personality Disorders, 34*, 122–142. https://doi.org/10.1521/pedi.2020.34.supp.122

Wheaton, M. G., & Ward, H. E. (2020). Intolerance of uncertainty and obsessive-compulsive personality disorder. *Personality Disorders: Theory, Research, and Treatment, 11*(5), 357–364. https://doi.org/10.1037/per0000396

Yakeley, J. (2019). Personality disorder: Complexity, countertransference and co-production. *Medicine, Science and the Law, 59*(4), 205–209. doi:10.1177/0025802419880782

5 Attention Deficit Hyperactive Disorder

Fredrick Dombrowski, Natasha Chung, and Robert Yates III

Introduction

Attention-deficit hyperactivity disorder (ADHD) is a neurodevelopmental disorder characterized by symptoms of inattention, hyperactivity and impulsivity, disorganization, and behavioral problems (5th ed.; *DSM-5*; American Psychiatric Association [APA], 2013). ADHD commonly presents in childhood and can be a risk factor in the development of a substance use disorder (Adisetiyo & Gray, 2017). ADHD has received greater attention since the 1980s and has shown an increase in diagnoses within the general population (Crunelle et al., 2018). Although ADHD may have more mainstream attention, very little is known about it by the general public, and many counselors may struggle to implement some traditional mental health or substance use tools as the individual's limited ability to focus prevents them from following up with certain recommendations (Quinn et al., 2017).

While the experience of ADHD can have some similarities across populations, variations in primary support, exposure to knowledgeable clinical staff and education, and specific individual areas of deficit can make assessment and diagnosis more difficult for the individual. ADHD is often considered a diagnosis for children and adolescents. Children and adolescents living with ADHD, as they grow and enter the adult world, still experience these symptoms, and thus, they can develop mental health diagnoses as they struggle to complete tasks and may often turn to illicit substances to cope with these symptoms. Consequently, early identification and treatment of ADHD is important to reduce the risk of concomitant substance use problems. This is especially true for males, who have higher rates of ADHD and who show increased risk for ADHD, substance use problems, and other mental or behavioral health problems when there is a positive family history of substance use (Glenn & Parsons, 1989). It is important for counselors to have knowledge of ADHD and how this impacts the treatment of co-occurring disorders. In this chapter, the diagnostic features of ADHD will be explored, age of onset and prevalence of ADHD will be examined, and the relationship between ADHD and substance use will be discussed with a focus on treatment and best practices related to ADHD.

Learning Objectives

- Identify key diagnostic features of ADHD
- Understand various struggles (interpersonal, vocational, etc.) that an individual living with ADHD can experience
- Identify how co-occurring disorders can manifest for those living with ADHD
- Identify adjustments in clinical treatment that need to be considered when attempting to meet the needs of those living with ADHD
- Identify national services available for those living with ADHD

DOI: 10.4324/9781003220916-6

Key Terms

Attention: The cognitive and behavioral actions of directly focusing on a topic, action, or event while simultaneously ignoring other stimuli.

Concentration: The act of harnessing one's attention to a topic, action, or event.

Conduct Disorder: A disorder first diagnosed prior to adulthood in which an individual shows signs of aggression, destructive behavior, lying, and violation of rules.

Executive Functioning: A set of cognitive skills that allows an individual to engage effectively in the world around them. These skills include the ability to self-monitor, cognitive flexibility, and working memory.

Hyperactivity: An individual state of seemingly constant activity including instances when the activity is not appropriate.

Impulsivity: A tendency to behaviorally respond to a trigger without applying cognitive processes to consider the outcomes of the actual behavior.

Oppositional Defiant Disorder: A disorder often diagnosed prior to adulthood in which an individual is prone to lose their temper, become easily annoyed or irritated with others, maintain an interpersonal hostile mood, and show vindictive or spiteful behaviors toward others.

Stimulants: A class of drugs that cause an increased rate of functions in the central nervous system. These substances can also provide euphoric feelings and assist with focus and concentration.

History, Prevalence, and Age of Onset

Compared to other sciences, the fields of psychology and counseling are relatively new, with increased study and attention emerging in the 1800s (Corey, 2018). In the past, the symptoms associated with ADHD were conceptualized from a behavioristic model while other diagnoses such as substance use and mental illnesses were conceptualized from a moralistic point of view (Doweiko, 2009). This indicated that individuals experiencing symptoms related to ADHD were considered to be showing behavioristic tendencies that required discipline from parents to extinguish such behaviors. A lack of concentration and an inability to sit still were viewed from the perspective of boys willfully not adhering to adult expectations. In the 1700s, some health workers identified struggles that individuals experienced with their ability to pay attention to certain tasks. As some behavioral presentations of ADHD change throughout adulthood, these symptoms remained interpreted as children (specifically boys) acting out as the model changed to focus on a lack of ability to apply moralistic responses to triggers (Maté, 2019; Wittenauer-Welsh et al., 2017).

As the field of psychology continued to develop in the twentieth century, so, too, did the conceptualization of the behaviors associated with ADHD. In the early twentieth century, the impulsive behaviors and inability to maintain stillness under certain circumstances prompted the development of the diagnosis of hyperkinetic disease of infancy (Smith, 2012). This conceptualization again changed to focus on descriptions of higher process problems such as 'brain damage' or 'brain dysfunction'. In the 1960s, these clusters of symptoms were then refocused on increased movement and inability to sit still (Maté, 2019).

The diagnosis of ADHD has increased toward the end of the twentieth century and the early twenty-first century. The prevalence of children diagnosed with ADHD increased by 42% between 2003 and 2011, from 7.8% to 11% (National Institute of Mental Health [NIMH], 2017). Currently, 9.4% of children ages two to seventeen have ever been diagnosed with ADHD. Boys are more likely than girls to be diagnosed (12.9% versus 5.6%) (Centers for Disease Control and Prevention [CDC], 2019). While the median age of onset varies, the median age of diagnosis for severe symptoms is four years. Children with moderate levels of symptoms are diagnosed at a median age of six years, and children with mild symptoms tend to be diagnosed at a median age of seven years (NIMH, 2017). There are some who may struggle throughout their childhood and early adult years without ever receiving a formal diagnosis or assessment.

Our modern conceptualization of ADHD was heavily influenced by the diagnostic criteria listed in the *DSM-III*, which focused more on a lack of attention individuals experience (APA, 1980). The diagnosis of attention deficit disorder (ADD) became the primary way of identifying this cluster of symptoms. However, this diagnosis added a qualifier for those living with ADD while also experiencing hyperactivity. In 1987, the revised version of the *DSM-III* formally changed this diagnosis to what we now know today as ADHD, including both lack of attention and hyperactive behaviors indicative of impulsivity (APA, 1987). The *DSM-IV* (APA, 2000) considered these ongoing symptoms and added subtypes (focusing primarily on lack of attention or on impulsive behaviors) and also added severity qualifiers to measure the rate at which an individual's daily functioning was impacted by these symptoms (Epstein & Loren, 2013). While ADHD was first considered to be an illness that primarily presented in childhood, additional research regarding this diagnosis found that symptoms persist into adulthood although some individuals find coping strategies to mask some of these problems (Arvidsson et al., 2019). The considerations for adults living with ADHD was addressed in the *DSM-5*, which adjusted some diagnostic criteria for adults, considering the implementation of coping strategies (APA, 2013). The evolution of the conceptualization of ADHD began from a disciplined specific behavioristic conceptualization indicating the need for punishment when symptoms were present. As the field of psychology grew and improved, these symptoms were quantified to focus on either hyperactivity or lack of ability to function. The modern perspective on ADHD occurred in 1987s diagnostic criteria. As time continued, it was found that these symptoms continue into adulthood. Adults living with ADHD and co-occurring mental health diagnoses are at greater risk for substance use disorders and co-occurring mental health diagnoses (Arvidsson et al., 2019).

Primary Symptomology

The primary symptomology of ADHD focuses on various aspects of an individual's ability to remain focused on certain tasks while also managing impulsive behaviors (Crunelle et al., 2018). While other symptoms of ADHD can appear, similar to those of other disorders such as conduct disorder, oppositional defiant disorder in childhood, and intermittent explosive disorder in adulthood, it is important to use comprehensive assessment to determine the symptoms that individuals with ADHD experience as the disorder is associated with higher levels of substance abuse as well as impaired academic, social, and occupational functioning (APA, 2013). As considered in the *DSM-5* (2013), an individual must show at least six of the following developmentally inappropriate symptoms for at least six months:

- Struggles to focus on specific details, causing continuous mistakes in education, work, or other activities
- Inability to maintain focus on certain tasks
- May not seem to listen when directly spoken to
- Struggles to adhere to instruction and often does not complete activities for work, school, etc. as they become sidetracked
- Struggles to organize tasks
- Avoids activities that require mental focus over long periods of time
- Misplaces tools needed to complete tasks
- Distracted with ease
- Forgetful in routine activities

The following set of symptoms focuses on hyperactivity and impulsivity (Epstein & Loren, 2013). In order to meet the threshold for diagnosis, those under the age of 17 must have at least six of the following symptoms. As adults may develop some coping strategies to manage these symptoms, those over the age of 17 must have at least five of the following symptoms:

- Struggles to maintain stillness (may tap fingers or feet or constantly adjust their body)
- Leaves position when it is required for them to stay in that position
- Feels restless, causing the individual to run or climb when not socially acceptable
- Struggles to maintain quiet during leisure activities
- Ongoing energy described as 'being on the go'
- Talks more than required for basic communication
- Answers questions before the question is completed
- Struggles to wait for their turn to engage in an activity
- Interrupts conversations or activities of others

The following criteria must also be met:

- Several symptoms presented before age 12
- Many symptoms are present in two or more settings
- Symptoms interfere with and reduce the quality of life
- Symptoms are not better explained by another disorder

The current diagnosis of ADHD has three subtypes. The first indicates a combined presentation of both attention deficit and hyperactivity. The following subtypes focus predominantly on inattentiveness and hyperactivity, respectively (ACA, 2014). ADHD can be diagnosed as mild, moderate, or severe, depending on the number of symptoms present and the level of functional impairment individuals experience as a result of their symptoms. Additionally, three different specifiers can be assigned in regard to presentation. Combined presentation is specified if criteria for inattention and hyperactivity-impulsivity have been met through appropriate assessment. If criteria for inattention are met but not criteria for hyperactivity-impulsivity, the specifier used is 'predominantly inattentive presentation'. If only criteria for hyperactivity-impulsivity are met, the specifier is 'predominantly hyperactive/impulsive presentation' (APA, 2013).

When conceptualizing the diagnosis of ADHD, the wording of the diagnosis can seem somewhat self-explanatory. Identifying the symptoms alone may not fully encapsulate the experience of the individual living with ADHD (Wimberley et al., 2020). The social interpretations of symptoms of ADHD can seem as if the individual is acting lazy or rude or showing a lack of regard for important aspects of society. The danger of this interpretation is the belief that the individual has the ability to choose which behaviors they can selectively focus on (Mitchell et al., 2018). Rather, counselors must adjust their conceptualization of ADHD to better understand the relationship of ADHD and co-occurring substance use and mental health diagnoses.

Practical Interpretation of Symptomology

For those living with ADHD, the ability to engage in executive functioning for certain activities is compromised (Maté, 2019). Most people will be able to engage in activities (even mundane or inconvenient); they will be able to mentally create a plan to approach these activities with a step-by-step process, even if this process is not spoken out loud, written, or recognized by the individual (Smith, 2012). For those living with ADHD, this process is constantly interrupted as the individual's attention and focus are pulled uncontrollably in different directions, causing them to get off task. These symptoms also impact the individual's ability to make interpersonal connections.

The *DSM-5* describes symptoms of inattention as off-task behaviors, wandering, disorganization, and lack of persistence or focus that does not occur due issues of comprehension or defiant behaviors. A person may seem distracted or forgetful, missing out on commitments they have made to friends and family. Hyperactivity can present as excessive and inappropriate motor activity in children and adults and as extreme restlessness in adulthood. Impulsivity includes actions that are hasty and initiated without forethought and that have potential to harm, as well as failure to consider long-term consequences and social intrusiveness (APA, 2013). While those living with ADHD may identify how illicit substance use can provide initial relief of symptoms, the compounding effects of ongoing substance use coupled with symptoms of co-occurring disorders on a bedrock of lack of attention and impulsivity indicates a need for multimodal treatment to assist those in this category (Maté, 2019).

ADHD presents, more often than not, as a comorbid diagnosis. As such, 64% of people diagnosed with ADHD are also diagnosed with another emotional, mental, or behavioral disorder. Indeed, it is estimated that five in ten children with ADHD present with behavioral or conduct problems, three in ten children present with symptoms of anxiety, and nearly two in ten have depressive symptoms. Given the often-complex needs of individuals with ADHD, an estimated 62% of children and adolescents take stimulant and non-stimulant ADHD medication, with 30% receiving medication treatment alone. Many youths also receive behavioral treatment. An estimated 47% receive behavioral health care, with 15% receiving behavioral treatment alone. Among this population, 32% of youth receive both medication and behavioral treatment, while 23% of youth diagnosed with ADHD receive no treatment at all (CDC, 2019).

Further complicating the diagnosis and treatment of ADHD, especially in adolescence and adulthood, is the prevalence of substance use. Forty percent of individuals with ADHD develop a substance abuse disorder at some point in their lives. Individuals with ADHD are more likely to develop a substance use disorder than individuals who do not have ADHD. Individuals with ADHD have a significantly higher chance of abusing nicotine, cannabis, and cocaine, though they are less likely than control groups to abuse alcohol (Vingilis et al., 2015).

Psychological Factors

Generally, ADHD is considered to be a neurodevelopmental disorder with origins involving genetic, biological, neurological, and developmental causes. However, psychological factors have been identified that are related to ADHD, including interaction with parents, temperament, and abuse in the home (Lambert & Hartsough, 1984). Children who are diagnosed with ADHD tend to be more moody, have a lower distress threshold, be less persistent than other children, be more active than other children, and struggle with adapting to changes. Children who have ADHD also tend to have a home environment that involves more social control and more frequent punishment. Parents of children with ADHD appear to be less involved in activities such as reading with their children, have lower aspirations for success, and move more frequently, resulting in their children attending more schools.

Individuals diagnosed with ADHD are more likely to engage in delinquency and substance use and are more likely to experience academic and social impairment (Walther et al., 2012). Research has shown that parent involvement and behavior management using behavior parent training and positive parenting practices can play a significant role in reducing the psychological and social consequences of ADHD. Parent involvement in their children's lives has a significant protective effect and can aid in reducing the risk of future substance use.

Psychological and social risk factors for ADHD have been found to include a history of maternal depression, family history of disruptive behavior problems, negative personality traits such as jealousy or clinginess in childhood, difficult temperament, frequent sadness, history of parental immigration, violence in the home, and low socioeconomic status (Grizenko & Pawliuk, 1994).

Protective factors that have been identified include having two or more hobbies, having a positive relationship with grandparents, ability to cope with stress, ability to adapt to change, ability to express feelings easily, and having an easy temperament.

Comorbidity of Substance Use and ADHD

Substance use and ADHD are complicated and interconnected issues. Though the research reports vary in the amount of risk, overall, youth with mental health disorders have an increased risk for developing substance-related disorders. Some studies report that ADHD, specifically, is associated with higher risk for alcohol-related disorders, while other studies do not support a higher risk for alcohol use (Vitulano et al., 2014). Most studies on the topics of SUD and ADHD report an elevated risk of nicotine-related disorders and any substance-related disorders (Groenman et al., 2017). ADHD has been linked youth smoking at an earlier age, even when SES, IQ, and psychiatric morbidity have been controlled for (Vitulano et al., 2014). A question remains as to whether ADHD is the risk factor for all substance abuse, however, because a mitigating factor like oppositional defiant disorder (ODD) increases the risk for substance use, which, in turn, increases the risk of substance use in individuals with ADHD who also experience behavioral disorders/disruption as children or adults (Groenman et al., 2017). Despite any mitigating factors that might impact the link between ADHD and substance use, youth with ADHD generally have an earlier onset of SUD (most commonly marijuana use). The recovery time for youth with ADHD in substance use treatment is two times as long as youth without ADHD. Research has indicated how early ADHD symptoms lead to peer rejection and/or internalizing problems. This combination of risk factors, in turn, can lead to early initiation of tobacco use and, subsequently, a more rapid acceleration of risk for use of marijuana and other substances (Vitulano et al., 2014).

Risk factors in youth should be taken into consideration, but many people do not seek treatment until faced with the challenges and responsibilities of adulthood. It is estimated that roughly 80% of adults living with ADHD also have comorbid mental health and/or substance use disorders (Katzman et al., 2017). Those living with symptoms of ADHD have reported earlier introduction to illicit substances and alcohol use (Molina et al., 2018). Adults living with ADHD are more likely to use nicotine, THC, and other substances than their peers without diagnoses (Wilens & Kaminski, 2018). Many people living with ADHD will also experience increased rates of depression, anxiety, and diagnosis of personality disorder (Anker et al., 2018). As those living with ADHD age into adulthood, their struggles with primary symptomology coupled with comorbid disorders will have major impacts on various aspects of their lives. Those living with ADHD were found to have increased struggles managing finances as they aged when compared to those without the diagnosis. Ongoing financial stress has also been a predicting factor of suicide among men living with ADHD (Beauchaine et al., 2020).

Those living with ADHD have identified various factors that have contributed to an increase in substance use. Some have indicated struggles to meet demands during childhood and adolescence contributed to their seeking emotional relief through substances (Smith, 2012). The impulsive response and struggles with long-term planning during adolescence and early adulthood have also been found to be predictors of substance use (Egan et al., 2017). Some individuals living with ADHD have reported that THC has the effect of reducing stress and anxiety as well as providing a calm effect to decrease impulsivity (Mitchell et al., 2018). In adulthood, between 25% and 55% of individuals diagnosed with ADHD report a history of drug use or dependence, compared to 15% to 18% of the general population. Clearly, adults with ADHD have been at earlier risk for the onset of substance abuse prior to adulthood and evidence a higher rate of substance abuse diagnoses. As with adolescents with ADHD, adults with ADHD also experience more difficulty remaining in treatment and require longer amounts of time in treatment for recovery (Nogueira et al., 2014).

Also, during adulthood, there remains a significant association between conduct problems, academic underachievement, and lifelong substance abuse. The association between an ADHD diagnosis and SUD is strongest with individuals who present with impulsivity. Individuals designated as inattentive types are least likely to develop SUD. Across individuals diagnosed with ADHD, the greater in severity the ADHD symptoms are, the higher the risk for substance abuse. Individuals who have comorbid diagnoses of ODD and CD in childhood have a higher risk of substance abuse, though substance use is still two times more prevalent, even when controlling for CD and ODD. Substance use is also increased in individuals with ADHD who also report childhood sexual abuse, school suspensions, family history of ADHD, family history of substance abuse, or being single (Nogueira et al., 2014).

Special Consideration

Counselors conducting intake assessments are required to engage in various tasks simultaneously. The counselor must establish a rapport while also obtaining information for a biopsychosocial assessment, establishing a case conceptualization, and providing the mental status exam (Corey, 2018). Because of these factors, concerns have been expressed about the ability to appropriately diagnose substance use or co-occurring disorders for those living with ADHD (Smith, 2012). In children and adolescents, ADHD can be misdiagnosed as oppositional defiant disorder or conduct disorder. The child's inability to complete tasks may be perceived as defiance, and pressures to complete such tasks can cause mood lability. This, coupled with impulsive reactions, can be misinterpreted as other childhood disorders (Manos et al., 2017). For adults, presentations of impulsivity, increased speech, and an inability to plan and complete tasks can be misinterpreted as symptoms of mania (Katzman et al., 2017). Despite the symptoms of ADHD that could potentially interfere with appropriate diagnosis, those living with ADHD can receive an appropriate diagnosis of other co-occurring disorders, especially if the diagnosis of ADHD is pre-existing (Van Oortmerssen et al., 2017). For counselors working with adults who have not received a previous diagnosis, connecting with collateral contacts (specifically family) can indicate a symptomology observable in childhood that is usually inconsistent with the onset of other mental health diagnoses. In such conditions, the counselor is advised to connect the client with a formal ADHD assessment from a psychologist who specializes in this area (Katzman et al., 2017). Those who receive a diagnosis and treatment at an earlier age have better treatment outcomes than those who are diagnosed later in life (Molina et al., 2018).

Gender Differences

It is evident that males are diagnosed with ADHD more frequently than females at all developmental levels, though the male predominance does decrease with age. Another gender difference that has been reported in the literature is that the positive symptoms of ADHD seem to stabilize for men in young adulthood, while positive symptoms decrease for women as they age. This difference is important to note because positive symptoms that persist over the lifespan are associated with adverse psychiatric, substance use, and social outcomes (Vingilis et al., 2015).

This gender difference, however, does not imply that women are not greatly impacted by ADHD symptoms in adulthood. In fact, research demonstrates that women are more likely to be impacted by inattentive-type symptoms in adulthood (Agnew-Blaise et al., 2013). Women also report more comorbid internalizing disorders than men (e.g., anxiety or depression), though internalizing issues tends to be problematic only if their ADHD symptoms persist beyond childhood (Owens et al., 2017). Women are more likely to report a history of treatment for comorbid psychiatric disorders and higher levels of impairment than men. Overall, men and women clinically diagnosed with ADHD have a four to nine times higher prevalence of bipolar disorder, anxiety, depression, schizophrenia, personality disorder, and substance abuse disorder than other adults. The comorbid diagnostic differences between adults with ADHD and adults without ADHD are greater with women than men, with women reporting a higher level of both ADHD symptoms and symptoms of comorbid disorders at higher rates than men (Agnew-Blaise et al., 2013; Solberg et al., 2018).

Men, who are more likely to be diagnosed with the combined subtype, are also more likely to be diagnosed with antisocial personality disorder or substance abuse disorder. Men are also more likely to be diagnosed with schizophrenia. The gender difference in schizophrenia diagnosis rates could be explained by the increase in likelihood that men have a comorbid substance use disorder, which could increase the likelihood of the presence of psychotic symptoms (Solberg et al., 2018).

Robust associations between childhood ADHD and substance use disorders in women are not consistently demonstrated in the literature. Overall, studies have not found that gender reliably explains differences in regard to the association between ADHD and SUD (Owens et al., 2017), though some studies have found that the lifetime prevalence of drug abuse and smoking might be increased among women with ADHD (Fuller-Thompson et al., 2016). Alternatively, research has also reported that ADHD is not associated with substance use amongst women, with control samples reporting higher rates of substance abuse than women with ADHD (Owens et al., 2017). The mixed findings in the research literature highlight the importance of looking at additional factors that impact women's presentation of ADHD. Paying attention to women with ADHD who present with less hyperactivity and fewer positive symptoms than men could prevent missed or inaccurate diagnoses (Solberg et al., 2018).

A sizable difference between women whose symptoms continue to persist after childhood and women without ADHD by the time women are in their mid-twenties has been reported. Women with ADHD symptoms, as compared to women without symptoms, present with increased internalizing and externalizing problems, self-injury, health problems, social impairment, and decreased educational attainment. Additionally, women with adult ADHD symptoms report increased rates of unplanned pregnancy and obesity. Unlike men with ADHD, who also present with increased social impairment and decreased educational attainment, women do not show increased adverse driving outcomes/tickets/accidents or decreased rates of employment. Women with ADHD report similar work hours as those without ADHD but also report lower levels of productivity and work quality (Owen, et al.). Women with ADHD are more likely to have a lower income than women without ADHD, are less likely to have a post-secondary degree, and have increased prevalence of sleep problems, chronic pain, physical limitations, mental health disorders, suicidal ideation, and incidents of past sexual or physical abuse victimization (Fuller-Thompson et al., 2016).

It is important to note, however, that despite gender differences, compared to non-ADHD adults, adults diagnosed with ADHD have higher rates of psychopathology, disruptive behavior, substance use, and criminal offenses. Adults with ADHD are less likely to enter college or to be employed and have lower income/socioeconomic status (SES). These differences hold especially true when a comorbid condition is present (Lee et al., 2011; Vingilis et al., 2015).

Counselor Experience

Counselors working with children and adults living with ADHD can experience difficulty as the client will struggle to stay on task (Maté, 2019). Traditional group counseling may be an avenue in which the client may struggle as it can be difficult for them to allow others to finish talking, and they can become easily distracted. It is recommended that counselors manage their own internal responses to children and adults living with ADHD. The countertransference that counselors can experience may cause them to approach the client in a way that indicates their annoyance or frustration (Corey, 2018). This can be difficult, especially for clinicians who have less experience as they are more likely not to openly ask for support in this area from their supervisors (Mehr et al., 2010). It is recommended that counselors learn and engage in regular mindfulness-based skills to interrupt these experiences in real time when they happen (Guest & Carlson, 2019). If countertransference is not appropriately managed, the therapeutic alliance can be damaged, contributing to an increased likelihood of treatment dropout on the part of the patient.

Evidence-Based Treatment

Many individuals living with ADHD who are linked with psychiatric care are often treated with various medications that increase the functions of the central nervous system (Quinn et al., 2017). It may seem counterintuitive that people who struggle to focus and sit still are given various stimulants. The use of stimulants has an unexpected effect that helps the individual improve focus and obtain the ability to work on larger tasks that require more mental acuity (Smith, 2012). For those not diagnosed with ADHD, these medications will have similar effects to other stimulants, and thus, these medications can be misused by both those with and without ADHD (Slobodin & Crunelle, 2019).

It has been hypothesized that the exposure to stimulants of individuals who are treated pharmaceutically for ADHD can result in increased risk for substance abuse and SUD. This hypothesis argues that individuals who take stimulants as medication therapy for ADHD become sensitized to the effect of their medication and are more likely to turn to additional substances to alleviate their symptoms. This hypothesis has not been supported over time. Indeed, the research literature reports that medication management of ADHD lowers the risk for substance-related problems. For men, long-term stimulant and non-stimulant therapy has been associated with an overall lower risk of substance-related problems. The research demonstrates less evidence of reduced risk of substance abuse for women who are prescribed and take stimulant or non-stimulant medications for ADHD but also reports no evidence that ADHD medication increases risk of substance abuse (Quinn et al., 2017). Males are more likely to initiate stimulant medication treatment than women. No gender differences are reported between men and women and the prevalence of non-stimulant therapy for ADHD (McCabe et al., 2016).

In the past, it was the predominating belief that starting medications later and taking medication holidays from stimulant medications constituted best practice. Current research contradicts these practices and indicates that medication that is administered starting before nine years of age and that continues for six or more years is associated with individuals being less likely to abuse substances during their lifetime. Later use of stimulant ADHD medication, starting between the ages of ten and fourteen or later, or a shorter-duration medication treatment (two years or less) is associated with increased risk for substance abuse in adolescence or adulthood. Early initiation of medication therapy is linked to lower substance abuse risk. Additionally, the longer individuals are treated with stimulants, the lower the likelihood that individuals with ADHD will abuse cocaine or misuse stimulants (McCabe et al., 2016).

Differential Diagnosis

ADHD shows comorbidity with several other mental health problems, including intellectual disability, specific learning disability, autism spectrum disorder, motor problems, conduct disorder, antisocial personality disorder, anxiety disorders, substance use disorder, and mood disorders (Thapar et al., 2013). Given the comorbidity between ADHD and several other common mental health problems, diagnosis of ADHD is complex. Diagnosis of ADHD commonly involves taking a complete developmental history and collateral informant interviews, the use of self- and informant-report inventories, tests of cognitive abilities, and the use of tests of attention performance. No one test is able to accurately capture a diagnosis of ADHD, and further, symptoms of ADHD should be present in more than one setting (APA, 2013). Because ADHD is a neurodevelopmental disorder, symptoms may present early in life and change at different points throughout the lifespan.

Due to the high comorbidity between ADHD and other mental health problems, which can range from 50% to 90% (Shokane et al., 2004), diagnosis of ADHD is multifaceted. Individuals who are diagnosed with ADHD may commonly present with one or more additional mental health problems. As a result, gaining insight into developmental history and reports of collateral informants are important to help guide diagnosis. Some mental health problems may present with symptoms that mimic ADHD, including bipolar disorder, anxiety disorders, and autism spectrum disorder, among others. Collateral informant reports are an important part of diagnosis and are commonly administered to parents, teachers, and other caregivers to collect data regarding behavioral performance in multiple settings. Tests of intellectual ability and academic achievement can be utilized to evaluate performance on measures related to problems with ADHD, such as working memory and executive function. Additionally, tests of attention performance that evaluate sustained attention can be utilized to attempt to directly measure attention ability to aid in differential diagnosis.

While diagnosis of ADHD is multifaceted and complex, combining the use of self- and informant-report instruments, tests of cognitive ability, and a detailed developmental history represents the current 'gold standard' for the diagnosis of ADHD. Diagnosis of ADHD may involve the diagnosis of additional comorbid mental health problems, but clinicians should work to ensure that a diagnosis of ADHD is consistent with an individual's functioning across two or more settings. Additionally, the law of parsimony should be applied when evaluating ADHD along with other mental health problems. Specifically, the simplest scientific explanation that fits the evidence should be utilized.

Resources for Families

Many family members of those living with ADHD may feel overwhelmed, especially during the early stages of diagnosis while treatment is still being formulated. The counselor can further assist the client and family by becoming linked with national resources to assist those living with ADHD and co-occurring disorders. The following links provide in-depth discussion of and resources for various aspects of ADHD, as well as helpful tips as to how family members and supports can assist those living with ADHD.

> https://add.org/
> https://chadd.org/
> https://edgefoundation.org/
> https://impactparents.com/
> www.adhdcoaches.org/circle/iaac-adhd-coach-certification/

Conclusion

ADHD in adults and children is often a misunderstood diagnosis. Although modern treatment has moved away from moralistic or punitive models of responding, many providers and educators can misinterpret these symptoms as being a sign of behavioral disobedience, causing inaccurate diagnosis in children. While ADHD predominantly impacts males, it also impacts females, and counselors must consider this when presented with a female who shows such symptoms. Those living with ADHD are at greater risk of comorbid mental health and substance use disorders. An appropriate early diagnosis has been found to improve long-term treatment and management of

ADHD and potential co-occurring disorders. Some clinicians may work with adults who have signs of ADHD who have not ever been diagnosed. It is important to refer such individuals for an appropriate evaluation as an affirmation of diagnosis helps inform the provider of modifications in treatment. Consequently, those with ADHD tend to benefit from longer treatment times and may struggle with their ability to sit still or pay attention in groups. Psychiatric treatment may require the use of prescribed stimulants, which have an inverse effect on the individual living with ADHD. However, access to these medications can make the individual at risk for selling them. It is recommended that counselors engage in ongoing internal assessment of their reaction when working with individuals living with ADHD, as well as receiving supervision as these symptoms can impact the treatment experience of others. Those living with ADHD benefit from connection to adjunct services, and national organizations can be a resource to help link such clients with appropriate supports.

Questions for Consideration

1. Are children with ADHD destined to develop substance use disorders in adulthood? Why or why not?
2. Untreated ADHD can lead to destructive coping behaviors in adulthood, are mood altering substances, prescription or non-prescription, the only solution?
3. What clinical consideration should be addressed when working with an adult living with ADHD and substance use disorders?

Case Study

Lance is a 19-year-old Caucasian male living with his parents and attending his first year of community college. When he was younger, Lance often struggled in school as he was unable to maintain focus on certain school-related topics. Although Lance excelled at his computer programming classes, he often struggled in classes such as English and social studies. Lance's parents reported that since he was a small child, he was unable to sit still and remain focused. Socially, Lance has always maintained a limited number of friends with a few close social supports. Upon entering community college, Lance attended a medical appointment where he was diagnosed with attention-deficit hyperactivity disorder. Lance was prescribed a stimulant that was reported to help him focus. Lance eventually created a small social network at his community college. This social network introduced Lance to marijuana, which he now uses daily. Lance reported an ongoing feeling of unhappiness about his life due to his ongoing disconnection from others and lack of enjoyment in activities. Lance will often trade his prescribed medications for THC. Lance is currently struggling with his classes as he maintains a 1.8 GPA. His parents have brought him to counseling as they are worried he is depressed.

Questions

1. What clinical areas of concern are described in Lance's case?
2. Lance has likely been living with ADHD for several years. What may have prevented Lance from being diagnosed earlier in his life? How might that have changed his college experience?
3. Marijuana is a commonly used drug for the self-medication of ADHD. In Lance's case, has the self-medication been effective? Why or why not?

Recommended Reading

Hallowell, E., & Ratey, J. (2011). *Driven to distraction: Recognizing and coping with attention deficit disorder from childhood through adulthood.* New York, NY: Anchor Books.

Tuckman, A. (2007). *Integrative treatment for adult ADHD: A practical, easy-to-use guide for clinicians*. Oakland, CA: New Harbinger Publications.

References

Adisetiyo, V., & Gray, K. M. (2017). Neuroimaging the neural correlates of increased risk for substance use disorders in attention-deficit/hyperactivity disorder: A systematic review. *The American Journal on Addictions, 26*, 99–111. doi:10.1111/ajad.12500

Agnew-Blaise, J., Seidman, L. J., & Buka, S. (2013). Adult ADHD: Persistence, symptom profile, and demographic characteristics. *Comprehensive Psychiatry, 54*(2013), E1. http://dx.doi.org/10.1016/j.comppsych.2012.07.016

American Counseling Association. (2014). *ACA code of ethics*. Author.

American Psychiatric Association. (1980). *Diagnostic and statistical manual of mental disorders* (3rd ed.). Author.

American Psychiatric Association. (1987). *Diagnostic and statistical manual of mental disorders* (3rd ed., rev.). Author.

American Psychiatric Association. (2000). *Diagnostic and statistical manual of mental disorders* (4th ed., text rev.). Author.

American Psychiatric Association. (2013). *Diagnostic and statistical manual of mental disorders* (5th ed., text rev.). Author.

Anker, E., Bendiksen, B., & Heir, T. (2018). Comorbid psychiatric disorders in a clinical sample of adults with ADHD, and associations with education, work and social characteristics: A cross-sectional study. *BMJ Open, 8*(3). doi:10.1136/bmjopen-2017-019700

Arvidsson, M., Dahl, M., Franck, J., Wiig, E., & Nielsen, N. (2019). Methylphenidate effects on processing speed in a clinical sample of adults with ADHD and substance use disorder: A pilot study. *Nordic Journal of Psychiatry, 73*(2), 118–124. doi:10.1080/08039488.2019.1573922

Beauchaine, T., Ben-David, I., & Bos, M. (2020). ADHD, financial stress, and suicide in adulthood: A population study. *Science Advances, 6*(40). doi:10.1126/sciadv.aba1551

Centers for Disease Control and Prevention. (2019). *Data and statistics about ADHD*. Retrieved from www.cdc.gov/ncbddd/adhd/data.html

Corey, G. (2018). *Theory and practice of counseling and psychotherapy* (10th ed.). Cengage Learning. ISBN: 978–1305263727

Crunelle, C. L., van den Brink, W., Moggi, F., Konstenius, M., Franck, J., Levin, F. R., . . . Matthys, F. (2018). International consensus statement on screening, diagnosis and treatment of substance use disorder patients with comorbid attention deficit/hyperactivity disorder. *European Addiction Research, 24*(1), 43–51.

Doweiko, H. (2009). *Concepts of chemical dependency* (7th ed.). Pearson Publishing.

Egan, T., Dawson, A., & Wymbs, B. (2017). Substance use in undergraduate students with histories of Attention-Deficit/Hyperactivity Disorder (ADHD): The role of impulsivity. *Substance Use & Misuse, 52*(10), 1375–1386. doi:10.1080/10826084.2017.1281309

Epstein, J. N., & Loren, R. E. (2013). Changes in the definition of ADHD in DSM-5: Subtle but important. *Neuropsychiatry, 3*(5), 455–458. https://doi.org/10.2217/npy.13.59

Fuller-Thompson, E., Lewis, D. A., & Agbeyaka, S. K. (2016). Attention-deficit/hyperactivity disorder casts a long shadow: Findings from a population-based study of adult women with self-reported ADHD. *Child: Care, Health, and Development, 42*(6), 918–927. doi:10.1111/cch.12380

Glenn, S. W., & Parsons, O. A. (1989). Alcohol abuse and familial alcoholism: Psychosocial correlates in men and women. *Journal of Studies on Alcohol, 50*(2), 116–127.

Grizenko, N., & Pawliuk, N. (1994). Risk and protective factors for disruptive behavior disorders in children. *American Journal of Orthopsychiatry, 64*(4), 534–544.

Groenman, A. P., Janssen, T. W. P., & Oosterlaan, J. (2017). Childhood psychiatric disorders as risk factor for subsequent substance abuse: A meta-analysis. *Journal of the American Academy of Child and Adolescent Psychiatry, 56*(7), 556–569. https://doi.org/10.1016/j.jaac.2017.05.004

Guest, J. D., & Carlson, R. G. (2019). Utilizing mindfulness strategies to manage negative countertransference and feelings of dislike while working with children exhibiting externalized behaviors. *Journal of Psychotherapy Integration, 29*(4), 426–439. https://doi.org/10.1037/int0000183

Hynd, G., Hern, K., Voeller, K., & Marshall, R. (1991). Neurobiological basis of attention-deficit/hyperactivity disorder. *School Psychology Review, 20*(2), 174–186.

Johnson, H. C. (1989). Disruptive children: Biological factors in attention deficit and antisocial disorders. *Social Work, 34*(2), 137–144.

Katzman, M. A., Bilkey, T. S., Chokka, P. R., et al. (2017). Adult ADHD and comorbid disorders: Clinical implications of a dimensional approach. *BMC Psychiatry, 17.* https://doi.org/10.1186/s12888-017-1463-3

Lambert, N. M., & Hartsough, C. S. (1984). Contribution of predispositional factors to the diagnosis of hyperactivity. *American Journal of Orthopsychiatry, 51*(1), 97–109.

Lee, S. S., Humphreys, K., Flory, R., Liu, R., & Glass, K. (2011). Prospective association of childhood Attention-Deficit/Hyperactivity Disorder (ADHD) and substance use and abuse/dependence: A meta-analytic review. *Clinical Psychology Review, 31*(3), 328–341. https://doi.org/10.1016/j.cpr.2011.01.006

Manos, M. J., Giuliano, K., & Geyer, E. (2017). ADHD: Overdiagnosed and overtreated, or misdiagnosed and mistreated? *Cleveland Clinic Journal of Medicine, 84*(11), 873–880. doi:10.3949/ccjm.84a.15051

Mariani, J., & Levin, F. (2007). Treatment strategies for co-occurring ADHD and substance use disorders. *American Journal of Addiction, 16*, 45–56. doi:10.1080/10550490601082783

Maté, G. (2019). *Scattered minds: The origins and healing of attention deficit disorder.* Random House.

McCabe, S. E., Dickinson, K., West, B. T., & Wilens, T. E. (2016). Age of onset, duration, and type of medication therapy for attention-deficit/hyperactivity disorder and substance use during adolescence: A multicohort national study. *Journal of the American Academy of Child and Adolescent Psychiatry, 55*(6), 479–486. doi:10.1016/j.jaac.2016.03.011

Mehr, K., LaDany, N., & Caskie, G. (2010). Trainee nondisclosure in supervision: What are they not telling you? *Counseling and Psychotherapy Research, 10*(2), 103–113.

Mitchell, J. T., Weisner, T. S., Jensen, P. S., Murray, D., Milina, B., Arnold, A., . . . Nguyen, J. (2018). How substance users with ADHD perceive the relationship between substance use and emotional functioning. *Journal of Attention Disorders, 22*(9), 49–60. doi:10.1177/1087054716685842

Molina, B. S., Howard, A. L., Swanson, J. M., Stehli, A., Mitchell, J. T., Kennedy, T. M., . . . Hoza, B. (2018). Substance use through adolescence into early adulthood after childhood-diagnosed ADHD: Findings from the MTA longitudinal study. *Journal of Child Psychology and Psychiatry, 59*, 692–702. https://doi.org/10.1111/jcpp.12855

National Institute of Mental Health. (2017). *Attention deficit/hyperactivity disorder (ADHD).* Retrieved from www.nimh.nih.gov/health/statistics/attention-deficit-hyperactivity-disorder-adhd.shtml#part_154901

Nogueira, M., Bosch, R., Valero, S. L., Gomez-Barros, N., Palomar, G., Richarte, V., . . . Ramos-Quiroga, J. A. (2014). Early age clinical and developmental features associated to substance use disorders in attention-deficit/hyperactivity disorder in adults. *Comprehensive Psychiatry, 55*, 639–649. http://dx.doi.Org/10.1016/j.comppsych.2013.12.002

Owens, E. B., Zalecki, C., Gilette, P., & Hinshaw, S. P. (2017). Girls with childhood ADHD as adults: Cross-domain outcomes by diagnostic persistence. *Journal of Consulting and Clinical Psychology, 85*(7), 723–736. http://dx.doi.org/10.1037/ccp0000217

Perugi, G., Pallucchini, A., Rizzato, S., De Rossi, P., Sani, G., Maremmani, A., Pinzone, V., & Maremmani, I. (2019). Pharmacotherapeutic strategies for the treatment of Attention-Deficit Hyperactivity (ADHD) disorder with comorbid Substance-Use Disorder (SUD). *Expert Opinion on Pharmacotherapy, 20*(3), 343–355. doi:10.1080/14656566.2018.1551878

Quinn, P., Chang, Z., Hur, K., Gibbons, R., Lahey, B., Rickert, M., . . . D'Onofio, B. (2017). ADHD medication and substance-related problems. *American Journal of Psychiatry, 174*(9), 877–885.

Shokane, M. J., Rataemane, L. U. Z., & Rataemane, S. T. (2004). Attention-deficit/hyperactivity disorder: Comorbidity and differential diagnosis. *South African Journal of Psychiatry, 10*(3), 67–72.

Slobodin, O., & Crunelle, C. (2019). Mini review: Socio-cultural influences on the link between ADHD and SUD. *Frontiers in Public Health, 7.* https://doi.org/10.3389/fpubh.2019.00173

Smith, M. (2012). *Hyperactive: The controversial history of ADHD.* Reaktion Books.

Solberg, B. S., Halmøy, A., Engeland, A., Igland, J., Haavik, J., & Klungsøyr, K. (2018). Gender differences in psychiatric comorbidity: A population-based study of 40,000 adults with attention deficit hyperactivity disorder. *Acta Psychiatrica Scandinavica, 137*, 176–186. doi:10.1111/acps.12845

Thapar, A., Cooper, M., Eyre, O., & Langley, K. (2013). Practitioner review: What have we learnt about the causes of ADHD? *The Journal of Child Psychology and Psychiatry, 54*(1), 3–16. doi:10.1111/j.1469-7610.2012.02611.x

Thapar, A., Cooper, M., Jefferies, R., & Stergiakouli, E. (2012). What causes attention deficit hyperactivity disorder? *Archives of Disease in Childhood, 97*, 260–265. http://dx.doi.org/10.1136/archdischild-2011-300482

Van Oortmerssen, K., Vedel, E., Kramer, F., Koeter, M., Schoevers, R., & Van Den Brink, W. (2017). Diagnosing ADHD during active substance use: Feasible or flawed? *Drug and Alcohol Dependence, 180*, 371–375.

Vingilis, E., Erickson, P. G., Toplak, M. E., Kolla, N. J., Mann, R. E., Seely, J., . . . Daigle, D. S. (2015). Attention deficit hyperactivity disorder symptoms, comorbidities, substance use, and social outcomes among men and women in a Canadian sample. *BioMed Research International, 2015*, 1–8. http://dx.doi.org/10.1155/2015/982072

Vitulano, M. L., Fite, P. J., Hopko, D. R., Lochman, J., Wells, K., & Asif, I. (2014). Evaluation of underlying mechanisms in the link between childhood ADHD symptoms and risk for early initiation of substance abuse. *Psychology of Addictive Behaviors, 28*(3), 816–827. http://dx.doi.org/10.1037/a0037504

Walther, C., Cheong, J., Molina, B., Pelham, W., Wymbs, B., Belediuk, K., & Pedersen, S. (2012). Substance use and delinquency among adolescents with childhood ADHD: The protective role of parenting. *Psychology of Addictive Behaviors, 26*(3), 585–598. doi:10.1037/a0026818

Wilens, T. (2006). Attention deficit hyperactivity disorder and substance use disorders. *American Journal of Psychiatry, 163*(12), 2059–2063.

Wilens, T., & Kaminski, T. (2018). The co-occurrence of ADHD and substance use disorders. *Psychiatric Annals, 48*(7), 328–332.

Wimberley, T., Agerbo, E., Horsdal, H. T., Ottosen, C., Brikell, I., Als, T. D., . . . Dalsgaard, S. (2020). Genetic liability to ADHD and substance use disorders in individuals with ADHD. *Addiction, 115*, 1368–1377. https://doi.org/10.1111/add.14910

Wittenauer-Welsh, J., Knight, J., Hou, S., Malowney, M., Schram, P., Sherritt, L., & Boyd, J. (2017). Association between substance use diagnoses and psychiatric disorders in an adolescent and young adult clinic-based population. *Journal of Adolescent Health, 60*(6), 648–652.

6 Process Use Disorders

Fredrick Dombrowski and Tara G. Matthews

Introduction

Similar to substance use disorders, process use disorders seek stimulus outside the self to change the feelings on the inside. The neurological experience of these behaviors can create a 'high' that can only be reached when seeking, thinking, or performing the identified behavior. Experiences of compulsion, excess, and continued behavior despite negative consequences are the cornerstone of all addictions. Process use disorders may lie underneath the surface and remain untreated as most are legal and socially acceptable activities, in moderation. Process use disorders are often exacerbated by the use of drugs and alcohol, which is why they often go hand in hand. The behaviors and research described in this chapter include sex and love, shopping, gambling, the internet, food, and exercise. The process use disorders explored herein are not meant to be exhaustive of all behaviors that can be problematic if performed with the same features of addiction.

Learning Objectives

* Identify similarities between process use disorders and substance use disorders
* Identify various behaviors that may fall under the process use disorders umbrella
* Identify the relationship between process use disorders and co-occurring mental health diagnoses
* Identify unique difficulties with treating process use disorders as many of these behaviors are unavoidable
* Identify evidenced-based treatment for process use disorders
* Learn about various groups researching and supporting those with process use disorders

Key Terms

Body Mass Index (BMI): Calculated by an individual's weight in kilograms divided by the square of height in meters. A healthy BMI is considered to be 18.5 < 25.
Obesity: When an individual's BMI is 30 or higher.
Morbid Obesity: When an individual's BMI is 40 or higher.
Overweight: A body mass index that is higher than deemed healthy for the height and weight of the person.
Oniomania: Term used to describe the compulsory behavior of shopping.
Process Use Disorder: Also known as a behavioral addiction. A behavior that becomes compulsive to an individual by which they mimic similar aspects of substance use disorders.

History of Process Use Disorders

Process use disorders (otherwise known as behavioral addictions) were considered in the twentieth century, although formal diagnostic attention was not given until the late twentieth century with

DOI: 10.4324/9781003220916-7

the recognition of gambling disorder (Andreassen et al., 2013). Updates in the *DSM-5* (APA, 2013) revamped the conceptualization of addictive behaviors as the new name 'substance-related and addictive disorders' replaced the name used in the *DSM-IV*, 'substance-related disorders' (Rosenburg & Feder, 2014). Despite these recent formal changes, process use disorders were conceptualized even in the early days of self-help as individuals considered how specific behaviors such as sex and gambling can manifest similar behavioral responses to those of substance use disorders (Karim & Chaudhri, 2012). As a result, several self-help groups have been created to assist individuals showing 'addictive behaviors' in the context of these actions. Gamblers Anonymous (founded in the 1950s) and Sex and Love Addicts Anonymous (founded in the 1970s) are community-based self-help groups designed to address such behaviors through traditional 12-step models (Doweiko, 2009). The need for self-help has evolved as additional technology and innovation have impacted how people interact with the world. With the increased availability of technology and ease of connection via gaming, Computer Gaming Addicts Anonymous has been a popular 12-step option to assist those struggling to control behaviors related to online gaming.

Primary Symptomology

The *DSM-5* (APA, 2013, p. 483) identifies several universal behaviors attributed to substance use and addictive disorders. These include engaging in the behavior more than intended, an inability to cut down or stop the behavior, instances when the behavior continues despite interpersonal problems, instances when the individual is unable to complete obligations as they are engaging in the behavior, the need for more of the behavior to obtain the same effect, and instances of mood alteration and impact in functioning when the behavior no longer occurs. One of the continued qualifiers for substance use and addictive disorders is that the specified behavior has caused a lack of functioning in various aspects of the individual's life (Atroszko et al., 2020).

Conceptualizing process use disorders is similar to conceptualizing substance use disorders as counselors are able to identify how the process (or behavior) has negatively impacted the individual's functioning (Alavi et al., 2012). Counselors are expected to identify how the behavioral pattern has contributed to the client's inability to follow up with obligations (Robbins & Clark, 2015). This may require the counselor to question how engaging in the behavior has contributed to the client being late for work, missing appointments, or not following up with important events. The counselor must ask the client about their attempts (if any) to cut down or limit the behavior. When considering tolerance, the counselor may need to ask about the client's reactions to the first time they engaged in the behavior and whether the behavior needs to be increased to obtain a similar initial effect (Sussman, 2012). Many clinicians may argue about the withdrawal experiences of a client who is attempting to stop a behavior. The engagement in specific behaviors still creates changes in brain chemistry and the reward system (Alavi et al., 2012). When the behavior is stopped, it is not uncommon for individuals to report increased irritability, struggles with sleeping, and inability to focus (Zilberman et al., 2018).

Types and Prevalence of PUDs

Sex and Love Addiction

It is difficult to treat some process disorders as the behaviors associated with these disorders are natural aspects of human behavior. Among these behaviors is the natural drive for humans to engage in sexual activity (Ajegena et al., 2018). The act of sexual intimacy can be described as pleasurable for much of the population. Sexual activity can be considered harmful when an individual experiences a hyper focus on sexual activity, continued engaging in sexual acts despite potential physical and interpersonal negative consequences, and inability to control or limit their sexual activity

(Carnes & Adams, 2020). In such instances, a counselor may engage with a client who has multiple sexual partners (despite being in committed relationships) who has experienced major life disruptions (work, obligations, and health) as a result of sexual activity (Zlot et al., 2018). The individual may engage in sexual acts with people they know and others whom they don't know very well. The client will continue to crave sexual activity despite incidents in which their bodies may feel physical pain from engaging in sex (Carnes & Adams, 2020). The client will also continue to engage in sexual encounters despite being exposed to sexually transmitted illnesses.

Ajegena and colleagues (2018) identify various types of sexual addictions. Some individuals may engage in seductive role sex, wherein they feel a sense of power by using seduction to convince others to engage in sexual activity. Some individuals may have voyeuristic tendencies in which they derive sexual pleasure from watching non-consenting individuals undress or engage in sexual acts. Others may have an exhibitionistic focus in which they derive pleasure from being observed by others as they engage in sexual activities (Carnes & Adams, 2020). Other individuals may engage in sadomasochism, in which they derive sexual pleasure from experiencing physical pain or inflicting physical pain on others. Others may engage in exploitive sex, in which they violate the rights of others to engage in sexual activity. Those who prefer exploitive sex may engage in rape or pedophilia. With these various types listed, it is important to state that all these types can be sexual preferences without meeting criteria for sexual addiction. The individual will need to compulsively engage in their preferred form of sex despite consequences to self or others, show an inability to control or cut down on these behaviors, and show a cognitive preoccupation with such acts (Woehler et al., 2018).

Although it is difficult to identify the specific statistics, Karila and colleagues (2014) estimate that 3% to 6% of the US population is living with some form of sex addiction, with the majority of these being male. Some research suggests that those who meet criteria for sex addiction have been victims of various forms of abuse. Roughly 81% report sexual abuse, 97% report emotional abuse, and 81% report physical abuse (Ajegena et al., 2018). It is further estimated that roughly 43% of those living with sex addiction also meet criteria for substance use disorders. Those living with sex addiction will also show increased rates of mental health diagnoses including anxiety, depression, and PTSD (Karila et al., 2014).

Shopping Addiction

Various aspects of Westernized culture may romanticize shopping and spending money as some pop culture references have used the term 'retail therapy' to describe the act of shopping to help people feel better after a difficult situation such as a breakup. Research conducted by Rick and colleagues (2014) found that shopping tended to make people feel better when experiencing real or imagined frustrations. Shopping is necessary when people must obtain basic needs to live healthy lives. Many people who experience compulsive shopping find themselves living in debt that they may never be able to pay off and experience interpersonal difficulties as a result of their spending (Hague et al., 2016). Others may find that their compulsive spending and cognitive focus on shopping has negatively impacted their ability to work and to follow up with obligations.

It is suggested that almost 6% of the US population experiences compulsive shopping (Aboujaoude, 2014). Research by Maraz and colleagues (2015) found that roughly 90% of compulsive shoppers were women while 8% were university students. This research also found that 58% have significant debt while 42% are unable to make their minimum debt payments. As a result, 45% percent report feelings of guilt regarding their shopping while 33% report having family problems as a result of their shopping. Finally, 8% experienced financial or criminal litigation as a result of their shopping. Some research suggests that the age of onset for compulsive shopping can vary from late teens to midlife (McElroy et al., 1994). Some research suggests that the majority of those living with compulsive shopping will live with a co-occurring mood disorder (depression and anxiety) while almost half live with a substance use disorder. Roughly 60% of those engaging in compulsive shopping also live with a co-occurring personality disorder (Black, 2007).

Gambling Disorder

Gambling disorder (GD) was the first process disorder identified in the *DSM* (APA, 2013). As several states within the US have some form of legal gambling, more research has been conducted on those living with GD than other process disorders. The North American Foundation for Gambling Addiction Help (2016) suggests that roughly ten million people live with GD, costing roughly $6 billion US to the economy. It is also reported that men live with GD disorder at roughly 12 times the rate of women. Those living with GD will often find themselves spending money set aside for other bills to engage in gambling. In many instances, they will spend money only available on credit cards and fail to follow up with monetary obligations (Swanton & Gainsburry, 2020).

Changes in technology have made it easier for individuals to engage in gambling without leaving home. Online websites and apps accessible via phone allow individuals to gamble while all their personal and financial information is linked with their technology (Hague et al., 2016). As many mobile devices are electronically linked to online banking information, it is easier for individuals to access savings through online connections, as opposed to having to withdraw cash from banks and then physically convert cash to casino currency such as monetary chips. Recent research has found that those who use their mobile devices to gamble had continued focus on gambling despite losses and lost more money as they spent more time on gambling apps (James et al., 2019). Access to gambling has changed from physical casinos to online apps available in the pocket of those with a smartphone.

Those living with GD are also more likely to have co-occurring mental health and substance use diagnoses (Swanton & Gainsburry, 2020). Research conducted by Rodriguez-Monguio and colleagues (2017) found that roughly 28% of those living with GD live with co-occurring anxiety disorders while 26% live with co-occurring substance use disorders. Many casinos may offer free alcoholic beverages to their patrons, which can further assist in the development of substance use disorders.

The problems that the individual living with GD experiences reverberate throughout the family unit as financial troubles can cause and exacerbate interpersonal difficulties (Doweiko, 2009). Research has suggested that intimate partner violence (IPV) is much higher in households that have an individual living with GD (Dowling et al., 2016). The research conducted by Dowling and colleagues (2016) indicates that roughly 38% of those living with PG have been victims of IPV while 36% have been perpetrators of IVP. Counselors working with individuals living with PG are strongly encouraged to engage in collateral contacts with family members while maintaining their appropriate duties to break confidentiality if there is concern about the potential of harm to the patient, their spouse, and children within the home.

Internet Addiction

Much of our daily lives is connected through the internet and through mobile devices. These devices and our connection to the internet are no longer luxuries as banking, looking for work, connecting with social supports, and even obtaining benefits for basic assistance are all completed through the internet. In many ways, the lives of the average US citizen have changed to more online and virtual presence. It is not uncommon for individuals to spend several hours per day on the internet completing work, connecting with others, or engaging in leisure activities. Concerns arise regarding internet use when the individual has made unsuccessful efforts to limit or cut down their internet use; fails to follow up with obligations; has interpersonal difficulties caused by the internet; and experiences instances of irritability, anxiety, and sleeplessness when they are unable to get online (Griffiths, 1998). With the explosion of home internet use in the 1990s, researchers have suggested serious consideration for internet addiction as many people spend many of their waking hours online (Griffiths, 2000). Concerns about internet addiction also occur as the internet serves as a nexus for various other forms of process disorders such as problematic gambling, pornography addiction, and gaming addiction (Li & Liu, 2021).

Recent research by the Pew Research Center (2021) found that roughly 80% of adults go online every day, with 31% reporting that they are constantly online and 47% reporting that they go online multiple times per day. These percentages vary by age as almost 50% of those ages 18 to 29 and 42% of those ages 30 to 49 reporting ongoing internet use. It is reported that those under the age of 10 will spend roughly eight hours per day engaging in various forms of media, including television, smartphones, and the internet (CCM, 2013). Many college students are required to engage in various forms of online learning, studying, and research while their social lives are also connected through social media. There are concerns that college students are at risk as much of their lives operates through an online platform (Li & Liu, 2021). Ongoing use of the internet for children and adolescents can be problematic as health problems such as increased eating of unhealthy food, troubles with vision, difficulties with sleeping, and obesity can result (Bener et al., 2019). Additional research has found that those who meet criteria for internet addiction have higher rates of ADHD, depression, and social phobia than their peers who do not meet this criteria (Yen et al., 2007). Substance use among adolescents (specifically nicotine and alcohol use) was found to be a predictor for individuals to eventually develop internet addiction (Lee et al., 2013).

Gaming Addiction

The use of video games has evolved as the internet has become more widely used, and improved technology allows people from different places to play the same game together synchronously. When considering the use of video games, many may assume that internet gaming disorder will primarily impact adolescents and young adults. However, research by Nasution and colleagues (2019) reiterates that this can occur in individuals spanning ages, genders, and backgrounds. Those living with gaming addiction will find themselves preoccupied with gaming, having instances of dishonesty about their engagement in gaming, having unsuccessful efforts to cut down on gaming, needing to spend more time gaming than when initially started, feelings of sadness or anxiety when unable to game, and continued gaming despite struggles to complete obligations or solve interpersonal problems caused by gaming. The research on internet gaming disorder is rather limited as this research is often coupled with internet addiction (Feng et al., 2017). However, the *DSM-5* recommends that gaming be pursued for further research regarding addictive behaviors (APA, 213).

Food Addiction

Although the process of eating is natural, the act of eating signals the brain to activate the dopamine system, allowing those eating to feel a sense of pleasure and satisfaction (Volkow et al., 2017). This process of dopamine rush is not dissimilar from the use of substances like opiates, although the use of these substances can have a much higher rate of dopamine activation within the brain (Pedram et al., 2013). Foods that have higher contents of sugars, salts, and fats will have an increased signal of dopamine in the brain than other foods (Gearhardt, 2009). While eating disorders such as anorexia nervosa and bulimia have been accepted into formal diagnostic criteria, there remains some lack of clarity regarding a full consensus on food addiction (Hebebrand et al., 2014). The *DSM-5* has identified that being overweight or obese can be a clinical focus if these conditions are clinically significant and contribute to a lack of appropriate functioning (APA, 2013, p. 726). Research by Pedram and colleagues (2013) found that among those sampled, almost 7% of women and 3% of men were found to meet criteria for food addiction. The likelihood of living with food addiction also increased with obesity among study participants. The short-term negative health effects of food addiction can include heartburn, nausea, and vomiting. The long-term negative health impacts of food addiction can include heart disease, diabetes, high blood pressure, and stroke. These health problems combined create higher mortality rates for those living with morbid obesity (Abdelaal et al., 2017).

Eating can become problematic when the individual is unable to cut down or control eating, is preoccupied with food, spends a large amount of time obtaining and eating food, reduces other pleasurable activities to spend time eating, needs larger amounts of food over time to feel satisfied, continues to engage in overeating despite physical health consequences, and experiences withdrawal symptoms when cutting down or controlling eating (Habebrand et al., 2014). Many individuals may be dishonest about their overall food intake or the types of foods being consumed. This can create ongoing difficulties with social supports and family members as the individual will experience increased isolation. Individuals living with food addiction also have higher rates of co-occurring mental health diagnoses: specifically, depression, anxiety, and personality disorders (Horsager et al., 2021).

Working with individuals living with food addiction can vary from working with individuals living with eating disorders such as anorexia and bulimia. The experience of those living with food addiction mirrors symptoms associated with substance use as indicated earlier. However, those living with anorexia nervosa or bulimia will experience a hyper focus on their body type, often seeing themselves as overweight despite living below the recommended BMI (Carter et al., 2019). Those living with bulimia or anorexia will attempt to purge food or drastically decrease their food intake to obtain an ideal body image. Those living with eating disorders can have instances in their lives when they also meet criteria for food addiction (Carter et al., 2019). Treatment for these disorders is different. Those living with traditional eating disorders are advised to follow up with a full team of professionals, considering the high mortality associated with eating disorders. These team members would include an individual counselor, group counselor, family counselor, nutritionist, and medical doctor and would use of family to assist with eating while at the home (Kazdin et al., 2017).

The treatment of individuals living with food addiction can be difficult as these individuals will have higher rates of mood disorders and personality disorders. With that said, society's response to individuals who meet criteria for morbid obesity has been counterintuitive for successful treatment (Davis, 2014). Those living with obesity and morbid obesity often experience criticism and social isolation due to their weight. The experience of ongoing 'fat shaming' makes it more likely that the individual will not follow up with treatment and will struggle to make progress managing their intake of food as eating has become their primary coping strategy for various life triggers (Edwards et al., 2019). It is recommended that counselors working with those living with food addiction, those who are obese or morbidly obese, or other marginalized populations engage in ongoing supervision, education, and consultation to provide appropriate treatment environments and modalities to meet the needs of various clients (Doweiko, 2009).

Exercise Addiction

Previously identified process disorders have focused on various behaviors such as eating, computer use, and gambling, which are traditionally viewed as negative when completed in excess. The concept of exercise is often viewed in a socially appropriate context in which individuals can be encouraged interpersonally and through external validation to engage in exercise. Business Wire (2021) reports that a record $78 billion US was spent on weight loss and diet control products in 2019 (experiencing a decline in 2020 due to COVID-19). These numbers are expected to rebound and break new records in the next five years. Although considered healthy, exercise can become problematic when the individual is unable to control or cut down on their exercise, continues to engage in exercise despite physical health problems, limits or stops other pleasurable activities to engage in exercise, misses obligations as a result of exercising, needs more exercise to obtain a satisfied feeling than when first started, has feelings of sadness or anxiety when not exercising, and continues exercise despite interpersonal problems caused by exercise (Mónok et al., 2012).

Those who experience addiction to exercise can experience various problems as a result of their focus on exercise. These problems can include damage to muscular and skeletal systems, dehydration impacting kidney and liver functioning, social impairment, heart problems, and irregular menses (Lichtenstein et al., 2017). The study of the negative side effects of overexercising can be difficult as there are high rates of co-occurring eating disorders such as anorexia or bulimia (almost 25%) for those living with exercise addiction (Trott et al., 2021). Counselors working with individuals who meet criteria for exercise addiction should also monitor for ongoing eating disorders. Those living with exercise addiction may experience higher rates of depression (Edwards et al., 2019). Counselors are also advised to consider the use of amphetamines and steroids among those who are living with exercise addiction (Trott et al., 2021). The research regarding treatment outcomes for those living with exercise addiction is rather limited. However, the limited research indicates a high dropout rate, and it is recommended that counselors use tools of motivational interviewing to help enhance the client's motivation to make changes in their exercise (Lichtenstein et al., 2017).

Evidence-based Treatment for Process Use Disorders

When considering evidenced-based treatment modalities associated with process use disorders, it is often recommended that an individual receive treatment from a team (including primary counselor, psychiatric consultant, and primary medical provider) in addition to using family and social supports (Ajegena et al., 2018). Many of the disorders listed have severe stigmas attached, which often prevent the individual from seeking treatment (Karim & Chaudhri, 2012). Stigma is exacerbated by the normalcy of many of these behaviors such as sex and food. Technology is a part of everyone's daily life and is nearly impossible to avoid completely. Additional treatment considerations are also impacted by challenges of modernity and the use of technology ongoing throughout the day, which can limit others from becoming aware of a struggle an individual is having with a process disorder (Hague et al., 2016). When concerns regarding such behavior are addressed, those living with these disorders may have greater ease in hiding their experiences based on updates in technology.

These reported diagnoses have received limited attention as the research committed to treatment of these disorders is far less than that focused on traditional substance use. However, metaanalysis has found the benefit of using various evidence-based practices, such as motivational interviewing and CBT, in conjunction with pharmaceutical implementation (Goslar et al., 2020). As is similar with substance use disorders, process use disorders will provide options for pleasurable activities, although these activities will have a detrimental impact on the individual's life. Motivational interviewing has been used to help individuals identify how their lives have been impacted by such behaviors (Pallesen et al., 2015) while for those engaging in online behaviors (gambling, gaming, internet use), treatment has often looked to assess the meaning and thoughts associated with these activities (King et al., 2017). Challenging these thoughts while helping identify other behavioral interactions has been helpful in improving outcomes for such disorders. Family members, social supports, etc. can also assist with maintaining limits on needed activities such as eating, shopping, and online usage. It is also important to assess the client for process use disorders that may cross the line into other diagnostic criteria, such as eating disorders, sexual dysfunctions, paraphilic disorders, and other conditions that may need clinical attention.

Conclusion

As with all use disorders, identification is key to effective treatment. Identification requires asking questions about coping behaviors that have caused problems in the client's life. Even behaviors that are fundamental to life, are legal, and/or are socially acceptable can morph into behavioral addictions. One of the symptoms of process use disorders is the withdrawal component that connects mood to the behavior. It is natural to want to feel better, be released from stressful situations, and lower feelings of anxiety. However, when a behavior hijacks the pleasure/reward system of the brain, it becomes a clinical issue that needs to be addressed. Effective treatment offers the opportunity to address underlying concerns and seek healthier coping.

Questions for Consideration

1. How can you develop expertise and support your clients if process use disorders are identified?
2. What tools can be used to screen for process use disorders?
3. If left untreated, how might the process use disorder be a trigger for substance use disorders and vice versa?
4. Explore how many behaviors associated with process use disorders are socially acceptable, which can lead to minimization and a return to use or behavior when clients are under stress.

Case Study

Alex is an unemployed, single, 26-year-old Caucasian male living with his parents. Alex has attended treatment at the behest of his parents as they worry about his inability to keep jobs and complete college. Upon entry into the treatment program, Alex's toxicology screen returned positive for THC. When asked about his use of marijuana, Alex simply states that it is part of his daily life as it is for everyone in his family. Alex reports that his parents are concerned specifically about the amount of time he spends playing video games. Alex admits that he enjoys playing video games as this provides him an opportunity to connect with friends online. Alex has identified that there have been several instances when he will wake up and immediately resume playing video games, taking breaks only to eat and go to the bathroom. During such instances, he will play video games all day into the early hours of the morning. As a result, he has missed work in the past and had days when he did not shower and forgot to call people back. Alex reported instances when he tried to limit his video game playing to only a few hours a day but was unsuccessful. He admits his video game playing has also caused ongoing struggles within his family. Alex does not feel his video game playing is a problem. However, in the rare instances when Alex is not able to play video games, he reports feeling anxious and irritable and thinking about playing video games.

Questions

1. What clinical concerns surface as you read about Alex?
2. The family wants him to get a job and/or go to college. Is a co-occurring disorder preventing him from meeting his family's goals?
3. Explore your beliefs about the addictive quality and the legality of video games and marijuana.

Resources and Recommended Reading

Sex and Love Addiction:

> https://saa-recovery.org/
> https://coda.org/
> https://slaafws.org/

Gambling Disorder:

> www.gamblersanonymous.org/ga/
> www.ncpgambling.org/programs-resources/resources/

Internet Addiction

> https://virtual-addiction.com/resources/
> http://netaddiction.com/

Gaming Addiction

> https://americanaddictioncenters.org/video-gaming-addiction
> www.netaddictionrecovery.com/video-game-addiction-treatment/

Food Addiction

> www.foodaddictionresources.com/
> https://foodaddictioninstitute.org/
> https://foodaddiction.com/

Exercise Addiction

> http://addictionexperts.com/types-of-addiction/exercise-addiction/

Recommended Reading

Ascher, M. S., & Levounis, P. (2015). *The behavioral addictions.* American Psychiatric Association Publishing.

References

Abdelaal, M., le Roux, C. W., & Docherty, N. G. (2017). Morbidity and mortality associated with obesity. *Annals of Translational Medicine*, *5*(7), 161. doi:10.21037/atm.2017.03.107

Aboujaoude, E. (2014). Compulsive buying disorder: A review and update. *Current Pharmaceutical Design*, *20*(25), 4021–4025. doi:10.2174/13816128113199990618

Ajegena, B., Victor, O., & Usman, B. (2018). Sex and sexual addiction in the United States of America: An overview of its epidemiology, management and prevention strategies. *Journal of Addiction Research & Therapy*, *9*(5). doi:10.4172/2155-6105.1000366

Alavi, S. S., Ferdosi, M., Jannatifard, F., Eslami, M., Alaghemandan, H., & Setare, M. (2012). Behavioral addiction versus substance addiction: Correspondence of psychiatric and psychological views. *International Journal of Preventive Medicine*, *3*(4), 290–294.

American Counseling Association. (2014). *ACA code of ethics.* Author.

American Psychiatric Association. (2000). *Diagnostic and statistical manual of mental disorders* (4th ed., text rev.). Author.

American Psychiatric Association. (2013). *Diagnostic and statistical manual of mental disorders* (5th ed., text rev.). Author.

Andreassen, C. S., Griffiths, M. D., Gjertsen, S. R., Krossbakken, E., Kvam, S., & Pallesen, S. (2013). The relationships between behavioral addictions and the five-factor model of personality. *Journal of Behavioral Addictions JBA*, *2*(2), 90–99. Retrieved May 22, 2021, from https://akjournals.com/view/journals/2006/2/2/article-p90.xml

Ascher, M. S., & Levounis, P. (2015). *The behavioral addictions.* American Psychiatric Association Publishing.

Atroszko, P. A., Demetrovics, Z., & Griffiths, M. D. (2020). Work addiction, obsessive-compulsive personality disorder, burn-out, and global burden of disease: Implications from the ICD-11. *International Journal of Environmental Research and Public Health*, *17*(2). http://dx.doi.org/10.3390/ijerph17020660

Bener, A., Yildirim, E., Torun, P., Çatan, F., Bolat, E., Alıç, S., . . . Griffiths, M. (2019). Internet addiction, fatigue, and sleep problems among adolescent students: A large-scale study. *International Journal of Mental Health and Addiction, 17,* 959–969. https://doi.org/10.1007/s11469-018-9937-1

Black, D. (2007). A review of compulsive buying disorder. *World Psychiatry, 6*(1), 14–18.

Burleigh, T. L., Griffiths, M. D., Sumich, A., Stavropoulos, V., & Kuss, D. (2019). A systematic review of the co-occurrence of gaming disorder and other potentially addictive behaviors. *Current Addict Report, 6,* 383–401. https://doi.org/10.1007/s40429-019-00279-7

Business Wire. (2021, March 26). *U.S. weight loss & diet control market report 2021: Market reached a record $78 billion in 2019, but suffered a 21% decline in 2020 due to COVID-19-Forecast to 2025-ResearchAndMarkets.com.* Retrieved from www.businesswire.com/news/home/20210326005126/en/U.S.-Weight-Loss-Diet-Control-Market-Report-2021-Market-Reached-a-Record-78-Billion-in-2019-but-Suffered-a-21-Decline-in-2020-Due-to-COVID-19-Forecast-to-2025-ResearchAndMarkets.com

Carnes, P., & Adams, K. (2020). *Clinical management of sex addiction* (2nd ed.). Routledge.

Carter, J., Van Wijk, M., & Rowsell, M. (2019). Symptoms of "food addiction" in binge eating disorder using the Yale Food Addiction Scale version 2.0. *Appetite, 133,* 362–369.

Corey, G. (2018). *Theory and practice of counseling and psychotherapy* (10th ed.). Cengage Learning. ISBN: 978-1305263727

Council on Communications and Media. (2013). Children, adolescents, and the media. *Pediatrics, 132*(5), 958–961. https://doi.org/10.1542/peds.2013-2656

Davis, C. (2014). Evolutionary and neuropsychological perspectives on addictive behaviors and addictive substances: Relevance to the "food addiction" construct. *Substance Abuse & Rehabilitation, 5,* 129–137. doi:10.2147/SAR.S56835

Doweiko, H. (2009). *Concepts of chemical dependency* (7th ed.). Pearson Publishing.

Dowling, N., Suomi, A., Jackson, A., Lavis, T., Patford, J., Cockman, S., . . . Max Abbott, M. (2016). Problem gambling and intimate partner violence: A systematic review and meta-analysis. *Trauma, Violence, & Abuse, 17*(1), 43–61. doi:10.1177/1524838014561269

Edwards, S., Lusher, J., & Murray, E. (2019). The lived experience of obese people who feel that they are addicted to food. *International Journal of Psychology and Cognitive Science, 5*(2), 79–87. ISSN: 2472-9450

Estévez, A., Jáuregui, P., Sánchez-Marcos, I., López-González, H., & Griffiths, M. D. (2017). Attachment and emotion regulation in substance addictions and behavioral addictions. *Journal of Behavioral Addictions, 6*(4), 534–544. Retrieved May 22, 2021, from https://akjournals.com/view/journals/2006/6/4/article-p534.xml

Feng, W., Ramo, D. E., Chan, S. R., & Bourgeois, J. A. (2017). Internet gaming disorder: Trends in prevalence 1998–2016. *Addictive Behaviors, 75,* 17–24. doi:10.1016/j.addbeh.2017.06.010

Gearhardt, A., Corbin, W., & Brownell, K. (2009). Preliminary evaluation of the Yale Food Addiction Scale. *Appetite, 52*(2), 430–436.

Goslar, M., Leibetseder, M., Muench, H. M., Hofmann, S. G., & Laireiter, A. (2020). Treatments for internet addiction, sex addiction and compulsive buying: A meta-analysis. *Journal of Behavioral Addictions, 9*(1), 14–43. Retrieved July 9, 2021, from https://akjournals.com/view/journals/2006/9/1/article-p14.xml

Grant, J., Potenza, M., Weinstein, A., & Gorelick, D. (2010). Introduction to behavioral addictions. *The American Journal of Drug and Alcohol Abuse, 36*(5), 233–241. doi:10.3109/00952990.2010.491884

Griffiths, M. (1998). Internet addiction: Does it really exist? In J. Gackenbach (Ed.), *Psychology and the internet: Intrapersonal, interpersonal, and transpersonal implications* (pp. 61–75). Academic Press.

Griffiths, M. (2000). Internet addiction: Time to be taken seriously? *Addiction Research, 8*(5), 413–418. doi:10.3109/16066350009005587

Hague, B., Hall, J., & Kellett, S. (2016). Treatments for compulsive buying: A systematic review of the quality, effectiveness and progression of the outcome evidence. *Journal of Behavioral Addictions, 5*(3), 379–394. doi:10.1556/2006.5.2016.064

Hebebrand, J., Albayrak, O., Adan, R., Antel, J., Dieguezc, C., de Jong, J., . . . Dicksong, S. (2014). "Eating addiction", rather than "food addiction", better captures addictive-like eating behavior. *Neuroscience & Biobehavioral Reviews, 47,* 295–306.

Horsager, C., Faerk, E., Lauritsen, M. B., & Østergaard, S. D. (2021). Food addiction comorbid to mental disorders: A nationwide survey and register-based study. *International Journal of Eating Disorders, 54*(4), 545–560. doi:10.1002/eat.23472. Epub 2021 Jane 17. PMID: 33458821

James, R. J. E., O'Malley, C., & Tunney, R. J. (2019). Gambling on smartphones: A study of a potentially addictive behaviour in a naturalistic setting. *European Addiction Research, 25*, 30–40. doi:10.1159/000495663

Karila, L., Wéry, A., Weinstein, A., Cottencin, O., Petit, A., Reynaud, M., & Billieux, J. (2014). Sexual addiction or hypersexual disorder: Different terms for the same problem? A review of the literature. *Current Pharmaceutical Design, 20*(25), 4012–4020. doi:10.2174/13816128113199990619. PMID: 24001295

Karim, R., & Chaudhri, P. (2012). Behavioral addictions: An overview. *Journal of Psychoactive Drugs, 44*(1), 5–17. doi:10.1080/02791072.2012.662859

Kazdin, A. E., Fitzsimmons-Craft, E. E., & Wilfley, D. E. (2017). Addressing critical gaps in the treatment of eating disorders. *International Journal of Eating Disorders, 50*, 170–189. doi:10.1002/eat.22670

King, D., Kaptsis, D., Delfabbro, P., & Gradisar, M. (2017). Effectiveness of brief abstinence for modifying problematic internet gaming cognitions and behaviors. *Journal of Clinical Psychology, 73*(12), 1573–1585.

Konkolÿ Thege, B., Hodgins, D. C., & Wild, T. C. (2016). Co-occurring substance-related and behavioral addiction problems: A person-centered, lay epidemiology approach. *Journal of Behavioral Addictions, 5*(4), 614–622.

Koran, L., Faber, R., Aboujaoude, E., Large, M., & Serpe, R. (2006). Estimated prevalence of compulsive buying behavior in the United States. *American Journal of Psychiatry, 163*(10), 1806–1812.

Lee, Y. S., Han, D. H., Kim, S. M., & Renshaw, P. F. (2013). Substance abuse precedes internet addiction. *Addict Behav, 38*(4), 2022–2025. doi:10.1016/j.addbeh.2012.12.024

Li, J., & Liu, X. (2021). Internet addiction and acculturative stress among international college students in the United States. *Journal of International Students, 11*(2), 361–376. https://doi.org/10.32674/jis.v11i2.2092

Lichtenstein, M. B., Hinze, C. J., Emborg, B., Thomsen, F., & Hemmingsen, S. D. (2017). Compulsive exercise: Links, risks and challenges faced. *Psychology Research and Behavior Management, 10*, 85–95. doi:10.2147/PRBM.S113093

Maraz, A., Griffiths, M., & Demetrovics, Z. (2015). The prevalence of compulsive buying: A meta-analysis. *Addiction, 111*(3). doi:10.1111/add.13223

McElroy, S. L., Keck, J. P. E., Pope, J. H. G., Smith, J. M., & Strakowski, S. M. (1994). Compulsive buying: A report of 20 cases. *Journal of Clinical Psychiatry, 55*(6), 242–248.

McGovern, M., Xie, H., Segal, S., Siembab, L., & Drake, R. (2006). Addiction treatment services and co-occurring disorders: Prevalence estimates, treatment practices, and barriers. *Journal of Substance Abuse Treatment, 31*(3), 267–275.

Mónok, K., Berczik, K., Urban, R., & Szabo, A. (2012). Psychometric properties and concurrent validity of two exercise addiction measures: A population wide study in Hungary. *Psychology of Sport and Exercise, 13*, 739–746.

Nasution, F. A., Effendy, E., & Amin, M. M. (2019). Internet Gaming Disorder (IGD): A case report of social anxiety. *Open Access Macedonian Journal of Medical Sciences, 7*(16), 2664–2666. doi:10.3889/oamjms.2019.398

North American Foundation for Gambling Addiction Help. (2016). *Statistics of gambling addiction: 2016.* Retrieved from https://nafgah.org/statistics-gambling-addiction-2016/

Pallesen, S., Lorvik, I. M., Bu, E. H., & Molde, H. (2015). An exploratory study investigating the effects of a treatment manual for video game addiction. *Psychological Reports, 117*(2), 490–495. https://doi.org/10.2466/02.PR0.117c14z9

Pedram, P., Wadden, D., Amini, P., Gulliver, W., Randell, E., Cahill, F., et al. (2013). Food addiction: Its prevalence and significant association with obesity in the general population. *PLoS One, 8*(9), e74832. https://doi.org/10.1371/journal.pone.0074832

Petry, N., Zajac, K., & Ginley, M. (2018). Behavioral addictions as mental disorders: To be or not to be. *Annual Review of Clinical Psychology, 14*(1), 399–423.

Pew Research Center. (2021, March 26). *Rates of internet use.* Washington, DC. Retrieved from https://pewrsr.ch/2Y5pwdX

Potenza, M. N. (2014). Non-substance addictive behaviors in the context of DSM-5. *Addictive Behaviors, 39*(1), 1–2. https://doi.org/10.1016/j.addbeh.2013.09.004

Rick, S., Pereira, B., & Burson, K. (2014). The benefits of retail therapy: Making purchase decisions reduces residual sadness. *Journal of Consumer Psychology, 24*(3), 373–380.

Robbins, T., & Clark, L. (2015). Behavioral addictions. *Current Opinion in Neurobiology, 30*, 66–72.

Rodriguez-Monguio, R., Errea, M., & Volberg, R. (2017). Comorbid pathological gambling, mental health, and substance use disorders: Health-care services provision by clinician specialty. *Journal of Behavioral Addictions*, *6*(3), 406–415. Retrieved June 4, 2021, from https://akjournals.com/view/journals/2006/6/3/article-p406.xml

Rosenburg, K., & Feder, L. (2014). *Behavioral addictions: Criteria, evidence, and treatment.* Elsevier Inc.

Sancho, M., De Gracia, M., Rodríguez, R., Mallorquí-Bagué, N., Sánchez-González, J., Trujols, J., Sanches, I., Jimenez-Murcia, S., & Menchón, J. (2014). Mindfulness-based interventions for the treatment of substance and behavioral addictions: A systematic review. *Frontiers in Psychiatry*, *9*. https://doi.org/10.3389/fpsyt.2018.00095

Sussman, S. (2012). Workaholism: A review. *Journal of Addiction Research & Therapy*, *S6*. doi:10.4172/2155-6105.S6-001

Sussman, S., Lisha, N., & Griffiths, M. (2011). Prevalence of the addictions: A problem of the majority or the minority? *Evaluation & the Health Professions*, *34*(1), 3–56. https://doi.org/10.1177/0163278710380124

Swanton, T., & Gainsburry, S. (2020). Gambling-related consumer credit use and debt problems: A brief review. *Current Opinion in Behavioral Sciences*, *31*, 21–31.

Trott, M., Johnstone, J., Firth, J., Grabovac, I., McDermott, D., & Smith, L. (2021). Prevalence and correlates of body dysmorphic disorder in health club users in the presence vs absence of eating disorder symptomology. *Eating and Weight Disorders*, *26*, 1169–1177. https://doi.org/10.1007/s40519-020-01018-y

Volkow, N. D., Wang, G.-J., Tomasi, D., & Baler, R. D. (2017). Overlaps between drug and food addiction. *Obesity Review*, *14*, 2–18. https://doi.org/10.1111/j.1467-789X.2012.01031.x

Walker, E., & Druss, B. (2017). Cumulative burden of comorbid mental disorders, substance use disorders, chronic medical conditions, and poverty on health among adults in the U.S.A. *Psychology, Health, & Medicine*, *22*(6), 727–735.

Woehler, E., Giordano, A., & Hagedorn, W. (2018). Moments of relational depth in sex addiction treatment. *Sexual Addiction & Compulsivity*, *25*(2–3), 153–169. doi:10.1080/10720162.2018.1476943

Yen, J. Y., Ko, C. H., Yen, C. F., Wu, H. Y., & Yand, M. J. (2007). The comorbid psychiatric symptoms of internet addiction: Attention deficit hyperactivity disorder, depression, social phobia, and hostility. *Journal of Adolescent Health*, *41*, 93–98.

Zilberman, N., Yadid, G., Efrati, Y., Neumark, Y., & Rassovsky, Y. (2018). Personality profiles of substance and behavioral addictions. *Addictive Behaviors*, *82*, 174–181.

Zlot, Y., Goldstein, M., Cohen, K., & Weinstein, A. (2018). Online dating is associated with sex addiction and social anxiety. *Journal of Behavioral Addictions*, *7*(3), 821–826. Retrieved June 4, 2021, from https://akjournals.com/view/journals/2006/7/3/article-p821.xml

Section II

Populations

Tara G. Matthews

Ethical counselors seek cultural humility as they engage with each of their clients. As all counseling is multicultural, both who we are as a counselor and the client matter in the therapeutic relationship. Understanding the dynamics of the power differential and the differences between your own life experiences and the client's story is key to connecting and treating the whole person. While a client may be the same gender, ethnicity, or even culture as the counselor, their experiences in the world are unique to them. Treatment assumptions may be ineffective as economic, geographic family dynamics and past treatment experiences play a role in access to resources and acceptance of support. Understanding their story will require the counselor to be open to the client's point of view, no matter how similar to or different from their own. Meeting the client where they are in their life's journey is vital to individualized treatment. Applying cultural humility, a counselor allows themselves to view the client through the client's own lens, allowing them to share their experiences without fear of judgment, thus opening the door to treating mental health, substance use, and underlying conditions with an integrated and individualized approach. Addressing underlying issues that may trigger symptomology of their co-occurring disorders requires an understanding of the needs of different populations. Each chapter in this section posits that gender, age, orientation, and culture carry specific traumas, life challenges, and considerations. Who the client is and how they experience the world cannot be taken for granted or addressed in isolative fashion. The co-occurring disorders should not be treated separately, but rather in an integrated, individualized program. This purpose of this section is not to define all cultural considerations for treatment, but rather to highlight unique sensitivities and concerns that will need to be addressed for treatment to be effective.

DOI: 10.4324/9781003220916-8

7 Women With Co-occurring Disorders

Tricia L. Chandler, Tara G. Matthews,
and Fredrick Dombrowski

Introduction

Over the past few decades, research has examined how and why men and women develop addictions, along with differences in underlying mental health disorders. The research concluded that women have special needs for co-occurring mental health issues and substance use disorder treatment, noting the difference in physiology, interpersonal issues, and risk factors (Becker, 2011; Gudrais, 2011; Kauffman et al., 1997). Additionally, the Substance Abuse and Mental Health Services Administration (SAMHSA, 2011) noted specific 'risk factors associated with substance abuse' in women, including having underlying posttraumatic stress, eating disorders, depression, and anxiety that contribute to increased sensation seeking. Further research suggests these additional risks are due to histories of trauma and childhood sexual abuse, as well as interpersonal abuse and socioeconomic issues, all related to the issues of regulating affect (Bloom & Covington, 1998; Chandler, 2010; Manhal-Baugus, 1998; Najavits, 2002; Nelson-Zlupko et al., 1995; US Department of Health and Human Services, 2000, 2003; SAMHSA, 2011). In addition to these concerns, women who have developed co-occurring disorders and are young, disadvantaged, and at risk for unplanned pregnancy have an increased risk of continuing to put themselves and their future children at risk by continuing to use alcohol and drugs while pregnant. All these concerns for women mean they may not have access to treatment, and even if they do, they may refuse long-term treatment due to their obligations to their families – both the younger and older generations – along with fears of what could happen to their children if they do not have support for them. This chapter will review various factors that must be considered in providing treatment to meet the unique needs of women.

Learning Objectives

- Early childhood trauma and abuse in women often lead to complex PTSD and a multitude of other disorders.
- Women have different treatment needs than men due to physiology, interpersonal relationships, and reasons for developing the co-occurring disorders.
- Multicultural considerations include misdiagnosis and how oppression and socioeconomic status may contribute to a lack of treatment options for women.
- Women have different stereotypical stigma issues when they have succumbed to substance use disorders than men, as well as many situations they must manage in their family and cultural obligations and less effective treatment access than men.

Key Terms

Fetal Alcohol Syndrome: A developmental syndrome that occurs during the development of a fetus if the pregnant mother is consuming alcohol. This syndrome often includes

DOI: 10.4324/9781003220916-9

slowed physical and mental development of the child, accompanied by abnormalities in the development of the skull and the face of the child.

Hysteroscopy: Medical procedure of removing the uterus due to various health concerns.

Menses: Time of menstruation.

Menopause: The time when a woman ceases to menstruate. During this time, the woman experiences various changes in hormones.

Osteoporosis: A health condition in which the body experiences a decrease in bone density or struggles to build bone to replace bone density. Primarily impacts women who have experienced menopause.

Pap Smear: A health test that requires cells scraped from the uterus to be tested for cancer.

Understanding the Unique Treatment Needs of Women

The following chapter section includes an overview of some important considerations when you provide treatment for women with co-occurring disorders. This section is guided by the content developed by the Substance Abuse and mental Health Services Administration (SAMHSA): Treatment Improvement Protocol 51, *Addressing the Specific Needs of Women* (2011). It is important to be cognizant that all women have their own personal story that should not be assumed based on gender, culture, or background. However, the general guidelines provided herein may be helpful in guiding the counselor's understanding of women's needs in treatment.

Psychological Issues

The University of Chicago Center for Health and Social Sciences sponsored two research studies (Engstrom et al., 2008; Schiff et al., 2002) that found, in interviewing over 400 women being treated for opiate addiction in a methadone clinic, that 58% had experienced childhood sexual abuse, 90% had experienced intimate partner violence, and 29% met the criteria for posttraumatic stress disorder. Similar findings have been substantiated by Robert Jamison (2011), a clinical psychologist at Harvard Brigham and Women's Hospital, who found correlations between women who abuse pain medications and having sexual and/or physical abuse histories, as well as psychological distress, as motivating factors for drug misuse. These findings further substantiate the complicated relationship between trauma, mental health disorders, and substance abuse for women that Dr. Gabor Mate' (2010) mentioned in clients he treated in Vancouver, Canada, over the past 15-plus years with substantial co-occurring disorders, all substantiating they have complex childhood trauma and abuse histories. While the percentage of women who have complex childhood histories of abuse and trauma may be difficult to know precisely, there is definitely a correlation between those childhood issues and the increased risk of developing co-occurring disorders, along with physiological issues, interpersonal problems, socioeconomic problems, and problems with both accessing and being able to maintain effective treatment historically for these issues.

Gender-Responsive Treatment

Based on years of research into women's special needs in substance abuse treatment, SAMHSA identified core principles for gender-responsive treatment (2011). These core principles include:

- Recognizing the importance and role of socioeconomic issues and differences among women
- Promoting cultural competence specific to women
- Recognizing the role and significance of personal relationships in women's lives
- Addressing the unique health concerns of women

- Endorsing a developmental perspective
- Attending to the relevance and presence of various caregiver roles that women assume throughout their lives
- Recognizing that ascribed roles and gender expectations across cultures affect societal attitudes toward women who abuse substances
- Adopting a trauma-informed perspective
- Using a strength-based model for women's treatment
- Incorporating an integrated and multidisciplinary approach to women's treatment
- Maintaining a gender-responsive treatment environment across settings
- Supporting the development of gender competency specific to women's issues

(SAMHSA, 2011/PIT 51, p. xviii)

While the need for gender-specific treatment has been identified, few protocols have been identified to treat the whole person related to the issues that women have in substance abuse treatment. The quality of life after treatment may be a better predictor of successful treatment outcomes than gender, but without further research, it would be difficult to determine (Glanton Holzhauer et al., 2020). This may contribute to why gender specific treatment is not the standard. However, an integrative treatment approach would include gender specific issues that are unique to women. A syndemic approach is needed. For example, chronic alcohol use has significant negative physical effects on women, including fluctuations in estrogen levels, which may be linked to an increase in impulsivity, issues with fertility, and an increase in sexual dysfunction (Glanton Holzhauer et al., 2020). These issues alone put women at a higher risk for unique traumas that need to be addressed in gender-responsive treatment.

Typically, residential treatment programs include both men and women whether these are predominantly substance use treatment programs or those that are considered integrative of both mental health issues and substance use disorders. One 12-week pilot study of substance abuse treatment done by Shelly Greenfield in connection with Harvard Medical School found that women's self-efficacy improved with a combined woman-centered approach and group dynamics in treatment (Gudrais, 2011). Even with effective gender-responsive treatment, there are still barriers to treatment as women balance the fears, responsibilities, and health insecurities of their lives.

Barriers to Treatment

While reasons behind substance abuse have been acknowledged as different for women, with relational and environmental influences being significant for women (Kauffman et al., 1997; SAMHSA, 2011), treatment protocols have been slow to acknowledge and change in accordance with the need for integrative treatment protocols specific to women's needs. Traditionally, substance abuse treatment has offered a specialized protocol that has been provided for both women and men in the same facility. While primary residential facilities state that women and men are treated separately, in actuality, most of these facilities intermingle groups, resulting in findings that women have a greater risk of relapse after completing treatment in these environments (Gudrais, 2011). Women are also at greater risk for intimate partner violence, food insecurity, and human trafficking.

Women who are experiencing co-occurring substance use and mental health diagnoses are less likely to adhere to women's specific services, such as regular medical visits, pap smears, and gynecology appointments (Mahoney et al., 2020). The lack of connection to these services could be a long-lasting detriment to the woman's health, which may reach beyond the incidents of substance use or mental health diagnosis. Lack of care in women's reproductive health additionally places the woman and her potential children at risk for ongoing health problems.

Young women who are pregnant and mothers to small children have additional barriers to treatment that put their children and fetuses at risk for many physiological and psychiatric issues due to being exposed to alcohol and drugs in the womb and lack of proper care, nutritional intake, and parenting skills for those children already born (SAMHSA, 2011). Women in this category can be teens or young adults and have childhood trauma histories that have contributed to mood disorders, anxiety disorders, body dysmorphic disorders, eating disorders, and interpersonal problems, along with other problems that include not being aware of or willing to use safe sex practices (Ackard & Neumark-Sztainer, 2003). Prenatal care may be minimal or non-existent, with women going to hospital emergency rooms to have their babies, and these women and their unborn babies are at great risk, which indicates a need for integrating health interventions of pre-natal care into mental health and substance use treatment (Lee King et al., 2015). It may be fairly common knowledge that drinking alcohol while pregnant can lead to having babies with alcohol fetal syndrome (Alati et al., 2006), but it may be less common knowledge what the long-term adverse effects are on children who were exposed to methamphetamines, crack cocaine, heroin, or other harsh substances.

Women who do not stop using while pregnant destine their children to potential learning dis-orders, mood disorders, and anxiety and personality disorders; those with the worst issues have little access to higher executive cognitive functioning. Being born without the abilities to access empathy and compassion for others, understanding of other people's rights, and a variety of other concerns is a red flag for conduct disorder and sociopathic tendencies showing up in many children born with some of these drugs in their systems. These women need special services that identify them early in their pregnancy and provide them with safe and long-term residential services to medically monitor the pregnancy; house any other children; and provide extensive integrative treatment that includes parenting classes, vocational training, mindfulness-based therapies, nutritional counseling, addiction recovery services, and access to services to help the mother graduate from the program with the abilities and skills to succeed in society as a healthy woman and mother (SAMHSA, 2011).

A recent study conducted on a diverse sample of 245 women looked at three treatment referral groups to see which leads to better retention in treatment programs for women with these issues and found those mandated by child protective services or court jurisdiction have better treatment retention than those who are not mandated for services, with those mandated by CPS being most receptive to treatment retention (Rivera et al., 2021). A finding from the study noted that part of the reason for increased treatment retention in those mandated to treatment may be because addi-tional services were offered the women that included case management, treatment planning, and interagency progress meetings with parenting classes, housing and transportation support, and social services that support the women and their children after treatment, along with retaining child custody rights or family reunification (Rivera et al., 2021). This information is relevant to demonstrating the need for integrative treatment for women with co-occurring disorders.

Multicultural Considerations

Appropriate person-centered treatment to meet the needs of women must consider whether there is generational trauma due to culture, spiritual considerations, and any other cultural reason for overall mistrust of the medical model and mental health treatment from that model. Leddy et al. (2021) reiterated the need for trauma-informed care when working with women as they are at greater risk for intimate partner violence, food insecurity, and HIV. Substance use becomes a cop-ing mechanism reenforcing a dangerous cycle of risky behavior or risky environmental exposure, exacerbating underling mental health conditions. Unhelpful partners, social isolation or ostra-cization, and violence in the living environment contribute to resistance to treatment or return to use (Boroumandfar et al., 2020). Women are more likely to become victims of sex crimes and abuse, particularly when under the influence themselves. To be competent to work with women from diverse backgrounds, one has to develop a holistic approach that is respectful of that diversity and develop a healthy curiosity about what the client feels is in their best interest and their family's.

While there may be various reasons that contribute to a lack of trust between treatment providers and those of marginalized backgrounds, women of color are less likely to follow up with treatment and support despite higher rates of sexual violence and increased rates of substance use (Taylor & Kuo, 2019). Within the cultural context, many women will take on various roles, such as primary care provider, nurturer, cook, and scholar. With some cultures viewing women as less than men, they may have limited rights and may not seek treatment for co-occurring disorders or abuse (Lopez et al., 2018). While treatment providers may not be trusted due to systemic issues and a male-dominated treatment perspective, many cultures may feel that it is taboo to discuss mental health or substance use issues, especially with women. Supportive multicultural treatment takes economics, resources, access, culture, and safety into consideration.

Psychological Disorders

Women who live with substance use disorders seldom struggle with substance use independent of psychological influences. Their lives are often riddled with complexities and unresolved traumas that can lead to avoidance. The anxiolytic effects of alcohol may contribute to why women drink as it can temporarily ease feelings of anxiety or reduce negative emotions (Zachry et al., 2019). Stigma associated with treatment can also prevent women from seeking help, especially women who perceive devaluation and discrimination (Matsumoto et al., 2021). Women are far more likely to have depression and anxiety underlying substance use disorders and often have three or more co-occurring disorders, including PTSD and eating disorders, that are associated with co-occurring substance use disorders (Agrawal et al., 2005).

Anxiety and Depression

Women with co-occurring mood disorders may present in treatment in a variety of ways. Women with depression and anxiety often seek treatment for somatic complaints, such as exhaustion, sleep problems, irritability, and chronic pain (SAMHSA, 2011). Both the physical and psychological symptoms of depression and anxiety can be exacerbated and triggered by substance use. A familial history of depression and anxiety may be a biological cause, but substance use can lead to ineffective coping and neurological changes. Substance use can also impact the neurotransmitters and result in the development of depression or anxiety as a withdrawal symptom or side effect of substance abuse. When working with women, it is imperative to explore substance use and mental health issues simultaneously as they go hand in hand. Biological considerations must also be addressed as they can impact the treatment and presentation of co-occurring disorders.

Pregnancy and motherhood can be central components of a women's identity. While not all women choose to have children, the societal pressures and assumptions surrounding childbearing may be present. This results in both a stigma associated with either choice and a societal judgment of the woman's use of substances. Additionally, a woman can experience major challenges in identity and life meaning if her ability to conceive and bear children as planned is disrupted (He et al., 2019). Women who have reported experiences of infertility and ongoing struggles to become pregnant and maintain pregnancy have reported increased symptoms of depression and anxiety. For women who bear children, the process of raising children can also be difficult as a lack of sleep experienced by the mother following the birth of a child can exacerbate and enhance symptoms of post-partum depression (Okun et al., 2018). Post-partum depression is unique to women, and for those already struggling with substance use disorders, the hormonal and physiological implications can be triggering. While in some cultures, women have familial or partner support during and after pregnancy, this is not the norm or the experience of all women. As women then struggle to raise children while they are experiencing their own anxiety and depression, they can become especially frustrated with themselves for experiencing such feelings and can turn to substance use to manage such feelings (Albert, 2015).

Symptoms of depression and anxiety can be impacted by various hormonal changes that occur naturally throughout a women's life. Around the age of menopause and beyond, women are found to be more at risk for symptoms of depression and anxiety (Mulhall et al., 2018). While changes in hormones can be somewhat expected, these hormone changes can be accompanied by other physical symptoms such as hot flashes and changes in mood. Consequently, these changes can be misinterpreted as a mental health diagnosis. Additionally, women who use substances prior to menopause may increase their substance use to cope with such changes (Milic et al., 2018). While the changes that women experience in menopause can be subtle and are primarily associated with reproductive functioning, cognitive shifts in focus and interests can also change through this life stage (Greendale et al., 2020). As women age after menopause, additional health concerns must be addressed, especially as women experience decreased bone density at higher rates than men, making them at higher risk for broken bones and osteoporosis (Kelly et al., 2019). Those who live with osteoporosis may be at greater risk of anxiety due to concerns about broken bones and at a higher risk for opiate use disorder as painkillers can be prescribed to manage pain associated with a broken bone. Ongoing linkage with a primary care physician should be recommended for all clients receiving care for mental health and substance use disorders. Women-specific care is also needed as these natural changes can impact substance use and co-occurring disorders.

Posttraumatic Stress Disorder (PTSD)

PTSD is a risk factor for substance use disorders (Guliyev et al., 2021), and the unique treatment needs of women include recognition of trauma- and gender-specific interventions. PTSD in women often goes untreated and underreported as research tends to focus on co-ed treatment facilities. In 2007, a gender-specific treatment was utilized, showing promise in decreasing symptomology (Toussaint et al., 2007). However, stigma and perceived discrimination can prevent women from seeking treatment. Matsumoto et al. (2021) found that women devalue and stigmatize themselves due to beliefs that most people consider those who use alcohol and drugs unreliable, dangerous, and not good people. Self-stigma may be a factor in fewer woman seeking treatment, despite an increased need for treatment of co-occurring disorders; this may be particularly true with younger women (Melchior et al., 2019).

Women are also at a higher risk for sexual exploitation when under the influence of drugs and alcohol. As alcohol and drugs lower inhibitions, they can also put women in vulnerable situations that can lead to retraumatization and/or new traumas. Narvaez et al. (2019) concluded that use of club drugs is strongly correlated with PTSD and may be a risk factor for exposure to risky sexual situations. These risky situations may trigger unresolved traumatizing experiences or vulnerability to new traumatizing situations.

Eating Disorders

Herzog et al. (2006) found clinical significance between drug abuse and diagnosed eating disorders. Eating disorders are categorized in the *DSM-5* as a separate and distinct disorder. Reviewing the criteria for eating disorders and receiving specialized training in the unique needs of those with eating disorders are strongly recommended. For those with eating disorders, co-occurring anxiety and/or PTSD is common. Piran and Gadalla (2007) suggested that eating disorders and substance abuse may go hand in hand. In this Canadian study of adult women, Piran and Gadalla (2007) found that, in women 25 to 44, alcohol abuse is four times more likely than occurring by chance alone, and for women 45 and up, alcohol abuse is eight times more likely than occurring on its own. These number are significant and should be taken into consideration during the assessment and treatment process. In college students, disordered eating has been connected to substance use (Perryman et al., 2018), each laying the foundation for future co-occurring disorders. A client may not present for treatment because of an eating disorder, but not inquiring about their history and screening for eating disorders would be a disservice.

Current Treatment

Various treatment programs may have gender-specific placement, where men and women would respectively be served in a unit or wing of a hospital or treatment center. There are some institutions where men and women may be housed in different wings of the same facility while having ample access to one another in group interactions and within the social context. The normal length of stay to address the substance abuse issues for both genders is usually 30 days, which does not begin to address all the biopsychosocial needs of women to work with complex co-occurring disorders. Primary treatment has traditionally included cognitive therapy and recovery-based protocols, with a strong element of 12-step indoctrination aimed solely at the substance abuse issue and deferring additional issues that the individual may have. Those programs that do attempt to incorporate an integrative approach at all are extremely expensive and not accessible to those individuals without significant financial resources. Funding grants from SAMHSA for substance abuse treatment are less available than they were years ago, when considering inflation, per Harold Pollack (faculty chair at the Center for Health Administrative Studies), which adds to the difficulty in accessing appropriate substance abuse treatment (SAMHSA, 2011).

Integrative Treatment

Integrative treatment for women from young through middle years must take into consideration not only the individual but also her family situation as she may be taking care of her children and/ or her parents, which will impede willingness to go into any form of long-term treatment. Having all services in one location with a variety of practitioners and professionals makes it easier for women to get transportation to appointments. The facility offering childcare makes it even more likely that young women will make and keep appointments, whether these are individual, group, or family therapy. Outpatient therapy often includes groups of many kinds that are great opportunities for women to bond with other women while learning about mindfulness, nutrition, parenting, and self-care, along with any therapeutic programming.

One international study in Germany looked at the cognitive behavioral approach of Seeking Safety to help women with co-occurring PTSD and SUDs consider the overall efficacy of the approach, either in a stand-alone treatment or accompanied by recovery programming and multidiscipline approaches like EMDR (Schafer et al., 2019). Outcome measures suggest that combining approaches increases the efficacy of treatment outcomes for PTSD while the Seeking Safety workbook and recovery measures did decrease substance use (Schafer et al., 2019). Another study researched trauma-informed treatment for women with co-occurring PTSD and substance use disorders with a randomized trial of 353 women (Lopez-Castro et al., 2015). The study suggested that 80% of women who seek treatment for substance use disorders have childhood histories of sexual and/or physical abuse leading to severe and complex psychiatric presentations, which interfere with treatment outcomes. The results of the study suggest that treatment must be specialized to the individual and that research needs to continue to develop so that the needs of these women are effectively addressed (Lopez-Castro et al., 2015).

Therapist Gender

Both as an individual treatment provider and a group counseling treatment provider, the therapist's gender is a factor. Women's experiences with previous counselors and previous men or women in their lives will impact their preconceived expectations of the counseling relationship. While assumptions are often made that woman are best supported by women therapists, these assumptions are not consistently empirically supported. In fact, NeSmith et al. (2000) suggested that there is no statistically significant difference between client self-acceptance in a treatment group with a male leader and a female leader. However, in the treatment group with a male leader, attitudes toward men significantly improved throughout therapy (NeSmith et al., 2000), thus reenforcing the value of the therapeutic relationship rather than the gender of the therapist themselves. According to SAMHSA (2011), creating a sense of safety, maintaining clear boundaries, consistently enforcing treatment rules, and maintaining trust are all key to facilitating effective treatment with women and avoiding retraumatization. This can be done by a counselor of any gender if self-reflection, self-awareness, and cultural humility are utilized. However, if the client has a preference concerning the therapist's gender and that preference can be met, it should be honored.

Conclusion

In an era of person-centered care, counselors must be willing to adjust treatment options to meet the needs of women of various backgrounds, ages, ethnicities, and circumstances. Women experience unique physical health experiences that impact the etiology of mental health and substance use disorders. Cultural expectations of women often require them to be the primary caregivers and nurturers while in other cultures, women may not have the same rights and privileges as men. These cultural expectations further exacerbate the stigma associated with mental health and substance use diagnoses. Despite natural changes that women experience through the process of pregnancy and aging, these ongoing changes can cause various disruptions in hormones, causing adjustments in mood and a greater risk of health problems. Women who are pregnant and living with mental health diagnoses may experience challenges related to treatment as some concerns may arise about how some psychotropic medications can impact the developing child. Women who are pregnant and living with ongoing substance use disorders may not seek treatment due to concerns about being separated from their children and limited support through social service agencies for recovery and family reinstatement. Concerns for treatment also arise regarding appropriate treatment implementation and using evidence-based practices that are designed to meet the needs of women. The therapeutic alliance can be further impacted by a disconnect that women may experience with male counselors who have limited understanding of women's needs and the responsibilities placed on them within their culture. Although the majority of counselors are women, all counselors working with women are advised to obtain their own supervision and support based on their own assumptions and expectations of women as these can come out negatively toward the client in a treatment session. The experiences of women are unique, and treatment must reflect the specific needs of the woman being treated.

Questions for Consideration

1. Pregnant women present unique clinical issues as stigma and fear prevent them from seeking treatment. Consider your own beliefs about substance abuse and pregnancy. What resources are needed to ethically treat women in this capacity? How could you address the stigma and fear?
2. Women are often treated in co-ed groups. What issues may be left untreated in co-ed groups?
3. Consider your own gender and how that would impact your work with women. Does your age matter? What about your ethnicity?

Case Study

Jennifer is a 24-year-old unmarried African American woman who is seeking treatment due to a recent arrest for driving under the influence. She reports that she has never been to treatment before and is just here for an assessment so she can get her license back. As you facilitate the assessment, you learn that Jennifer has a significant history of trauma and anxiety. Her drinking has increased to daily over the past year after a recent sexual encounter at work. When you inquire about anything other than her drinking behavior, she becomes defensive and tells you that it is none of your business. Her court paperwork indicates that her BAC upon arrest was .29, and her urine drug screen at the time of her assessment shows that she has marijuana in her system.

Questions

1. What clinical information is needed to make treatment recommendations for Jennifer?
2. What co-occurring disorders might play a role in her substance use behavior?
3. Based on your gender, ethnicity, and age, what challenges would you face working with Jennifer?

References

Ackard, D. M., & Neumark-Sztainer, D. (2003). Multiple sexual victimizations among adolescent boys and girls: Prevalence and associations with eating disorders and psychological health. *Journal of Child Sexual Abuse, 12*(1), 17–37.

Agrawal, A., Gardner, C. O., Prescott, C. A., & Kendler, K. S. (2005). The differential impact of risk factors on illicit drug involvement in females. *Social Psychiatry and Psychiatric Epidemiology, 40*(6), 454–466.

Alati, R., Al, M. A., Williams, G. M., O'Callaghan, M., Najman, J. M., & Bor, W. (2006). In utero alcohol exposure and prediction of alcohol disorders in early adulthood: A birth cohort study. *Archives of General Psychiatry, 63*(9), 1009–1016.

Albert, P. (2015). Why is depression more prevalent in women? *Journal of Psychiatry and Neuroscience, 40*(4), 219–221. doi:10.1503/jpn.150205

Becker. (2011). *Differences of treatment amongst men and women.* Retrieved from http://abcnews.go.come/Health/story?id=116913&page=1

Bloom, B., & Covington, S. (1998). *Gender-specific programming for female offenders: What is it and why is it important?* Paper presented at the 50th Annual Meeting of the American Society of Criminology, Washington, DC.

Boroumandfar, Z., Kianpour, M., & Afshari, M. (2020). Ups and downs of drug rehab among women: A qualitative study. *BMC Women's Health, 20*(1), 1–10. https://doi-org.libauth.purdueglobal.edu/10.1186/s12905-020-00946-2

Chandler, P. (2010). *Resilience in healing from childhood sexual abuse.* Dissertation presented to Faculty at Saybrook University for Partial Fulfillment of Requirements for the Degree of Doctor of Philosophy (Ph.D.) in Psychology, UMI Dissertation Services.

Engstrom, M., El-Bassel, N., Go, H., & Gilbert, L. (2008). Childhood sexual abuse and intimate partner violence among women in methadone treatment: A direct or mediated relationship? *Journal of Family Violence, 23*(7), 605–617.

Glanton Holzhauer, C., Cucciare, M., & Epstein, E. E. (2020). Sex and Gender Effects in Recovery from Alcohol Use Disorder. *Alcohol Research: Current Reviews, 40*(3), 1–19. https://doi-org.libauth.purdueglobal.edu/10.35946/arcr.v40.3.03

Greendale, G., Karlamangla, A., & Maki, P. (2020). The menopause transition and cognition. *JAMA, 323*(15), 1495–1496. doi:10.1001/jama.2020.1757

Gudrais, E. (2011, July–August). Women and alcohol. *Harvard Magazine.*

Guliyev, C., Kalkan, Ö., Tekin, K., Tuna, Z. O., & Ögel, K. (2021). Comparison of individuals with and without the risk of post-traumatic stress disorder in terms of substance use features and psychological problems according to their substance preferences. *Alpha Psychiatry, 22*(3), 153–158. https://doi-org.libauth.purdueglobal.edu/10.5455/apd.14413

He, L., Wang, T., & Xu, H. (2019). Prevalence of depression and anxiety in women with recurrent pregnancy loss and the associated risk factors. *Archives of Gynecology and Obstetrics, 300,* 1061–1066. https://doi.org/10.1007/s00404-019-05264-z

Herzog, D. B., Franko, D. L., Dorer, D. J., Keel, P. K., Jackson, S., & Manzo, M. P. (2006). Drug abuse in women with eating disorders. *International Journal of Eating Disorders, 39*(5), 364–368. https://doi-org.libauth.purdueglobal.edu/10.1002/eat.20257

Jamison, R. N. (2011). *Just how do gender differences show up relative to a particular drug that's abused?* Retrieved from www.healthfinder.gov/News/newsstory.aspx?docid=638574

Kauffman, S. E., Silver, P., & Poulin, J. (1997). Gender differences in attitudes toward alcohol, tobacco, and other drugs. *Social Work, 3*(42), 231–241.

Kelly, R., McDonald, L., Jensen, N., Sidles, S., & LaRue, A. (2019). Impacts of psychological stress on osteoporosis: Clinical implications and treatment interactions. *Frontiers in Psychiatry, 10.* https://doi.org/10.3389/fpsyt.2019.00200

Leddy, A. M., Zakaras, J. M., Shieh, J., Conroy, A. A., Ofotokun, I., Tien, P. C., & Weiser, S. D. (2021). Intersections of food insecurity, violence, poor mental health and substance use among US women living with and at risk for HIV: Evidence of a syndemic in need of attention. *PLoS One, 16*(5), 1–19. https://doi-org.libauth.purdueglobal.edu/10.1371/journal.pone.0252338

Lee King, P., Duan, L., & Amaro, H. (2015). Clinical needs of in-treatment pregnant women with co-occurring disorders: Implications for primary care. *Maternal & Child Health Journal, 19*(1), 180–187.

Lopez, V., Sanchez, K., Killian, M., & Eghaneyan, B. (2018). Depression screening and education: An examination of mental health literacy and stigma in a sample of Hispanic women. *BMC Public Health, 18.* https://doi.org/10.1186/s12889-018-5516-4

Lopez-Castro, T., Hu, M., Papini, S., Ruglass, L. M., & Hien, D. A. (2015). Pathways to change: Use trajectories following trauma-informed treatment of women with co-occurring post traumatic stress disorder and substance use disorders. *Drug and Alcohol Review, 34,* 242–251.

Mahoney, K., Reich, W., & Urbanek, S. (2019). Substance use disorder: Prenatal, intrapartum and postpartum care. *The American Journal of Maternal/Child Nursing, 44*(5), 284–288. doi:10.1097/NMC.0000000000000551

Manhal-Baugus, M. (1998). The self-in-relation theory and women for sobriety: Female specific theory and mutual help group for chemically dependent women. *Journal of Addictions and Offender Counseling, 18*(2), 78–85.

Mate', G. (2010). *In the realm of hungry ghosts: Close encounters with addiction.* North Atlantic Press.

Matsumoto, A., Santelices, C., & Lincoln, A. K. (2021). Perceived stigma, discrimination and mental health among women in publicly funded substance abuse treatment. *Stigma and Health, 6*(2), 151–162. https://doi-org.libauth.purdueglobal.edu/10.1037/sah0000226

Melchior, H., Hüsing, P., Grundmann, J., Lotzin, A., Hiller, P., Pan, Y., . . . Schäfer, I. (2019). Substance abuse-related self-stigma in women with substance use disorder and comorbid posttraumatic stress disorder. *European Addiction Research, 25*(1), 20–29. https://doi-org.libauth.purdueglobal.edu/10.1159/000496113

Milic, J., Glisic, M., Trudy, V., Pletsch Borba, L., Asllanaj, E., Rojas, L., . . . Franco, O. (2018). Menopause, ageing, and alcohol use disorders in women. *Maturitas, 111,* 100–109.

Mulhall, S., Andel, R., & Anstey, K. (2018). Variation in symptoms of depression and anxiety in midlife women by menopausal status. *Maturitas, 108,* 7–12.

Najavits, L. M. (2002). "Seeking safety": Therapy for trauma and substance abuse. *Corrections Today, 64*(6), 136–139.

Narvaez, J. C. de M., Remy, L., Bermudez, M. B., Scherer, J. N., Ornell, F., Surratt, H., Kurtz, S. P., & Pechansky, F. (2019). Re-traumatization Cycle: Sexual Abuse, Post-Traumatic Stress Disorder and Sexual Risk Behaviors among Club Drug Users. *Substance Use & Misuse, 54*(9), 1499–1508. https://doi-org.libauth.purdueglobal.edu/10.1080/10826084.2019.1589521

Nelson-Zlupko, L., Kauffman, E., & Dore, M. M. (1995). Gender differences in drug addiction and treatment: Implications for social work intervention with substance-abusing women. *Social Work, 40*(1), 45–54.

NeSmith, C. L., Wilcoxon, S. A., & Satcher, J. F. (2000). Male leadership in an addicted women's group: An empirical approach. *Journal of Addictions & Offender Counseling, 20*(2), 75. https://doi-org.libauth.purdueglobal.edu/10.1002/j.2161-1874.2000.tb00144.x

Okun, M. L., Mancuso, R. A., Hobel, C. J., Schetter, C. D., & Cousonns-Read, M. (2018). Poor sleep quality increases symptoms of depression and anxiety in postpartum women. *Journal of Behavioral Medicine*, *41*, 703–710. https://doi.org/10.1007/s10865-018-9950-7

Perryman, M., Barnard, M., & Reysen, R. (2018). College students' disordered eating, substance use, and body satisfaction. *College Student Journal*, *52*(4), 516–522.

Piran, N., & Gadalla, T. (2007). Eating disorders and substance abuse in Canadian women: A national study. *Addiction*, *102*(1), 105–113. https://doi-org.libauth.purdueglobal.edu/10.1111/j.1360-0443.2006.01633.x

Rivera, D., Dueker, D., & Amaro, H. (2021). Examination of referral source and the retention among women in residential substance use disorder treatment: A prospective follow-up study. *Substance Abuse Treatment, Prevention, and Policy*, *16*(1), 1–11.

SAMHSA. (2011). Women have special needs in substance abuse treatment. *Treatment Improvement Protocols (TIP) 51*. The Substance Abuse and Mental Health Services Administration (SAMHSA).

Schafer, I., Lotzin, A., Hiller, P., Sehner, S., Driessen, M., Hillemacher, T., . . . Grundmann, J. (2019). A multisite randomized controlled trial of seeking safety vs relapse prevention training for women with co-occurring posttraumatic stress disorder and substance use disorders. *European Journal of Psychotraumatology*, *10*(1), 1–15.

Schiff, M., El-Bassel, N., Engstrom, M., & Gilbert, L. (2002). Psychological distress and intimate physical and sexual abuse among women in methadone maintenance treatment programs. *Social Service Review*, *76*(2), 302–320.

Taylor, R. E., & Kuo, B. C. H. (2019). Black American psychological help-seeking intention: An integrated literature review with recommendations for clinical practice. *Journal of Psychotherapy Integration*, *29*(4), 325–337. https://doi-org.libauth.purdueglobal.edu/10.1037/int0000131

Toussaint, D. W., VanDeMark, N. R., Bornemann, A., & Graeber, C. J. (2007). Modifications to the Trauma Recovery and Empowerment Model (TREM) for substance-abusing women with histories of violence: Outcomes and lessons learned at a Colorado substance abuse treatment center. *Journal of Community Psychology*, *35*(7), 879–894. https://doi-org.libauth.purdueglobal.edu/10.1002/jcop.20187

US Department of Health and Human Services. (2000). *Gender differences in drug abuse risks and treatment*. U.S. Department of Health and Human Services, National Institutes of Health, National Institute on Drug Abuse.

US Department of Health and Human Services. (2003). *Treatment methods for women*. U.S. Department of Health and Human Services, National Institutes of Health, National Institute on Drug Abuse.

Zachry, J. E., Johnson, A. R., & Calipari, E. S. (2019). Sex differences in value-based decision making underlie substance use disorders in females. *Alcohol & Alcoholism*, *54*(4), 339–341.

8 Men With Co-occurring Disorders

Tara G. Matthews and Tom Alexander

Introduction

The treatment of individuals living with co-occurring disorders must consider the identified gender of the client in order to help create appropriate person-centered goals. While there are some universal needs shared by men and women, each group also has unique biological needs and cultural expectations. Because of these biological differences, men will have different responses to substance use than women as body weight and mass are usually higher. While this chapter is meant to identify treatment that can enhance the ways men receive treatment for co-occurring disorders, it recognizes that culture, subculture, race, ethnicity, and sexuality also impact an individual. While the information provided is general in nature, it can be a good starting point to meet the needs of men living with co-occurring disorders. The treatment needs for men are quite extensive as they are more likely to complete suicide than women while also living with various expectations regarding masculinity (SAMHSA, 2013a). Men can also maintain rigid stigmas which can be barriers to seeking treatment for co-occurring disorders.

Learning Objectives

- Understand unique factors that contribute to co-occurring disorders among men
- Integrate best practices for treatment with the understanding of co-occurring disorders among men
- Recognize critical elements of co-occurring disorders that contribute to prevalence among men
- Outline barriers to treatment and recovery for men with co-occurring disorders
- Identify key concerns related to the role of psychological trauma in contributing to co-occurring disorders among men

Key Terms

Body Mass Index: A calculation used to identify the ratio between one's weight and height. The BMI has been essential to understanding how various substances can impact the human body.

Male: For the ease of the reader, the term 'male' will refer to individuals who are born with XY chromosomes. This text respects those born with XX chromosomes or a combination of chromosomes who identify as men. Considering the biological specificities of those living with XY (such as increased body mass, testosterone level in blood, variance in brain structures), the use of the term 'male' in this chapter will be specific to those living with XY chromosomes.

Suicide Attempt: An attempt (including an aborted attempt) by an individual to end their own life.

Suicide Completion: The act of an individual ending their own life.

DOI: 10.4324/9781003220916-10

Men With Co-Occurring Disorders

The following chapter addresses considerations for men with co-occurring disorders. Factors related to the prevalence of both mental health and substance use conditions are addressed, along with the impact of traumatic experiences. Specific considerations for several key treatment-related factors are discussed. The therapeutic alliance and the importance of multicultural competency are explored.

The needs of men are often assumed in treatment as many treatment models and psychological modalities were created by white men of Western origin. Despite these assumptions, men experience unique needs for treatment that must take into consideration, their socio-cultural expectations coupled with genetic determinants. The experience of working with males can vary by age, depending on developmental stage and biological factors such as the specific hormonal interactions. Treatment of men living with co-occurring mental health and substance use disorders can be complicated as the vast majority of counselors are women, thus creating a disconnect in some respects while also causing struggles in some clients to accept and understand the boundaries of counseling. As many men may struggle to be open about their intrapersonal experiences and may maintain previously held stigmas about treatment, establishing an open and non-judgmental therapeutic rapport is essential to help engage in treatment.

Multicultural and Social Justice Competency

It is of utmost importance to consider that each person is different. The conceptualization, perception, and expression of masculinity or femininity are influenced by a vast array of cultural and social justice considerations. Reflecting on your own beliefs about masculinity or male roles as well as your own gender role will allow you to work with men with cultural humility rather than with preconceived ideas. Exploring 'attitudes, beliefs, and knowledge' is key to multicultural competencies endorsed by the American Counseling Association. Ratts et al. (2016) discussed that 'privileged and marginalized counselors are aware of clients' worldview, assumptions, attitudes, values, beliefs, biases, social identities, social group statuses, and experiences with power, privilege, and oppression' (p. 6). As you continue through this chapter, you are encouraged to consider the way that each aspect of a client's worldview, as outlined by Ratts et al. (2016), impacts the unique lived experience of a man with co-occurring disorders.

Prevalence

Mental Health Disorders

The Substance Abuse and Mental Health Services Administration (SAMHSA, 2013b) indicates that mental health disorders are more prevalent among women than men. However, rates of illicit substance use and suicide are higher among males than females (SAMHSA, 2013b). Treatment for mental health disorders is accessed at lower rates for men than women, which contributes to the possibility of lower prevalence rates based on volume related to diagnosable episodes of care. To understand the overall prevalence of mental health disorders among men, one must consider some of the most commonly diagnosed conditions: depression, anxiety, bipolar disorder, and posttraumatic stress disorder.

Depression

Depression is diagnosed among women (10.4%) at approximately twice the rate that it is among men (5.4%) (Brody et al., 2018; Parker & Brotchie, 2010). This disparity in prevalence rate has brought some researchers to believe that gender-based differences in the expression of depressive symptomatology have contributed to lower rates of diagnosed depression among males (Call & Shafer, 2018). Call and Shafer (2018) discuss that male-typical symptoms of depression are often diagnosed as a separate mental health disorder. Symptoms like anger and substance use as a coping strategy to mitigate the effects of depression can be easily overlooked by clinical professionals and cataloged as something other than depression. The lack of diagnostic clarity is exacerbated by the fact that men are less likely to seek help and much more likely to initially seek help for depression from their primary care provider when they do reach out (Call & Shafer, 2018). Primary care providers, though experts in their scope of practice, may sometimes lack proficiency in accurately diagnosing, treating, and following up with men who may be exhibiting signs and symptoms of depression. Call and Shafer refer to the lower likelihood of asking for help and the decreased chance of receiving adequate follow-up care when they do seek help as a form of 'double-jeopardy' (p. 47). Along with depression, diagnoses related to anxiety are common among men as well.

Anxiety

The National Institute of Mental Health (NIHM) (2017a) indicates that approximately 19% of adults in the United States have experienced symptoms indicative of an anxiety disorder in the past year. Of the 19%, over 23% are female compared to over 14% who are male. As with depression, the diagnostic rate for women with any anxiety disorder significantly exceeds the rate for men. Current literature on gender differences in the prevalence of anxiety disorders is lacking. Moreover, specific considerations for the diagnosis and treatment of men with anxiety disorders are underrepresented in scholarly research as well. Some of the most recent research on gender differences and anxiety disorders was conducted by McLean et al. (2011). McLean, Asnaani, and Hofmann found that the burden of illness related to anxiety disorders among men created some substantial differences for men with anxiety versus men without anxiety.

Specifically, men with anxiety disorders were significantly more likely to visit the emergency department, an urgent care, or even their doctor than men without anxiety (McLean et al., 2011). However, men with anxiety were found to visit the ED, urgent care, or physician at a much lower rate than women, leading to the consideration of either under-diagnosis or stigma-related barriers to men seeking help. Furthermore, the researchers found that men with anxiety are significantly more likely to seek help due to a substance use or emotional concern than men who do not have an anxiety disorder. Thus, the presence and prevalence of anxiety disorders among men can create frequent health-related concerns and possibly contribute to lower quality of life and health status. In addition to depression and anxiety, bipolar disorder is considered a mental health condition that is prevalent among men.

Bipolar Disorder

Bipolar disorder is much less prevalent in the general population than both anxiety and depression. Rates of bipolar disorder for the general population are approximately 2.8%. Women are diagnosed with bipolar disorder at a rate of 2.8%, whereas men are diagnosed at the slightly higher rate of 2.9% (National Institute of Mental Health, 2017b). Though men are diagnosed at a higher rate, women with bipolar disorder are more likely to experience multiple comorbidities related to physical and mental health conditions (Patel et al., 2018). The presence of bipolar disorder in men can lead to difficulties in functioning, work, relationships, and social interaction. Men with bipolar disorder may choose to address symptoms through the use of substances, further complicating the symptomatology and clarification of diagnosis. Both men and women may engage in substance use to counter the symptoms associated with depression and/or mania. Essentially, the symptoms of bipolar disorder can remain masked by the use of substances, to the extent that the disorder may be overlooked as a SUD only or misdiagnosed altogether.

Posttraumatic Stress Disorder (PTSD)

The role of trauma in the development of both substance use disorder and an array of mental and physical health conditions is significant. The Adverse Childhood Experiences Study (Felitti et al., 1998) confirmed in a longitudinal study of over 17,000 participants that a positive correlation exists between childhood trauma/adversity and health-related conditions like substance use and mental health disorders later in life. In essence, trauma can be viewed as foundational to the development of many of the disorders that are discussed in this chapter. At times, trauma will result in a diagnosis of posttraumatic stress disorder (PTSD).

Prevalence rates for PTSD are approximately 3.6% for the general population in the United States (NIMH, 2017c). Olff (2017) indicates that gender differences in the diagnosis of PTSD range from 10% to 12% for women and 5% to 6% for men. As with depression and anxiety, men are much less likely to be diagnosed with PTSD than women. However, some of the same concerns persist with regard to under-diagnosis of men who have experienced both early-life and late-life trauma. Calear et al. (2017) discuss that help-seeking behavior is much less common in males than females, which may contribute to higher rates of suicide among males than females. The experience of trauma, especially trauma that is related to sexual abuse, can create an enormous amount of shame among survivors. One can make the assumption that due to stigma and lower rates of help-seeking behavior, the prevalence of PTSD, along with depression and anxiety, may indeed be higher than the current data indicate.

Depression, anxiety, bipolar disorder, and PTSD are not the only mental health disorders that have gender differences in prevalence rates and overall impact. However, this chapter does not address each disorder in depth due to the fact that subsequent chapters of this text explore components of co-occurring disorders as they relate to the general population, including some gender-based differences as well as cultural considerations. It is important to note that, although some of the most common mental health disorders are more prevalent among women than men, substance use disorders are much more commonly diagnosed in males. The following section explores the prevalence rates of various types of substances, leading to subsequent content that examines prevalence rates of co-occurring mental health and substance use disorders among men.

Substance Use Disorders

While the criteria for substance use disorders remain consistent between males and females, the way men become connected to substances and their lived experiences struggling with substance use disorders are unique. It is important to identify how these disorders can impact specific behaviors of men as they are at greater lethality risk than their women counterparts (CDC, 2016).

Alcohol Use Disorder

The Centers for Disease Control and Prevention (CDC) (2016) states that men have a significantly higher likelihood of excessive drinking than women. Overall, the CDC indicates that approximately 4.5% of men and 2.5% of women can be classified as having an alcohol use disorder in a given year (CDC, 2016). Further, 23% of men engage in binge drinking, approximately twice the rate that women do (CDC, 2016). In regard to mortality risks, men are more likely to die of either suicide or a fatal vehicle accident than women due to excessive alcohol use and alcohol use while operating a motor vehicle (CDC, 2016). Along with the mortality rate, men have higher occurrences of hospitalizations due to excessive alcohol use and are at higher risk for certain types of cancer and other physical health conditions. Finally, men are more likely to engage in violence and aggression due to excessive alcohol use (CDC, 2016). In addition to alcohol use, men are more likely to use illicit substances than women.

Illicit Substances

Illicit substances are drugs considered to be illegal: cocaine, methamphetamine, heroin, marijuana, and other street-based drugs (National Institute on Drug Abuse (NIDA), 2018). Illicit substances can also include the misuse of prescription medications (NIDA, 2018). However, prescription medication use is addressed in the following section due to the vast increase in prescription opioid misuse and the need to specifically address the topic in more depth. Thus, for the purpose of this section, illicit substances will consist of illegal drugs other than prescription medications that are misused.

Males have consistently demonstrated higher rates of illicit drug use than females in the general population. The National Survey on Drug Use and Health (SAMHSA, 2013b) indicates that 11.5% of males utilized an illicit substance compared to 7.3% of females. Moreover, the data indicate that males were also much more likely to be using multiple illicit substances at the same time. The use of illicit substances places men at a higher likelihood of experiencing multiple episodes of emergency department care and increased possibility of overdose death (NIDA, 2018). In the 2018 Annual Report of Drug-Related Risks and Outcomes, the CDC (2018) reports the following data for gender and specific type of illicit substance use in the past year among the general population in the United States:

Table 8.1 Past Year Illicit Substance Use by Gender (CDC, 2018)

	Marijuana	*Heroin*	*Methamphetamine*	*Cocaine*
Female	6.7%	0.1%	0.2%	0.4%
Male	11.3%	0.2%	0.3%	1.0%

Source: CDC, 2018

Prescription Medications

The misuse of prescription medications in the US has reached epidemic proportions in the previous two decades, especially with regard to opioid-based medications. Mortality rates from opioid overdose continue to peak (CDC, 2018). Perhaps the most concerning trend across the spectrum of both mental health and substance use for men is the extreme level of mortality due to opioid overdose. Data as recent as 2016 highlight the fact that the opioid overdose mortality rate per 100,000 persons in the US is approximately 13.3. Of the 13.3, the rate is 18.1 for males and 8.5 for females. The disparity in overdose mortality exists despite the fact that there is no significant difference between the rates of prescription opioid use disorder among men and women in the US (Griesler et al., 2019). Thus, substantial concern exists in the areas of prevention, diagnostic, and treatment efforts to address opioid use disorder among men and women in the US, especially with regard to mortality rates.

Aside from the misuse of prescription opioids, there are additional prescription medications that are of concern among the general population. Some of the primary prescription medications that are often misused are sedatives and tranquilizers. The misusage rate differs slightly between men and women in the population at large. Men report misuse of prescription tranquilizers at a rate of 2.2%, whereas women report a higher rate of 2.3% within the past year. Regarding prescription sedatives, males indicated a rate of 0.5% and females 0.6% within the past year (CDC, 2018). Overall, women trend higher on misuse of prescription medications with the exception of opioids. Men appear to be at extreme risk for both opioid misuse and subsequent mortality from overdose in the general population. Along with differences in prevalence, side effects from substance use vary for men and women.

Sex/Gender–Specific Side Effects of Substance Use

Men and women experience the effects of substance use in different ways. Agabio et al. (2016) conducted an exhaustive review of literature related to the side effects of substances like alcohol, heroin, cocaine, marijuana, and nicotine. The researchers examined the sex/gender–specific effects and subsequent differences between men and women. Overwhelmingly, women experienced significantly greater side effect–related sequelae. Moreover, women demonstrated a higher risk than men with regard to negative side effects of medication-assisted treatment drugs such as naltrexone, complicating and adding barriers to the treatment and recovery process for some women (Agabio et al., 2016). Ultimately, the key understanding related specifically to men is that, although men are found to use illicit substances and misuse prescription opioids at a higher rate than women, women experience a higher burden of disease. These are key factors to understand when approaching medical, behavioral, and substance use treatment for both men and women; understanding the short- and long-term side effects and their presentation among men and women can be critical to recovery.

Prevalence of Co-occurring Disorders Among Men

Within the US alone, approximately 8.7 million adults age 18 or older were estimated to have a co-occurring substance use and mental health disorder in 2016; 2.6 million were found to have a serious mental illness, which includes a diagnosis of schizophrenia/schizoaffective, bipolar, or major depressive disorder (SAMHSA, 2017). These particularly alarming statistics on the prevalence of co-occurring disorders (COD) contribute to considerable concern for both men and women in the US. The National Survey on Drug Use and Health (SAMHSA, 2013b) found that co-occurring mental health and substance use disorders among males (4.1%) were higher than among females (3.1%). Thus, as we review the aforementioned statistics on prevalence of mental health disorders and substances use disorders, we find that men have a significantly higher number of co-occurring disorders. This is particularly concerning when one considers that men with co-occurring SUD and serious mental illness are both less ready to change when seeking treatment and stay in treatment for a shorter amount of time than women (Choi et al., 2015; Drapalski et al., 2011). The following section explores this treatment-related concern in detail.

Treatment Seeking and Retention Considerations

Treatment-Seeking Behaviors and Characteristics

In reviewing the literature for gender-based differences among men and women with co-occurring disorders, the research seems to indicate that there are more resemblances than there are variances between genders (Drapalski et al., 2011). For example, when examining reasons for seeking treatment, Drapalski et al. (2011) found that there were no significant differences between women and men. However, there are a few key differences that are worth highlighting with regard to men in treatment for co-occurring disorders. (Drapalski et al., 2011) found that, in a sample of treatment-seeking men and women who have co-occurring disorders, women were more likely to possess a significantly higher level of readiness to change.

We know that readiness to change can have a tremendous impact on treatment outcomes in an array of clinical settings (Krampe et al., 2017). In essence, higher levels of readiness to change can contribute to a greater likelihood of treatment success. Therefore, this is an important consideration regarding men with COD who have entered a treatment setting. Further research is needed to explore the variations in readiness to change and perhaps address the need for more specific treatment aimed at increasing readiness to change among both male and female persons.

In addition to readiness to change, women and men also differ in some aspects of treatment-based retention or attrition, especially regarding residential treatment services for substance use and mental health disorders. Treatment retention is a critical factor that can impact the overall success of the treatment process itself and the long-term recovery journey for persons with COD.

Treatment Retention and Characteristics

Entering treatment is a significant step for a person who is living with substance use and mental health disorders. Beginning a residential treatment program can be a tremendous step toward health and improved quality of life for a person with COD. Significant challenges and barriers to beginning the residential treatment process can abound for many individuals in need of clinical and social services. Thus, it becomes critical for health professionals to collaborate with persons who have COD in order to maximize the positive impact that a treatment intervention might have. Choi et al. (2015) found that men with COD tend to stay in residential treatment significantly fewer days than women with COD. The researchers discuss that men averaged 30.17 days in residential treatment, compared to women, who averaged close to 34.85 days, about 4.5 days more than men with co-occurring disorders. Further, Choi et al. (2015) elucidate that women with COD had a greater likelihood overall of remaining in residential treatment for at least 30 days.

For males in residential treatment, Choi et al. (2015) indicate that both age and employment issues were moderating factors. Specifically, older men were found to stay in residential treatment for a longer period of time than younger men. Furthermore, concerns with employment issues were a significant factor for men in a residential treatment program. Each of these factors can be addressed through providing treatment protocol that is aimed specifically at addressing unique needs among the clientele. Both women and men can benefit from treatment programs that are tailored to addressing both progress- and retention-related factors, leading to possible improvements in the outcome of treatment at multiple levels of care, not solely at the residential level. Along with treatment-seeking behavior and factors associated with retention, the role and impact of trauma in men with co-occurring disorders are key factors to consider.

The Moderating Effect of Trauma

An Overview

Giordano et al. (2016) highlight the critical fact that persons who engage in substance use have often experienced a significantly higher amount of trauma. This fact is underpinned by the landmark adverse childhood experiences (ACE) study that found a positive correlation between early-life trauma and health concerns that include mental and substance use disorders later in life (Felitti et al., 1998). The preponderance of research evidence has supported the moderating effect of trauma on the development of both mental health and substance use disorders. For example, Halpern et al. (2018) report that individuals who survive sexual abuse are approximately 73% more likely to develop a substance use disorder. Moreover, Halpern and colleagues found that those who survived physical abuse are at higher risk for substance use disorders at a rate of 74% compared to the general population. Concerning gender-based prevalence of trauma among persons with a substance use disorder, significant evidence in the literature demonstrates that women have overwhelmingly experienced more trauma and the effects of trauma than males.

Gender-Specific Prevalence

Some of the specific data related to gender-based variations have been elucidated in recent research. Cosden et al. (2015) report data identifying that women who have a substance use disorder have survived significantly higher rates of sexual abuse than men with a substance use disorder. Trauma related to sexual abuse can have tremendously detrimental effects on a person's health, well-being, and perspective of themselves. Along with sexual abuse, women also report surviving physical abuse at higher rates than men do as well. Cosden et al. (2015) indicate that women in a particular sample of persons in substance use treatment reported rates of physical abuse of almost 70%, whereas men reported rates slightly over 20%.

Similar to sexual abuse, physical abuse can also have highly negative effects on the health and well-being of an individual. Finally, an article by Keyser-Marcus et al. (2015) found that women were as much as five times more likely to indicate surviving past trauma than their male counterparts in substance use treatment. There are a few types of trauma that men were reported to have experienced at higher rates than women: specifically, trauma related to natural disasters and witnessing violence.

Male Survivors of Witnessing Violence

Giordano et al. (2016) reported that within a sample of individuals with substance use disorders attending an outpatient treatment program, men experienced significantly more trauma related to witnessing violence. We know from recent research that witnessing violence as a child or adolescent can affect substance use behavior. Löfving-Gupta et al. (2018) found a positive correlation between the severity of violence witnessed and the severity of substance use. This finding confirms the critically negative effects that witnessing violence can have on a person's overall health and well-being. Providing clinical interventions for men who have witnessed violence may need to be specifically tailored to the impact that violence exposure can have on a person. Both substance use and mental health treatment professionals must be mindful of the impact that violence may have had on male and female clientele alike.

Male Survivors of Natural Disasters

Hetzel-Riggin and Roby (2013) indicate that males have a higher likelihood of experiencing trauma resulting from a natural disaster. Though men are more likely to experience trauma related to a natural disaster, the psychological effects of a disaster are more severe for older adults, women, and children (Makwana, 2019). Makwana (2019) discusses that exposure to disasters, whether man made or naturally occurring, can contribute to the development of an array of mental health and substance use concerns, such as depression, alcohol use, and increased overall stress on the survivor.

Treating the Male Survivor of Trauma

Treatment for male survivors of trauma can be guided by most evidence-based practices for addressing traumatic experiences and subsequent symptoms of PTSD. Treatment approaches like cognitive processing therapy, prolonged exposure, cognitive behavioral therapy, and eye movement desensitization and reprocessing can be effective approaches to addressing trauma. Animal-assisted therapies continue to demonstrate efficacy in the treatment of trauma and are explored later in this text. One aspect to consider is gender-specific group treatment for male survivors of trauma. Røberg et al. (2018) conducted a study that found that men may benefit from gender-specific groups with regard to stabilizing symptoms of trauma. Ultimately, best practice in addressing trauma involves consulting directly with the client on his preference for modality of treatment that aligns with unique needs and preferences.

Understanding the Unique Treatment Needs of Men

The following chapter section includes an overview of some common concerns and challenges that may arise when providing treatment for men with co-occurring disorders. The section is strongly guided by content developed by the Substance Abuse and Mental Health Services Administration (SAMHSA): Treatment Improvement Protocol 56, *Addressing the Specific Behavioral Health Needs of Men* (2013a). Keep in mind when reading the following content that each person has a lived experience that is unique and does not, by any means, always fit into the common barriers and considerations discussed here.

Therapist Gender

At the onset of treatment for men with co-occurring disorders, SAMHSA (2013a) indicates that it is important to consider the role of gender dynamics in the process of counseling. Challenges related to transference and countertransference must be considered by the clinical professional, and any issues arising in treatment should be addressed promptly in the therapeutic setting. Some consider it best practice to address whether the male client has any gender preference with regard to selecting a counselor. Specifically, SAMHSA (2013a) encourages professionals to combine the topics of prior treatment experience and gender preference in a primary therapist within the initial assessment at the beginning of the treatment process. Early discussion of gender-related dynamics in the counseling process can communicate to the client that his personal experience in treatment is important to the clinician (SAMHSA, 2013a).

As a clinical professional working with a male client, it is important to consider that both male and female clinicians may experience countertransference throughout the treatment process. SAMHSA (2013a) cites Scher (2005) in stating that concerns related to countertransference may be more significant when a male counsels another male than when a woman counsels a man. Moreover, SAMHSA (2013a) discusses that due to some socially defined expectations of masculinity, 'male counselors might be reluctant to bring up feelings of warmth, love, and emotional attraction for male clients' in the context of addressing countertransference in clinical supervision (p. 35). Ultimately, it is important for clinical supervisors to cultivate an environment of trust when supervising male counselors, adding opportunity for male clinicians to open up in ways that they may also be reluctant to do because of established cultural expectations related to masculinity (SAMHSA, 2013a). Both male and female counselors need to be cognizant of their own bias and stereotypes, be willing to explore emotions as a clinical consideration, and to explore countertransference in clinical supervision (SAMHSA, 2013a, p. 33).

Men and Emotion

Another significant factor when working with men who have co-occurring disorders is related to difficulty in recognizing and communicating emotional experiences. Not all men experience difficulty in emotional recognition and communication, but some experience barriers in this area. For men who do have challenges with emotional expression, these barriers are experienced in differing levels of severity. Specifically, SAMHSA (2013a) shares that some men may experience an almost complete lack of emotions, where others have minor difficulty recognizing and sharing certain emotional experiences. Emotional sharing is further complicated by the judgment that some men face when actually disclosing emotional experiences. McKenzie et al. (2018) conducted a qualitative analysis related to masculinity, mental health, and the social connectedness of men. The researchers disclose a powerful finding in the statement that 'Among men, emotional sharing was likely to be ridiculed and dismissed' (McKenzie et al., 2018, p. 1252). One of the key tips that SAMHSA (2013a) offers to clinicians who work with men is to focus on emotions that the client is already able to identify and express. From a clinical standpoint, focusing on already-identifiable emotions can help ensure that the male client is comfortable throughout the initial phase of the treatment process, possibly leading to the identification and expression of different or more complex emotions.

Men and Shame

Counselors working with men who have co-occurring disorders must be aware of the effects of shame on the male clientele. Shame is a complex emotion and is influenced and experienced in various ways based on cultural differences (SAMHSA, 2013a). As early as infancy, relationships with others lay the foundation of shame (Bradshaw, 1988). Shame allows people to get their needs met, recognize limitations, and shape decisions. The way people react to our needs will determine what role shame will play in our lives (Bradshaw, 1988). Both healthy and unhealthy shame are used to guide decisions on how to meet basic needs. Survival, love and belonging, self-worth, freedom, and fun are basic needs (Wubbolding & Brickell, 1999) that can be met in both healthy and self-destructive ways. Since caregivers are the first to provide for our survival needs, our sense of shame begins in early childhood. This further emphasizes the role of early childhood experiences and the impact shame has throughout men's lives.

SAMHSA (2013a) also clarified that the cultural stigma that occurs when men go outside gender expectations can create a sense of shame. Bradshaw (1988) indicated that healthy shame allows us to see our limitations and boundaries and can inspire us to seek more knowledge. Healthy shame could be interpreted as humility. Unfortunately, shame can be toxic and create a self-fulling prophecy with a toxic shame, toxic behavior cycle. If men have a shame identity and seek to numb the feelings of shame, this may be a normal reaction to pain, but it can be self-defeating. The compulsive activity itself simply reinforces the shame identity and sense of worthlessness; shame becomes the root and the cause and perhaps even exacerbates the need for compulsion and addictive behaviors. Further, shame may be experienced at varying intensities based on the overall socialization and lived experience of the client as well. Shepard and Rabinowitz (2013) highlight the fact that men who seek treatment for depression, which co-occurs frequently with SUD, may be dealing with shame that is connected to a sense of 'failure or inadequacy' (p. 456).

Toxically shamed people often remain stagnant in life (Bradshaw, 1988) and may struggle to move on or improve the quality of their lives. This stagnation may be derived from an underlying belief of unworthiness or hopelessness. Kaufman (1992) indicated that shame lies hidden beneath the surface and is seldom communicated verbally. This isolation can lead to a lack of self-worth and failure identity. Both SAMHSA (2013a) and Shepard and Rabinowitz (2013) suggested the use of group work or mutual help support groups as an intervention to address shame among men who are seeking behavioral health treatment.

Additionally, SAMHSA (2013a) points out that therapists who are in SUD recovery can serve as models for how to both accept and work through a behavioral health condition. Thus, connecting a male client who might be experiencing severe shame with a clinician who is in recovery could be beneficial in addressing the component of shame and reducing a significant barrier to ongoing treatment and recovery for the male client. The experience and expertise of the counselor, the client's preferences, and the therapeutic alliance must also be taken into consideration when determining how best to address shame with men. Shame impacts men's understanding of self and influences their relationship to self and others.

Men and Violence

Society is filled with people who do not know how to handle complex emotions, perpetuate unhealthy coping skills (such as drinking, fighting, or escaping), and expect everyone to deal with stress the same way. Self-esteem and identity are affected by our ability to deal with the stress in our lives. Based on this phenomenon, violence is increasing, and negative emotions are spreading (Silvan S. Tomkins Institute, 2003). Men of all cultures have the potential to be victims of or to perpetuate violence as a means of unhealthy coping. SAMHSA (2013a) highlighted that, although violence is not by any means exclusive to the male gender, men are more likely to demonstrate physical violence than women. Criminally violent behavior has been found to be positively correlated with the use of substances (SAMHSA, 2013a). Specifically, of all substances, alcohol has the highest correlation with criminally violent behavior. Combining the use of alcohol with a co-occurring mental health condition can potentially increase the risk for engaging in violent behavior among men. With regard to treatment considerations, SAMHSA (2013a) and Easton et al. (2018) discussed that CBT can be effective for men who engage or have engaged in violent behavior. Providing CBT combined with group therapy offers evidence-based treatments to address violent behavior in men with co-occurring disorders. Clinicians who treat men with a history of violent behavior must be aware that violent behavior may occur in the treatment setting as well and that it is important to clearly identify unacceptable behaviors at the onset of treatment, including clarification of potential sanctions, such as removal from treatment if necessary for the safety of the client and others (SAMHSA, 2013a).

Conclusion

Although there are some generalized experiences between men and women living with co-occurring disorders, it is essential for the counselor to create person-centered care that takes into account the unique needs of those being served. Counselors providing treatment to men are tasked with considering the biopsychosocial factors that are unique to this population while also considering how the individual has been impacted by their own cultural values. As most counselors are women, providing gender-specific care can have a lasting impact on the individual, family system, and community. While gender inequities exist in various vocational and societal aspects, the counselor helps enhance ongoing social change by working through treatment-related stigmas that many men will experience. Having an understanding of how substance use and mental health disorders can manifest in men also provides counselors with the ability to link with adjunct care as needed. Successful treatment is evidence based and made within the goals, needs, and values of the individual being served. In order to provide this treatment to men, counselors must be committed to enhancing their knowledge and skills to facilitate overall recovery from co-occurring disorders.

Questions for consideration

1. Based on the unique needs of men, what are your beliefs about single-gender groups? Would the gender of the therapist matter in this group?
2. Preconceived ideas about men can lead to misguided treatment expectations and reenforce the shame that the client carries into the treatment room. How could you best address men's unique needs?
3. Co-occurring disorders are very prevalent among the male population. What cultural barriers may exist for men in addition to gender? What role does stigma play in getting help?

Case Study

Matthew is a 59-year-old veteran who has been taught his entire life that crying is a weakness. A few years ago, he lost his wife, and his drinking increased significantly. His friends and family are concerned about his increase in drinking, and with his recent arrest for driving under the influence, he has been forced to meet with a counselor. He explains that he has everything under control and that it was the officer's fault that he was arrested. Upon further inquiry, you discover that his job is also at risk due to missed days and reactivity to coworkers.

Questions

1. What are your clinical concerns for Matthew?
2. What information would you like to know to further explore potential diagnosis or treatment planning with Matthews?
3. Based on the information shared, is Matthew a client you would feel comfortable working with? Why or why not?

References

Agabio, R., Campesi, I., Pisanu, C., Gessa, G. L., & Franconi, F. (2016). Sex differences in substance use disorders: Focus on side effects. *Addiction Biology, 21*(5), 1030–1042. https://doi.org/10.1111/adb.12395

Bradshaw, J. (1988). *Healing the shame that binds you.* Health Communications. ISBN: 0932194869

Brody, D. J., Pratt, L. A., & Hughes, J. P. (2018). Prevalence of depression among adults aged 20 and over: United States, 2013–2016. *Centers for Disease Control and Prevention.* (CDC): NCHS data brief no. 303. Retrieved from www.cdc.gov/nchs/products/databriefs/db303.htm

Calear, A. L., Banfield, M., Batterham, P. J., Morse, A. R., Forbes, O., Carron-Arthur, B., & Fisk, M. (2017). Silence is deadly: A cluster-randomised controlled trial of a mental health help-seeking intervention for young men. *BMC Public Health, 17*, 1–8. https://doi.org/10.1186/s12889-017-4845-z

Call, J. B., & Shafer, K. (2018). Gendered manifestations of depression and help seeking among men. *American Journal of Men's Health, 12*(1), 41–51. http://dx.doi.org.libauth.purdueglobal.edu/10.1177/1557988315623993

Centers for Disease Control and Prevention. (2016). *Alcohol and public health: Excessive alcohol use and men's health.* Retrieved from www.cdc.gov/alcohol/fact-sheets/mens-health.htm

Centers for Disease Control and Prevention (CDC). (2018). 2018 annual surveillance report of drug-related risks and outcomes. *CDC U.S. Department of Health and Human Services.* Retrieved from www.cdc.gov/drugoverdose/pdf/pubs/2018-cdc-drug-surveillance-report.pdf

Choi, S., Adams, S. M., Morse, S. A., & MacMaster, S. (2015). Gender differences in treatment retention among individuals with co-occurring substance abuse and mental health disorders. *Substance Use & Misuse, 50*(5), 653–663. https://doi.org/10.3109/10826084.2014.997828

Cosden, M., Larsen, J. L., Donahue, M. T., & Nylund-Gibson, K. (2015). Trauma symptoms for men and women in substance abuse treatment: A latent transition analysis. *Journal of Substance Abuse Treatment, 50*, 18–25. doi:10.1016/j.jsat.2014.09.004

Drapalski, A., Bennett, M., & Bellack, A. (2011). Gender differences in substance use, consequences, motivation to change, and treatment seeking in people with serious mental illness. *Substance Use & Misuse, 46*(6), 808–818. doi:10.3109/10826084.2010.538460

Easton, C. J., Crane, C. A., & Mandel, D. (2018). A randomized controlled trial assessing the efficacy of cognitive behavioral therapy for substance-dependent domestic violence offenders: An integrated substance abuse-domestic violence treatment approach (SADV). *Journal of Marital & Family Therapy, 44*(3), 483–498. https://doi.org/10.1111/jmft.12260

Felitti, V. J., Anda, R. F., Nordenberg, D., Williamson, D. F., Spitz, A. M., Edwards, V., . . . Marks, J. S. (1998). Relationship of childhood abuse and household dysfunction to many of the leading causes of death in adults: The adverse childhood experience study. *American Journal of Preventive Medicine, 14*(4), 245–258. https://doi.org/10.1016/S0749-3797(98)00017-8

Gawda, B., & Czubak, K. (2017). Prevalence of personality disorders in a general population among men and women. *Psychological Reports, 120*(3), 503–519. https://doi.org/10.1177/0033294117692807

Giordano, A. L., Prosek, E. A., Stamman, J., Callahan, M. M., Loseu, S., Bevly, C. M., . . . Chadwell, K. (2016). Addressing trauma in substance abuse treatment. *Journal of Alcohol & Drug Education, 60*(2), 55–71. Retrieved from https://search-ebscohost-com.libauth.purdueglobal.edu/login.aspx?direct=true&db=a9h&AN=118492634&site=ehost-live

Griesler, P. C., Hu, M.-C., Wall, M. M., & Kandel, D. B. (2019). Medical use and misuse of prescription opioids in the US adult population: 2016–2017. *American Journal of Public Health, 109*(9), 1258–1265. https://doi.org/10.2105/AJPH.2019.305162

Halpern, S. C., Schuch, F. B., Scherer, J. N., Sordi, A. O., Pachado, M., Dalbosco, C., . . . Von Diemen, L. (2018). Child maltreatment and illicit substance abuse: A systematic review and meta-analysis of longitudinal studies. *Child Abuse Review, 27*(5), 344–360. https://doi.org/10.1002/car.2534

Hetzel-Riggin, M. D., & Roby, R. P. (2013). Trauma type and gender effects on PTSD, general distress and peritraumatic dissociation. *Journal of Loss and Trauma, 18*, 41–53. doi:10.1080/15325024.201 2.679119

Kaufman, G. (1992). *Shame: The power of caring* (3rd ed.). Schenkman. ISBN: 0870470531

Keyser-Marcus, L., Alvanzo, A., Rieckmann, T., Thacker, L., Sepulveda, A., Forcehimes, A., . . . Svikis, D. S. (2015). Trauma, gender and mental health symptoms in individuals with substance use disorders. *Journal of Interpersonal Violence, 30*, 3–24. doi:10.1177/0886260514532523

Krampe, H., Salz, A. L., Kerper, L. F., Krannich, A., Schnell, T., Wernecke, K. D., & Spies, C. D. (2017). Readiness to change and therapy outcomes of an innovative psychotherapy program for surgical patients: Results from a randomized controlled trial. *BMC Psychiatry, 17*(1), 417. doi:10.1186/s12888-017-1579-5

Löfving-Gupta, S., Willebrand, M., Koposov, R., Blatný, M., Hrdlička, M., Schwab-Stone, M., & Ruchkin, V. (2018). Community violence exposure and substance use: Cross-cultural and gender perspectives. *European Child & Adolescent Psychiatry, 27*(4), 493–500. https://doi.org/10.1007/s00787-017-1097-5

Makwana, N. (2019). Disaster and its impact on mental health: A narrative review. *Journal of Family Medicine & Primary Care, 8*(10), 3090–3095. https://doi.org/10.4103/jfmpc.jfmpc_893_19

McKenzie, S. K., Collings, S., Jenkin, G., & River, J. (2018). Masculinity, social connectedness, and mental health: Men's diverse Patterns of practice. *American Journal of Men's Health, 12*(5), 1247–1261. doi:10.1177/1557988318772732

McLean, C. P., Asnaani, A., Litz, B. T., & Hofmann, S. G. (2011). Gender differences in anxiety disorders: Prevalence, course of illness, comorbidity and burden of illness. *Journal of Psychiatric Research, 45*(8), 1027–1035. doi:10.1016/j.jpsychires.2011.03.006

National Institute of Mental Health. (2017a). *Any anxiety disorder*. Retrieved from www.nimh.nih.gov/health/statistics/any-anxiety-disorder.shtml

National Institute of Mental Health. (2017b). *Bipolar disorder*. Retrieved from www.nimh.nih.gov/health/statistics/bipolar-disorder.shtml

National Institute of Mental Health. (2017c). *Post-traumatic stress disorder*. Retrieved from www.nimh.nih.gov/health/statistics/post-traumatic-stress-disorder-ptsd.shtml

National Institute on Drug Abuse (NIDA). (2018). *Sex and gender differences in substance use*. Retrieved from www.drugabuse.gov/publications/research-reports/substance-use-in-women/sex-gender-differences-in-substance-use

Olff, M. (2017). Sex and gender differences in post-traumatic stress disorder: An update. *European Journal of Psychotraumatology*. https://doi.org/10.1080/20008198.2017.1351204

Parker, G., & Brotchie, H. (2010). Gender differences in depression. *International Review of Psychiatry, 22*, 429–436. doi:10.3109/09540261.2010.492391

Patel, R. S., Virani, S., Saeed, H., Nimmagadda, S., Talukdar, J., & Youssef, N. A. (2018). Gender differences and comorbidities in U.S. adults with bipolar disorder. *Brain Sciences (2076–3425), 8*(9), 168. https://doi.org/10.3390/brainsci8090168

Ratts, M. J., Singh, A. A., Nassar, M. S., Butler, S. K., & McCullough, J. R. (2016). Multicultural and social justice counseling competencies: Guidelines for the counseling profession. *Journal of Multicultural Counseling & Development, 44*(1), 28–48. https://doi.org/10.1002/jmcd.12035

Røberg, L., Nilsen, L., & Røssberg, J. I. (2018). How do men with severe sexual and physical childhood traumatization experience trauma-stabilizing group treatment? A qualitative study. *European Journal of Psychotraumatology, 9*(1), 1541697. doi:10.1080/20008198.2018.1541697

Scher, M. (2005). Male therapist, male client: Reflections on critical dynamics. In Brooks, G. R., & Good, G. E. (Eds.), *The new handbook of psychotherapy and counseling with men: A Comprehensive guide to settings, problems, and treatment approaches* (2nd ed., pp. 308–320). Jossey-Bass.

Shepard, D. S., & Rabinowitz, F. E. (2013). The power of shame in men who are depressed: Implications for counselors. *Journal of Counseling & Development, 91*(4), 451–457. https://doi.org/10.1002/j.1556-6676.2013.00117.x

Silvan S. Tomkins Institute (Producer). (2003). *Managing shame, preventing violence: A call to our clergy* [DVD]. Retrieved from www.tomkins.org

Substance Abuse and Mental Health Services Administration. (2013a). *Addressing the specific behavioral health needs of men*. Treatment Improvement Protocol (TIP) Series 56. HHS Publication No. (SMA) 13–4736.

Substance Abuse and Mental Health Services Administration. (2013b). *Results from the 2012 national survey on drug use and health: Mental health findings*. NSDUH Series H-47. HHS Publication No. (SMA) 13–4805.

Substance Abuse and Mental Health Services Administration. (2017). *Key substance use and mental health indicators in the United States: Results from the 2016 National Survey on Drug Use and Health*. HHS Publication No. SMA 17–5044, NSDUH Series H-52. for Behavioral Health Statistics and Quality, Substance Abuse and Mental Health Services Administration. Retrieved from www. samhsa.gov/data/

Wubbolding, R. E., & Brickell, J. (1999). *Counselling with reality therapy*. Speechmark Publishing.

9 Adolescents With Co-occurring Disorders

Tricia L. Chandler and Fredrick Dombrowski

Introduction

Adolescence is the time between childhood and adulthood from 12 to 17+ years of age when youth are actively growing into their adult physiology through hormonal and physical growth changes, exploring their own values and beliefs that may be separate from their cultural and familial beliefs, and developing a sense of identity through their peer interactions along with identifying their sexual orientation. Developmentally, this is the time of life when childhood experiences begin to be integrated into the schemas of the youth, and with increasing ability for abstract reasoning, youth are pondering their self-identity within the framework of family values and expectations while also exploring their social world of peers (Berk, 2018). Considering the myriad ways youth are growing, it is no surprise that the years involved are fraught with increased risks and risk-taking, and any childhood trauma, abuse, neglect, poor attachment issues, and/or potential learning disorders will increase risk for mental health issues, substance use disorders, and body dysmorphic disorders. In some cases, there is increased risk of suicidal ideation and developing maladaptive behaviors such as non-suicidal self-injury and eating disorders (American Psychiatric Association, 2013). Additionally, by the end of adolescence, any personality disordered traits will have emerged as diagnosable, yet these traits will be causing interpersonal issues prior to diagnosis.

Learning Objectives

- Recognize various developmental aspects of adolescence that impact treatment implementation and outcomes
- Identify how childhood trauma develops into maladaptive behaviors for adolescents, increasing risk of the development of mental health and substance use issues
- Understand current evidence-based treatment practices that have shown efficacy in integrative treatment for adolescents

Key Terms

Adolescent: An individual who is enduring the long-term stage of puberty who has not yet developed full adulthood characteristics identified with physical, neurological, and cognitive development.

Parental Attachment: The connection a child has with their parent(s), which helps shape psychological well-being, skill building, confidence, and independence.

Puberty: A stage of development in which a child experiences physical, neurological, and cognitive changes as they progress over time from child to adult. Puberty is most notable for physical health changes in the body, in which an individual obtains more pronounced primary and secondary sex characteristics while also experiencing an increase in physical and sexual attraction to others.

DOI: 10.4324/9781003220916-11

Biological Factors

The Centers for Disease Control and Prevention (CDC) view adolescent development in two stages, with the first stage including youth between the ages of 12 and 14 and the second stage between 15 and 17 years old (CDC.gov). Developmental milestones during the first stage of adolescence begin with hormonal changes as puberty starts with physical changes in appearance. Boys' voices beginning to deepen, and both facial and pubic hair grow. Girls tend to grow pubic hair, develop breasts, and begin having menses. Growth patterns can be erratic as girls tend to grow height in measured routine incremental patterns while boys can grow taller in spurts, which may be slower or faster depending on each individual's genetics and overall physical health. These physical changes can be problematic for some youth as they are concerned with their appearance being acceptable to peers, which can lead to anxiety, dysregulated moods, and maladaptive behaviors like eating disorders and engaging in substance use to attempt to fit in with peers. Adolescent perspectives of closeness and relationships change as they tend to develop more intense relationships with peers and spend less time with parents. When youth feel they are not acceptable to peers, especially if they're bullied, these issues can become worse, leading to co-occurring disorders and suicidal ideation.

The 15-to-17-year-old adolescent stage is a time of consolidation of physical changes in the body, and the youth is developing more psychological maturity with a greater ability to identify preferences sexually and think through constructs and ideology to form their own opinions separate from parents' beliefs and values, and engaging in peer relationships is even more important to the adolescent (CDC.gov). Physically, adolescents are stronger and faster than they were as children, with improved immune systems and increased capacity to withstand cold, heat, injury, and physical stress; however, comorbidity and risks of death increase as well (Berk, 2018). The youth is developing more independence and responsibility in the attempt toward greater personal freedom from parents and may be involved in romantic and/or sexual relationships. Any unresolved issues that have carried over from childhood trauma and co-occurring disorders may reach more profound demonstrations of behavioral dysfunction, and increased risk taking can lead to adolescent pregnancy, sexually transmitted diseases, and more experimentation with substances.

Psychological and Neurological Factors

The typical youth who is developing in a supportive family environment will transition through a stage of development that is fraught with uncertainty and increased risk taking as biological changes are accompanying changes in the neural systems of emotion and motivation due to neural plasticity during puberty and adolescence (Berk, 2018). The neurological changes create normal neurobehavioral changes as the brain is continuing to develop. The changes in the circuits that are used for executive functioning in decision making enhance a proclivity toward high-intensity feelings, which lead to seeking experiences to contribute to high-intensity feelings due to enjoying excitement and arousal. As researchers have been considering the underpinnings of risk-taking behaviors in adolescence, the explanations for these behaviors look at issues with executive control and the understanding that the frontal lobe and prefrontal cortex are the last regions of the brain to develop, both structurally and functionally (Luciana & Collins, 2012; Luciana, 2013). Along with the desire to experience thrill-seeking and adult behaviors, such as sexual encounters and substance use, youth have the mental construct of 'magical thinking', or a tendency to minimize the potential consequences of engaging in high-risk activities. Thus, the dangers of sexual activity leading to pregnancy or sexually transmitted diseases, driving while texting, risk taking on social media, and indulging in substance use that could potentially lead to developing substance use disorders are not considered likely to occur. Swadi (1999) suggested that the constellation of traits that can be linked to higher risk for substance use in adolescents includes low self-esteem, aggression, high novelty seeking, low harm avoidance, and high reward dependence, along with stressful or traumatic life events and comorbid psychiatric disorders.

Depression and Anxiety

A few studies noted by the NIH demonstrated that depression often predates adolescents using alcohol and other drugs, with as many as 73% of those in treatment for SUDs having comorbid depression (Deas-Nesmith et al., 1998a), and others have observed that depression is a risk factor for adolescents to self-medicate (Burke et al., 1994). Anxiety is another psychiatric disorder that has been researched as a comorbid disorder that increases risks for developing alcohol and drug (AOD) use disorders. The two anxiety disorders that have been noted most in adolescents who use substances are social anxiety and posttraumatic stress disorder (PTSD). Deas-Nesmith et al. (1998b) found that social anxiety was the most persistent psychiatric disorder found in adolescents, with 60% of those with AOD use meeting criteria for the social anxiety disorder. In a 2000 study by Kilpatrick et al., investigators found that youth with PTSD were at increased risk for abusing drugs to cope with the trauma they had experienced. Clark et al. (1997a) found risks for adolescents increased between 6% and 12% if they experienced physical abuse and 18% and 21% if there was a history of sexual abuse, as well as finding alcohol abuse The was higher in females with PTSD than in males in another study (Clark et al., 1997b). A more recent study noted in clinical settings showed that adolescents who have co-occurring disorders include comorbid mood disorders with statistics noting males at 29% and females at 49% (Wu et al., 2011). Comorbid anxiety disorders for those displaying SUDs in males is 9% and females at 19% (Wu et al., 2011). Findings suggest that co-occurring disorders increase substance use severity and can lead to treatment being unsuccessful (Chan et al., 2008; Wise et al., 2001).

DSM-5 Criteria

Major depressive disorder and persistent depressive disorder (American Psychiatric Association, 2013, pp. 160–169) are the two most prevalent depressive disorders among adolescents. The difference between the two is that major depressive disorder is quite dramatic in presentation and acute, with symptoms of loss of pleasure or depressed mood impacting weight, sleep patterns, psychomotor agitation, loss of energy, feelings of worthlessness, diminished ability to concentrate or think, and recurrent thoughts of death, and these symptoms develop quickly within a two-week period of time. Persistent depressive disorder is more chronic in nature, with symptoms perhaps being less severe but being present daily for at least two years.

Social anxiety disorder (American Psychiatric Association, 2013, pp. 202–205) has been moved into the anxiety disorders category that include phobias and panic disorder due to the criteria of fear of social situations and negative evaluation. Additionally, criteria for the disorder include being afraid of being humiliated or embarrassed in interactions with peers as well as adults. The fears, anxiety, or avoidance becomes worse over time and persists in a variety of settings, with symptoms persisting for at least six months.

Posttraumatic stress disorder (American Psychiatric Association, 2013, pp. 271–277) has been moved into a chapter in the *DSM-5* with acute stress disorder due to these disorders developing due to experiencing or witnessing significant trauma, abuse, and significant adverse events. PTSD can develop in very young children, adolescents, and adults, but the significance of early childhood trauma, abuse, and neglect in contributing to the risks for co-occurring psychiatric and substance use disorders has been well researched (Banyard et al., 2001; Briere & Richards, 2007; Kolbo, 1996; van der Kolk, 1994, 2006a, 2006b). The *DSM-5* criteria for PTSD include: experiencing or witnessing a traumatic event that learning of a death or violence, experiencing repeated or extreme exposure to aversive events contribute to developing the disorder, along with the presence of intrusive and distressing memories of the event, dissociative reactions, psychological distress at exposure to internal or external cues that symbolize the trauma, persistent avoidance of stimuli, negative alterations in mood and cognition, with marked alterations in arousal and reactivity associated with the traumatic event(s) that has lasted more than a month with impairment in occupational, social, and/or other areas of functioning. Those with this disorder are at far greater risk for developing additional psychiatric disorders and for numbing the psychic and emotional pain with the use of substances (American Psychiatric Association, 2013).

Living with various mental health diagnoses poses additional problems within the family, school, and interpersonal relationships of the adolescent (Clayborne et al., 2019). In the past, the medical community often approached the treatment of children and adolescents as if they were smaller adults. This approach is far too narrow and limited. Many adolescents who are living with co-occurring disorders may show lower grades in school, lack of accountability to chores, increased moodiness, and struggles with parents (Johnson et al., 2018). As the adolescent is not living in a home that they own, they usually have to adhere to rules imposed by parents. Adults living in their own homes who endure depression have the ability to spend the day in bed. Adolescents will be prompted to engage in activities despite their symptoms. Because of this, the observation of some symptoms may be inaccurate, and the adolescent may be viewed as being 'rebellious' as opposed to living with mental health diagnoses.

Conduct Disorder and ADHD

Conduct disorder is a reference to antisocial behavior in youth and, if diagnosed prior to adolescence, has a direct correlation with having had extreme adversity in the home environment and is indicative of developing an antisocial personality disorder as the youth becomes an adult (American Psychiatric Association, 2013). CD has been linked with early abuse of alcohol in adolescents and is a disorder found more prevalently in males (Clark et al., 1997b). Those with attention-deficit hyperactivity disorder (ADHD) and lower cognitive functioning were found to have higher risks for developing AOD use (Span & Earleywine, 1999; Dawes et al., 2000). When considering the higher risk for substance use in those with ADHD, it has been noted that treating ADHD with stimulant medications like amphetamine will reduce impulsive behaviors, fidgeting, and inability to concentrate early on, but the research is inconclusive on whether the children who have taken such medications will develop substance use disorders later in life due to the brain changes caused by taking prescription amphetamine, with some preliminary studies suggesting this will not occur (Nelson & Galon, 2012; Zulauf et al., 2014) and others suggesting that psychotropic medications of this sort will lead to chronic brain disabling if used long term (Breggin, 2011).

DSM-5 Criteria

Conduct Disorder (American Psychiatric Association, 2013, pp. 469–169)

Conduct disorder falls into the category of disruptive, impulse-control, and conduct disorders, which include oppositional defiant disorder (ODD) and intermittent explosive disorder; combined with CD, intermittent explosive disorder is the most problematic of the three disorders diagnosed in children and youth. Typically, a youth who has been diagnosed with CD has additional diagnoses of ODD, mood disorders, and possibly learning disabilities or ADHD due to the significant adverse events going on in the home. To be diagnosed with CD, a youth has to have had at least three criteria present during the past year, and a youth who has been given that diagnosis prior to age 15 is considered to have the necessary traits to be diagnosed with antisocial personality disorder by the time young adulthood has been attained. Primarily, this disorder is found in males with an uncontrolled temperament as infants and lower-than-average intelligence.

The family environment is fraught with risk factors due to parental abuse, neglect, and rejection, along with many of the adverse childhood events noted in the ACEs study (Felitti et al., 1998). *DSM-5* criteria for CD include four categories of demonstrating aggression toward people and animals, destruction of property, deceitfulness and theft, and serious violation of rules, along with a general lack of remorse for one's actions and a lack of empathy for the rights of others (American Psychiatric Association, 2013, pp. 469–471).

Gender Differences and Prevalence

While working in a co-occurring residential treatment facility for adolescents and simultaneously being the art therapist and mental health professional on a National Institute of Health–funded educational grant to present the correlations between substance use disorders and sexually transmitted diseases like HIV (Chandler, 2005–2006), the statistics at that time in the US stated that young men, especially those of minority ethnicity, were the fastest-growing population contracting HIV. The information provided at that time was that the majority of the males were heterosexual and passing the virus to their unprotected girlfriends. The male adolescents who were part of the study were in a juvenile detention setting, with many of them having gang affiliation outside the facility, and the demographics of the males were 95% Hispanic/Latino, 4% African American, and only 1% Caucasian. Primarily, these youth met criteria for conduct disorder, anxiety disorders, learning disorders, and substance use disorders. What impressed this researcher about assessing, diagnosing, and working with the males in this study was how much they expressed a need for any adult who would care about them, gratitude that they were receiving any attention from the staff involved in the research study listening to them, and how hopeless they were that they could go back to their neighborhoods and change the trajectory of their lives. While the males in the study are one population of adolescents with co-occurring disorders who found themselves incarcerated for criminal activity while engaging in substance use, this group had both externalizing and internalizing traits associated with conduct disorder, along with anxiety and depression, which have been noted as creating higher risks for developing co-occurring substance use disorders (Clark et al., 1997b). Additionally, exposure to community violence and its correlation with hopelessness in minority males with delinquent behaviors support the findings noted in the youth in the 2005–2006 study (Burnside & Gaylord-Harden, 2018).

The female adolescents in the study were from a high school with modified curriculums for specialized education for girls who were pregnant, girls with young children, and girls who were pregnant again. The ethnic mix of the females in the study were roughly 46% Hispanic/Latino, 44% African American, and 10% Caucasian. The females discussed with this researcher that they knew all about sexually transmitted diseases, and some of them had contracted vaginal warts, herpes, gonorrhea, or syphilis from their sexual partners. When asked why they did not use protection and make their boyfriends use condoms, they were quick to say that the males did not like using them, and the girls would not risk losing their boyfriends over self-protection. As for the drugs they used, many of these girls stated that their reason for using methamphetamine was to lose weight. The females in the study demonstrated problems with anxiety and depression, along with body dysmorphic issues, a tendency toward eating disorders, and low self-esteem as they were more than willing to put their lives at risk for their relationships with their boyfriends (Clark et al., 1997a; Burke et al., 1994).

DSM-5

Eating Disorders (American Psychiatric Association, 2013, pp. 338–349)

The two most serious eating disorders in the *DSM-5* are anorexia nervosa and bulimia nervosa, and both of these are considered to be connected to inappropriate and negative self-evaluation about body weight while being tied to body dysmorphic disorder, social anxiety, and obsessive-compulsive disorder. Those who engage in disordered eating by minimizing food intake and avoiding food can exhibit significant weight loss and nutritional deficiencies that can become life threatening, which is anorexia nervosa. Those who develop bulimia nervosa binge on large portions of food, then purge by forcing themselves to throw up what they have eaten or by using diuretics to force diarrhea to eliminate the food eaten. These disorders rarely develop in children but are more common in adolescent females and young women as a means to control their weight. They can also be an attempt to have some control in a life that otherwise appears to have nothing the individual can control. Eating disorders are difficult to successfully treat as the mindset of the youth must change to the point that an accurate ability to see changes to the body is possible, and the underlying causes for these disorders must be successfully treated. Some family members of those living with eating disorders may make an attempt to assist the individual by linking them up with traditional outpatient mental health treatment. The nature of eating disorders is so severe that an outpatient treatment program may not be sufficient. It is recommended that a full team of clinicians work together with the adolescent and their family to assist in the recovery process. An eating disorders treatment team usually consists of individual counselors, group counselors, nutritionists, medical doctors, family counselors, psychiatrists, and social workers to appropriately support all aspects of the adolescent's life (Kazdin et al., 2017).

Non-Suicidal Self-Injury (American Psychiatric Association, 2013, pp. 803–805)

The NSSI disorder in past decades was associated as a symptom of those diagnosed with borderline personality disorder (BPD) and was indicative of cutting one's self but now includes any minor to moderate self-harm inflicted with no intent toward suicide. To be diagnosed with the disorder requires five consecutive days of engaging in some form of self-inflicted bodily harm, which has become an approach that adolescents may use to sublimate emotional pain or interpersonal difficulty with temporary physical pain. While adolescent females are associated with the disorder, the *DSM-5* states that statistics have found that females and males use these types of behaviors. Often, parents or adults may misperceive non-suicidal self-injury as a cry for help. This may often invalidate the experience of the adolescent engaging in this type of behavior. It is recommended that counselors conceptualize this from the perspective of a coping strategy. The adolescent may feel very overwhelmed emotionally, and lacking the skills to manage this, they may resort to non-suicidal self-injury to focus on the physical pain as opposed to being emotionally overwhelmed (Miller et al., 2007).

Socio-cultural Considerations and Barriers to Treatment

There are cultural trust issues in many minority cultures around mental health treatment in general and especially using allopathic approaches that do not demonstrate understanding or acceptance of multicultural values. A current study has suggested that racism has pervasive mental health impacts for African American youth and propose a culturally informed Adverse Childhood Experiences (ACEs) model C-ACE to look at the impact of intergenerational racism as public health risk for these youth to develop mental health and substance or process use disorders (Bernard et al., 2021). A study on adolescent trauma and disenfranchised grief suggests that adapting therapeutic interventions for African American and Latino youth and delivering them in school settings by trained counselors could improve the mental, emotional, and social well-being of the students, along with potentially improving academic success while preventing legal involvement for the youth (Dutil, 2019). This could potentially provide greater access to treatment services for these youth.

A study researched the prevalence of mood disorders, anxiety disorders, and exposure to interpersonal violence along with substance use and delinquency in Hispanic and non-Hispanic black adolescents and found that trauma-related adversity may differ for the adolescents in how they may internalize or externalize symptoms of trauma (Lopez et al., 2017). A study by Judith Siegel (2015) determined a critical factor that predisposed youth to psychiatric and substance use disorders was lack of emotional regulation that corresponds to the traumas noted in Felitti et al. (1998) on traumas and adverse events that contribute to higher risk for co-occurring mental health and substance use disorders (Felitti, 2004). Siegel suggests that the emerging research on the lack of emotional regulation contributes to both externalizing and internalizing factors involved in both psychiatric and substance use disorders and that more research is needed in this area (Siegel, 2015). Additionally, addictive processes are not just around illicit substances but include addiction to behavioral processes that create an obsession with social media, shopping, sex, and eating disorders that can become problematic for many adolescents.

Adolescents only have access to treatment if their parents have the means and desire to get treatment for their youth or if they are in legal trouble and court ordered to treatment. Adolescents from minority cultures, especially those of First Nation or indigenous cultures, may have no trust in allopathic treatment even if they have access to treatment facilities. Additionally, there are few long-term integrated treatment facilities that specialize in adolescent recovery and treatment and even fewer that engage in a holistic approach.

Integrated Treatment Approaches and Best Practices

It has been found that, while research has increased in recent decades on the correlation between co-occurring psychiatric and substance use disorders, there is still a minimal number of empirical studies done with adolescents. Those studies have noted only modest improvement in adolescent clients with the current treatment approaches, and research on long-term treatment that is empirically controlled is almost non-existent, with a great many adolescents returning to substance use once out of treatment (Barnett et al., 2012; Winters et al., 2011). The treatment approaches that have been traditionally used with adolescents with co-occurring disorders have included cognitive behavioral therapy (CBT), motivational interviewing (MI), and multidimensional family therapy (MDFT), yet these have not been fully effective for adolescent recovery of co-occurring disorders (Chorpita et al., 2009; Rotheram-Borus et al., 2012; Weisz et al., 2012).

Hulvershorn et al. (2015) recommend integrated treatment in one facility assessing and diagnosing all comorbid disorders and treatment being individualized, with components of CBT, MI, MDFT, and other therapeutic approaches as are deemed appropriate for the adolescent, including psychotropic medications where applicable. We suggest that mindfulness-based behavioral therapy like dialectic behavioral therapy, which teaches regulating moods, impulse control, increasing interpersonal skills, distress tolerance, and mindfulness and has shown efficacy in adult populations with personality disorders, mood and anxiety disorders, and substance use disorders be clinically studied with the adolescent population in integrated treatment protocols (Dimeff & Linehan, 2008). A pilot study done with high school students found that by modifying the DBT protocols to short-term mindfulness interventions to promote emotion regulation and impulsivity interventions resulted in low attrition rates, improved treatment outcomes, and evidence that these forms of intervention should be studied more for use with adolescents (Russell et al., 2019). Creative arts therapies and somatic expressive therapies are also viable approaches that are effective with adolescents, and nutritional counseling should be a part of the approach, in addition to the aforementioned treatment approaches to rule out vitamin and amino acid deficiencies prior to putting youth on psychotropic medications, as well as improving their dietary choices to whole foods that support brain chemistry (Procyk, 2016; Walsh, 2014). Additionally, outdoor therapies and animal-assisted therapies have shown efficacy in adolescents.

Conclusion

Adolescents are no longer children, but they are not adults either. The teen years are riddled with tremendous physiological, neurological, and intellectual changes occurring along with increased peer relationship development and development in understanding one's own identity. Interest in intense emotional encounters and thrill-seeking activity can make this population extremely vulnerable to co-occurring disorders. Early childhood trauma, abuse, and neglect contribute to the increased risk of maladaptive coping mechanisms, high-risk behaviors, and subsequent issues. Integrated treatment approaches that teach adolescents emotional regulation, distress tolerance, and interpersonal skills and uses creative and somatic therapies to heal from a whole-brain approach are needed for those who have developed co-occurring disorders. Individual, group, and family therapy approaches in either inpatient or outpatient settings, depending on the severity of issues, can assist adolescents in their recovery and in developing meaningful and healthy lives.

Questions for Consideration

1. Based on the risk and vulnerability of the adolescent population to co-occurring disorders, what can be done to promote health during these challenging years?
2. Once adolescents have been exposed to mood-altering substances, some will develop substance use disorder very quickly while others do not seem to exhibit the negative consequences of use. How is this possible?
3. The brain is so placid during the adolescent years and is particularly vulnerable to mood-altering substances. Can their brains heal? Why or why not?
4. Mood-altering substances are illegal for adolescents. Do you think this contributes to the allure and risk-taking behavior associated with use?

Case Study

Caleb is a 15-year-old African American young man who has always done well in school and excelled in sports. During his first year of high school, he joined the football team and seemed to make a lot of friends. His family encouraged sports and academics as they believed that he could earn a scholarship and be the first person in the family to go to college. Over the past year, his attitude, grades, and mood have all changed. He is staying out later, skipping practice, and lying about what is going on. His mother is concerned. She has requested a comprehensive evaluation because she is concerned about the drugs she has found in his room, his fluctuating grades, and his recent obsession with eating. When you meet with Caleb, his toxicology screen shows a high level of marijuana, traces of steroids, and low levels of methylphenidate. Caleb shares that he borrowed some pills from his friend, smokes a little, and tried steroids when his coach encouraged him to get bigger for the big game. 'Oh, yeah, and we all drink, a lot'.

Questions

1. What are your clinical concerns with Caleb?
2. His substance use would impact his brain development and functioning. However, there may be something else going on. What information would you like to know about Caleb that could help clarify a diagnosis?
3. What type of treatment interventions could be appropriate for Caleb? What role would his family play in any treatment recommendations?

References

American Psychiatric Association. (2013). *Diagnostic and statistical manual of mental disorders* (5th ed.). American Psychiatric Association.

Banyard, V. L., Williams, L. M., & Siegel, J. A. (2001). The long-term mental health consequences of child sexual abuse: An exploratory study of the impact of multiple traumas in a sample of women. *Journal of Traumatic Stress*, *14*(4).

Barnett, E., Sussman, S., Smith, C., Rohrbach, L. A., & Spruit-Metz, D. (2012). Motivational interviewing for adolescent substance use: A review of the literature. *Addict Behavior*, *37*(12), 1325–1334.

Berk, L. E. (2018). *Development through the lifespan* (7th ed.). Pearson.

Bernard, D. L., Calhoun, C. D, Banks, D. E, Halliday, C.A., Hughes-Halbert, C, & Danielson, C. K. (2021). Making the "C-ACE" for a culturally informed adverse childhood experiences framework to understand the pervasive mental health impact of racism on black youth. *Journal of Child and Adolescent Trauma*, *14*, 233–247. https://doi.org/10.1007/s40653-020-00319-9

Breggin, P. R. (2011). Psychiatric drug-induced Chronic Brain Impairment (CBI): Implications for long-term treatment with psychiatric medication. *Journal of Risk & Safety in Medicine*, *23*(4), 193–200.

Briere, J., & Richards, S. (2007). Self-awareness, affect regulation, and relatedness: Differential sequels of childhood versus adult victimization experiences. *The Chicago Journal of Nervous and Mental Disease*, *19*(6), 497–508.

Burke, J. D., Burke, K. C., & Rae, D. S. (1994). Increased rates of drug abuse and dependence after onset of mood or anxiety disorders in adolescence. *Hospital and Community Psychiatry*, *45*(5), 451–455.

Burnside, A. N., & Gaylord-Harden, N. K. (2018). Hopeless and delinquent behavior as predictors of community violence exposure in ethnic minority male adolescent offenders. *Journal of Abnormal Child Psychology*, *47*(2), 11.

Chan, Y. F., Dennis, M. L., & Funk, R. R. (2008). Prevalence and comorbidity of major internalizing and externalizing problems among adolescents and adults presenting to substance use treatment. *Journal of Substance Abuse Treatment*, *34*(1), 14–24.

Chandler, T. (2005–2006, January). *Education on the correlation between substance use disorders and sexually transmitted diseases for at risk youth. Researcher/mental health facilitator on a National Institute of Health grant for community mental health & substance use disorder treatment facility*. Findings were presented at the SAMHSA Conference, Washington, DC.

Chorpita, B. F., & Daleiden, M. L. (2009). Mapping evidence-based treatments for children and adolescents: Application of the distillation and matching model to 615 treatments from 322 randomized trials. *Journal of Consulting Clinical Psychology*, *77*(3), 566–579.

Clark, D. B., Lesnick, L., & Hegedus, A. M. (1997a). Traumas and other adverse life events in adolescents with alcohol abuse and dependence. *Journal of the American Academy of Child & Adolescent Psychiatry*, *36*(9), 1744–1751.

Clark, D. B, Pollock, N., Bukstein, O. G., Mezzich, A. C., Bromberger, J. T., & Donovan, J. E. (1997b). Gender and comorbid psychopathology in adolescents with alcohol dependence. *Journal of the American Academy of Child & Adolescent Psychiatry*, *36*(9), 1195–1203.

Clayborne, Z., Varin, M., & Colman, I. (2019). Systematic review and meta-analysis: Adolescent depression and long-term psychosocial outcomes. *Journal of the American Academy of Child & Adolescent Psychiatry*, *58*(1), 72–79.

Dawes, M. A., Antelman, S. M, Vanyukov, M. M., Giancola, P., Tarter, R. E., Susman, E. J., Mezzich, A, & Clark, D. B. (2000). Developmental sources of variation in liability to adolescent substance use disorders. *Drug and Alcohol Dependence*, *61*, 3–14.

Deas-Nesmith, D., Brady, K., & Campbell, S. (1998a). Substance use disorders in an adolescent inpatient psychiatric population. *Journal of the National Medical Association*, *90*, 233–238.

Deas-Nesmith, D., Campbell, S., & Brady, K. (1998b). Comorbid substance use and anxiety disorders in adolescents. *Journal of Psychopathology and Behavioral Assessment*, *20*(2), 139–148.

Dimeff, L. A., & Linehan, M. M. (2008). Dialectical behavior therapy for substance abusers. *Addiction Science & Clinical Practice*, *4*(2), 39.

Dutil, S. (2019). Adolescent traumatic and disenfranchised grief: Adapting an evidence-based intervention for Black and Latinx youths in schools. *Children & Schools*, *41*(3), 179–187. https://doi.org/10.1093/cs/cdz009

Felitti, V. J. (2004). *The origins of addiction: Evidence from the adverse childhood experiences study.* Retrieved from www.nijc.org/pdfs/Subject%20Matter%20Articles/Drugs%20and%20Alc/ACE%0Study% 20-%20OriginsofAddiction.pdf

Felitti, V. J., Anda, R. F., Nordenberg, D., Williamson, D. F., Spitz, A. M., Edwards, V., . . . Marks, J. S. (1998). Relationship of childhood abuse and household dysfunction to many of the leading causes of death in adults: The Adverse Childhood Experiences (ACE) study. *American Journal of Prevention Medicine, 14*(4), 245–258.

Hulvershorn, L. A., Quinn, P. D., & Scott, E. L. (2015). Treatment of adolescent substance use disorders and co-occurring internalizing disorders: A critical review and proposal model. *Current Drug Abuse Review, 8*(1), 41–49.

Johnson, D., Dupuis, G., Piche, J., Clayborne, Z., & Colman, I. (2018). Adult mental health outcomes of adolescent depression: A systematic review. *Depression & Anxiety, 35*, 700–716. https://doi.org/10.1002/da.22777

Kazdin, A. E., Fitzsimmons-Craft, E. E., & Wilfley, D. E. (2017). Addressing critical gaps in the treatment of eating disorders. *International Journal of Eating Disorders, 50*, 170–189. doi:10.1002/eat.22670

Kolbo, J. R. (1996). Risk and resilience among children exposed to family violence. *Violence and Victims, 11*(2), 113–128.

Lopez, C. M., Andrews, A. R., Chisolm, A. M., de Arellano, M. A., Saunders, B., & Kilpatrick, D. G. (2017). Racial/ethnic differences in trauma exposure and mental health disorders in adolescents. *Cultural Diversity and Ethnic Minority Psychology, 23*(3), 382–387.

Luciana, M. (2013, November). Adolescent brain development in normality and psychopathology. *Developmental Psychopathology, 25*(4 Pt 2), 1325–1345. doi:10.1017/S0954579413000643. PMID: 24342843. PMCID: PMC4076820

Luciana, M., & Collins, P. F. (2012). Incentive motivation, cognitive control, and the adolescent brain: Is it time for a paradigm shift? *Child Development Perspectives, 6*(4), 392–399.

Miller, A., Rathus, J., & Linehan, M. (2007). *Dialectic behavior therapy with suicidal adolescents.* The Guilford Press.

Nelson, A., & Galon, P. (2012). Exploring the relationship among ADHD, stimulants, and substance abuse. *Journal of Child and Adolescent Psychiatric Nursing Office for the Public Association of Child and Adolescent Psychiatric Nurses Incorporated, 25*(3), 113–118.

Procyk, A. (2016). *Nutritional and integrative interventions for mental health disorders.* CMI Education Institute, Inc.

Rotheram-Borus, M. J., Swendemann, D., & Chorpita, B. F. (2012). Disruptive innovations for designing evidence-based interventions. *American Psychologist, 67*(6), 463–476.

Russell, B. S., Hutchison, M., & Fusco, A. (2019). Emotion regulation outcomes and preliminary feasibility evidence from a mindfulness intervention for adolescent substance use. *Journal of Child & Adolescent Substance Abuse, 28*(1), 21–31. https://doi.org/10.1080/1067828X.2018.1561577

Siegel, J. P. (2015, March/April). Emotional regulation in adolescent substance use disorders: Rethinking risk. *Journal of Child & Adolescent Substance Abuse, 24*(2), 67–79. doi:10.1080/1067828X.2012.761169

Span, S. A., & Earleywine, M. (1999). Cognitive functioning moderates the relation between hyperactivity and drinking habits. *Alcoholism: Clinical and Experimental Research, 23*, 224–229.

Swadi, H. (1999). Individual risk factors for adolescent substance use. *Drug and Alcohol Dependence, 55*, 209–224.

van der Kolk, B. A. (1994). The body keeps the score: Memory and the evolving psychobiology of post-traumatic stress. *Harvard Review of Psychiatry, 1*, 253–265.

van der Kolk, B. A. (2006a). Clinical implications of neuroscience research in PTSD. [Electronic version]. *Annuals of the New York Academy of Sciences, 17*(1), 277–293.

van der Kolk, B. A. (2006b). Developmental trauma disorder: A new, rational diagnosis for children with complex trauma histories. [Electronic version]. *Psychiatric Annals, 200X*, 2–8.

Walsh, W. J. (2014). *Nutrient power: Heal your biochemistry and heal your brain.* Skyhorse Publishing, Inc.

Weisz, J. R., Chorpita, B. F., Palinkas, L. A., Schoenwald, S. K., Miranda, J., Bearman, S. K., Daleiden, E. L., Uqueto, A. M., Ho, A., Martin, J., Gray, J., Alleyne, A., Langer, D. A., Southam-Gerow, M. A., Gibbons, R. D., & Research Network on Youth Mental Health (2012). Testing standard and modular designs for psychotherapy treating depression, anxiety and conduct problems in youth: A randomized effectiveness trial. *Archival of General Psychiatry, 69*(3), 274–282.

Winters, K. C., Botzet, A. M., & Fahnhorst, T. (2011). Advances in adolescent substance abuse treatment. *Current Psychiatric Research*, *13*(5), 416–421.

Wise, B. K., Cuffe, S. P., & Fischer, T. (2001). Dual diagnosis and successful participation of adolescents in substance abuse treatment. *Journal of Substance Abuse Treatment*, *21*(3), 162–165.

Wu, L. T., Gersing, K., Burchett, B., Woody, G. E., & Blazer, D. G. (2011). Substance use disorders and comorbid Axis I and II psychiatric disorders among your psychiatric patients: Findings from a large electronic health records database. *Journal of Psychiatric Research*, *45*(11), 1453–1462.

Zulauf, C. A., Sprich, S. E., Safren, S. A., & Wilens, T. E. (2014). The complicated relationship between attention deficit/hyperactivity disorder and substance use disorders. *Current Psychiatry Reports*, *16*(3), 436.

10 Co-occurring Disorders Among the Older Adult Population

Karlene Barrett and Tricia L. Chandler

Introduction

The world population has been rapidly aging, with the older adult population being estimated to double between 2015 and 2050 from 900 million to 2 billion people over the age of 60. In the United States alone, there are approximately 46 million adults 65 years or older, with those in the baby boomer group (those born between 1946 and 1964) representing the fastest-growing population in the country (Eden, 2012; Mather et al., 2015; Mignon, 2015). In 2021, this baby boomer group is between the ages of 57 and 75, and over 80 million people in the United States are considered to be in midlife adulthood through the elder adult stage of life (Lachman, 2004). This population also includes a huge group of people who were born before 1946, who comprise the true elder population and who are living longer due to medical advances. The advances in medical health that contribute to longer life have created a treatment gap in meeting the needs of the expanding aging population.

Learning Objectives

- Identify various issues specific to the fastest-growing population in the US (older adults) living with co-occurring disorders
- Recognize current barriers to treating older adults living with co-occurring disorders
- Identify specific adjunct services to enhance the treatment of older adults living with co-occurring disorders
- Recognize appropriate evidenced-based treatment models for older adults living with co-occurring disorders

Key Terms

Acute Pain: Pain that is the response to an immediate trigger. The pain goes away relatively quickly but can last up to six months, based on the severity of the injury/illness. The pain is resolved when the body appropriately heals.

Baby Boomer Generation: This is the fastest-growing population segment, born after WWII between 1946 and 1964.

Chronic Care Model: Chronic medical and mental health issues need long-term coordinated treatment using a team approach that includes a primary care physician (PCP) and professionals in the mental health and addiction fields

Chronic Pain: Ongoing pain lasting more than six months. Can continue when the source of injury or illness has been resolved

Generativity: A focus that transcends the individual, allowing them to care for younger and older generations.

Failure to Thrive: A development state in older adults with various areas of decline that can be caused by chronic diseases and functional impairments

DOI: 10.4324/9781003220916-12

Hospice Care: Treatment focusing on enhancing the quality of life for patients (and their families) living with life-ending illnesses

Older Adult Abuse: Interpersonal violence on an older adult in which they are subject to physical, emotional, financial, and sexual abuse. The older adult can also experience deprivation and neglect

Palliative Care: Specialized medical care focusing on pain relief from significant illness to improve the quality of life for patients and their families

Stagnation: A state of being that lacks ongoing personal growth or development

Socio-cultural Considerations

This age group has several considerations that set it apart from other adult populations, as baby boomers were the first generation of people who were born under the threat of nuclear war, as well as the first population to be raised with pharmaceutical directives of 'better living through chemistry', which affected medication, nutrition, and the explosion of experimenting with substances during the 1960s and beyond (Colliver et al., 2006; Wu & Blazer, 2011). The feminist movement, civil rights, the Vietnam War, questioning authority figures of mainstream cultures, experimentation with consciousness-raising activities, and experimentation with substances are all part of the socio-cultural changes that occurred with this population called baby boomers. Many people in this age category are still actively working; however, they may have a very different attitude toward alcohol use and pharmaceutical and illicit drugs, along with a reluctance to seek out psychotherapeutic treatment for mental disorders or substance use disorders (Segal et al., 2005). An additional consideration with this population is that as they age, there is more risk of medical concerns that contribute to mental health issues, cognitive declines, socioeconomic changes, and overuse of medications. Those individuals that are in their 80s and older may develop medical issues that can give rise to both mood and anxiety disorders, as well as leading to the overuse of psychotropic medications for pain, insomnia, and anxiety.

As adults age, they become vulnerable to elder abuse, which can include physical, verbal, psychological, financial and sexual abuse; abandonment; neglect; and loss of dignity and respect, which also increases depression and anxiety that is often undiagnosed. Despite these issues, there is an underuse of mental health services often due to older adults holding negative views of mental illness, along with the perceived stigma and shame involved with seeking out psychiatric services (Hannaford et al., 2018; Preville et al., 2015; Segal et al., 2005). Often older adults will seek medication from primary care physicians rather than seeking psychotherapy for their mental disorders.

Biological Factors

Biological factors of aging can create multiple issues for older adults to manage. As people age, they may experience reduced mobility, chronic pain, cardiovascular disease complications, diabetes, chronic immune system impairment, cancer, and a variety of other health conditions for which they are taking some form of medication to manage the symptoms, indicating the potential need for long-term care to treat the elderly to manage the overuse of prescription drugs in the United States (Bogunovic, 2012). Chronic pain and higher levels of pain intensity have been correlated with elevated depression symptoms, which contribute to the use of opiates and benzodiazepine medications to manage pain symptoms, which in some cases increase the risk of dementia (Brooks et al., 2019; Tampi & Bennet, 2021). These pain substances, along with other psychotropic medications prescribed for anxiety and depression, can lead to reduction in an older adult's quality of life due to increases in drowsiness, weakness, and confusion; problems with coordination; and injuries due to falls (Tournier et al., 2019).

Older adults living with chronic pain often seek treatment from their medical providers (Hser et al., 2017). Older adults are less likely to seek medications or substances from friends and family than those under the age of 50. Living with chronic pain contributes to instances of isolation and disconnection from family supports among the older adult population (Makaroun et al., 2020). Ongoing isolation and disconnection make it difficult for family members and medical providers to assess for the potential misuse of prescribed medications (Chhatre et al., 2017). Issues regarding treatment of older adults can then be exacerbated as many primary care physicians may lack in-depth education regarding the treatment of older adults, substance use, or mental health disorders (Sedhome & Barile, 2017). The coalescence of the limitations of primary care, access to connections, struggles with ongoing physical pain, and interactions with family greatly contribute to ongoing psychological factors among older adults.

Psychological Factors

While mental health issues can occur at any point in life, stressors for older adults include increased bereavement, depression, and anxiety in dealing with the increased medical issues they face (Blackburn et al., 2017). Additionally, loneliness, isolation, and other psychological distresses occur more frequently in this population, along with increasing risks for dementia (Bogunovic, 2012). Those with diagnosed mental disorders such as bipolar disorder, schizophrenia, depression, and anxiety disorders are at greater risk for adverse outcomes like premature death, cancer, substance abuse, and suicide (Brooks et al., 2019; Powell, 2011).

Changes in biology and environment can be contributors to factors emulating symptoms of mental health. It can become increasingly difficult to diagnose and treat such factors as symptoms associated with depression (such as a lack of enjoyment in activities, increased need for sleep, and decreased appetite) that may naturally manifest in older adults who may be experiencing major life changes or developments of neurological disorders (Onyike, 2016). Appropriate existential concerns such as wrestling with one's mortality and making decisions regarding end-of-life care and plans for the individual's assets following their passing can cause appropriate and expected levels of anxiety (Romo et al., 2017). Clinicians attempting to work with older adults can struggle to navigate several of these factors when attempting to make treatment considerations. Ongoing additional stress, disconnection from family, lack of treatment, and exacerbated medical health problems can also contribute to the neurobiological factors an older adult faces.

Neurobiological Factors

Mental and neurological disorders among older adults account for 6.6% of the total disability for this age group, with the most common issues being dementia, depression, and anxiety. These are among the most problematic disorders, ranging from 3% to 7%; substance use issues affect almost 1% of those over 60 years of age, and a lifetime prevalence of mental health issues over 47% in the US (Chhatre et al., 2017; Mattson et al., 2017; Tournier et al., 2019). Living with these issues may place an increased burden on caregivers as they attempt to meet the basic needs of their aging family members. Many individuals caring for aging family members have little understanding of diagnosis, prognosis, and treatment of their loved ones, which manifests in additional interpersonal problems or struggles to adhere to treatment as recommended (Whitlatch & Orsulic-Jeras, 2018). Adhering to medication regimens including painkillers and psychotropics can be confusing to caregivers. Problems with adherence to medications can contribute to the development of substance use disorders and problems with mental health care and, when medications are inaccurately provided, can cause unintentional death.

Rate of Occurrence

Eden suggested (Eden & The Institute of Medicine [U.S.], 2012) that approximately 20% of older Americans experience co-occurring disorders. There is a further estimate that by 2030, up to 14 million Americans over the age of 65 will have co-occurring disorders; however, the number of psychiatrists who work with the elder population is decreasing (Bartels & Naslund, 2013). Chronic pain and painful disorders such as cancer have led to the increased use of cannabis among the elderly (Dinitto & Choi, 2011; Han et al., 2017; Mahvan et al., 2017; Noel, 2017; van den Elsen et al., 2014; Walsh et al., 2017; Williamson & Evans, 2000). The baby boomer group of older adults are among the people who may tend toward self-medicating with illicit substances and use cannabis despite potential cognitive issues developing from the substance and the limited understanding of the long-term outcome of its use (Fahmy et al., 2012; Gerberich et al., 2003; Kostadinov & Roche, 2017; Vacaflor, 2020). While women tend to use more pharmaceutical substances and men tend toward using stimulants, sedatives, and tranquilizers, alcohol is the most abused substance in the older adult population (Mattson et al., 2017; Powell, 2011; Tournier et al., 2019). Treatment is often not available for older adults who experience substance abuse, and when it is, it is rarely accredited (Morgen et al., 2015). It is therefore judicious to improve our understanding of how alcohol and illicit drugs intersect with older adults' mental health challenges and explore best practices to address this public health issue.

Barriers to Treatment

As has been noted, one of the biggest barriers to accessing mental health and substance use disorders treatment for older adults is the stigma around accepting psychotherapy, and most often, older adults prefer to seek help from their primary care physician (Hannaford et al., 2018). An additional issue with this preference is that older adults will present with somatic issues but will be less likely to report mental health or substance issues (Hannaford et al., 2018). There are few integrated facilities to treat co-occurring disorders to begin with and even fewer that older adults have access to, with fewer psychiatrists treating this population (Bartels & Naslund, 2013). Many physicians treating older adults may have limited experience working with mental health and substance use disorders. The physician may interpret certain symptoms (such as isolation from others and lack of enjoyment of activities) as evidence of age-related physical decline.

Many older adults may rely on family members for assistance to attend needed medical appointments. Whereas primary care physicians can see an individual once every three to six months, mental health and substance use treatment usually relies on weekly individual sessions in addition to weekly groups (Schepis et al., 2018). The frequency of treatment can be a barrier, especially if the primary mental health/substance use provider has limited experience working with older adults. A lack of attendance may be misinterpreted as resistance to change (Sedhom & Barile, 2017). It is recommended that treatment providers be aware of services for aging adults within their communities to assist with transportation as needed.

Special Considerations

As approximately 20% of older Americans experience co-occurring disorders and as many as 25% of older adults have access to prescription drugs that can be abused (e.g., narcotic pain medication, sedatives), with even more using over-the-counter pain medication, it is incredibly important to consider how to overcome these barriers to treatment access (Eden, 2012). Eden and The Institute of Medicine (U.S.) (2012) propose addressing the health- and mental health–care needs of older adults by first dealing with the dearth of trained and qualified health workers for the geriatric population at a legislative level. This will help bring needed attention to a neglected area of health care, in addition to the personal distress this population experiences, that will have significant social and economic impact in the long term. This will present opportunities for the development of resources (training programs, educational materials, evidence-based research protocols, etc.) that may motivate the engagement of workers in this field. Qualls's (2015) approach also includes building competencies but expands this to those already in practice.

Although it may be slowed as humans age, development continues throughout the lifespan. Consideration must be given to the life experiences of older adults and how these may have shaped or impacted their mental and emotional development. Chronic illnesses and the experience of traumatic life events such as war, natural disasters, abuse, racism, other forms of discrimination, etc. can have profound consequences for adults. If they are not addressed, the individual continues to live with the effect into older adulthood. One example of this can be seen in the special needs of veterans, especially those who have experienced posttraumatic stress (Carrola, 2015).

Negative mood, isolation, and grief are strong predictors of substance misuse among older adults (Schonfeld & MacFarland, 2015). The older one gets, the more likely it is that one loses loved ones. For older adults who outlive family and friends, there can be a sense of profound isolation, grief, and loss. In addition to the functional limitations that aging may generate, older adults may feel inadequate or ineffective. Many may also grieve the loss of vitality. In addition, the world is constantly changing, and this can present challenges to persons as they age and may not be able or willing to keep up with the pace of change. If this causes anxiety, older adults may self-medicate using alcohol or tobacco (SAMHSA, 2020).

Where older adults live can also impact their mental health. Someone aging at home with a supportive family may face mental health challenges differently than someone who lives in an institution such as a nursing home or assisted-living facility. Someone whose family has predeceased them may have a different experience of aging than someone whose family is alive and supportive. Even when an older family member lives at home, there are the considerations of the impact on the family and vice versa. Caretakers of parents and their own children are known as the sandwich generation, and such responsibility may present additional stressors on all family members (O'Sullivan, 2015).

Older adults are at increased risk of abuse from caregivers when compared to younger adults (Evans et al., 2017). Clinicians may inappropriately assume that abuse of older adults will be physical (skin abrasions, black eyes, etc.). While physical abuse does occur among older adults, various other forms of abuse occur, such as emotional abuse, financial abuse, sexual abuse, verbal abuse, and neglect. Some older adults relying on assistance from family members may be unaware that their finances are being misused or that their basic needs are being neglected (Han & Mosqueda, 2020). It is recommended that counselors engage with caregivers when assessing the needs of the older adult patient. As counselors are mandated reporters, older adults are among populations for whom abuse must be reported to the appropriate state and local authorities.

Treatment Approaches

The Substance Abuse and Mental Health Services Administration (SAMHSA, 2020) recommends screening for both SUD and mental illness among older adults, using appropriate tools for both substance use and mental illness. Since older adults may experience mental illness in ways that differ from the general population, specialized tools will be appropriate. These may include the Geriatric Depression Scale, the Geriatric Anxiety Scale, and the Elder Abuse Suspicion Index.

Assessments of co-occurring disorders should also consider age-related disorders whose disease pathway may have elements of cognitive or emotional decline (SAMHSA, 2020). For example, Parkinson's disease may also include symptoms of hallucination and depression (American Psychiatric Association, 2013; Chang et al., 2020; Han et al., 2018). A chronic illness such as chronic obstructive pulmonary disease (COPD), which can be caused or exacerbated by smoking, can be accompanied by symptoms of anxiety (Fuller-Thomson & Lacombe-Duncan, 2016).

Schonfeld and MacFarland (2015) report that isolation and lack of mobility may make it difficult to detect when older adults are misusing substances. This presents challenges in assessment and treatment. They recommend utilizing assessment approaches that consider somatic symptoms (e.g. sleep patterns, hepatic function, speech patterns) and collateral resources that may support more efficient diagnosis and treatment of older adults with co-occurring disorders.

As telehealth becomes more integrated into health care, there are possibilities for older adults to have access to mental health care via this means. However, this may not be a viable option for them due to cost constraints and limits in their ability to use technology. Auditory and visual challenges may also limit their ability to engage in telehealth.

Best Practices

Eden and The Institute of Medicine (U.S.) (2012) recommends a chronic care model since older adults typically experience chronic (rather than acute) disease and benefit most from long-term approaches. The conundrum is that most health and mental health treatment approaches are periodic, episodic, or short term. Older adults need treatment that considers the chronic nature of their illnesses and offers ongoing longer-term care. They also tend to seek treatment most often from a primary care physician (PCP). It is therefore important for the treatment of co-occurring disorders among older adults to consider how to engage not only mental health and SUD treatment partners but also primary care providers. Likewise, the PCPs may benefit from training and incentives to utilize a chronic care model that also integrates co-occurring disorders.

Similarly, Miller et al. (2019) suggest a biopsychosocial (BPS) approach. Although their area of focus was primarily individuals with HIV/AIDS, they focused on the aging population and their ongoing chronic health needs. A BPS approach integrates treatment of the physical health needs (e.g., chronic pain) in a holistic manner that considers the social, cognitive, emotional, and behavioral context of the older adult. This also includes integrating treatment of mental health and substance use. Essentially, the BPS model reflects the need for an integrated approach utilizing a multidisciplinary team; however, for seniors, because of the chronic physical health issues, the primary care providers need to be even more involved.

Schonfeld and MacFarland (2015) indicate the value of a relapse-prevention approach that engages older adults in support groups for people their own age, not age-integrated groups. This approach also focuses on using assessment as a means of identifying not only substance use but also other behaviors that may indicate mental health or other areas for treatment. They recommend a functional behavioral analysis, tools developed for specific use with older adults, an evidence-based approach such as cognitive behavioral therapy or applied behavioral analysis, and individualized treatment.

Best practices involve a coordinated approach to care in which services are easily accessible and consider mobility needs. With older adults, mobility may include not only transportation but also their physical mobility. Those who are located in senior residences or institutions or who are homebound may need an additional layer of services. Including mental health and substance misuse services within these institutions and to individuals at home will help address this need. Services may also include community-based engagements such as adult day programs or senior centers. Health-care institutions may include case management or other wrap-around services specifically for older adults. Agencies or organizations may provide other types of support such as home visits, adopt-a-grandparent programs, and support groups for substance use and mental health needs including trauma, grief, and loss.

Services for Older Adults

It is recommended that counselors become familiar with 211.org and local services to enhance the lives of the older adults they serve.

Conclusion

Older adults, like the rest of the population, are vulnerable to experiencing co-occurring disorders. However, the presence of a co-occurring disorder may go undetected because of difference in presentation, lack of training of clinicians, and lack of coordination of care among treatment professionals. Likewise, their treatment needs often differ from those of the general population and should include age-related developmental or lifespan needs; life experience and culture; assessment that considers physical health, mental health, and substance use; and integration of evidence-based approaches developed for older adults.

Questions for Consideration

1. Why do you suppose the older population born before 1946 will not consider psychotherapy for their co-occurring disorders?
2. What treatment approaches do you feel need to be better developed for the older adult population?
3. What treatment skills are needed for those counselors who wish to work with the older adult population?
4. What special skills does one need to work effectively as a counselor with someone who is not of your culture, religion, gender, or sexual orientation, particularly in the older generation?

Case Study

Daniel sat back on the couch and let out a sigh. He was frustrated. Angry most likely. He had met his counselor today. Why he even needed to see a 27-year-old to talk about his life made him even more frustrated. He had served his country, honorably discharged. He had never complained when he could not keep a job because of his war-related illness. That was what made him begin to drink in the first place. Then came the pills for the pain. But he had held it together for over 30 years. Now his best buddy from those days in the trenches had died, and Daniel felt his life also draining away from him. That was when he began drinking again – a lot – and his children insisted he get help. They had all the right reasons, but young people just did not understand. They were busy with their own families, wanting to pawn him off on this treatment program where there were even more young people. Nobody understood what it is like to grow old and watch your life melting away. The next day, as Daniel walked into the office, Sam smiled, invited him to take a seat, and said, 'Hi, Dan, so good of you to come in today'. Daniel winced. It was going to be a long hour.

Questions to Consider

1. As Daniel's counselor, how can you help him address his concerns about treatment?
2. What are some potential issues from the case study that may need to be included in his care plan?
3. What resources are available to support him and his family?

Resources

There are national resources available for older adults:

U.S. Department of Health and Human Services: www.hhs.gov/programs/social-services/
  programs-for-seniors/index.html
The National Council on Aging: www.ncoa.org/
Eldercare Locator: https://eldercare.acl.gov/Public/About/Aging_Network/Services.aspx
Volunteers Association of America: www.voa.org/older-adults
Elder Abuse | National Institute on Aging: www.nia.nih.gov/health/elder-abuse
Growing Older: Providing Integrated Care for An Aging Population: https://store.samhsa.
  gov/sites/default/files/d7/priv/sma16-4982.pdf
Mental health of older adults – WHO | World Health Organization: www.who.int/news-room/
  fact-sheets/detail/mental-health-of-older-adults
The State of Mental Health and Aging in America: www.cdc.gov/aging/pdf/mental_health.pdf
Working with Older Adults: What mental health providers should know: www.apa.org/pi/
  aging/resources/guides/practitioners-should-know

References

American Psychiatric Association. (2013). *Diagnostic and statistical manual of mental disorders* (5th ed.). American Psychiatric Press.

Bartels, S. J., & Naslund, J. A. (2013). The underside of the silver Tsunami: Older adults and mental health care. *New England Journal of Medicine, 368*, 493–496.

Blackburn, P., Wilkins-Ho, M., & Wiese, B. (2017). Depression in older adults: Diagnosis and management. *British Columbia Medical Journal, 59*(3), 171–177.

Bogunovic, O. (2012). As we are faced with a growing population of older adults, a better understanding of issues they confront is crucial. *Psychiatric Times, 29*(8).

Brooks, J. M., Polenick, C. A., Bryson, W., Naslund, J. A., Renn, B. N., Orzechowski, N. M., . . . Bartels, S. J. (2019). Pain intensity, depressive symptoms, and functional limitations among older adults with serious mental illness. *Aging & Mental Health, 23*(4), 470–474.

Carrola, P., & Corbin-Burdick, M. F. (2015). Counseling military veterans: Advocating for culturally competent and holistic interventions. *Journal of Mental Health Counseling, 37*(1), 1–14.

Chang, Y. P., Lee, M. S., Wu, D. W., Tsai, J. H., Ho, P. S., Lin., C. R., & Chuang, H. Y. (2020, July 27). Risk factors for patients with Parkinson's disease: A nationwide nested case-control study. *PLoS One, 15*(7), 1932–6203. PubMed.

Chhatre, S., Cook, R., Mallik, E., & Jayadevappa, R. (2017). Trends in substance use admissions among older adults. *BMC Health Services Research, 17*, 584–592.

Colliver, J. D., Compton, W. M., Gfroerer, J. C., & Condon, T. (2006). Projecting drug use among aging baby boomers in 2020. *Annals of Epidemiology, 16*(4), 257–265.

Dinitto, D. M., & Choi, N. G. (2011). Marijuana use among older adults in the U.S.A.: User characteristics, patterns of use, and implications for intervention. *International Psychogeriatric, 23*(5), 732–741. doi:10.1017/S1041610210002176

Eden, J., & The Institute of Medicine (U.S.). (2012). *The mental health and substance use workforce for older adults: In whose hands?* National Academies Press.

Evans, C., Hunold, K., Rosen, T., & Platts-Mills, T. (2017). Diagnosis of elder abuse in U.S. emergency departments. *Journal of the American Geriatrics Society, 65*(1), 91–97.

Fahmy, V., Hatch, S. L., Hotopf, M., & Stewart, R. (2012). Prevalences of illicit drug use in people aged 50 years and over from two surveys. *Age Ageing, 41*(4), 553–556. doi:10.1093/ageing/afs020

Fuller-Thomson, E., & Lacombe-Duncan, A. (2016). Understanding the association between chronic obstructive pulmonary disease and current anxiety: A population-based study. *Journal of Chronic Obstructive Pulmonary Disease, 13*(5), 622–631. www.tandfonline.com/doi/full/10.3109/15412555.2015.1132691

Gerberich, S. G., Sidney, S., Braun, B. L., Tekawa, I. S., Tolan, K. K., & Quesenberry, C. P. (2003). Marijuana use and injury events resulting in hospitalization. *Annual Epidemiology, 13*(4), 230–237. doi:10.1016/S10472797(02)00411-8

Han, B. H., Sherman, S., Mauro, P. M., Martins, S. S., Rotenberg, J., & Palamar, J. J. (2017). Demographic trends among older cannabis users in the United States, 2006–13. *Addiction, 112*(3), 516–525. doi:10.1111/add.13670

Han, J. W., Ahn, Y. D., Kim, W., Shin, C. M., Jeong, S. J., Song, Y. S., . . . Kim, J. M. (2018). Psychiatric manifestation in patients with Parkinson's disease. *Journal of Korean Medical Science, 33*(47). doi:10.3346/jkms.2018.33.e300

Han, S. D., & Mosqueda, L. (2020). Elder abuse in the COVID-19 era. *Journal of the American Geriatrics Society, 68*(7), 1386–1387. https://doi.org/10.1111/jgs.16496

Hannaford, S., Shaw, R., & Walker, R. (2018, July). Older adults' perceptions of psychotherapy: What is it and who is responsible? *Australian Psychologist, 54*, 37–45.

Hser, Y., Mooney, L., Saxon, A., Miotto, K., Bell, D., & Huang, D. (2017). Chronic pain among patients with opioid use disorder: Results from electronic health records data. *Journal of Substance Abuse Treatment, 77*, 26–30.

Kostadinov, V., & Roche, A. (2017). Bongs and baby boomers: Trends in cannabis use among older Australians. *Australian Journal on Ageing, 36*(1), 56–59. doi:10.1111/ajag.12357

Lachman, M. (2004). Development in midlife. *Annual Review Psychology, 55*, 303–331.

Mahvan, T. D., Hilaire, M. L., Mann, A., Brown, A., Linn, B., Gardner, T., & Lai, B. (2017). Marijuana use in the elderly: Implications and considerations. *Consultant Pharmacist, 32*(6), 341–351. doi:10.4140/TCP.n.2017.341

Makaroun, L. K., Bachrach, R. L., & Rosland, A. M. (2020). Elder abuse in the time of COVID 19-Increased risks for older adults and their caregivers. *The American Journal of Geriatric Psychiatry, 28*(8), 876–880. https://doi.org/10.1016/j.jagp.2020.05.017

Mather, M., Jacobsen, L. A., & Pollard, K. M. (2015). Population bulletin. *Population Reference Bureau, 70*(2). Retrieved from https://prb.org

Mattson, M., Lipari, R. N., Hays, C., & Van Horn, S. L. (2017). *A day in the life of older adults: Substance use facts.* The CBHSQ Report: May 11, 2017. Center for Behavioral Health Statistics and Quality, Substance Abuse and Mental Health Services Administration.

Mignon, S. (2015). *Substance abuse treatment: Options, challenges, and effectiveness.* Springer Publishing Company.

Miller, T. R., Halkitis, P. N., & Durvasula, R. (2019, March). A biopsychosocial approach to managing HIV-related pain and associated substance abuse among older adults: A review. *Ageing International, 44*(1), 74–116. Complementary Index Database.

Morgen, K., Denison-Vesel, K., Kobylarz, A., & Voelkner, A. (2015). Prevalence of substance use disorder treatment facilities specializing in older adult and trauma care: N-SSATS data 2009 to 2011. *Traumatology, 21*(3), 153–160.

Noel, C. (2017). Evidence for the use of "medical marijuana" in psychiatric and neurologic disorders. *Mental Health Clinician, 7*(1), 29–38. doi:10.9740/mhc.2017.01.029

Onyike, C. U. (2016). Psychiatric aspects of dementia. *Continuum (Minneapolis, Minn.), 22*(2 Dementia), 600–614. https://doi.org/10.1212/CON.0000000000000302

O'Sullivan, A. (2015). Pulled from all sides: The sandwich generation at work. *Work, 50*(3), 491–494.

Powell, J. (2011). *Alcohol and drug abuse issues in older persons as revealed through the comprehensive drug, alcohol, and mental health treatment systems.* Springer Publishing Company.

Preville, M., Tahiri, S. D. M., Vasiliadis, H. M., Quesnel, L., Gontijo-Guerra, S., Lamoureux Lamarche, C., & Berbiche, D. (2015). Association between perceived social stigma against mental disorders and use of health services for psychological distress symptoms in the older adult populations: Validity of the STIG scale. *Aging & Mental Health, 19*(5), 464–474.

Qualls, S. H. (2015). Building competencies in professional geropsychology: Guidelines, training model, and strategies for professional development. In P. A. Areán (Ed.), *Treatment of late-life depression, anxiety, trauma, and substance abuse* (pp. 11–48). American Psychological Association.

Romo, R., Allison, T., Smith, A., & Wallhagen, M. (2017). Sense of control in end-of-life decision making. *Journal of the American Geriatrics Society, 65*(3), 70–75.

Schepis, T. S., McCabe, S. E., & Teter, C. J. (2018). Sources of opioid medication for misuse in older adults: Results from a nationally representative survey. *Pain, 159*(8), 1543–1549. https://doi.org/10.1097/j. pain.0000000000001241

Schonfeld, L., & MacFarland, N. S. (2015). Relapse prevention treatment for substance abuse disorders in older adults. In P. A. Areán (Ed.), *Treatment of late-life depression, anxiety, trauma, and substance abuse* (pp. 211–234). American Psychological Association.

Sedhom, R., & Barile, D. (2017). Teaching our doctors to care for the elderly: A geriatrics needs assessment targeting internal medicine residents. *Gerontology & Geriatric Medicine, 3*, 2333721417701687. https://doi.org/10.1177/2333721417701687

Segal, D. L., Coolidge, F. L., Mincic, M. S., & O'Riley, A. (2005). Beliefs about mental illness and willingness to seek help: A cross-sectional study. *Aging & Mental Health, 9*(4), 363–367.

Substance Abuse and Mental Health Services Administration. (2020). TIP 26: Treating substance use disorder in older adults. *Treatment Improvement Protocol, 26*. Retrieved from https://store.samhsa.gov

Tampi, R. R., & Bennett, A. (2021, January). Benzodiazepine use and the risk of dementia. *Psychiatric Times, 38*(1), 16–18.

Tournier, I., Hanon, C., Vasseur-Bacle, S., Deloyer, J., Moraitou, M., Tzanakis, E., . . . Fond-Harmant, L. (2019). Mental health care networks in older adults: A narrative review. *Journal Plus Education, 25*(2), 179–187.

Vacaflor, B. E., Beauchet, O., Jarvis, G. E., Schavietto, A., & Rej, S. (2020). Mental health and cognition in older cannabis users: A r. *Canadian Geriatrics Journal: CGJ, 23*(3), 242–249. https://doi.org/10.5770/cgj.23.399

Van den Elsen, G.A.H., Ahmed, A.I.A., Lammers, M., Kramers, C., Verkes, R. J., van der Marck, M. G., & OldeRikkert, M.G.M. (2014). Efficacy and safety of medical cannabinoids in older subjects: A systematic review. *Ageing Research Review, 14*, 56–64. doi:10.1016/j.arr.2014.01.007

Walsh, Z., Gonzalez, R., Crosby, K., Thiessen, M. S., Carroll, C., & Bonn-Miller, M. O. (2017). Medical cannabis and mental health: A guided systematic review. *Clinical Psychological Review, 51*, 15–29. doi:10.1016/j.cpr.2016.10.002

Whitlatch, C. J, & Orsulic-Jeras, M. A. (2018). Meeting the informational, educational, and psychosocial support needs of persons living with dementia and their family caregivers, *The Gerontologist, 58*(1), 58–73. https://doi.org/10.1093/geront/gnx162

Williamson, E. M., & Evans, F. J. (2000). Cannabinoids in clinical practice. *Drugs, 60*(6), 1303–1314. doi:10.2165/00003495-200060060-00005

Wu, L. T., & Blazer, D. G. (2011). Illicit and nonmedical drug use among older adults: A review. *Journal of Aging and Health, 23*(3), 481–504.

11 LGBTQIA+ and Co-occurring Disorders

Fredrick Dombrowski

Introduction

Although the exact data is not known, the number of adults in the United States who identify as LGBT is pushing 10 million. There are concerns that this data may be inaccurate as stigma may prevent individuals from disclosing their sexual preferences or gender identity. Roughly 19 million Americans have reported engaging in at least some same-sex sexual behavior while roughly 26 million Americans have acknowledged some form of same-sex attraction (American Psychiatric Association, 2017). While a heavy emphasis is placed on cultural humility and culturally sensitive treatment, all counselors benefit from challenging their own perspectives and bias when working with clients from the lesbian, gay, bisexual, transgender, queer/questioning, intersex, and asexual (LGBTQIA) communities. As members of the LGBTQIA communities have fought to obtain the same rights as their straight and cisgender counterparts, there remains a lack of knowledge of appropriate treatment approaches and considerations when working with LGBTQIA clients (Overby, 2014). This lack of knowledge in treatment providers has caused many LGBTQIA individuals to avoid treatment (Spack, 2013). In the event that LGBTQIA individuals did obtain treatment, many reported their role as a primary educator to their treatment provider as providers lacked LGBTQIA-specific knowledge (Teich, 2012).

In this chapter, we will discuss factors that are facing LGBTQIA populations, as well as addressing how institutional stigmas continue to permeate programs causing inadequate treatment for co-occurring disorders. This chapter will also provide knowledge to differentiate the needs of members of the LGBTQIA communities. This chapter will review factors specific to co-occurring treatment and discuss potential treatment options. Finally, we will review the benefits of social supports and provide information regarding national supports for the LGBTQIA communities.

Learning Objectives

* Identify the role of institutional stigma in influencing treatment provision
* Review co-occurring disorders that exist among LGBTQIA individuals
* Identify factors associated with increased mental health and substance use diagnoses
* Provide evidence and recommendations for appropriate treatment considerations
* Provide lists of national support services available for LGBTQIA individuals

Key Terms

Androgyny: A person with masculine and feminine physical traits
Asexual: An individual who lacks sexual attraction or a desire for partnered sexuality
Bisexual: An individual who experiences sexual attraction to those of the same and other genders
Cisgender: An individual whose gender identity is the same as their sex assigned at birth.

DOI: 10.4324/9781003220916-13

Gay: Traditionally used for men, describes those who have a primary sexual attraction to those who share their gender.

Gender Dysphoria: *DSM-5* diagnosis indicating that an individual has a gender identity not the same as their assigned birth sex (APA, 2013). Many of those in this category have experienced limitations in their ability to function effectively as the disconnect between their sense of self and assigned sex causes one or more areas of their life to not reach maximum potential. The diagnosis provides the individual an opportunity to be linked with adjunct services, to assist in gender transition such as hormone replacement therapy, official name and identification changes, and potential surgeries. Having an identity not the same as the sex assigned at birth is not the focus of this diagnosis. Rather, the dysphoria caused by this is the clinical focus.

Gender Fluid: An individual whose gender identity shifts from traits associated with assigned birth sex and traits associated with other genders.

Gender Nonconforming: People who do not adhere to societal expectations of gender role and expression.

Intersex: An individual born with a mix of traditionally male and female anatomy without any medical intervention. In some instances, the outer anatomy will not be consistent with the inner anatomy traditionally associated with the individual's interpreted sex. In some cases, the individual may have cells that have XX chromosomes and other cells that have XY chromosomes.

Lesbian: Term used to describe women who show primary sexual attraction to other women.

Microaggressions: Brief and commonplace daily verbal, behavioral, or environmental indignities, whether intentional or unintentional, that communicate hostile, derogatory, or negative slights and insults about one's marginalized identity/identities (Sue et al., 2019).

Queer: A self-identification indicating that the individual has multiple aspects and identities that are outside the traditional cisgender and heterosexual norms.

Questioning: Exploring one's romantic attractions, gender identity, or gender expression.

Unique Groups

Often when clinicians consider the needs of people who identify as LGBTQIA, they will lump these diverse populations into one group with homogeneous needs, beliefs, cultural values, and preferences. However, each individual population has diversity of culture, members with varying political ideologies, varied spiritual perspectives, and specific needs. For example, a woman who identifies as lesbian will have needs that are not shared by an individual who identifies as gay. People who identify as bisexual have reported their own experiences in which they may have felt invalidated by gay or lesbian individuals who feel that a bisexual is just a gay person lying to themselves and trying to maintain a somewhat heterosexual lifestyle (Bostwick, 2012). An individual who experiences gender dysphoria may be inadvertently lumped with those with hetero-variant sexualities. However, experiencing gender dysphoria is not related to the sexuality of the individual (Alegria & Ballard-Reish, 2013). In other words, a transgender person does not transition to a gender other than their birth sex because of preference of sexual attraction but rather as a result of living with gender dysphoria. The needs of intersex individuals are entirely separate from those of other groups as those who are born intersex have a biological mix of male and female chromosomes that impact the development of primary and secondary sex characteristics (Griffiths, 2018). To fully explore the needs of each group represented in this chapter, full texts on each group would provide the most comprehensive review. The purpose of this chapter is to discuss commonalities shared among these communities.

In some instances, the LGBTQIA populations may be addressed as LGBT, LGBTQ+, or LGBTQIA. For the purpose of this chapter, LGBTQIA will be used.

Institutional Stigma

Currently best recommendations for treatment of LGBTQIA individuals requires all clinicians to become aware of their own views of and bias regarding members of these communities (Levounis et al., 2012). Traditional religious and cultural norms have rejected these groups, causing members to be disowned by their families, children, friends, spiritual supports, and careers (Kuper et al., 2014). Despite moves to validate the experiences of these communities, ongoing stigmas persist within mental health treatment programs. These stigmas have contributed to barriers to members of the LGBTQIA communities receiving treatment for co-occurring disorders.

Despite changes in the *Diagnostic and Statistical Manual* 5th edition (APA, 2013), institutional stigma in mental health treatment has been established as the previous versions of the *DSM* stated that homosexuality, non-heterosexism, and a gender identity outside an individual's assigned sex at birth were diagnosable mental health disorders (APA, 1952). As a result of previous assumptions about LGBTQIA individuals, many treatment providers attempted to engage in treatment preventing the individual from having a sexual attraction outside the realm of heterosexuality or having a gender identity outside cisgender norms and expectations. Many treatment strategies, including conversion therapy, were used to help treat sexualities and gender identities that were outside heterosexual and cisgender norms. These treatment attempts caused individuals to feel more alienated, increased depression, increased substance use, internalized homophobia and transphobia, and often contributed to an increase in suicide attempts and suicide completions (Goodrich et al., 2017). In the third version of the *DSM* (APA, 1980) homosexuality was removed as a diagnosable disorder. Changes in the *DSM* regarding homosexuality were muddied as many clinicians struggled to conceptualize sexuality from a non-binary perspective.

The difficulty conceptualizing gender dysphoria and those having a gender identity outside their assigned sex or outside the binary has been consistent throughout previous versions of the *DSM* (APA, 1952, 1980, 1990). Identifications such as transvestic fetishism and associations with gender expression and sexuality were prevalent in the *DSM*s I and II. Changes occurred in the *DSM-III* as the term 'transsexualism' was used as a diagnosis. However, this diagnosis was specifically for those who had a gender identity that was not traditionally associated with their assigned sex at birth and gender identity from childhood. Being placed in the disorders specifically related to childhood invalidated those individuals who experienced a later onset of dysphoria. The changes in the *DSM-IV* recognized the experiences of both children and adults, officially changing the diagnosis to gender identity disorder, with a specification for children and/or adults (APA, 1990). The use of the word 'disorder', however, implied that the individual's gender identity was wrong as they did not comply with the expectations of the assigned birth sex. Although this term maintained stigma regarding those living with gender dysphoria, it also helped establish the expectations and conditions associated with gender transition and best practices of clinical treatment as identified win the *Harry Benjamin International Gender Dysphoria Association Standards of Care* now known as the *World Professional Association for Transgender Health Standards of Care (WPATH)*. As ongoing research was conducted on those experiencing gender dysphoria, the *WPATH* recommendations for transgender treatment became more flexible and specific to the individual (Coleman et al., 2011).

In an attempt to destigmatize the experiences of this population, the *DSM-5* (APA, 2013) changed the diagnosis from gender identity disorder to gender dysphoria. The changes in this diagnosis were meant to highlight the belief that having a gender identity outside one's assigned birth sex in itself is not the disorder, but rather the dysphoria and disconnected feelings that the individual experiences as consequences of this identity. The attempt to destigmatize the experience of transgender, gender-fluid, and gender-nonconforming individuals also provides the benefit of an official diagnosis of gender dysphoria, making treatments such as hormone replacement therapy and some surgeries coverable by insurance carriers. The actual term 'gender dysphoria' may have been changed to end stigmatization, but common inaccurate beliefs about transgender individuals and the assumptions that an individual will transition to a different sex based solely on sexual fetishism persist (Alegria & Ballard-Reish, 2013).

Co-Occurring Disorders in the LGBTQIA Communities

It is no wonder that members of the LGBTQIA populations are at higher risk for mental health and substance use disorders as roughly 40% have reported being disconnected from their families and support system as a result of disclosing their sexual preferences and/or gender identity (Pew Research Center, 2013). LGBTQIA individuals experience depression, anxiety, and substance use disorder at a rate of roughly 2.5 times greater than their cisgender and heterosexual counterparts (APA, 2017). Members of these groups are much more likely to consider suicide than those who are cisgender or heterosexual. Roughly 30% of transgender individuals have considered suicide, and roughly 40% of the entire LGBTQIA population has identified experiencing a mental health disorder within the past year (Anxiety and Depression Association of America, 2017; NAMI, 2020). Members from the LGBTQIA communities who are not from Caucasian backgrounds experience more victimization, mental health disorders, and substance use than Caucasian members of the LGBTQIA communities (APA, 2017). The data suggests that members of the LGBTQIA communities are at higher risk for co-occurring disorders, although treatment centers are limited in their expertise in helping these populations (Baams et al., 2015).

A survey conducted by SAMHSA (2016) concluded that those who identify as sexual minorities have reported increased substance use compared to sexual majorities. The survey found that sexual minorities used cocaine, heroin, hallucinogens, opiates, prescription drugs, and inhalants at higher rates than sexual majorities. Sexual minority populations were found to have greater percentages of those living with alcohol use disorder, substance use disorder, and opiate use disorder than sexual majorities. The percentage of sexual minorities who meet criteria for substance use treatment (for any substance) is higher than the percentage of sexual majorities.

Members of the LGBTQIA communities experience ongoing disconnection from their families and supports while living in a heteronormative/cisgender Westernized society that has traditionally invalidated the experiences of these populations (Bartoş et al., 2014). Ongoing minority stress coupled with open homophobia and transphobia contribute to increased risk of depression, anxiety, and other mental health disorders (Hughes, 2017). As members of the LGBTQIA communities may feel disconnected from service providers, they may turn to alcohol and drug use to cope with these experiences. As a result, research has indicated that members of these communities experience higher co-occurring substance use and mental health disorders than sexual majority populations.

Factors Related to Co-occurring Disorders for LGBTQIA Populations

Members of the LGBTQIA communities face multiple roadblocks to mental wellness and sobriety as they are living in a heteronormative gender-binary culture (Baams et al., 2015). LGBTQIA communities face higher rates of physical assault, bullying, and discrimination than their heterosexual and cisgender counterparts (Levounis et al., 2012). Within these communities, those who are from marginalized backgrounds and those with physical and or intellectual disabilities will experience increased isolation, thoughts of suicide, and feelings of disconnection from the world around them (Brechwald & Prinstein, 2011). Finally, adult members of the LGBTQIA populations experience a higher risk of homelessness and unstable living environments (NAMI, 2020).

The stress associated with these groups exists in adolescents as members will experience bullying, marginalization, assault, lack of support, and even hate crimes (Levounis et al., 2012). With multiple stressors placed on them, a focus on academic development and prosocial behaviors can be impeded for members of these groups as isolation and substance use become coping strategies from an early age. Many schools have worked to create inclusive environments for LGBTQIA youth, providing safe spaces away from bullying, varying bathroom options, and acceptance on sports teams of the identified gender of the student. However, these steps are not universal, and inclusion alone does not fully stop the harassment of LGBTQIA youth (Diamond et al., 2011). In the high school and adolescent cultures, ongoing invalidating language such as 'That's so gay' or 'She looks like a man' continues to send messages of disconnection and disapproval to these populations, although schools try to limit such behaviors (Chonody et al., 2012; Duncan & Hatzenbuehler, 2014). For minority LGBQIA students living in urban centers, the lack of funds associated with scholastic or other activities further contributes to isolation and limits the ability to create bonds with other students (Burns et al., 2015). Additional limits to mental health treatment and inappropriate cultural competence within these areas drives a further wedge between the individual and the treatment provider (Fernando, 2012).

The problems associated with LGBTQIA populations are not limited to adolescents and adults; even seniors within these populations experience disparities compared to their cisgender and heterosexual counterparts (Levounis et al., 2012). Senior LGBTQIA populations experience exacerbated feelings of isolation as those from previous generations have tended to be more intolerant to LGBTQIA communities, and people who may have been comfortably open about their gender identity or sexuality may have been placed 'back in the closet', attempting to pass as heteronormative in shared living spaces (Stevens et al., 2018). Seniors in LGBTQIA populations experience increased loneliness as they may not feel comfortable engaging in activities with other seniors. LGBTQIA seniors also face struggles to connect as they may not be able to navigate current social media software (Hughes, 2017).

Treatment Recommendations

Members of the LGBTQIA populations have been willing to seek mental health and substance use disorders treatment (NAMI, 2020), although treatment centers have fallen behind in providing informed care. There are a multitude of recommendations that can be made to create a treatment environment that is fully inclusive for these populations. Recommendations to improve treatment of the LGBTQIA populations range from the micro (internal responses of treatment providers) to macro (formal policies and legislative advocacy). For co-occurring disorders treatment, it is important for clinicians to be aware of available community and national resources for these populations.

Considering the internal experience of clinicians working with LGBTQIA populations, providers may experience countertransference in several ways (Levounis et al., 2012). A treatment provider may feel uncomfortable when discussing LGBTQIA-related issues, or in some instances, those who belong to LGBTQIA communities may overidentify with those for whom they are providing treatment. Balancing and recognizing the clinician's internal responses while also placing an emphasis on patient goals and showing a sincere willingness to learn about and appreciate the experience of the patient are key to providing care within the cultural humility perspective (Goodrich et al., 2017). Many clinicians may have belief systems that seem contradictory to the experiences of LGBTQIA communities. Despite the belief system of the clinician, every patient deserves 100% clinically appropriate care and also is entitled to the best care from the clinician, despite personal thoughts, feelings, and beliefs.

To assess a clinician's readiness to work with members of the LGBTQIA communities, they can complete the *Self-Assessment Checklist for Personnel Providing Services and Supports to LGBTQ Youth and Their Families* (Georgetown University Center for Child and Human Development, 2012). This checklist assesses the attitudes and values of clinicians by asking them to rate how often they engage in certain behaviors. Some of the behaviors concern personal interactions (using preferred pronouns), agency-related issues (such as having affirming LGBTQ policies), and macro issues such as advocating on behalf of patients and their families. A copy of this assessment can be found at the following link:

https://nccc.georgetown.edu/documents/Final%20LGBTQ%20Checklist.pdf

Many treatment providers may struggle to ask questions related to sexuality and gender expression (Levounis et al., 2012). Avoiding such discussions will prevent the clinician from being fully aware of the experience of the patient while also invalidating the patient experience. Asking questions from a treatment perspective must be done with respect and unconditional positive regard, creating an environment that is conducive to treatment. Clinical supervisors are expected to provide LGBTQIA training and support to frontline staff while also preventing worsening stigma within a treatment center.

To create an inclusive treatment environment, it is recommended that visible posters indicating commitment to the treatment of LGBTQIA communities be present in waiting rooms. Resources such as pamphlets, workbooks, and community services for LGBTQIA patients should be readily available in the treatment program. This will require agency workers to be knowledgeable of and build relationships with local LGBTQIA resources. In the absence of local resources, national resources are also available, and information regarding these resources will be provided at the end of this chapter. To further provide LGBTQIA-competent care, it is recommended that an agency at least have a liaison who specializes in the treatment of these populations (Coleman et al., 2012). The liaison can provide LGBTQIA-specific treatment groups and use informed evidence-based practices for individual sessions. Having this liaison assists in the clinical development of and competence of other clinicians in the treatment of LBTQIA groups.

Figure 11.1 shows a positive space poster that signifies the areas to be affirming of LGBTQIA+ identities while also inferring that staff are committed to respect of and advocacy for these groups.

Figure 11.1 Positive Space Poster for the LGBTQ Community

Community and National Supports

Considering the isolation and stigma experienced by members of the LGBTQIA communities, it is recommended that members be linked to community and national resources for support and peer connection (Bartos et al., 2014). Many midsize-to-large cities have community providers for LGBTQIA populations. To find such resources, a clinician can log on to 211.org and submit the patient's town of residence to find the closest services. In remote and rural areas where these resources are lacking, clinicians should be aware of national agencies as well as groups that can be accessed remotely via social media. The following is a list of national LGBTQIA supports:

> The Trevor Project: Providing 24-hour crisis assistance to LGBTQIA youth via telephone and online at 1-866-488-7386 and www.thetrevorproject.org/
> Family Equality: Advocating for equal rights for same-sex couples and families. Available at www.familyequality.org/
> The LGBT National Help Center: Providing free and confidential support and connection to local resources. Available at www.glnh.org/
> PFLAG: Providing national support and advocacy. Available at https://pflag.org/
> Transgender Law: Providing legal connection to services and advocacy. Available at https://transgenderlawcenter.org/

Conclusion

Members of the LGBTQIA populations are at higher risk for substance use and mental health disorders. Members of these groups experience multiple roadblocks, enhancing minority stress and increasing depression and anxiety, which often causes the individual to self-medicate using alcohol or other substances. The treatment needs of these groups are different from their cisgender and heterosexual peers. LGBTQIA youth, adults, and seniors are provided with treatment options that often don't validate these populations. Treatment centers must work to promote LGBTQIA-sensitive care ranging from providers who practice cultural humility to agency policy providing appropriate access to basic needs such as bathrooms and validating language used by staff. Treatment providers can enhance their programs by having access to local and national LGBTQIA supports as well as creating a welcoming environment through the use of visible posters. Clinicians benefit from linking LGBTQIA patients with appropriate community supports as needed. It is essential that providers are aware of and build a connection with such supports.

Questions for Consideration

1. Stigma prevents many people from seeking clinical help for mental health and substance use disorders. What additional layers of stigma may prevention LGBTQIA people in your community from seeking help?
2. What additional trainings and/or local resources may be needed to best serve this growing population?
3. As you consider the limitations of many treatment providers in your area, it may not be realistic to have LGBTQIA treatment groups. How would an integrated group be beneficial? How might an integrated group limit honestly, self-expression, and treatment?

Case Study

Chris is a 26-year-old person who has struggled with drugs, alcohol, and depression since adolescence. During the assessment, the counselor seemed open and non-judgmental but did not ask about gender identity or sexuality. Chris was hesitant to share anything outside of the basic questions due to unpredictable responses when sharing with people in the past. After the assessment, group treatment was recommended in an outpatient program that meets three times a week. Chris put on a public face and went to group treatment. While sitting in the group before the first session, Chris overheard a few of the other group members talking about the counselor.

> Group member #1 – 'I think the counselor is gay. Did you see her wife was here?'
> Group member #2 – 'How could you tell?'
> Group member #1 – 'She/he was dressed like a man'.
> Group member #2 – 'Gays are so weird. Why do they need to get married; what is the point?'

As the counselor walked into the group space, Chris stood up and walked toward the door, stating, 'I don't feel like this is the right place for me'.

Questions

1. 'I don't think this is the right place for me'. What is Chris really saying?
2. What immediate clinical concerns do you have for Chris?
3. Does this mean that Chris is not a good fit for group counseling? How could treatment have been better tailored to Chris' needs?

Recommended Reading

Beatti, M., Lenihan, P., & Dundas, R. (2018). *Counseling skills for working with gender diversity and identity*. Philadelphia, PA: Kingsley Publishers. ISBN-13: 978–1785927416
Ginicola, M., Smith, C., & Filmore, J. (2017). *Affirmative counseling with LGBTQI+ people*. Alexandria, VA: Wiley Publishing. ISBN: 978–1556203558
Wolters, L. (2020). *Voices of LGBTQ+: A conversation starter for understanding, supporting, and protecting gay, bi, trans, and queer people*. Herndon, VA: Mascot Books. ISBN: 9781645431480

References

Alegria, C., & Ballard-Reish, D. (2013). Gender expression as a reflection of identity reformation in couple partners following disclosure of male-to-female transsexualism. *International Journal of Transgenderism*, *14*(2), 49–65.
American Psychiatric Association. (1952). *Diagnostic and statistical manual of mental disorders* (1st ed.). Author.
American Psychiatric Association. (1980). *Diagnostic and statistical manual of mental disorders* (3rd ed.). Author.
American Psychiatric Association. (1990). *Diagnostic and statistical manual of mental disorders* (4th ed.). Author.
American Psychiatric Association. (2013). *Diagnostic and statistical manual of mental disorders* (5th ed., text rev.). Author.
American Psychiatric Association. (2017). *Mental health disparities: LGBTQ*. American Psychiatric Association.
Anxiety and Depression Association of America. (2017). Retrieved from https://adaa.org/find-help/by-demographics/lgbtq#Facts
Baams, L., Bos, H. M., & Jonas, K. J. (2014). How a romantic relationship can protect same-sex attracted youth and young adults from the impact of expected rejection. *Journal of Adolescence*, *37*, 1293–1302.
Baams, L., Grossman, A., & Russell, S. (2015). Minority stress and mechanisms of risk for depression and suicidal ideation among lesbian, gay, and bisexual youth. *Developmental Psychology*, *51*, 688–696.
Bartoş, S. E., Berger, I., & Hegarty, P. (2014). Interventions to reduce sexual prejudice: A study-space analysis and meta-analytic review. *Journal of Sex Research*, *51*, 363–382. doi:10.1080/00224499.2013.871625
Bostwick, W. (2012). Assessing bisexual stigma and mental health status: A brief report. *The Journal of Bisexuality*, *12*(2), 214–222. doi:10.1080/15299716.2012.674860

Brechwald, W., & Prinstein, M. (2011). Beyond homophily: A decade of advances in understanding peer influence processes. *Journal of Research on Adolescents, 21*, 166–179.

Burns, M., Ryan, D., Garofalo, R., Newcomb, M., & Mustanski, B. (2015). Mental health disorders in young urban sexual minority men. *Journal of Adolescent Health, 56*, 52–58.

Chauvin, I., McDaniel, J., Banks, A., Eddlemon, O., & Cook, L. (2013). Writing a commemoration: A technique for restoring equilibrium after a crisis. *Journal of Creativity in Mental Health, 8*(4), 416–427.

Chonody, J. M., Kavanagh, P., & Woodford, M. (2016). Does closeness to someone who is gay, lesbian, or bisexual influence etiology beliefs about homosexuality? *Journal of Homosexuality, 63*(12), 1726–1748.

Chonody, J. M., Rutledge, S. E., & Smith, K. S. (2012). "That's so gay": Language use and sexual prejudice. *Journal of Gay and Lesbian Social Services, 24*, 241–259.

Coleman, E., Bockting, W., Botzer, M., Cohen-Kettenis, P., DeCuypere, G., Feldman, J., . . . Zucker, K. (2012). Standards of care for the health of transsexual, transgender, and gender-nonconforming people: Version 7. *International Journal of Transgenderism, 13*, 165–232.

Cunningham, G. B., & Melton, E. N. (2013). The moderating effects of contact with lesbian and gay friends on the relationship among religious fundamentalism, sexism, and sexual prejudice. *Journal of Sex Research, 50*, 401–408. doi:10.1080/00224499.2011.648029

Diamond, G. M., Diamond, G. S., Levy, S., Closs, C., Ladipo, T., & Siqueland, L. (2012). Attachment-based family therapy for suicidal lesbian, gay, and bisexual adolescents: A treatment development study and open trial with preliminary findings. *Psychotherapy, 49*, 62–71.

Diamond, G. M., Shilo, G., Jurgensen, E., D'Augelli, A., Samarova, V., & White, K. (2011). How depressed and suicidal sexual minority adolescents understand the causes of their distress. *Journal of Gay and Lesbian Mental Health, 15*, 130–151.

Duncan, D., & Hatzenbuehler, M. (2014). Lesbian, gay, bisexual, and transgender hate crimes and suicidality among a population-based sample of sexual-minority adolescents in Boston. *American Journal of Public Health, 104*, 272–278.

Fernando, S. (2012). Race and culture issues in mental health and some thoughts on ethnic identity. *Counseling Psychology Quarterly, 25*(2), 113–123.

Fishman, S. L., Paliou, M., Poretsky, L., & Hembree, W. C. (2019). Endocrine care of transgender adults. In L. Poretsky & W. Hembree (Eds.), *Transgender medicine: Contemporary endocrinology*. Humana Press.

Frias-Navarro, D., Monterde-i-Bort, H., Pascual-Soler, M., & Badenes-Ribera, L. (2015). Etiology of homosexuality and attitudes toward same-sex parenting: A randomized study. *Journal of Sex Research, 52*, 151–161. doi:10.1080/00224499.2013.802757.

Georgetown University Center for Child and Human Development. (2012). *Self-assessment checklist for personnel providing services and supports to LGBTQ youth and their families*. National Center for Cultural Competence. Retrieved from https://nccc.georgetown.edu/documents/Final%20LGBTQ%20Checklist.pdf

Goodrich, K., Farmer, L., Watson, J., Davis, R., Luke, M., Dispenza, F., . . . Griffith, K. (2017). Standards of care in assessment of lesbian, gay, bisexual, transgender, gender expansive, and queer/questioning (LGBTGEQ+) persons. *Journal of LGBT Issues in Counseling, 4*, 203–211.

Griffiths, D. (2018). Shifting syndromes: Sex chromosome variations and intersex classifications. *Social Studies of Science, 48*(1), 125–148.

Hughes, M. (2017). Loneliness and the health and well-being of LGBT seniors. *Innovation in Aging, 1*, 606–612. doi:10.1093/geroni/igx004.2122

Kuper, L. E., Coleman, B. R., & Mustanski, B. S. (2014). Coping with LGBT and racial-ethnic-related stressors: A mixed-methods study of LGBT youth of color. *Journal of Research on Adolescence, 24*, 703–719.

Levounis, P., Drescher, J., & Barber, M. (2012). *The LGBT casebook*. American Psychiatric Association Publishing.

Lewis, J., Ratts, M., Paladino, D., & Toporek, R. (2011). Social justice counseling and advocacy: Developing new leadership roles and competencies. *Journal for Social Action in Counseling and Psychology, 3*(1), 5–16.

Marshal, M. P., Dietz, L. J., Friedman, M. S., Stall, R., & Smith, H. A. (2011). Suicidality and depression disparities between sexual minority and heterosexual youth: A meta-analytic review. *Journal of Adolescent Health, 49*, 115–123. Comprehensive meta-analysis of studies of depression and suicidality among sexual minority youth.

Medley, G., Lipari, R. N., Bose, J., Cribb, D. S., Kroutil, L. A., & McHenry, G. (2015). Sexual orientation and estimates of adult substance use and mental health: Results from the 2015 national survey on drug use and health. *SAMHSA Data Review*. Retrieved from www.samhsa.gov/data/sites/default/files/NSDUH-SexualOrientation-2015/NSDUH-SexualOrientation-2015/NSDUH-SexualOrientation-2015.htm

Mitchell, R. W., & Dezarn, L. (2014). Does knowing why someone is gay influence tolerance? Genetic, environmental, choice, and "reparative" explanations. *Sexuality & Culture, 18*, 994–1009. doi:10.1007/s12119-014-9233-6

Mustanski, B., Birkett, M., Greene, G. J., Hatzenbuehler, M. L., & Newcomb, M. E. (2014). Envisioning an America without sexual orientation inequities in adolescent health. *American Journal of Public Health, 104*, 218–225.

National Alliance on Mental Illness. (2020). *LGBTQIA*. Retrieved from https://www.nami.org/Your-Journey/Identity-and-Cultural-Dimensions/LGBTQI

Overby, L. M. (2014). Etiology and attitudes: Beliefs about the origins of homosexuality and their implications for public policy. *Journal of Homosexuality, 61*(4), 568–587.

Pew Research Center. (2013). *A survey of LGBT Americans*. Social and Demographic Trends. Retrieved from www.pewsocialtrends.org/2013/06/13/a-survey-of-lgbt-americans/

Russell, S., & Fish, J. (2016). Mental health in Lesbian, Gay, Bisexual, and Transgender (LGBT) youth. *Annual Review of Clinical Psychology, 12*, 465–487.

Spack, N. P. (2013). Management of transgenderism. *JAMA, 309*(5), 478–484.

Stevens, G., Nguyen, T., & Fajardo, F. (2018). LGBT senior health disparities: Information resources to bridge the gap. *Journal of Consumer Health on the Internet, 22*(2), 150–157. https://doi.org/10.1080/15398285.2018.1451143

Substance Abuse and Mental Health Services Administration. (2016). *Sexual minorities: 2015–2016 NSDUH Summary Sheet*. Retrieved from https://www.samhsa.gov/data/report/2015-2016-nsduh-sexual-orientation-summary-sheets

Sue, D. W., Sue, D., Neville, H. A., & Smith, L. (2019). *Counselling the culturally diverse* (8th ed.). Wiley Publishing.

Teich, N. (2012). *Transgender 101: A simple guide to a complex issue*. Columbia University Press.

Tomita, K. K., Testa, R. J., & Balsam, K. F. (2019). Gender-affirming medical interventions and mental health in transgender adults. *Psychology of Sexual Orientation and Gender Diversity, 6*(2), 182–193. https://doi.org/10.1037/sgd0000316

12 Multicultural Perspectives in Co-occurring Treatment

Natasha Chung, Karlene Barrett, and Tara G. Matthews

Introduction

Therapeutic efficacy depends on professional competence. Multicultural competence and perspective involve the provision of culturally competent services that allow therapy to be effective. In order to explore this topic, it is important to acknowledge that most therapists have good intentions when it comes to learning about and accepting the cultural differences of others. While good intentions are a place to start, they are not linked to therapeutic efficacy (Rogers-Sirin et al., 2015). Multicultural perspectives begin with an openness to reflect on self and to learning from others. The focus of this chapter is to increase awareness of multicultural issues in dual diagnosis treatment and to link personal awareness to clinical skills so that the therapists do not simply think that they are culturally effective practitioners but so that clients experience the therapist as being effective as well.

Learning Objectives

- Identify and explore the benefits of approaching clinical treatment from the perspective of cultural humility to meet the needs of a diverse clientele
- Identify the ways in which diverse populations experience co-occurring disorders
- Identify how minority stress and systemic racism can contribute to the development of various mental health and substance use diagnoses
- Identify ways of advocating to meet the needs of marginalized individuals
- Explore clinical tools that can enhance the therapeutic alliance between the counselor and clients of various cultural and ethnic backgrounds

Key Terms

Bias: A preference, especially an unfair or preconceived one, for something or someone compared to another.

Culture: Includes the dynamic pattern of knowledge, shared behavior, common interactions, social norms, and characteristics acquired by socialization within a group of people.

Cultural Influence: Any individual or series of familial, environmental, historical, societal, or geographical factor(s) that impact the client and that might affect the process of assessment and intervention.

Culturally Responsive Treatment: The capacity of practitioners to consider cultural and social factors in assessment and treatment, including client culture, practitioner culture, and how the two might interact to impact the therapeutic relationship.

Ethnicity: Groups that share language, culture, or other identity-based ancestry, including migration patterns, religion, customs, and beliefs.

DOI: 10.4324/9781003220916-14

Implicit Bias: Can occur when individuals unknowingly harbor attitudes toward or associate stereotypes with a social group. This form of bias can be acquired at a young age and is the result of social learning and conditioning.

Multicultural Competence: A professional skill set that includes behavior, attitudes, ongoing education and exposure, and the use of evidence-based practice that facilitates successful work and practice among more than one cultural dimension.

Race: A system of social categorization related to skin color and other phenotypical characteristics. Racial taxonomies are not valid at the DNA level. The definition of race varies from culture to culture.

Reflective Local Practice: A practical framework that can be used in training and practice to improve cultural competence. This approach emphasizes personal insight, skills training, and the utilization of local and historical resources.

Self-Evaluation: The ability or skill to look at one's own development, progress, and learning in order to determine personal strengths and needs.

Transtheoretical Model of the Stages of Change: A model of intentional behavioral change that focuses on six stages of change that individuals move through over time. This model assumes that people change behaviors gradually, in steps.

Importance of Clinician Competency in Treating Individuals From a Multicultural Perspective

The population of the United States has become more diverse in the past few decades than in any other period of its history, and this trend is projected to continue. According to the US Census Bureau (2015), in the next 25 years, the population is expected to comprise more than 50% non-white Americans. By 2060, it is projected that approximately 20% of the population will comprise foreign-born individuals. This means that racial and ethnic diversity is increasingly becoming the norm. Socio-cultural and generational factors also play a role in the diversity of clientele, and no two clients will experience their lives the same way. Effective treatment approaches should reflect this.

Racial and ethnic differences are one way to understand diversity. Within each racial and ethnic group, there are also different practices, languages/dialects, and nuances of culture. Likewise, there are differences based on the level of acculturation of families and individuals or whether they are first-, second-, or third-generation Americans. Economic experiences of a client's upbringing will also play a role in their experiences. A multicultural perspective accepts and respects that these differences are important to the persons and groups involved, as well as to effective professional practice.

Results from the National Epidemiologic Survey on Alcohol and Related Conditions (NESARC) indicate that access to and use of mental health and substance use treatment services vary along ethnic and non-white group lines (Le Cook et al., 2017). Blacks and Latinos are less likely to receive treatment for co-occurring disorders (Nam et al., 2017). Disparities in access to and utilization of treatment may be impacted by the types of treatment available and economic inequalities, and different ethnic groups may prefer or utilize different types of treatment modalities. Ethnic groups may face discrimination, lack of access to quality mental health treatment, and cultural stigma or stereotyping about mental illness. There are also significant deficits in service delivery by clinicians who do not understand ethnic diversity, and these include possible misdiagnosis and inappropriate treatment (American Psychiatric Association, 2019).

Prevalence of Co-occurring Disorders in Multicultural Populations

According to the 2013 NSDUH report of individuals 12 years or older, the rate of illegal drug use differs among different ethnic and racial groups, as does the rate of treatment use (SAMHSA,

2013). The occurrence of mental illness also varies, along with how each group may experience symptoms and be motivated to seek treatment. In the US in 2017, there were 8.5 million persons (or 3.4% of population) who had a co-occurring disorder (SAMHSA, 2018). However, co-occurring disorders also vary among different ethnic groups. Mericle, Ta, Holck, and Arria (2012) found the following incidence of a lifetime co-occurring disorder: Whites 8.2%, Blacks 5.4%, Hispanics 5.8%, and Asians 2.1%. Using a multicultural perspective, one might question whether proper diagnosis and access to treatment have influenced these statistics.

Ethnic and racial minorities do not have the same access to treatment as the majority race, and treatment is frequently not tailored to their specific needs (American Psychiatric Association, 2019). But competency in multicultural treatment also must include other groups that are defined not by ethnicity or race, but by being unlike or other than ourselves. This approach can eliminate the majority-minority perspective and embrace a more holistic approach that encourages us to step outside the comfort zone of what we know based only on who we are. It motivates us to explore and engage in the lived experience of others from their unique cultural perspective.

Multicultural Dimensions

In 2002, the American Psychological Association Council of Representatives introduced the Guidelines for Multicultural Education, Training, Research, Practice, and Organizational Change for Psychologists. As the ethical mandate among professionals to include multicultural services has advanced, the research has proliferated. Since their publication in 2003, the guidelines have been cited approximately 900 times in empirical research articles. But does this mean that the field has become more culturally aware and effective? Fouad et al. (2017) found that of the 895 studies that mentioned the guidelines, only 34 articles mentioned specific guidelines. Most other articles mentioned the guideline document as a whole, mainly as a means to document the importance of considering culture as part of the topic of the individual article. The authors concluded that the guidelines, though aspirational and important, have not substantively influenced psychological research on cultural factors. Though the guidelines emphasize the importance of culture to all members of the field, alternative or new standards must be being used practically in the areas of research and practice.

The idea that a newer, more integrated approach to multicultural competence is needed and is foundational to this chapter. Principle IV of the NAADAC Code of Ethics (2021) emphasizes the need to practice with cultural humility and to provide services that are culturally driven rather than relying on conventional approaches if not best suited for their clients. In order to understand what we need to know, we need to be able to conceptualize, use, and integrate culturally relevant themes and influences into psychological treatment. Cultural influences include the many factors that dual-diagnosis treatment providers need to address multicultural needs that are related to psychological assessment and treatment. These influences include:

- Values
- Gender roles
- Counseling expectations
- Communication patterns and language
- Behavioral norms
- Geographic location
- History and heritage
- Family and kinship
- Values and traditions
- Worldview
- Cultural identification and level of acculturation

- Education
- Social economic status (SES)
- Immigration, migration, and acculturation stress
- Religion and spirituality
- Standards for illness, healing, and health

(SAMSHA, 2014, TIP 59)

Therapist-Client Match

The exploration of cultural influences that impact clients has led some in our field to consider whether therapists can achieve increased efficacy in terms of meeting the cultural needs of clients by simply matching clients' and therapists' ethnicity or gender. Research on therapist-client matching has found that things are not as simple as they might seem. Reviews of racial, ethnic, and cultural therapist-client match literature, for example, have not found clinically meaningful effects on overall therapeutic outcome. These findings are not surprising in that it is nearly impossible to achieve perfect matches on any identity variables between clients and therapists in general. Furthermore, it is a rather large assumption that such a match would produce a meaningful similarity that directly leads to increased mutual understanding, which, in turn, leads to increased therapeutic efficacy or outcomes, especially because differing cultural influences (e.g., ethnicity, gender, sexual orientation, acculturation level, etc.) could be more or less important to each individual client (Ertl et al., 2019).

Generally, studies on this topic show that when client symptom severity and demographic values are controlled for, therapists show the same patterns of efficacy. Some therapists are more effective in general. Some therapists are more effective with racially and ethnically diverse clients. Individual disparities between therapists can be attributed to some therapists simply being more skilled than others. These findings suggest that some therapists are more culturally competent than others, and looking at whether or not therapists who have certain cultural factors produce better outcomes will not produce the answers to why therapists have disparate levels of effectiveness across clients. Indeed, it is possible for one therapist to show no disparity in treatment efficacy from one cultural group to another but to be equally ineffective with all clients. It is also possible for another therapist to demonstrate a larger difference between efficacy across people of different cultural influences but to still be more effective overall with each group than other therapists are (Imel et al., 2011).

These findings lead toward the identification of possible characteristics of multiculturally competent therapists that go beyond matching clients and therapists along one or more cultural dimensions. Berger et al. (2014) found that individual therapist behaviors and characteristics were related to increased cultural competence. In their study, no difference was found in therapy skills and knowledge among therapists, but one main component of cultural efficacy was therapists putting in increased time serving diverse clientele. More time spent and experience amassed with diverse populations set therapists on a developmental trajectory toward increased cultural awareness, by which they broadened their views beyond academic and therapy perspectives. In addition to increased multicultural practice, the authors noted that those therapists who indicated they had increased involvement in the communities that they served and who used an eclectic treatment orientation also demonstrated increased cultural awareness and efficacy. It is likely that therapists who use an inclusive and diverse treatment orientation that considers the individual needs of the client and involves collaborative planning/aligning with the client are seen by clients to be more impactful. Overall, it is clear that the cultural background of the therapist is not the only or primary factor that needs to be considered for multicultural competence; rather, multicultural competence is a skill set that is important to develop across all treatment providers.

Multicultural Incompetence

Before looking at cultural competence, it is important to examine what a culturally incompetent provider can look like. It is fair to say that all people have cultural influences and needs. Therapy providers and clients alike spend their lives moving through different cultural influences, and all people, as a result, are multicultural and have the ability to move fluidly from one culture to another. This normal social ability lays a foundation for practitioners to build discipline-specific multicultural skills. It is not enough for practitioners to rely on good intentions or their own worldview as their primary source of multicultural skills.

Reliance on the wrong skills set or failure to develop multicultural competence can result in clinical incompetence. Incompetence can lead to maleficence, no matter the intent. Signs of a lack of multicultural skills include:

- Not providing clarity about the expectations of therapy and what therapy involves overall
- Direct discrimination
- The use of microaggressions
- The assumption that one has adequate cultural knowledge while making incorrect assumptions that negatively impact clients
- Pathologizing cultural differences or viewing client beliefs or behaviors that are part of the client's cultural system/worldview as problematic
- Failing to address obvious cultural issues and needs
- Discounting how one's own cultural background influences initial impressions, assessment, and diagnosis of clients
- Intentional or unintentional use of one's own cultural norms and experiences as standards to judge or assess client symptoms, presentation, or experiences
- Minimizing the impact or importance of cultural experiences on individual clients
- Failing to systematically identify the cultural needs of clients and to offer appropriate treatment services
- Using a superior perspective, stereotype, or bias to judge or view client behavior
- Minimizing or limiting the exploration of the impact of bias, stereotypes, or discrimination on the client during the assessment or the treatment process

(Rogers-Sirin et al., 2015; SAMSHA, 2014, TIP 59)

Some examples of multicultural incompetence would include labeling a client as resistant when they are culturally not trusting of the counseling relationship or questioning 'why can't you simply (an action)' that may not be available or accessible due to the client's cultural beliefs. Implying that a clear economic or uninformed solution could 'solve' their challenges is both ineffective and unethical. While no one likes to believe they are incompetent, focusing on what skills are needed rather than what is lacking may inspire development of multicultural competence.

Multicultural Competence

Multicultural competence flows from the deliberate acquisition of a skill set that allows each counselor to thrive in a multicultural setting. Multicultural competence is critical to effective and ethical professional practice. It has been common for cultural training to focus on content and normative information on various cultural groups. This training has often been delivered from the perspective that treating professionals emerge from a dominant culture and are learning how to treat a minority, disempowered, or underprivileged cultural group. It is just as important to acknowledge that providers are multicultural and that all counseling relationships are multicultural by nature. This requires a shift to understanding that cultural needs are universal. Those learning about cultural competence should not be assumed to be from a dominant culture as psychology is a growing, diverse field (Sandeen et al., 2018). It is also important to note that simply because a client 'looks like you' doesn't mean that their cultural experiences have been similar. All counselors should approach their clients with cultural humility, leading with a sense of openness to the client's life experiences.

Multicultural competence is an ethical necessity, the absence of which can cause providers to make mistakes that limit or prevent client benefit. Well-equipped practitioners will have to understand more than a discrete skill set or knowledge base about a specific culture and engage in an ongoing process of self-evaluation. Professional growth can only be achieved through a combination of increased self-awareness and content-based information about specific cultural issues and groups. Therapists will need to strive to understand history; group power structures; multigenerational differences, experiences, and challenges; overt/covert/institutional racism; and expressions of privilege that impact client experiences. Ultimately, all this is learned alongside the understanding that bias is universal to all people. All types of bias, including implicit bias, occur with all humans, not as part of one culture (Sandeen et al., 2018). This means that recognizing your own bias will help you develop into a more ethical counselor.

Rogers-Sirin et al. (2015) suggest that cultural competence starts with being proactive and open to learning, making an effort to seek knowledge from the client about his or her cultural needs at the start and throughout the therapy process. Therapists build on the information they learn by using culture appropriately to address how cultural needs might impact therapy while developing an empathetic connection with the client. During the therapeutic process, the therapist would avoid assuming multicultural competence with clients based on past experiences, readings, or trainings. Therapists emphasize the development of genuine, warm, empathetic, and safe therapeutic environments where clients do not perceive they are discriminated against, misunderstood, or stereotyped. This level of competence can be accomplished through the use of a reflective local practice (RLP) approach (Sandeen et al., 2018).

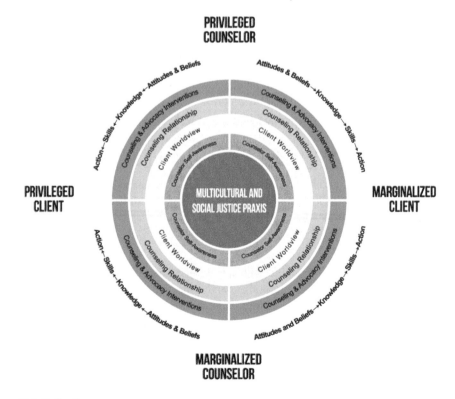

Figure 12.1 Reflection

Dual-diagnosis therapists engage in a reflective process that increases self-awareness of biases, assumptions, and experiences. It is understood that bias is a natural part of being human and that it is different from malicious intent. Bias must be addressed to provide competent care to clients (Sandeen et al., 2018).

Local

Multicultural competency includes knowledge and experiences with local cultures that are relevant to an individual therapist's practice (Sandeen et al., 2018). Practitioners expand their knowledge with activities that can include, but are not limited to:

- Learning local history and vocabulary
- Reading literature and reading local
- Reflecting on the power dynamics of one's culture in the local area

(Sandeen et al., 2018)

To avoid the potential for stereotyping people, therapists use specific content and learning about cultures for hypothesis testing with clients rather than for making assumptions about clients who belong to or identify with particular cultural groups. Consistent with recommendations of exposure to diversity, cultural immersion is recommended in counseling training programs, and participants have indicated they had a shift in cultural self-awareness (Lorelle et al., 2021).

Practice

Therapists learn culturally relevant skill sets and actively compensate for individual implicit bias. Skills can include, but are not limited to:

- Introducing the topic of culture during therapy
- Responding to cultural questions and needs of clients
- Addressing racism and the effects of racism on the client
- Habitually identifying and challenging assumptions of the therapist

(Sandeen et al., 2018)

Multicultural counseling competence requires ongoing reflection of one's ethnic identity, awareness of blind spots, and clinical supervision. Matthews et al. (2018) found that there is a correlation between multicultural self-efficacy and ethnic identity development, which suggests that counselors are trending in the right direction, toward multicultural counseling competence. However, this trend may be a result of years of practice in the field and exposure to multicultural training (Matthews et al., 2018).

It is possible to build on the RLP approach by adding that reflection requires ongoing self-evaluation in which one is aware of one's own cultural groups and the related assumptions, biases, and values. A practitioner must understand how their own background impacts their ability to provide culturally sensitive and effective services. Individual provider worldviews shape practitioner perspectives, and multiple people's worldviews interact during the treatment process to shape perceptions of health, normality/abnormality, prognosis, treatment interventions, and treatment outcomes. Therapists who are multiculturally competent identify and address client concerns early in the therapeutic process by providing comfortable opportunities to discuss and process trust and power, current needs, experiences, practice abilities, and any limitations regarding populations and treatment issues that they are qualified to treat (SAMHSA, 2014, TIP 59).

Ultimately, the culturally competent therapist must be able to use the knowledge of culturally relevant, responsive treatment principles to:

- Assess for co-occurring disorders
- Engage clients
- Educate and familiarize clients and families with the assessment and treatment process
- Use a collaborative approach to engage clients and families in assessment and treatment planning
- Elicit and integrate culturally relevant information and themes into therapeutic services
- With client permission, gather and include culturally relevant collateral information from sources other than the client
- Select and use culturally appropriate screening and assessment tools, including translated or adapted tools that have been validated for professional use
- Determine client motivation/readiness for change through the use of the motivational interviewing process, utilizing techniques likely to advance the client through the stages of change
- Use culturally competent case management techniques and/or referrals that focus on the individual needs of the clients and their families
- Use strength-based strategies to incorporate cultural factors into treatment planning

(TIP 59)

Developing Multicultural Competencies Using the Stages of Change: A Practical Approach

Since the therapeutic alliance is repeatedly validated as a strong predictor of treatment outcomes across different types of mental health disorders (Fluckiger et al., 2013), the value of clinician cultural competence should not be disregarded. Moving from ignorance of the need for cultural competency as a clinician through implementing a culture-sensitive approach and then becoming a person who consistently integrates this perspective can occur using a stage-of-change approach.

Students learning about multicultural perspectives and who desire to implement cultural awareness into their work with clients often feel overwhelmed at the scope of diversity and confused about how much they are expected to know about other cultures in order to be culturally competent. Students who are members of a minority culture may also feel confused as they may already be practiced in implementing measures to adapt to a majority culture and now are asked to adapt to other cultures as well.

It is important to know that the skills acquired over the course of studies can be connected to developing cultural competency. For example, students already have research skills and are often adaptable and curious. Students also belong to their own culture and are aware of how to maneuver and adjust among their family members, peers, social groups, and society. Consciously adapting these skills can be useful in developing multicultural competency. It is also important to know that once they begin learning about and/or working with even one people group that is different than their own, they initiate a process of change that can translate positively to overall growth and maturity in multicultural competence.

In the transtheoretical model of the stages of change, individuals can be guided through a process of developing new behaviors (Prochaska & DiClemente, 1982). By identifying first which stage of change an individual is located in, clinicians can utilize different techniques to help that person move toward and maintain change or new behaviors. Techniques may include questioning, introspection, and reflection to identify perceptual and cognitive barriers to change and education and motivation to address these barriers. The stages of change include pre-contemplation, contemplation, preparation, action, and maintenance. The idea is that a sequential movement forward encourages and sustains change because it is based on an acquisition of the knowledge and skills necessary for long-lasting behavior modification. The model has had substantial success across disciplines and in various contexts (Krebs et al., 2018). It is presented here to provide a method to help clinicians conceptualize and develop multicultural competencies.

Pre-contemplation

Clinicians in the pre-contemplation stage of change are unaware of their need to develop cultural competence. They may be aware of their own ethnic and cultural heritage and practices and take them as given without considering that others may do life differently than they do. They engage in activities specific to their worldview without openness to knowing about or considering others unlike them, who may have different approaches to life. In the extreme case, they may discount the value of other lifestyles that do not imitate their own or may be prejudiced or racist. At the other extreme, they may be cliquish, naïve, or oblivious. In other words, cultural awareness is not on their radar.

Reflection Questions and Activities in the Pre-contemplation Stage

Some questions to ask oneself in this stage include:

> *Reflection Question #1*: Have I ever interacted with someone of a different cultural group in a social context or with curiosity to learn more about them?
> *Reflection Question #2*: What are some of the barriers that keep me from knowing or interacting with others from different cultures?

Some steps to assist in moving through the pre-contemplation stage of change may include education and learning about another culture of interest from members of, or experts in, that culture through reading or viewing documentaries. The reading material may include texts and also any literature that helps foster an understanding of their worldview.

Contemplation

If these activities lead to contemplating the value of further engagement with another culture, then the education can proceed to a deeper level.

Reflection Questions and Activities in the Contemplation Stage

Questions to ask at this stage of change include:

> *Reflection Question #3*: What do I know or believe about a cultural group other than my own?
> *Reflection Question #4*: How did I come to know this, and is it true?

This form of reflection addresses not only the lack of knowledge about but also stereotypes of other cultures. Some steps to assist in moving through the contemplation stage of change include exploration: seeking more knowledge and understanding of other cultures by continued reading and healthy curiosity or perhaps seeking out someone from another culture and engaging positively with them, attending an event, or sharing a meal with the goal of developing understanding.

Preparation

If these activities lead to a decision to develop multicultural competence, the next step is to prepare for this significant change. Preparation includes self-evaluation and continued education. Completing a self-assessment of our own cultural experience is an important step in bridging the cultural divide between ourselves and others. Hays (2016) presents compelling evidence of the efficacy of this approach, as well as steps that can be taken to accomplish self-evaluation. In the preparation stage of change, spending time in reflection on how we present to the world and how this impacts those we engage with can be a benchmark step in professional as well as multicultural development. Hays identifies not only a self-assessment based on age, development, ethnicity or race, socioeconomic status, sexual identification, indigenous heritage, national origin, and gender (the ADDRESSING model) but also on how culture and privilege factor into the clinical work we do.

Reflection Question and Activities in the Preparation Stage

A question to ask at this stage of change is:

> *Reflection Question #5*: Have I engaged in a self-assessment of my own cultural experiences? Why or why not?

Steps to assist in moving through the preparation stage of change include a self-assessment. For each of Hays's (2016) categories of self-assessment listed here (age, development, ethnicity or race, socioeconomic status, sexual identification, indigenous heritage, national origin, gender) and social privilege, discuss how your personal experiences and perspective influence your life. Discuss how this information will potentially influence your professional work. An honest self-assessment will help identify blind spots and growth opportunities for multicultural competence. Identifying resources for learning and skill development becomes a priority at this stage and, consequently, moves the clinician toward action.

Action

In the action stage of change, the clinician is motivated and begins to engage in the process of developing skills and working with others of different cultures. Steps that foster growth in this stage include a focus on the cultural influences (TIP 59) discussed in the *Multicultural Dimensions* section of this chapter.

Reflection Questions and Activities in the Action Stage

Questions to ask at this stage of change include:

> *Reflection Question #6*: Have I purposefully sought out training and professional experiences related to multicultural practice?
> *Reflection Question #7*: Am I aware of and able to utilize the network of multicultural resources in my area of practice?

One step to assist in moving through the action stage of change is engagement. Joining in social and educational activities with persons of different cultures, learning about cultural customs, food, music, and heritage, may present opportunities to learn while experiencing important traditions and values. In the clinical context, obtaining guidance from culturally aware supervisors or colleagues can also foster multicultural growth.

Maintenance

Once multicultural competence is developed, it is necessary to continue growing through education, engagement, reflection, and embracing.

Reflection Questions and Activities in the Maintenance Stage

Questions to ask at this stage of change include:

> *Reflection Question #8*: What ongoing professional or personal activities can contribute to my active use of culturally competent skills?
>
> *Reflection Question #9*: Am I remaining open and teachable when I encounter a novel experience or an individual need?

Steps to assist in moving through the action stage of change include embracing. Multicultural competence is best developed in the context of a lifelong learning experience. By being open to new experiences and maintaining a worldview that values each person and culture, multicultural competence can be maintained.

Conclusion

Multicultural competence is foundational to efficacy in mental health treatment, including working with persons who have co-occurring disorders. Acquiring multicultural competence requires a proactive and integrated approach that considers the conceptualization, utilization, and integration of culturally relevant themes and influences into treatment. It also requires a mindset that values humans in the context of their culture and works consistently to develop a workable skill set. Beginning with an understanding of their own culture and biases, clinicians can learn by engaging openly with individuals and groups that are different from their own. Through a process of self-evaluation, they can develop self-awareness related to their cultural and ethnic worldview. They can utilize the transtheoretical stages of change to help develop competence in engagement and treatment of a multicultural clientele. When all is said and done, it is the clients who matter most, and developing skills to be more effective in working with them should encompass not only clinical techniques but also multicultural competence.

Questions for Consideration

1. Explore your own culture. What are the strengths and challenges presented to you as a counselor based on your cultural identity?
2. All counselors have blind spots in their competence. What can you do to ensure that you are aware of those blind spots and create an action plan to identify growth opportunities?
3. Lifelong learning is required to achieve multicultural competence. However, we are surrounded by culture changes and evolution every day. What can you do to maintain cultural competence? What challenges do you face?

Case Study

Mani is 24-year-old first-generation American. His parents immigrated from Turkey and have held on to the traditional cultural beliefs of their homeland. Mani was raised in a Muslim household, and although alcohol is consumed in his culture, drugs are strictly forbidden. Reaching the age of expected marriage, he has begun to struggle with his American life and the cultural expectations his parents are trying to reenforce. In high school and college, Mani drank alcohol and began experimenting with club drugs. Two weeks ago, Mani was arrested for driving under the influence (DUI) of alcohol and drugs after driving the wrong way down a one-way street in the city. Luckily, no one was hurt. This was his second DUI, and because he has a history of other drug use, he was referred for an evaluation for treatment. When asked about his alcohol and drug use, Mani stated that he needed to escape the life his parents had planned for him, and when he was partying was the only time he felt 'normal'.

Questions

1. What are your clinical concerns for Mani?
2. What information would you need to develop a preliminary diagnosis?
3. What challenges would you face when working with Mani?
4. What challenges would he face working with you?

References

American Psychiatric Association. (2019). *Mental health disparities: Diverse populations.* Retrieved from www.psychiatry.org/psychiatrists/cultural-competency/education/mental-health-facts

Berger, L. K., Zane, N., & Hwang, W. (2014). Therapist ethnicity and treatment orientation differences in multicultural counseling competencies. *Asian American Journal of Psychology, 5*(1), 53–65. https://doi.org/10.1037/a0036178

Ertl, M. M., Mann-Saumier, M., Martin, R. A., Graves, D. F., & Altarriba, J. (2019). The impossibility of client therapist "match": Implications and future directions for multicultural competency. *Journal of Mental Health Counseling, 4*(4), 312–326. https://doi.org/10.17744/mehc.41.4.03

Fouad, N. A., Santana, M., & Ghosh, A. (2017). Empirical influence of the multicultural guidelines: A brief report. *Cultural Diversity and Ethnic Minority Psychology, 23*(4), 583–587. http://dx.doi.org/10.1037/cdp0000136

Hays, P. (2016). *Addressing cultural complexities in practice: Assessment, diagnosis, and therapy* (3rd ed.). American Psychological Association.

Imel, Z. E., Baldwin, S., Atkins, D. C., Owen, J., Baardseth, T., & Wampold, B. E. (2011). Racial/ethnic disparities in therapist effectiveness: A conceptualization and initial study of cultural competence. *Journal of Counseling Psychology, 58*(3), 290–298. http://doi.org/10.1037/a0023284

Krebs, P., Norcross, J. C., Nicholson, J. M., & Prochaska, J. O. (2018). Stages of change and psychotherapy outcomes: A review and meta-analysis. *Journal of Clinical Psychology, 74*(11), 1964–1979.

Le Cook, B., Trinh, N., Li, Z., Hou, S. S.-Y., & Progovac, A. M. (2017). Trends in racial-ethnic disparities in access to mental health care, 2004–2012. *Psychiatric Services, 68*(1).

Lorelle, S., Atkins, K., & Michel, R. (2021). Enhancing social justice and multicultural counseling competence through cultural immersion: A guide for faculty. *The Journal of Counselor Preparation and Supervision, 14*(1). Retrieved from https://repository.wcsu.edu/jcps/vol14/iss1/4

Matthews, J. J., Mehta Barden, S., & Sherrell, R. S. (2018). Examining the relationships between multicultural counseling competence, multicultural self-efficacy, and ethnic identity development of practicing counselors. *Journal of Mental Health Counseling, 40*(2), 129–141. https://doi-org.libauth.purdueglobal.edu/10.17744/mehc.40.2.03

Mericle, A. A., Ta, V. M., Holck, P., & Arria, A. M. (2012). Prevalence, patterns, and correlates of co-occurring substance use and mental disorders in the US: Variations by race/ethnicity. *Comprehensive Psychiatry, 53*(6).

NAADAC, the Association for Addiction Professionals. (2021). *NAADAC/NCC AP code of ethics.* NAADAC.

Nam, E., Matejkowski, M., & Lee, S. (2017). Racial/ethnic differences in contemporaneous use of mental health and substance use treatment among individuals experiencing both mental illness and substance use disorders. *The Psychiatric Quarterly, 88*(1), 185–198.

Prochaska, J. O., & DiClemente, C. C. (1982). Transtheoretical therapy: Toward a more integrative model of change. *Psychotherapy: Theory, Research & Practice, 19*(3). PsychARTICLES database.

Rogers-Sirin, L., Melendez, F., Refano, C., & Zegarra, Y. (2015). Immigrant perception of therapists' cultural competence: A qualitative investigation. *Professional Psychology Research and Practice, 46*(4), 258–269. http://dx.doi.org/10.1037/pro0000033

Sandeen, E., Moore, K. M., & Swanda, R. M. (2018). Reflective local practice: A pragmatic framework for improving culturally competent practice in psychology. *Professional Psychology: Research and Practice, 49*(2), 142–150. http://doi.org/10.1037/pro0000183

Substance Abuse and Mental Health Services Administration. (2013). *Results from the 2012 national survey on drug use and health: Mental health findings.* Retrieved from www.samhsa.gov/data/sites/default/files/NSDUHmhfr2012/NSDUHmhfr2012.pdf

Substance Abuse and Mental Health Services Administration. (2014). Improving cultural competence. *Treatment Improvement Protocol 59*. Retrieved from https://store.samhsa.gov/system/files/sma14-4849. pdf

Substance Abuse and Mental Health Services Administration. (2018). *Results from the 2017 national survey on drug use and health: Mental health findings*. Retrieved from www.samhsa.gov/data/release/2017-national-survey-drug-use-and-health-nsduh-releases

U.S. Census Bureau. (2015). *Projections of the size and composition of the population: 2014–2060*. Retrieved from www.census.gov/library/publications/2015/demo/p25-1143.html

Section III

Integrative Treatment Approaches for Those With Co-occurring Disorders

Tricia L. Chandler

Over the course of the twentieth century, there was a separation of how illnesses were treated in the medical and mental health fields, with substance use disorders and mental illness treated as if they were completely separate disorders, and mental health issues treated as if they are separate from overall health care. Since neuropsychology and neurobiology have evolved, there is an increased understanding that these co-occurring disorders are interrelated, and the driving force for this phenomenon is early childhood trauma and abuse. Trauma can be defined in many ways, but when activated by fear of dying, witnessing abuse, experiencing abuse, etc., the limbic brain, known as our survival instinct, takes control. When the limbic brain is activated through an adverse or perceived adverse event, the survival brain takes over and puts the higher executive cognitive functioning found in the prefrontal cortex into a more auxiliary position. This function supports the survival drive but is not what helps an individual function with the rational logical mind. As the mesolimbic brain is so important to understanding the process of addiction, and neurotransmitters are so important in our functioning well as humans, those studying co-occurring disorders need to be cognizant of the complexity of human frailty and how helping people heal requires a holistic and whole-person approach to treatment.

The need for effective integrative treatment for the populations being served with co-occurring disorders is dire in this country. There is no one-size-fits-all way to treat those with co-occurring disorders, but understanding the neurobiology and neuropsychology involved with a variety of mental disorders and trauma can assist the counselor in considering causal issues involved with having substance use and process use disorders, along with mental health disorders to develop individualized treatment that addresses all biopsychosocial issues. This section of the text provides an overview of the traditional therapies and approaches that have been used to treat mental illness and substance abuse disorders, along with the newer approaches that have evolved over the past 30 years. Often, individuals with co-occurring disorders will need to be treated with several different approaches that include nutrition, somatic and creative arts therapies, mindfulness-based therapies, energy psychology approaches, and recovery models to effect real change. The following chapters will address the level of care needed for most effective treatment.

DOI: 10.4324/9781003220916-15

13 Assessment of Co-occurring Disorders, Levels of Care, and ASAM Requirements

Elizabeth Reyes-Fournier, Tara G. Matthews, and Tom Alexander

Introduction

The clinical assessment is a crucial part of ethical, effective, and evidenced-based treatment of co-occurring disorders. Assessments are the first opportunity to hear the client's history and needs and to lay the foundation for clinical work. While the assessment process can feel invasive, if rooted in respectful curiosity, the counseling professional can gather vital information that will guide future clinical treatment with the whole client. Whether we are determining levels of care, determining readiness for early intervention, or doing an intake with a court-ordered client, assessment seeks to collect data from interviews, observations, histories, and established measurements to accurately diagnose a client so that the practitioner can effectively treat the individual.

The assessment process relies on a practitioner's ethics and evidenced-based practices and can be dangerous when conducted by individuals who are untrained or biased. The first step in working with individuals with co-occurring disorders is to accurately assess them. Without proper assessment, there is no proper treatment. If the assessment approach is too rigid, short, biased, or dismissive, critical pieces of information can easily be missed such as nutrition, early childhood experiences, current living situation, or cultural influence. The practice of assessment is not a blunt tool but a refined system of data collection that works best when it is organized and founded on evidence that justifies each assertion. The assessment process is the first opportunity to demonstrate professionalism and a genuine curiosity with the client and, done with care, will begin the process of developing a therapeutic rapport, in which the client develops trust in the counselor.

Once assessment is complete and diagnosis, along with severity of symptoms, has been determined, the next part of the process is determining necessary level of care for effective treatment of the individual. The specific levels of care are guided by the American Society of Addiction Medicine (ASAM) criteria, edited by Ries et al. (2014). Each level of care is meant to provide the best possible treatment approach for clients in the least intrusive environment.

Learning Objectives

1. Identify various types of treatment offered to individuals with co-occurring disorders
2. Recognize intrapersonal factors experienced by the client that help provide a path for linkage to the appropriate level of care
3. Understand a current model of integrated co-occurring disorders treatment to assist with linking clients to the correct level of care based on their unique needs

Key Terms

Detox Services: This is the unofficial name provided to medical services provided to individuals to help remove all traces of alcohol or other substances from their bodies. This

DOI: 10.4324/9781003220916-16

service is designed to assist in managing symptoms of withdrawal, often through medicine, primarily completed at inpatient hospital units.

Inpatient Treatment: A level of care often provided at a hospital in which an individual stays for a duration of 10 to 28 days. The purpose of this level of care is to decrease the most severe symptoms associated with substance use or mental illnesses while allowing patients to transition to long-term treatment.

Outpatient Treatment: Treatment module that is provided within the community, usually allowing the individual to stay with their families, engage in work, and engage with self-help while also obtaining ongoing treatment for mental health or substance use disorders.

Residential Treatment: Treatment provided at a shared home or apartment building to which the individual has 24-hour access. This level of care assists the individual with obtaining skills of basic living while also translating tools of recovery for long-term use.

Assessment in Substance Abuse Counseling

All assessments in substance abuse counseling need to be rooted in genuine curiosity about how best to serve the client and be guided by professional competencies and ethical considerations. 'Addiction counselors encounter clients with CODs [co-occurring disorders] as a rule, not an exception' (Substance Abuse and Mental Health Services Administration (SAMHSA), 2020a, p. xi). Clinical evaluation is the first practice dimension of a professional substance abuse counselor (Center for Substance Abuse Treatment, 2006). The role of the substance abuse counselor must always be to assess the individual's current state and possible risk. Guided by the NAADAC Code of Ethics Principle V (NAADAC, 2021), the tools used to assess the client must be reliable, be effective, and take personal and cultural influences into consideration.

The ability to screen and assess a client is key to providing them effective treatment. This process ideally will begin with collecting data concerning the individual's behavior and history from the client, their significant others, and referral agencies. This data, in combination with established, reliable, and valid measures, forms the basis of a comprehensive diagnosis. Assessment is an ongoing process that does not end with one clinical interview. The initial session will have the counselor establish rapport to assess a client's level of functioning; history, include information like their mental health and use disorder issues; and family, social, and medical information. Every session will contain an assessment of the client's current status, progress, and risk (Center for Substance Abuse Treatment, 2006). Clients with co-occurring disorders are at a greater risk for harming themselves or others. A practice of risk assessment at every session is best practice for the clinician (SAMSHA, 2020a).

It is estimated that approximately 3.3% of the population of the United States has co-occurring substance use and mental health disorders. More than half of those 7.7 million individuals will not receive any treatment, and less than 10% receive integrated treatment (Han et al., 2017). The difficulty in assessing co-occurring disorders begins with ignoring the prevalence of this phenomenon. From the perspective of treating severe mental illness, there has been a tendency to omit questions regarding potential use with clients (Chen et al., 1992). From the perspective of the substance abuse counselor, many indicators of severe mental illness may appear as severe use or withdrawal symptoms (Mueser & Gingerich, 2013). The reality is that exclusion of either the mental illness or the substance abuse in the treatment of those with co-occurring disorders results in a considerable risk that the individual will relapse, reoffend, or be hospitalized (Perry et al., 2019). Understanding that any assessment in a substance abuse setting must include a mental health screening is key to properly diagnosing the individual. Additionally, any mental health assessment would need to rule out substance use disorders to better understand the symptomatology presented.

Categorical Versus Dimensional Concepts in Diagnosing

Unlike medical conditions that are diagnosed with a laboratory test separating a bacteria or virus from normal cells, mental disorders are not distinct categories but rather a range of symptoms with an overarching hallmark of disability (Widiger & Samuel, 2005). For example, a client complains of sleep disturbances, fatigue, difficulty concentrating, and feeling agitated. What category would you automatically assume that this client's diagnosis would fall under? These symptoms are not unique, and, as has been noted by psychological professionals for decades, the overlap of symptoms can result in faulty assessments. (See Table 13.1.) This is but one example of several from previous iterations of the *DSM*.

The categorical model of diagnosing was based on symptoms belonging to categories that created distinct diagnosing. The goal of the model was to present diagnoses that were unique and distinct from other diagnoses in the *DSM* (Widiger & Samuel, 2005). The obvious limitations of this model were that many symptoms in the *DSM* are ubiquitous. Also, the attempt to present a diagnosis as separate and apart from other abnormal moods, behaviors, or disturbances limited the detection of co-occurring disorders (Blashfield, 1998). Despite the previous iterations of the *DSM* attempting to quash issues by providing guidance in differential diagnostics, separating one diagnosis from another, the similar symptoms, and the tendency to stick with faulty diagnosing, this system of viewing mental disorders is faulty and results in poor and ineffective treatment for our clients (Widiger & Samuel, 2005).

When comparing major depressive disorder and general anxiety disorder criteria in the *DSM-5* (APA, 2013), both disorders have similar issues with sleep disturbances, psychomotor agitation and feelings of restlessness, fatigue or loss of energy daily, and diminished ability to sleep or concentrate with mind going blank at times. The dimensional model of diagnosing considers the degree of severity of symptoms, number of symptoms, duration, and degree of dysfunction to provide a diagnosis that notes not only the diagnosis but also specifiers and severity (American Psychiatric Association, 2013). The obvious reason for employing a dimensional approach to

Table 13.1 Biopsychosocial data collection table

Domain	Area	Collected Information
Biological	Medical Information	History of illness, surgeries, injuries, disabilities, hospitalizations
	Genetic Information	Family history of illness, diseases, deaths, use disorders, mental illness, homicidal/suicidal ideation and attempts, family criminal background
	Developmental Information	Developmental delays in speech, milestones, type of birth, other developmental delays
	Substance Use Information	Use of legal and illegal substances, age of first use, current use, administration, frequency, and amount
Psychological	Mental Status	Current diagnosis, current presentation
	History	Age of onset, trauma, and family trauma
	Hospitalizations	Any commitment due to mental health (voluntary and involuntary)
	Medications	Use of prescribed medications for mental health treatment
	Strengths/ Limitations	Client's self-perception of strengths and areas in need of development
Social	Social	Friends, supports, family connections including parents, siblings, and extended family
	Cultural	Family culture, languages, foods, rituals
	Education/Vocation	Education level (including GED), work history, current work, and vocational goals
	Criminal	Detailed personal criminal history, including juvenile history
	Religious/Spiritual	Client's connection to spirituality or religion (passive or active)

diagnosing is when comparing individuals with similar diagnoses. The overarching diagnosis is similar, but the features, symptoms, and severity give us a deeper understanding as to the dysfunction of the individual (Widiger & Samuel, 2005). This method of assessment forces the psychological professional to avoid 'yes-no' questions and employ a crosscutting-symptoms style of measurement in both interviews and use of established measures.

Which Came First?

Professionals are tempted to answer that very question. Which came first – the use disorder or the mental health disorder? A mental illness can force an individual to find relief of their symptoms with the use of a substance (self-medication). A use disorder can induce a mental illness like a substance-induced bipolar disorder (Revadigar & Gupta, 2021). A co-occurring disorder can have a third cause, like an illness, chronic pain, or a yet-to-be-uncovered posttraumatic stress disorder (SAMSHA, 2020a). Considering that 90% of all Americans have experienced a traumatic experience at some point in their lives, the real possibility of yet another explanation for the presentation of the symptoms of an individual should be anticipated (Kilpatrick et al., 2013). The obvious issue with this question belies the underlying issue: If the best form of treatment for co-occurring disorders is integrative treatment, why would it matter which came first? What behooves the practitioner is properly assessing the individual to provide a comprehensive diagnosis to create and carry out an effective treatment plan.

Biopsychosocial Model

The biopsychosocial assessment of co-occurring disorders is a measure of the whole individual. The assessment includes information on the client from the biological, psychological, and social domains. The assessment can be completed with a structured/semi-structured instrument (e.g., Global Appraisal of Individual Needs-Initial (GAIN-I)). The professional can also complete this assessment through an interview, making sure to collect necessary data in all domains. (See Table 13.1.) The wealth of information gathered from a biopsychosocial assessment is unrivaled and crucial for both assessment and treatment planning.

Established Measures

The field of psychology is replete with measures. A psychological measure is an assessment that seeks to quantify a specific construct. In the case of co-occurring disorders, the measures in question will measure a client's biopsychosocial history, drug use, or mental disorders. The difference between the aforementioned biopsychosocial assessment and the GAIN-I is that the former is a set of unstructured questions that will gather information for the professional to write their client report and treatment plan while the latter is a psychological measure that has been tested and shown to have reliability and validity and is used to screen, justify, and support a possible diagnosis. An established measure will have been tested repeatedly to assure that it is reliable (consistent) and is valid (measures what it purports to measure) on specific populations (e.g., adults, adolescents, adults with a known use disorder).

Types of Measures

There are various types of measures that are used readily in the assessment process. Each type is specific to the measure or the purpose of the assessment.

Clinical Interview (a.k.a. Unstructured Interview): This term is used to refer to the type of assessment done by a practitioner in which they use open-ended questions to elicit responses from the client to obtain information. The clinician will ask general questions regarding thoughts, feelings, and behaviors while systematically ruling out possible domains of disorders. As the client answers questions, the clinician mentally refines their questions to arrive at a tentative diagnosis. This is done during the screening and intake process, in which an initial diagnosis must be completed.

Structured Interview: This is a form of administering a measure with set questions in which the items are close ended (specific responses are expected: e.g., yes/no, a specific number). These are measures that can be done by anyone with minimal training.

Semi-Structured Interview: This is a form of administering a measure with set questions in which the items are closed ended, but the interviewer can ask clarifying questions to expand the response (e.g., 'Can you tell me more about how you feel when you experience this?'). These are measures that are done by trained clinicians.

Self-report: These are measures in which the respondent is asked to report their feelings, beliefs, attitudes, and experiences using the scale provided. Self-reports use Likert scales, true/false, or semantic differentials (e.g., a system to assess the respondent's connotative meaning of certain words to obtain a precise understanding). Self-reports are widely used in psychological measures and can be administered with paper/pencil or computer or read to the client in the case of limited reading ability.

Use Disorder Diagnoses in the Dimensional System

The criteria for diagnosing any use disorder are the same. The distinctions are substance, severity, and level of remission. Dimensional systems allow the professional to make the distinction between an individual who has been using a substance and endured consequences because of their use that have affected them medically, socially, and psychologically and if there is an underlying mental health diagnosis.

Diagnostic Criteria for Use Disorders from the *DSM-5* (American Psychiatric Association, 2013).

A problematic pattern of substance use leading to clinically significant impairment or distress, as manifested by at least two of the following, occurring within a 12-month period:

1. Substance is often taken in larger amounts or over a longer period than was intended.
2. There is a persistent desire or unsuccessful efforts to cut down or control substance use.
3. A great deal of time is spent in activities necessary to obtain substance, use substance, or recover from its effects.
4. Craving, or a strong desire or urge to use substance.
5. Recurrent substance use resulting in a failure to fulfill major role obligations at work, school, or home.
6. Continued substance use despite having persistent or recurrent social or interpersonal problems caused or exacerbated by the effects of substance.
7. Important social, occupational, or recreational activities are given up or reduced because of substance use.
8. Recurrent substance use in situations in which it is physically hazardous.
9. Substance use is continued despite knowledge of having a persistent or recurrent physical or psychological problem that is likely to have been caused or exacerbated by substance.
10. Tolerance, as defined by either of the following:

    • A need for markedly increased amounts of substance to achieve intoxication or desired effect.
    • A markedly diminished effect with continued use of the same amount of substance.

11. Withdrawal, as manifested by either of the following:

  • The characteristic withdrawal syndrome for substance. (The essential feature is the development of a substance-specific problematic behavioral change, with physiological and cognitive concomitants, that is due to the cessation of, or reduction in, heavy and prolonged substance use. The substance-specific syndrome causes clinically significant distress or impairment in social, occupational, or other important areas of functioning.)

  • Substance (or a closely related substance) is taken to relieve or avoid withdrawal symptoms.

Specifier:
Mild: Presence of 2–3 symptoms.
Moderate: Presence of 4–5 symptoms
Severe: Presence of 6 or more symptoms

The addition of a severity index to the current diagnosing system considers that some individuals are less involved than others. With as few as two symptoms, an individual can be diagnosed with a use disorder. It is entirely possible at this point to diagnose any individual who has used alcohol normally throughout their life, who now requires more alcohol to feel 'drunk' and experience a hangover, with a mild alcohol use disorder. This would, of course, be a mistake and abuse of the system. The severity index was created to acknowledge that there is a continuum in diagnostics. Unfortunately, the research has not supported the effectiveness of the severity index as providing a more precise treatment plan (Lane et al., 2016). However, these findings are more of a reason for the professional to thoroughly analyze the level of dysfunction of an individual. Any assessment of an individual must include the apparent and reported dysfunction of the individual.

Mental Health Disorders

Mental illness is common in the United States. This is a bold statement, and yet the data supports this assertion. One in five people are living with a mental illness at any given time in the US (SAMSHA, 2020b). Proper diagnosis of these mental illnesses is still a primary concern for practitioners. To effectively treat, we must properly assess. The *DSM-5* introduced a series of measures for mental health disorders and a medically inspired cross-cutting system measure, which focuses on the client's report of their thoughts, feelings, and behaviors. The goal of using these systems is to ultimately provide data that will accurately show efficacy (Narrow & Kuhl, 2011). The idea is that if mental illness is accurately assessed and the treatment results are positive, then we can deduce that the diagnosis was correct. Using this form of evidence-based measurement is not new to the research of psychology, but there has been a history of lax or quick diagnostics in the practice that have affected the efficacy of treatment (Flynn & Brown, 2008).

Use of Cross-cutting System Measure

The *DSM-5* (APA, 2013) has introduced several measures that are to be used to assist in the assessment of individuals. The cross-cutting system measure is available in both the print and electronic *DSM-5*. The measure is a 23-item self-report that can narrow down potential mental health diagnoses (depression, emotional distress, anger, mania, anxiety, somatic symptoms, suicidal ideation, psychosis, sleep problems, memory issues, repetitive thoughts and behaviors, dissociation, personality issues, substance use) (APA, 2013). These areas of dysfunction demonstrate the dimensional concept previously mentioned. The results of the cross-cutting system measure will then prompt a secondary measure to rule out, clarify, or quantify a diagnosis. For example, the Level 2 Depression Adults (PROMIS Emotional Distress-Depression-Short Form) consists of seven items, answered on a five-point Likert Scale, that ask the individual if they have experienced certain feelings within the last seven days (APA, 2013). The *DSM-5*'s introduction of a series of the patient reporting outcome (PRO) measures is an attempt to increase accuracy and reliability in assessment.

NOTE: These measures can be found in the electronic and print versions of the *Diagnostic Statistical Manual*, 5th edition.

Sample of Measures for Use Disorders and Mental Disorders

WHO Disability Assessment Schedule 2 (WHODAS 2.0): This measure is a 12-item, self-report that was created by the World Health Organization. It measures the individual's level of disability due to physical issues, substance use, or mental disorders (Axelsson et al., 2017). It is important to note that the WHODAS 2 was created to screen for and measure disability issues based on the International Classification of Functioning of Disability and Health (ICF), which is the companion to the International Classification of Disease (ICD) that provides the internationally recognized coding system for all diseases and illnesses. The WHODAS 2 was included in the *DSM-5*, marking a change in the *DSM* history, which marked the alignment of the *DSM* coding to that of the ICD 11 codes (APA, 2013).

CAGE: Consists of 4 questions to screen for potential alcohol use disorder. The letters stand for cut down (C), annoyed (A), guilty (G), and eye-opener (E) (Ewing, 1984).

1. Have you ever felt you should cut down on your drinking?
2. Have people annoyed you by criticizing your drinking?
3. Have you ever felt bad or guilty about your drinking?
4. Have you ever had a drink first thing in the morning to steady your nerves or to get rid of a hangover (eye-opener)?

CAGE-AID: This is like the CAGE but is for other substance use (Brown & Rounds, 1995).

1. Have you ever felt you ought to cut down on your drinking or drug use?
2. Have people annoyed you by criticizing your drinking or drug use?
3. Have you felt bad or guilty about your drinking or drug use?
4. Have you ever had a drink or used drugs first thing in the morning to steady your nerves or to get rid of a hangover (eye-opener)?

Global Appraisal of Individual Needs-Initial (GAIN-I): This is a structured and semi-structured, standardized, biopsychosocial assessment that also serves as a diagnostic aid. The measure has over 1,000 items and has 100 subscales (Dennis et al., 2002).

Substance Abuse Subtle Screening Inventory 4 (SASSI-4): The SASSI-4 is a validated measure and diagnostic tool that assesses substance use, including prescription medication misuse (Lazowski & Geary, 2019).

Minnesota Multiphasic Personality Inventory 2 (MMPI-2): The MMPI-2 is considered one of the most researched and widely used assessment in the world. It is used both for screening and diagnostic purposes. It consists of 567 true-false questions. It has ten scales with numerous subscales that measure mental illness. Three subscales specifically assess use disorders (Miller et al., 2007).

Beck's Depression Inventory (BDI): The BDI is a widely used 21-item self-report that screens and measures the severity of depression in an individual (Beck et al., 1996).

Generalized Anxiety Disorder 7 item (GAD 7): The GAD 7 is a 7-item self-report that screens and measures generalized anxiety disorder (Spitzer et al., 2006).

Positive and Negative Syndrome Scale (PANSS): The PANSS is a semi-structured interview of 30-item scale that was created to measure the severity of the positive and negative symptoms of schizophrenia (Kay et al., 1988). This measure requires training to administer and score.

Young Mania Rating Scale: This scale is a clinical interview that takes less than 30 minutes to complete. It is used to measure the severity of mania and done primarily in hospital settings. It is not a screening tool and must be done by a trained clinician (Young et al., 1978).

Posttraumatic Stress Disorder (PCL-C, S, M): The PCL-C is a widely used, 17-item checklist for the screening and diagnosing of PTSD. It has versions for specific trauma (S) and for military personnel (M) (Lang et al., 2012).

Bipolar Spectrum Diagnostic Scale (BSDS): The BSDS is a 20-item self-report that is sensitive to subtle bipolar disorder symptoms (Nassir Ghaemi et al., 2005).

Eating Disorder Diagnostic Scale (EDDS): The EDDS is a scale designed to be used on clients from ages 13 to 65 to screen and diagnose eating disorders after treatment. It is a 22-item self-report (Stice et al., 2000).

Once the initial evidenced-based assessment has been completed, diagnosis and treatment can begin. Be mindful that the assessment process is an ongoing process that may need to be revisited throughout treatment. For example, a client entering treatment under the influence of mood-altering substances would need to be detoxed prior to completing the comprehensive assessment. Immediate treatment needs can be assessed based on specific criteria present at the time of entry into the treatment program. Based on the symptomology present, there are various levels of care available to clients.

Residential and Inpatient Treatment for Co-occurring Disorders

Persons with co-occurring disorders may receive treatment from an array of service providers at differing levels of care. One of the primary goals of health-care professionals is to establish effective treatment that is provided at the least restrictive level of care. When lower levels of care like outpatient counseling, medication management, intensive outpatient, and partial hospitalization will not meet the treatment needs of a person with co-occurring disorders, alternate and higher levels of care are considered. Two of the higher levels of care are residential treatment and inpatient hospitalization. The following content explores variations in residential and inpatient levels of care and their subsequent application to the treatment of persons with co-occurring psychiatric and substance use disorders. The specific levels of care are guided by the American Society of Addiction Medicine (ASAM) criteria, edited by Ries et al. (2014). Prior to discussing the variations in levels of inpatient and residential treatment, it is imperative to fully outline the six dimensions utilized by ASAM to determine the appropriateness of each level of care.

ASAM Assessment Dimensions and Co-occurring Disorders

Prior to discussing the inpatient and residential levels of care, it is important to consider some foundational tenets of the ASAM criteria, which can be found within the specific assessment dimensions. The ASAM assessment dimensions provide a picture of both the level of care that may be needed by a person with co-occurring disorders and the type of focus that treatment may take (Ries et al., 2014). The following content will address each dimension, along with a discussion of ways in which a person with co-occurring disorders might present with treatment-related concerns in each assessment dimension. The descriptive factors of each assessment dimension have been developed by ASAM and provide guidance for treatment and recovery (Ries et al., 2014).

Dimension 1: Acute Intoxication and/or Withdrawal Potential

When a person with co-occurring disorders presents for treatment, one of the primary areas assessed is related to intoxication and withdrawal (Ries et al., 2014). Both intoxication and withdrawal can significantly affect the initial phase of treatment due to the medical and psychological risks that can be presented for withdrawal from certain types of substances like alcohol, benzo-diazepines, and opioids. For example, Kosten and Baxter (2019) discuss that opioid withdrawal can include components of both anxiety and depression, along with an array of additional physi-ological challenges throughout the process. Moreover, Kosten and Baxter discuss that insom-nia is a common symptom of opioid withdrawal. Insomnia can have an immense effect on the mental health status of a person with co-occurring disorders. Bonnet and Preuss (2017) confirm similar effects of cannabis withdrawal on mental health symptomatology. Specifically, Bonnet and Preuss (2017) indicate that insomnia, anxiety, and depression can occur for persons who are withdrawing from cannabis use. For persons with co-occurring disorders, the inclusion of with-drawal-based symptoms that affect mental health can complicate the treatment process, espe-cially in the initial phase. Such effects on the treatment process demonstrate the need to include withdrawal management as a specific dimension to assess at the onset of treatment and recovery.

Dimension 2: Biomedical Conditions and Complications

Included in the assessment of a person with co-occurring disorders should be an evaluation of medical conditions that affect treatment, recovery, and quality of life (Ries et al., 2014). An array of physical health conditions can present along with co-occurring mental and substance use disorders. Chronic pain is a primary example of one type of biomedical condition that may be present for a person seeking treatment, especially in regard to opioid use disorder. Barry et al. (2016) provided an analysis of the prevalence of types of psychiatric diagnoses among persons with chronic pain and opioid use disorder. Barry et al. (2016) conducted a study of 170 persons in treatment for chronic pain and opioid use disorder. Of the 170 participants in the study, the researchers found that 91% reported a lifetime diagnosis of a psychiatric disorder, not including personality disorders. The specifics of the 91% were broken down to 52% anxiety, 57% mood, and 78% SUD other than OUD (Barry et al., 2016).

Thus, when looking only at chronic pain as a biomedical condition, it can be easily seen that the prevalence of co-occurring medical, mental health, and substance use conditions is concern-ing among patients seeking treatment. Aside from chronic pain, an array of additional medical concerns could be present as well, including diabetes, chronic obstructive pulmonary disease, chronic heart failure, and many others. Ultimately, biomedical conditions and complications inform the need for both residential and inpatient services for persons with co-occurring dis-orders. Ideally, all health conditions should be managed in an integrated treatment approach (Ries et al., 2014), including collaboration between health-care providers and the person with co-occurring disorders.

Dimension 3: Emotional, Behavioral, or Cognitive Conditions and Complications

Perhaps one of the most important factors of assessment for persons with co-occurring disorders are the emotional, behavioral, and cognitive conditions dimension of the ASAM criteria. Dimen-sion 3 provides an opportunity to comprehensively assess a person with co-occurring disorders to understand the psychological factors that may influence the need for residential or inpatient treatment (Ries et al., 2014). Essentially, gaining as full an understanding as possible about the psychological and cognitive challenges facing a person with co-occurring disorders is a criti-cal aspect of the success of treatment and recovery. One specific example of the importance of understanding emotional and cognitive conditions is associated with suicidal ideation. The risk of attempting suicide is significantly higher for persons with a mental health disorder than for the general population (Hoertel et al., 2015). Further, in an extensive meta-analysis, Poorolajal et al. (2016) found that SUD is positively correlated with suicidal ideation, suicide attempt, and death from suicide. Suicide risk is only one aspect of a constellation of emotional and behavioral factors that may affect a person with co-occurring disorders who is seeking residential or inpatient treatment. Along with suicidal ideation, factors related to depression, anxiety, trauma sequelae, psychosis, and other symptomatology must be considered prior to engagement in any level of care, especially inpatient or residential treatment. Again, ASAM encourages integrated treatment for persons who have co-occurring substance use, emotional, behavioral, and cognitive conditions (Ries et al., 2014).

Dimension 4: Readiness to Change

When assessing a person with co-occurring disorders for residential or inpatient treatment needs, it is important to consider overall readiness to change (Ries et al., 2014). Choi et al. (2013) found that readiness to change is significantly correlated with overall residential treatment retention among persons with co-occurring substance use and mental health conditions. Thus, a person's readiness to change should be assessed at the onset of treatment to determine whether or not residential or inpatient treatment should be an option as the most effective and least restrictive level of care. De Weert-van Oene et al. (2015) conducted a study that confirms the results found by Choi et al. (2013), indicating that aspects of motivation for treatment and change can significantly affect a person's likelihood of remaining in treatment. Van Oene et al. (2015) suggest that persons who are not as motivated to change could perhaps be considered for increased focus in treatment that aims to reduce the likelihood of early attrition. Overall, the ASAM dimension for assessing readiness to change provides vital knowledge that can inform patients and health professionals about the most appropriate option for treatment, especially when considering the option of residential or inpatient services.

Dimension 5: Resumed Substance Use, Continued Use, or Continued Problem Potential

Potential for substance use recurrence is a critical dimension to be assessed according to ASAM criteria (Ries et al., 2014). One of the key factors assessed in this dimension is related to impulsivity. Impulsivity can be understood as an individual's ability to refrain from substance use despite cravings and repeated treatment interventions. Loree et al. (2015) conducted a meta-analysis of research data aimed at the correlation between impulsivity and substance use disorder treatment outcomes. The researchers found that impulsivity is negatively correlated with treatment outcomes for substance use disorder. As impulsivity increases, the likelihood of successful treatment outcomes decreases. Conceptualizing the risk for continued substance use is important for managing treatment for both substance use and mental health disorders. For example, if a client were to present for treatment with a high potential for substance use recurrence, it may behoove the health professionals to consider residential treatment or inpatient services as a more viable option than outpatient services. Though more restrictive, inpatient and residential treatment can provide more structure, stability, and accountability regarding substance use treatment and recurrence prevention than most outpatient services.

Dimension 6: Recovery Environment

ASAM Dimension 6 provides consideration for the type of environment that the person with co-occurring disorders will be living in during the recovery process (Ries et al., 2014). Environmental factors are critical in regard to potential for continued substance use, especially the quality and quantity of supportive relationships that the recovering person is involved in throughout the process (Menon & Kandasamy, 2018). Menon and Kandasamy (2018) specifically state that 'Negative social support in the form of interpersonal conflict and social pressure to use substances has been related to an increased risk for relapse' (p. S475). Persons with co-occurring disorders should be carefully assessed for problem potential in the areas of interpersonal relationships, pressure to use substances by family or peers, or other social factors in the recovery environment. Again, potential use of residential or inpatient services for persons with co-occurring disorders can be considered when the recovery environment is considered to be very high risk and has the potential to significantly disrupt or eliminate treatment progress in an outpatient setting alone.

Understanding the ASAM dimensions is vital to conceptualizing the need for both residential and inpatient services for persons with co-occurring disorders. The following chapter content explores the specific types of residential and inpatient treatment levels and the similarities and differences between each level of care. Ultimately, it is important to understand that the most appropriate level of care should be guided by the patients themselves, with supportive assistance provided by professional mental health and substance use disorder treatment personnel.

Residential Treatment

Those living with ongoing mental health diagnoses and/or substance use face several challenges in their attempts to resume a life focused on recovery. The impact of their ongoing struggles indicates that basic needs and activities of daily living have been limited. The skills associated with self-care, family engagement, chore completion, and personal finance management have been limited as a result of the struggles of living with co-occurring disorders. While individuals living in residential treatment engage in individual and group counseling sessions, additional focus is needed to help enhance and appropriately resume these essential daily living skills, which are foundational to maintaining recovery. Residential living can enhance these basic skills while also helping the individual obtain and use skills to manage mental health symptoms and tools to engage in recovery.

Clinically Managed Low-Intensity Residential

Low-intensity residential treatment is the initial and lowest level of residential services. Low-intensity residential treatment is provided in a setting that offers 24-hour care. The ASAM criteria specifically call for an emphasis on community re-entry in the low-intensity residential treatment environment. Throughout treatment at this level of care, ASAM calls for the availability of health-care staff who are appropriately trained and a minimum of five hours of treatment during a week of residential services (Ries et al., 2014). Despite calling for only five hours of clinical treatment per week, residential services offer overall structure, which is often much needed for individuals who have co-occurring disorders. Persons with co-occurring disorders and persons with substance use disorder only can receive treatment services from low-intensity residential. Length of stay is often guided by treatment progress or regression, combined with input from managed-care organizations or other external payer sources and stakeholders (Ries et al., 2014).

Clinically Managed Population-Specific High-Intensity Residential

Population-specific high-intensity residential treatment is an appropriate level of care for persons who present for treatment with an element of imminent harm (Ries et al., 2014). For a person with co-occurring disorders, this could include risk related to substance use, acute medical concerns, or suicidal or homicidal ideation. The population-specific aspect of this level of care is clarified as being related to the provision of treatment for persons who may have a functional impairment that limits engagement in a full range of intensity of residential treatment services (Ries et al., 2014). This level of care also maintains a living structure that allows the resident to plan their days while having staff support, ability to connect with treatment, and use skills associated with self-help such as AA or NA. Again, 24-hour structured treatment is offered at this level of care, including the use of counselors who are trained to deliver needed services (Ries et al., 2014).

Clinically Managed High-Intensity Residential

High-intensity residential treatment is similar to population-specific residential with the exception of the inclusion of the full range of intensity of services (Ries et al., 2014). The component of imminent danger is also present, with treatment services guided by clinically trained therapists. The direction of treatment is to ensure symptom stability with the goal of stepping the client down to a lower level of outpatient treatment post-discharge. Group work and therapeutic community structure are provided (Ries et al., 2014).

Inpatient Treatment

Medically Monitored Intensive Inpatient

At times, persons with co-occurring disorders may need a more medically intensive monitoring program. Thus, the inpatient level of care offers a shift from clinical management to medical management of treatment oversight (Ries et al., 2014). The component of medical management involves the utilization of both physician and nursing care in a 24-hour setting (Ries et al., 2014). Additionally, physician and nursing care is combined with clinical treatment that includes trained counselors. ASAM criteria call for counseling and clinical treatment to be available in the medically monitored intensive inpatient level of care at least 16 hours per day (Ries et al., 2014).

Medically Managed Intensive Inpatient

Persons with co-occurring disorders may present to treatment with health-related concerns and risks that are highly severe and in need of acute stabilization. When the individual with a co-occurring disorder has severely unstable symptoms related to withdrawal or medical or mental health conditions, treatment at the medically managed intensive inpatient level of care may be appropriate. Again, 24-hour nursing and physician care is available in this level of treatment, along with availability of clinical counseling staff (Ries et al., 2014). Those receiving this level of care also receive support through ongoing contact with various staff and structure, otherwise known as the therapeutic milieu.

Withdrawal Management

It is important to note that both the residential and inpatient levels of care also offer specific withdrawal management services (Ries et al., 2014). Many persons with co-occurring disorders who seek treatment may need medical oversight of withdrawal symptoms to ensure that clinical risk is mitigated, along with an improvement in ability to engage immediately with treatment resources. Overall, withdrawal management is often a significant component of the treatment process, especially in the initial stage of treatment when substance use may have been more recent and intense. The effects of substance use withdrawal on mental health–related symptomatology are discussed in a previous section of this chapter. It is important for counselors to consider that services used to specifically manage withdrawal symptoms can help an individual become linked with ongoing forms of treatment. However, the focus of this level of care is to assist the individual with managing symptoms of withdrawal to be able to engage in ongoing treatment to improve recovery-related skills. This level of treatment alone does not provide the same type of support and skills enhancement as other and longer forms of treatment.

Integration of Care

At the inpatient and residential levels of care, it is crucial to ensure that, to the greatest extent possible, patients with co-occurring disorders have access to integrated treatment (Ries et al., 2014). McKee et al. (2013) discuss that a preponderance of research indicates that integrated treatment for co-occurring disorders is preferential and provides better outcomes for patients. Moreover, McKee et al. (2013) cite Hogan (2011) in stating that the access to and availability of fully integrated treatment models for persons with co-occurring disorders is lacking. Though such programs appear to be currently lacking, McKee et al. (2013) conducted an integrated treatment implementation study and discussed that:

> A traditional residential service was transformed to an integrated treatment program for co-occurring disorders in such a way that participation in the program led to clients exhibiting clinically significant improvements in symptoms, gains in relevant knowledge and skills, and high satisfaction.

(p. 257)

Based on the study and conclusions presented by McKee et al. (2013), it is imperative for mental health and substance use professionals, administrators, and medical staff to seek the best way possible to establish integrated care for persons with co-occurring disorders, especially in residential and inpatient treatment milieus. Integrated treatment provides the best opportunity for individuals with co-occurring disorders to experience care that is centered on their unique needs, resulting in a greater opportunity for successful treatment outcomes and patient satisfaction (McKee et al., 2013).

Deciding Level of Care

Up until recently (and perhaps still in some parts of the country), the prevailing approach to working with individuals living with co-occurring substance use and mental health diagnoses has been focused on separately treating each illness (Ding et al., 2018). Those living with co-occurring substance use and mental health diagnoses often began by focusing on substance use treatment before fully addressing mental health diagnoses. Co-occurring disorders had been conceptualized in a linear approach in which, in order for an individual to make long-term progress on their mental health, they must first stop using substances that could exacerbate mental health symptoms (O'Connell et al., 2020). This conceptualization in some ways makes sense, especially if treatment for mental health disorders included controlled substances that carry high risk for abuse. However, conceptualization of treatment coupled with abstinence-based recovery programs often left individuals who used substances to cope with mental health symptoms without a primary coping strategy often contributing to high dropout rates and resumed substance use. As opposed to a linear perspective of care, recent models have argued for a combined approach to treating co-occurring disorders based on the client's unique symptoms, substance use, and various risks.

Deciding which level of care to use to meet the client's needs can be difficult to decide, especially if the individual has a lack of resources such as limited or no health insurance or lack of childcare or employment. The recommendations to be made must also be flexible enough to consider these unique factors associated with the client in order to provide them the best opportunity to make progress in various aspects of their lives.

The Four-Quadrant Model Approach

The linear conceptualization of co-occurring disorders treatment often left people feeling over-whelmed with mental health diagnoses while trying to find skills to prevent substance use. An integrated approach to treatment in which the individual's mental health symptoms are addressed and tools for recovery are created is the preferred method for working with those living with co-occurring disorders (Doweiko, 2018).

The model shown here is from SAMHSA's TIP 42 (2005) recommendations for working with individuals with co-occurring substance use and mental health diagnoses.

Alcohol and Other Drug Abuse Categories

Category I

Mental health disorders less severe
Substance abuse disorders less severe
System of care: Primary health-care systems

Category II

Mental health more severe
Substance abuse disorders less severe
System of care: Mental health system

Category III

Mental health less severe
Substance abuse disorders more severe
System of care: Substance abuse system

Category IV

Mental health more severe
Substance abuse disorders more severe
System of care: Hospitals, prison, emergency rooms

When considering this model, mental health and substance use symptoms are viewed on a con-tinuum of severity. It is a combination of these severities that help link the individual with an appropriate level of care.

Individuals with substance use disorder mild and co-occurring mild mental health diagnoses are often treated in primary-care facilities as their level of current functioning may not be severe enough to prompt a higher level of care for both substance use and mental health. Individuals meeting criteria in these settings may also receive treatment in outpatient mental health and sub-stance use facilities. Treatment at such agencies would most likely include individual treatment with an emphasis on education to reduce risk while enhancing commitment to personal care without substance use (SAMHSA, 2005).

Those living with more severe mental health symptoms while also living with substance use disorder mild most likely would be linked with a primary outpatient mental health treat-ment provider. Treatment in these agencies would include individual and group counseling, linkage with psychiatric care, and additional family-related treatment as needed. The outpa-tient mental health focus would be to have individuals obtain skills to manage their mental health symptoms without the use of substances while also meeting various other personal goals (Doweiko, 2018).

Individuals living with moderate to severe substance use disorders while also living with mild mental health diagnoses are considered to receive primary treatment in substance use facilities. Treatment at such programs can include intensive outpatient treatment, which requires the individual to attend treatment several days a week (in some instances, one two-hour group per day for six days per week, plus an additional individual session). Based on the severity of substance use symptoms such as withdrawal symptoms, detox services must be considered (SAMHSA, 2005).

The most restrictive level of care would be for those living with both severe mental health and substance use diagnoses. For many individuals, the severity of their co-occurring symptoms may have caused them to lose their primary housing, and they may be arrested as their symptoms manifest in the streets or other community areas (Ding et al., 2018). As many of these individuals most likely have not adhered to medication management for mental health symptoms while simultaneously engaging in illicit substance use, their presentations upon arrest would require that they be seen and treated at a local emergency room. Usually, after the initial assessment, the individual is referred to inpatient psychiatric care, where they would be treated for immediate substance use concerns such as withdrawal while also being treated for primary mental health diagnoses. The time needed for symptom amelioration is a predictor of length of stay; this can usually range between 10 to 28 days (SAMHSA, 2005). After discharge, the client is usually linked with outpatient substance use treatment and outpatient mental health treatment. Counselors should consider more enhanced levels of care such as residential treatment for those who have met criteria for several episodes of such a high level of care, especially if their home environments (or lack thereof) are related to resuming substance use or lack of follow through with mental health treatment.

Conclusion

The assessment process needs to be grounded in ethics and professional competencies. The validity and reliability of each instrument selected needs to be taken into consideration according to Principle V-2 (NAADAC, 2021). The key to ethical practice is to diagnose only within your scope of practice (Principle V-7) (NAADAC, 2021) and to seek referral and supervision during this critical process. No one assessment tool is finite, nor will one tool give you the complete picture of the client. Most importantly, when facilitating assessments, it is important to 'recognize the potential for substance use disorders to mimic a variety of medical and mental health conditions and the potential for medical and mental health conditions to coexist with addiction and substance abuse' (Center for Substance Abuse Treatment, 2006, Competency 4). Assessment leads to determining diagnostic criteria for disorders, which is needed to determine the level of care needed for the least intrusive treatment for co-occurring disorders. Levels of care go from the intensity of inpatient hospitalization and residential to intensive outpatient and outpatient services. While labeling an individual with disorder(s) is fraught with problems if those professionals are not thorough with diagnosing properly, the caveat is that only once the problems have been clearly diagnosed can individualized treatment plans be developed for the client. Level of care is determined for medical necessity to be indicated as this will provide the client with appropriate treatment approach.

Questions for Consideration

1. At some facilities, there are separate professionals who complete the assessment and facilitate treatment. What benefits or drawbacks would there be to having an assessment completed by a professional who is not also providing the treatment?

2. Facilitating assessments often requires different professional skills than providing treatment. What strengths do you possess that would help you be an effective assessor?
3. Diagnosis is a substantial responsibility and must be done professionally and ethically. What challenges do you foresee in diagnosing co-occurring disorders?

Case Study

Phil is a 56-year-old African American man who has recently been arrested for driving under the influence. He is a married father of two boys and owns a power washing company. His wife and his primary care doctor have warned him against drinking. As his diabetes continues to worsen and the pandemic shut down his business temporarily, he has found himself drinking more and more. His arrest followed a car accident in which his car was totaled. His neighbors called emergency services when he crashed into their mailbox and did not get out of the car. Emergency services drove him to the hospital, and a blood test revealed a .30 blood alcohol content (BAC). Phil woke in the hospital to find that he was handcuffed to the bed with no recollection of what had happened. The hospital doctors have advised the police that Phil needs to be detoxed prior to being taken to jail to prevent any dangerous withdrawal symptoms and to stabilize his blood sugar. The police are eager to arrest him as this is not the first time he has been in trouble with the law. Over the past year, he has received a drunk in public charge and a possession of marijuana charge when he was found wandering his neighborhood at 3:00 a.m.

Before he can be discharged from the hospital, you have been called in to determine if treatment is recommended and what level of services would be suited to his needs.

Questions to Consider

1. As Phil's assessor, what information do you think would be pertinent to obtain before he is discharged from the hospital?
2. What type of assessment tools would be best suited for a comprehensive assessment at this time?
3. What recommendations may need to be made for Phil in terms of level of care or services needed?

Recommended Reading and Websites for Training

American Society of Addiction Medicine. (2021). *The ASAM criteria.* Retrieved from www.asam.org/asam-criteria
NAADAC, the Association for Addiction Professionals. (2021). *NAADAC free webinar series.* Retrieved from www.naadac.org/webinars

References

American Psychiatric Association. (2013). *Diagnostic and statistical manual of mental disorders* (DSM-5). American Psychiatric Pub.
Axelsson, E., Lindsäter, E., Ljótsson, B., Andersson, E., & Hedman-Lagerlöf, E. (2017). The 12-item self-report World Health Organization Disability Assessment Schedule (WHODAS) 2.0 administered via the internet to individuals with anxiety and stress disorders: A psychometric investigation based on data from two clinical trials. *JMIR Mental Health, 4*(4), e58. https://doi.org/10.2196/mental.7497
Barry, D. T., Cutter, C. J., Beitel, M., Kerns, R. D., Liong, C., & Schottenfeld, R. S. (2016). Psychiatric disorders among patients seeking treatment for co-occurring chronic pain and opioid use disorder. *The Journal of Clinical Psychiatry, 77*(10), 1413–1419. doi:10.4088/JCP.15m09963
Bastiaens, L., & Galus, J. (2018). The DSM-5 self-rated level 1 cross-cutting symptom measure as a screening tool. *The Psychiatric Quarterly, 89*(1), 111–115. https://doi.org/10.1007/s11126-017-9518-7

Beck, A. T., Steer, R. A., & Brown, G. K. (1996). *Manual for the beck depression inventory-II*. San Psychological Corporation.

Blashfield, R. K. (1998). Diagnostic models and systems. In A. S. Bellack & M. Hersen (Eds.), *Comprehensive clinical psychology: Foundations* (4th ed., pp. 57–80). Pergamon.

Bonnet, U., & Preuss, U. W. (2017). The cannabis withdrawal syndrome: Current insights. *Substance Abuse and Rehabilitation, 8*, 9–37. doi:10.2147/SAR.S109576

Brown, R. L., & Rounds, L. A. (1995). Conjoint screening questionnaires for alcohol and other drug abuse: Criterion validity in a primary care practice. *Wisconsin Medical Journal, 94*(3), 135–140.

Center for Substance Abuse Treatment. (2006). *Addiction counseling competencies: The knowledge, skills, and attitudes of professional practice. Technical Assistance Publication (TAP) series 21* ((SMA) 15–4171). Substance Abuse and Mental Health Services Administration (SAMHSA).

Center for Substance Abuse Treatment: Substance Abuse and Mental Health Services Administration. (2005). *Substance abuse treatment for persons with co-occurring disorders (Treatment Improvement Protocol (TIP) series)*, 42. Retrieved from www.ncbi.nlm.nih.gov/books/NBK64184/figure/A74172/

Chen, C., Balogh, M., Bathija, J., Howanitz, E., Plutchik, R., & Conte, H. R. (1992). Substance abuse among psychiatric inpatients. *Comprehensive Psychiatry, 33*(1), 60–64. https://doi.org/10.1016/0010-440x(92)90081-z

Choi, S., Adams, S., MacMaster, S., & Seiters, J. (2013). Predictors of residential treatment retention among individuals with co-occurring substance abuse and mental health disorders. *Journal of Psychoactive Drugs, 45*(2), 122–131. https://doi.org/10.1080/02791072.2013.785817

Dennis, M., Titus, J., White, M., Unsicker, J., & Hodgkins, D. (2002). Global Appraisal of Individual Needs (GAIN): Administration guide for the GAIN and related measures. *Chestnut Health Systems*. [Online]. Retrieved from www.chestnut.org/li/gain/gadm1299.pdf

de Weert-van Oene, G. H., Gongora, V., von Sternberg, K., & de Jong, C. A. J. (2015). Motivation for treatment and motivation for change in substance-dependent patients with co-occurring psychiatric disorders. *Journal of Psychoactive Drugs, 47*(5), 393–400. https://doi.org/10.1080/02791072.2015.1079669

Ding, K., Slate, M., & Yang, J. (2018). History of co-occurring disorders and current mental health status among homeless veterans. *BMC Public Health, 18*, 751. https://doi.org/10.1186/s12889-018-5700-6

Doweiko, H. (2018). *Concepts of chemical depency* (10th ed.). Cengage Publishing.

Ewing, J. A. (1984). Detecting alcoholism: The CAGE questionnaire. *JAMA, 252*(14), 1905–1907.

Flynn, P. M., & Brown, B. S. (2008). Co-occurring disorders in substance abuse treatment: Issues and prospects. *Journal of Substance Abuse Treatment, 34*(1), 36–47. https://doi.org/10.1016/j.jsat.2006.11.013

Han, B., Compton, W. M., Blanco, C., & Colpe, L. J. (2017). Prevalence, treatment, and unmet treatment needs of US adults with mental health and substance use disorders. *Health Affairs, 36*(10), 1739–1747. https://doi.org/10.1377/hlthaff.2017.0584

Hoertel, N., Franco, S., Wall, M., Oquendo, B. T., Kerridge, F., Limosin, F., & Blanco, C. (2015). Mental disorders and risk of suicide attempt: A national prospective study. *Molecular Psychiatry, 20*, 718–726. doi:10.1038/mp.2015.19

Kay, S. R., Opler, L. A., & Lindenmayer, J. (1988). Reliability and validity of the positive and negative syndrome scale for schizophrenics. *Psychiatry Research, 23*(1), 99–110. https://doi.org/10.1016/0165-1781(88)90038-8

Kilpatrick, D. G., Resnick, H. S., Milanak, M. E., Miller, M. W., Keyes, K. M., & Friedman, M. J. (2013). National estimates of exposure to traumatic events and PTSD prevalence usingdsm-ivanddsm-5Criteria. *Journal of Traumatic Stress, 26*(5), 537–547. https://doi.org/10.1002/jts.21848

Kosten, T. R., & Baxter, L. E. (2019). Review article: Effective management of opioid withdrawal symptoms: A gateway to opioid dependence treatment. *The American Journal on Addictions, 28*(2). Retrieved from https://onlinelibrary.wiley.com/doi/full/10.1111/ajad.12862

Lane, S. P., Steinley, D., & Sher, K. J. (2016). Meta-analysis of DSM alcohol use disorder criteria severities: Structural consistency is only "skin deep". *Psychological Medicine, 46*(8), 1769–1784. https://doi.org/10.1017/s0033291716000404

Lang, A. J., Wilkins, K., Roy-Byrne, P. P., Golinelli, D., Chavira, D., Sherbourne, C., . . . Stein, M. B. (2012). Abbreviated PTSD checklist (PCL) as a guide to clinical response. *General Hospital Psychiatry, 34*(4), 332–338. https://doi.org/10.1016/j.genhosppsych.2012.02.003

Lazowski, L. E., & Geary, B. B. (2019). Validation of the adult Substance Abuse Subtle Screening Inventory-4 (SASSI-4). *European Journal of Psychological Assessment, 35*(1), 86–97.

Loree, A. M., Lundahl, L. H., & Ledgerwood, D. M. (2015). Impulsivity as a predictor of treatment outcome in substance use disorders: Review and synthesis. *Drug & Alcohol Review, 34*(2), 119–134. https://doi.org/10.1111/dar.12132

McGovern, M., Xie, H., Acquilano, S., Segal, S. S., Siembab, L., & Drake, R. (2007). Addiction treatment services and co-occurring disorders: The ASAM-PPC-2R taxonomy of program dual diagnosis capability. *Journal of Addictive Diseases, 26*(3), 27–37.

McKee, S. A., Harris, G. T., & Cormier, C. A. (2013). Implementing residential integrated treatment for co-occurring disorders. *Journal of Dual Diagnosis, 9*(3), 249–259. doi:10.1080/15504263.2013.807073

Menon, J., & Kandasamy, A. (2018). Relapse prevention. *Indian Journal of Psychiatry, 60*, S473–S478. https://doi.org/10.4103/psychiatry.IndianJPsychiatry_36_18

Miller, C. S., Shields, A. L., Campfield, D., Wallace, K. A., & Weiss, R. D. (2007). Substance use scales of the Minnesota multiphasic personality inventory: An exploration of score reliability via meta-analysis. *Educational and Psychological Measurement, 67*(6), 1052–1065.

Mueser, K. T., & Gingerich, S. (2013). Treatment of co-occurring psychotic and substance use disorders. *Social Work in Public Health, 28*(3–4), 424–439. https://doi.org/10.1080/19371918.2013.774676

NAADAC, the Association for Addiction Professionals. (2021). *NAADAC/NCC AP code of ethics.* NAADAC.

Narrow, W. E., & Kuhl, E. A. (2011). Dimensional approaches to psychiatric diagnosis in DSM-5. *The Journal of Mental Health Policy and Economics, 14*(4), 197.

Nassir Ghaemi, S., Miller, C. J., Berv, D. A., Klugman, J., Rosenquist, K. J., & Pies, R. W. (2005). Sensitivity and specificity of a new bipolar spectrum diagnostic scale. *Journal of Affective Disorders, 84*(2–3), 273–277. https://doi.org/10.1016/s0165-0327(03)00196-4

O'Connell, M., Flanagan, E., Delphin-Rittmon, M., & Davidson, L. (2020). Enhancing outcomes for persons with co-occurring disorders through skills training and peer recovery support. *Journal of Mental Health, 29*(1), 6–11. doi:10.1080/09638237.2017.1294733

Perry, A. E., Martyn-St James, M., Burns, L., Hewitt, C., Glanville, J. M., Aboaja, A., . . . Swami, S. (2019). Interventions for drug-using offenders with co-occurring mental health problems. *Cochrane Database of Systematic Reviews.* https://doi.org/10.1002/14651858.cd010901.pub3

Poorolajal, J., Haghtalab, T., Farhadi, M., & Darvishi, N. (2016). Substance use disorder and risk of suicidal ideation, suicide attempt and suicide death: A meta-analysis. *Journal of Public Health, 38*(3), 282–291. https://doi.org/10.1093/pubmed/fdv148

Revadigar, N., & Gupta, V. (2021, February 6). *Substance induced mood disorders – StatPearls – NCBI bookshelf.* National Center for Biotechnology Information. Retrieved from www.ncbi.nlm.nih.gov/books/NBK555887/

Ries, R., Miller, S. C., Saitz, R., & Fiellin, D. A. (2014). *The ASAM principles of addiction medicine* (5th ed.). Wolters Kluwer Health.

Spitzer, R. L., Kroenke, K., Williams, J. B., & Löwe, B. (2006). A brief measure for assessing generalized anxiety disorder. *Archives of Internal Medicine, 166*(10), 1092. https://doi.org/10.1001/archinte.166.10.1092

Stallvik, M., & Nordahl, H. M. (2014). Convergent validity of the ASAM criteria in co occurring disorders. *Journal of Dual Diagnosis, 10*(2), 68–78. doi:10.1080/15504263.2014.906812

Stice, E., Telch, C. F., & Rizvi, S. L. (2000). Development and validation of the eating disorder diagnostic scale: A brief self-report measure of anorexia, bulimia, and binge-eating disorder. *Psychological Assessment, 12*(2), 123–131. https://doi.org/10.1037/1040-3590.12.2.123

Substance Abuse and Mental Health Services Administration (SAMHSA). (2020a). *Substance use disorder treatment for people with co-occurring disorders. Treatment Improvement Protocol (TIP) series, No. 42* (PEP20-02-01-004). SAMHSA. Retrieved from https://store.samhsa.gov/sites/default/files/SAMHSA_Digital_Download/PEP20-02-01_004.pdf

Substance Abuse and Mental Health Services Administration (SAMHSA). (2020b). *Key substance use and mental health indicators in the United States: Results from the 2019 National Survey on Drug Use and Health* (HHS Publication No. PEP20-07-01-001). Rockville, MD: Center for Behavioral Health Statistics and Quality, Substance Abuse and Mental Health Services Administration. Retrieved from www.samhsa.gov/data/sites/default/files/reports/rpt29393/2019NSDUHFFRPDFWHTML/2019NSDUHFFR1PDFW090120.pdf

Widiger, T. A., & Samuel, D. B. (2005). Diagnostic categories or dimensions? A question for the diagnostic and statistical manual of mental disorders – fifth edition. *Journal of Abnormal Psychology, 114*(4), 494–504.

Young, R. C., Biggs, J. T., Ziegler, V. E., & Meyer, D. A. (1978). A rating scale for mania: Reliability, validity and sensitivity. *British Journal of Psychiatry, 133*(5), 429–435. https://doi.org/10.1192/bjp.133.5.429

14 Recovery Programming

12 Steps, Cognitive Behavioral Therapy, and Motivational Interviewing

Fredrick Dombrowski, Tom Alexander, and Tricia L. Chandler

Introduction

Treatment for mental health and substance use disorders has continued to evolve with greater research and application of evidence-based practices. While counselors work to improve mental health and substance use symptoms, they also work to connect the client to various supports to help maintain treatment goals and assist during long-term recovery. These social supports can come from community-based self-help groups such as AA or peer-organized activities. The advent of AA provided individuals attempting to engage in recovery with peer support at various hours and times, whereas treatment was generally limited to the authorized treatment schedule. While community-based organizations are helpful, treatment centers are tasked with providing evidence-based practice, using counseling tools that are not found in peer-run self-help groups. This chapter will briefly review the history of AA while also identifying how cognitive behavioral therapy and motivational interviewing are used in the treatment of co-occurring disorders.

Learning Objectives

- Understand the development of the 12-step recovery model
- Understand the cognitive behavioral therapy approach
- Understand the addition of motivational interviewing and stages of change

Key Terms

Ambivalence: The state in which an individual feels conflicted about making changes or engaging in certain behaviors.

Automatic Thoughts: Thoughts that are a direct reaction to a trigger and molded by an individual's core beliefs.

Cognitive Restructuring: The process of objectively assessing the accuracy of thoughts regarding triggers to find more accurate ways to assess a situation.

Core Beliefs: A set of values, expectations, and beliefs held by an individual to create an understanding of the world and of the individual. An individual's core beliefs may be at direct odds with their spiritual beliefs and regularly dictate reactions to triggers.

Evidence-Based Practice: Summarizing and applying research-supported treatment modalities to client care.

Metacognition: The process of an individual thinking about their own thoughts.

Motivation: The desire or willingness an individual has to accomplish a specific behavior.

Pre-contemplation: The stage in which an individual is ambivalent about making changes to their life although they may be able to identify how some behaviors are negatively impacting them and those around them.

Rolling with Resistance: A method in which a counselor is able to validate client concerns while also helping enhance the client's motivation for change.

DOI: 10.4324/9781003220916-17

Schema: A pattern of thought that organizes societal, interpersonal, and intrapersonal expectations.

Self-Help Groups: Groups held in the community that are conducted by peer members to help focus on managing a specific life problem. These groups are not led by treatment providers, do not maintain documented progress of members, and can have autonomy among groups, despite sharing the group's prominent name.

Self-Help Sponsor: An individual who has made progress on their recovery, adhering to the recommended modality of the self-help group. This individual shares their knowledge and support with other members who are attempting to take steps in their recovery. The sponsor can help the individual attend self-help groups and can be available during instances when an individual is feeling an urge to resume substance use.

Socratic Questioning: A form of dialogue that relies on the counselor and individual critically exploring the accuracy and meaning of a thought.

The Foundations of Self-Help

The recovery model began with the development of Alcoholics Anonymous (1939) by Bob Smith (a physician) and Bill Wilson (a businessman), who both lived with alcohol use disorder. After many instances of connecting with each other and additional individuals with a similar desire to quit using alcohol, they wanted to develop a manual to help maintain sobriety and published a book, *Alcoholics Anonymous: The Story of How More Than One Hundred Men Have Recovered from Alcoholism* (1939). Within this text are the 12 steps, which were created as the basis of the self-help program: that peers can assist one another in maintaining sobriety with a community of like supporters. The 12 steps incorporate the AA premise that those living with alcohol use disorder or other substance use disorders must recognize the diseased brain and that only through admitting one is powerless over the use of the substance and accepting that abstinence is the way to recovery can one begin the process of reclaiming one's life free of alcohol and other substances (Wilson, 1952, 1981).

The 12 steps are heavily influenced by Christian spirituality, causing such core aspects as 'turn one's life over to a higher power', 'a searching and fearless moral inventory of ourselves', and 'remove all defects of character' to be criticized as this wording is indicative that those living with substance use disorder are morally flawed (Dodes & Dodes, 2014; Wilson, 1952, 1981). Prior to the development of AA, those living with substance use disorders were often housed in sanitariums, fully limiting the freedom of the individual. AA was the first program to approach recovery from the perspective of mutual support and commitment, allowing members to enter groups, discuss their experiences with alcohol use, and apply the 12 steps to their daily lives. As therapeutic approaches have developed in the past several decades, the focus of research has been on these therapeutic interventions, whereas self-help groups, being mainly community supports, have been revered by personal and anecdotal evidence (Dodes & Dodes, 2014).

Regardless of the self-help nature of AA and other 12-step groups, many recovery programs incorporate and, at times, insist that those seeking treatment for substance use disorders seek out these programs as well. This makes sense clinically as linking the client with sober social supports allows them to connect with others and avoid isolation when most likely experiencing triggers for substance use during times when day treatment centers are not open (Doweiko, 2009). While this approach can certainly support recovery for many people, it is not a panacea for all with substance use disorders and has a spiritual perspective overall. Self-help programs such as AA are community peer groups that are heavily focused on spirituality conceptualizing substance use as a response to a deficiency in this area of the individual's life.

Many people in recovery can point to their own subjective experience as evidence to support the benefits of AA. However, AA and other 12-step groups are not therapeutic, evidence-based practices, and therefore, counselors applying aspects of these spiritual programs to their clinical work are not providing evidence-based clinical care. As there are thousands of chapters of AA, each chapter operates as their own individual cell. While each chapter may use *The Big Book* and adhere to similar meeting structures, the fluidity between chapters, changes in peer leadership, and the core value of anonymity make it difficult to follow up with long-term research on AA. Some research has found that AA can be a good ally to enhance evidence-based practices as the individual can remain in AA throughout their lifespan without financial or insurance limitations (Kelly, 2017). This chapter will review the current evidence-based psychotherapeutic approaches of cognitive behavioral therapy, motivational interviewing, and the stage of change models.

Cognitive Behavioral Therapy

Cognitive behavioral therapy (CBT) is one of the most widely used forms of treatment for co-occurring disorders (Hayes & Hofmann, 2017). Given the focus on observable and measurable behavioral activities providing evidence for changes in automatic thoughts and core beliefs, many treatment facilities and programs use treatment plans heavily influenced by CBT. Practitioners of CBT expect ongoing research and evidence to show the value and effectiveness of CBT (Warfield, 2013). With meta-analytic research confirming the benefits of CBT when working with those living with varying psychological and substance use disorders Cuijpers et al., 2016), many counselors in training will learn about the basic aspects of this form of treatment (Beck, 2011). CBT is applied to varying populations and treatment levels, including telehealth (Dobkin et al., 2020).

The emphasis on CBT cannot be understated in current treatment of co-occurring disorders. While there may be much discussion and appreciation of the outcomes that CBT can provide, many clinicians may use some aspects of CBT without adhering to the strict CBT process. Therefore, clinicians will use tools associated with CBT in an eclectic manner in an attempt to meet the needs of what they are discussing with the patient in the moment (Reiser & Milne, 2013). Applying eclectic skills of CBT, such as thought challenging, is not in alignment with the step-by-step CBT process, and therefore, clinicians may experience limited outcomes in treatment (Beck, 2011).

This section on CBT provides the reader with information regarding the basic components of CBT. Discussing the formation of CBT, this chapter will contrast CBT with other forms of treatment. Through this review, the reader will be able to identify the specific systematic process as to how to apply this treatment modality to those living with co-occurring disorders. This chapter also reviews the limitations to using CBT and provides recommendations for adjustment of CBT provision based on the need of the client. Finally, additional CBT resources will be provided to the reader.

History of CBT

Early conceptualization for cognitive hypothesis is traceable back to ancient philosophers such as Aristotle and Plato. These ancient philosophers attempted to understand the world and the universe specifically through the interpretations and thoughts of an individual. These early philosophers stressed that how an individual thinks about the world determines the nature of reality. In order to understand reality, each other, and themselves, it is necessary for an individual to understand their own thought process. Metacognition, or the process of 'thinking about thinking', is one of the cornerstones of CBT (Lee & Edget, 2012).

The field of psychology is in its relative infancy when compared to other sciences. Treatment of mental health and substance abuse disorders has drastically changed over the last 100 years as the field has moved away from institutionalization and practices that are not evidence based (Doweiko, 2009). Previous counseling theories conceptualized mental health and substance abuse problems from a perspective of subconscious desires and needs resulting from problems experienced with parental attachment in one or more psychosexual stages. Therefore, treatment was prescribed several times per week for years at a time with the belief that experiences of catharsis were primarily responsible for positive changes in the individual (Karpiak et al., 2016).

Although the traditional psychodynamic view of mental health was the primary way of treating patients in the early twentieth century, many psychologists, in an effort to further advance the scientific practice of psychology, sought to objectively observe and measure behaviors, which would be associated with thoughts (Corey, 2018). Prior psychodynamic-related treatment rested heavily on unobservable concepts such as thoughts, dreams, and childhood sexual stages. The behavioral model measured environmental rewards and punishments as being determinants of behavior while ignoring unobservable thoughts. Through this research, many scientists were able to control and predict the behavior of animals and some people by modifying environmental triggers, rewards, and punishments (David et al., 2018a).

Given the empirical support obtained through rigorous scientific study of behaviorism, some twentieth-century clinicians believed that behaviorist assumptions and determinations were limited as humans were not animals and experienced thoughts despite an inability to objectively see, hear, taste, smell, or touch a thought. Aligning with the belief in the value of research regarding mental health treatment, as well as the need for changes in behavioral outcomes, early behavioral therapists combined cognitive aspects in their treatment. In Albert Ellis's rational emotive behavioral therapy (REBT) and Aaron Beck's cognitive behavior therapy (CBT), an individual's thoughts and feelings ultimately determine their actions (David et al., 2018b). If clinicians could effectively challenge the distorted thinking of the client, the client would experience mood improvement, allowing them to select new and more effective behaviors as a response to a trigger. Using these new successful behaviors as a response to triggers causes the client to challenge and modify their core beliefs (Roychowdhury, 2016).

The theoretical orientation of CBT is different from that of other forms of therapy. The expectations of the client, roles of the therapist, and purpose of treatment also differ when comparing CBT to other treatment modalities. In traditional psychodynamic therapy, the clinician was viewed as a blank screen to allow the client to project their subconscious struggles. The clinician played the role of the expert, guiding the client through cathartic experiences to improve symptoms. In this modality, therapy occurred multiple times per week for several years and possibly a lifetime to help undo damage that occurred in a client's earlier psychosexual stages (Corey, 2018). Person-centered counseling differed in that the client was viewed as the expert in their own life, and the clinician's role was to provide unconditional positive regard to the client, allowing them a safe space to process life experiences and improve symptoms. Treatment would last as long as needed (often several years), and sessions would not be structured but open and flexible to respond to anything the client wanted to talk about (Doweiko, 2009).

Drastically differing from these forms of treatment, CBT is a preferably time-limited orientation in which clients identify and work on objective and measurable goals (Beck, 2011). The clinical session itself is not viewed as the instance in which change occurs. Rather, the client's using skills discussed during the session while engaging in their daily lives contributes to improvement in symptoms. Clinicians practicing CBT use the time-focused and homework-intensive approach to ultimately give the client the skills to become their own therapist and no longer need ongoing treatment. This is accomplished through the step-by-step CBT process causing the client to challenge their thoughts, use new and more effective coping strategies, and change core beliefs.

Basic Components of CBT

Counselors working with clients are aware that there are often multiple factors that contribute to a behavioral outcome. From the perspective of the clinician using CBT, the 'schema' or core beliefs of an individual often cause automatic thoughts following a trigger (Lee & Edget,

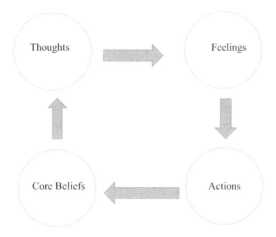

Figure 14.1 Biopsychosocial Data Collection Table

Source: Dombrowski (2021)

2012). Whereas subconscious desires and internal struggles can be difficult to access, focusing on immediate responses to a trigger shows insight into a client's individual core beliefs. Core beliefs are created by the personal experience of the individual along with cultural values, norms, and assumptions based on the world around them (Beck, 2011).

When an individual receives a trigger, their core beliefs generate an automatic thought. For example, an individual who is living with co-occurring disorders may experience depression and alcohol use disorder. When asked to engage in an outside activity with a friend, the individual living with co-occurring depression and alcohol use disorder may have thoughts such as 'I don't feel like it. This will be annoying. I just want to sit home and drink'. These thoughts then contribute to feelings of sadness, loneliness, and hopelessness, with which the individual then copes by using additional alcohol (Suveg et al., 2018). The core belief of this individual may be that they are destined to be unhappy. Core beliefs generate their thoughts. Additionally, the actions that this individual will take, such as isolation and continued substance use, act to strengthen the core beliefs (Beck, 2011).

Figure 14.1 shows the reciprocal relationship between core beliefs, thoughts, and actions.

The CBT Feedback Loop

The time span between a trigger and an action can be very quick. In such instances, many people may not be fully aware of their thought process. In many instances an individual will have a trigger and immediately react based on their immediate emotion. While the individual may not always consider what they are thinking during this time, they have an automatic thought as a response to the trigger. The job of the counselor using CBT is to slow down the time between trigger and action to help the individual become aware of their automatic thoughts. The automatic thoughts of an individual during a trigger are often distorted by core beliefs. Although core beliefs are unique to each individual, there are multiple distortions that are shared between individuals (David et al., 2018b). Among these distortions are:

All-or-Nothing Thinking: The perspective of viewing a situation or an individual as a total failure if they are not completely perfect.

Arbitrary Inferences: Concluding a trigger or a person's characteristics without direct evidence to support this conclusion.

Blaming: The inability of an individual to identify their own role in a difficult situation or problem.

Catastrophizing: Inadvertently making situations out to be worse than they actually are.

Emotional Reasoning: Reacting to an event based on the feeling of the individual as opposed to considering aspects beyond the feeling. An individual's emotions are real, but these emotions to do not always represent reality.

Fallacy of Fairness: A core belief dictating that fairness, equality, and equity are universal concepts employed by other individuals, nature, and spirituality.

Filtering: A thought process in which only one aspect (often negative) about a trigger is utilized.

Jumping to Conclusions: Assuming the outcome of an event without actually knowing.

Overgeneralizing: Making broad assumptions about people or situations based on a limited sample size.

Personalization: When an individual believes events out of their control are their fault.

Should Statements: Expecting standards based on one's own preferences (Beck, 2011).

The distortions listed here will cause an individual to have an emotional reaction. For example, people can have different reactions to the same event. Two individuals may be informed that their business is shutting down, and they will become unemployed. The first individual may have a set of core beliefs built on a lack of trust in others and may have an automatic response such as 'This isn't fair. I am not going to find a new job'. The first individual will experience sadness and anger. These feelings may contribute to such actions as interpersonal arguments with supports, isolation, and substance use. The second individual may have a set of core beliefs built on the efficacy of hard work. When presented with the information that they will lose their job, the second individual will have a thought such as 'This is a good opportunity for me to see what else is out there'. These thoughts can contribute to feelings of motivation, challenge, and determination. As a result, they may work on their resume, connect with supports to network, and look for additional jobs. The variance in thoughts in each individual causes different feelings; individual one has negative feelings followed by difficult interpersonal interactions, whereas individual two has motivated feelings, causing them to take steps to look for work and connect with others. In this hypothetical case, the automatic thoughts experienced by individual one can be in alignment with such cognitive distortions such as all-or-nothing thinking, jumping to conclusions, and the fallacy of fairness. Thoughts contribute to the development of emotions, and emotions dictate behavioral responses (Easton et al., 2018).

CBT Treatment Process

The process by which CBT is applied may vary slightly based on the population and level of care of the individual. Despite these slight variations, there remains an appropriate step-by-step process for applying this form of treatment. As identified in many studies, the need for the therapeutic alliance is paramount when providing any form of treatment as a strong alliance is necessary for the client to return to treatment and follow up with homework in between sessions (Duncan et al., 2003). Establishing a rapport between the counselor and client is based on a focus on the client's goals, a genuine desire to understand the client from their own perspective, and a commitment to understanding the role of the client's culture in their own experience (Warfield, 2013). When the therapeutic alliance is set and goals are established, the counselor can then move to the additional steps of CBT.

The counselor must orient the client to CBT and present to the client the CBT model, which indicates the relationship between triggers, thoughts, feelings, and actions. Triggers, thoughts, feelings, and actions are all separate processes but often become lumped together when people experience triggers. When a counselor asks a client to identify their thoughts associated with an event, it is not uncommon for the client to list feelings. The counselor should help the client distinguish between thoughts and feelings (Lee & Edget, 2012). By reviewing common scenarios, the counselor can help the client separate thoughts and feelings with practice.

It is appropriate for the counselor to use scenarios based on the client's own experiences in order to show how this treatment can be applied to instances that are important to the client. The client can be encouraged to read texts or worksheets about CBT in between sessions one and two to help them become aware of the type of treatment and the roles of both the counselor and the client in treatment (Beck, 2011). Additional worksheets allowing the client to record their experiences with triggers can be used between sessions to reinforce the CBT process.

Figure 14.2 shows a daily trigger diary that can be used to help clients become aware of their daily triggers and responses.

While the vast majority of people may not be paying attention to their core beliefs, counselors use the session to break down instances in which the individual experienced an automatic thought as a response to a trigger. Triggers can occur multiple times per day and may have a lasting impact on the mood and behavior of the client throughout the following days (Linehan, 1993). As the client has worked to complete the trigger diary, the counselor works with the client to explore and identify the automatic thoughts of the client when compared to a list of cognitive distortions. The counselor can introduce to the client a worksheet to provide psychoeducation

Trigger Journal

Day	Trigger	Feelings (1 to 10 intensity)	Thoughts
Monday			
Tuesday			
Wednesday			
Thursday			
Friday			
Saturday			
Sunday			

Figure 14.2 CBT Daily Trigger Diary

Source: Dombrowski (2021)

Thought Challenging and New Actions Worksheet

Triggers	Thoughts	Feelings (1 to 10)	Actions
What distortions am I experiencing?	New Thoughts	New Feelings	New Actions

Figure 14.3 Blank CBT Worksheet

Source: Dombrowski (2021)

regarding cognitive distortions. (Multiple free sources of information about cognitive distortions exist on the internet.) When reviewing the list of cognitive distortions, it is recommended that the counselor reconnect to an instance that the patient has provided and directly work with the patient on identifying which distortions they have experienced (Beck, 2011).

As the client works to identify their thoughts associated with cognitive distortions, the counselor works to help the client identify what feelings are generated because of these thoughts. If an individual identifies experiencing the fallacy of fairness, the counselor then asks the patient to identify how these thoughts make them feel. Specifically, the counselor asks the client to list the name and intensity of the feeling. The hypothetical client mentioned previously who is losing his job may have the thought that 'This isn't fair'. The client is asked to identify how this thought makes him feel and rate the thought on a scale of 1 (does not bother the client at all) to 10 (the feeling is overwhelming). In this hypothetical case, the client could state that he feels frustrated with an 8 rating and sad with a 6 rating. The counselor then works with the client to identify the actions that they take as a result of these thoughts and feelings. In the hypothetical case, the client will isolate and may have interpersonal problems with those whom they care for. The problems caused by these interpersonal difficulties make the client feel worse and strengthen core beliefs (Lee & Edget, 2012). The counselor works with the patient to identify how these actions are detrimental to the overall goals of the client. A full worksheet can be used to help the client document this experience.

Figure 14.3 shows a blank CBT worksheet. This worksheet allows clients to list their triggers, thoughts, feelings, and actions while also listing alternative internal and external responses to triggers.

After the client is asked to process their entire experience from trigger to thought, thought to feeling, and feeling to action, the counselor works with the client to challenge their automatic thoughts associated with the trigger (Beck, 2011). A completed CBT worksheet will look like Figure 14.4:

Thought Challenging and New Actions Worksheet

Triggers	Thoughts	Feelings (1 to 10)	Actions
Loss of job	I can't trust people Life isn't fair Nothing works out Things won't get better	Frustrated 8 Sad 8	Isolate Argue with family Use alcohol Ignore obligations
What distortions am I experiencing?	New Thoughts	New Feelings	New Actions

Figure 14.4 Completed CBT Process without Alternative Responses

Source: Dombrowski (2021)

This completed CBT worksheet shows how an individual experienced a trigger, listed their automatic thoughts as a response to the trigger, and identified how their emotions were impacted by their thoughts and lists behavioral outcomes as a response to thoughts and feelings.

Directly challenging a client's thought process can be potentially invalidating to the client, and thus a good therapeutic alliance and good interpersonal skills are necessary on the part of the counselor (Linehan, 1993). The counselor uses Socratic questioning to help the client find validity or inaccuracies in their automatic thoughts. In some instances of cognitive distortions, a counselor can feel tempted to directly point out the inaccuracy of a client's thought. For example, an individual living with co-occurring anxiety and alcoholism may stress their use of alcohol to help calm them in social situations as the client identifies a belief that others are judging them. While the client is experiencing the distortion of mind reading, directly telling the client that they are mind reading is an ineffective way to have the client adjust their thought. Rather, the counselor uses thought-challenging questions that generate alternative responses by the client. The following is a list of thought-challenging questions:

> **What is the evidence for or against this thought?**
> **How have I handled it in the past?**
> **Is there a potential other thought the individual can be having?**
> **How would I tell others to respond to this?**
> **How does my spirituality guide me in a response to this?**
> **Does thinking this way help me or hurt me?**
> **Will this situation matter in a month, a year, five years from now?**
> **What are other potential factors that could be contributing to the situation?**
>
> (Beck, 2011)

The thought-challenging questions listed here allow the client to generate new and more accurate thoughts. For the hypothetical client who is losing their job, using these questions above will

Thought Challenging and New Actions Worksheet

Triggers	Thoughts	Feelings (1 to 10)	Actions
Loss of job	I can't trust people Life isn't fair Nothing works out Things won't get better	Frustrated 8 Sad 8	Isolate Argue with family Use alcohol Ignore obligations
What distortions am I experiencing?	New Thoughts	New Feelings	New Actions
Overgeneralizing Fallacy of fairness Jumping to conclusions Focusing on negatives	Thinking this way doesn't help I've been through worse I can find work I have friends in the field I would tell others to look for work	Frustrated 3 Sad 2 Hopeful 7 Motivated 8	Apply to 2 jobs this week Reach out to friends in the field Attend job fair

Figure 14.5 Completed CBT Worksheet with Alternative Responses

Source: Dombrowski (2021)

generate new thoughts, such as 'Thinking this way doesn't help me', or 'I have been through tougher times. I have good skills. I can find a new job'. When using such questions to challenge cognitive distortions, in most instances, a client will have a reduction in the severity of their feelings or a full change in their emotion (Lee & Edget, 2012). The hypothetical client losing their job will have different feelings following their new thoughts. The new feelings can be a reduction in previous feelings as well as additional new feelings of hope and motivation. After identifying new feelings, the client is then asked to provide new behaviors they can engage in relatively soon to help them respond to their trigger. When considering new behaviors for the client, it is important to help the client identify behaviors that are observable and measurable and are important to the client. For this client, they would identify new behaviors such as looking for work and networking with vocational supports. This process completes the full CBT worksheet, as identified in Figure 14.5.

As the client uses new behaviors, they will have improved feelings and find evidence to challenge inaccurate thoughts. When using more appropriate behaviors, clients experience better outcomes, contributing to mood improvement. The new outcomes are evidence against core beliefs, and therefore, the client's schema is modified. Whereas the client may have a core belief that 'Life isn't fair', success with new actions allows modifications in core beliefs, such as 'Although life may not be fair, I do have some control over my circumstances'. In instances when a client's behavior may not be effective, the counselor will work with the client to challenge distortions related to ineffective behaviors in order to help the client process their experience and modify behaviors for better outcomes.

Barriers to CBT

In order for clients to use CBT, they must not be in a current state of psychosis or withdrawal. It is necessary for such clients to follow up with recommended medical care to stabilize symptoms, thus allowing them to become oriented to treatment (Doweiko, 2009). Limitations to CBT may also occur when working with a client who is unable to read and write. In such instances, it may be appropriate for the counselor to link the client with educational supports to help them obtain this necessary life skill. However, the counselor can still introduce the client to the CBT process through repetition in the individual session, specifically highlighting the process of trigger, thought, feeling, and action. Treatment for such a client will take more time as the client may be limited in their full application of the CBT process in between sessions.

There are some instances in which a client may not be experiencing a cognitive distortion as a result of a trigger. For example, when a client is presented with a major life-altering experience such as a death or a terminal diagnosis, the automatic thought of 'Things will not be the same' is not a distortion. If an individual loses a loved one and has the thought 'I will not see them again for the rest of my life', they are not having a distortion. In such instances, a person-centered approach creating a validating atmosphere can allow an individual the opportunity to explore potential behavioral options that are appropriate for them and are in alignment with their own belief system. The counsellor must use delicacy and empathy with such issues.

Available CBT Resources

With CBT being a structured form of therapy, the use of worksheets and homework is necessary to assist the client with becoming acclimated to the CBT process and using CBT-related skills in between sessions. The popularity of CBT, coupled with the meta-analysis supporting this form of treatment, has helped create various resources available to clinicians and clients alike. Additional CBT resources can be found at the following sites:

> https://beckinstitute.org/get-informed/tools-and-resources/professionals/
> www.therapistaid.com/therapy-worksheets/cbt/none
> https://positivepsychology.com/cbt-cognitive-behavioral-therapy-techniques-worksheets/

An Overview of the Stages of Change

Conceptualizing the Stages of Change Model

The foundation of motivational interviewing is found in the transtheoretical model (TTM) or stages of change, developed and conceptualized by Prochaska et al. (1992). This seminal work on the stages of change provided an outline by which persons in addiction treatment could go about the process of recovery and change. In order to fully understand how motivational interviewing might work for a person with co-occurring disorders, one must be well versed in the stages of change model. The following content will explore an overview of the stages of change, directly from Prochaska, DiClemente, and Norcross's work (1992). Additionally, the following content will delve into some practical application of the stages of change through motivational interviewing for persons living with co-occurring disorders. Also included are some of the limitations and challenges in the stages of change model. Although often conceptualized for the treatment of substance use disorders, the stages of change can also be considered for those living with various mental health or even physical health diagnoses (Krebs et al., 2019).

Pre-contemplation

One of the primary hallmarks of the pre-contemplation stage is a general lack of awareness that a problem exists. Persons in pre-contemplation may present for treatment due to external pressure from the justice system, family, friends, or occupational entities (Prochaska et al., 1992). A change may be made when experiencing external pressure but could potentially be retracted when the external stress is no longer present (Prochaska et al., 1992). Oftentimes, clients experiencing ambivalence to change can be viewed as resistant to treatment. However, the stages of change do not conceptualize the individual as resistant, but rather that they must work to resolve ambivalence to enhance their motivation (West, 2005). Counselors using the stages of change model are aware that there are usually various aspects of the client's life that impact their decisions to engage in change. In order to enhance the client's commitment and resolve ambivalence, the counselor must develop a good therapeutic rapport with the patient (Krebs et al., 2018).

Contemplation

The contemplation stage of change is highlighted by the awareness that something is in need of change, coupled with a lack of readiness to make any changes in the moment (Prochaska et al., 1992). Persons in contemplation could potentially remain in this stage for a significant duration of time. Ultimately, contemplation is defined by an understanding that a problem is present but a lack of clear conceptualization of what it may take to make significant changes (Prochaska et al., 1992). Many clients may stay in this stage as they may have worries as to how change would impact their lives. For many individuals engaging in substance use, their use (although detrimental) can be their main coping strategy. Considering options for change can make the individual feel overwhelmed and unprepared for change. As the individual contemplates options for change, the counselor enhances their motivation through ongoing questioning and support (Doweiko, 2009).

Preparation, Action, and Maintenance

The preparation stage can be viewed as an early precursor to the action stage, possibly encompassing some very small preparatory changes (Prochaska et al., 1992). Prochaska and colleagues indicated that the preparation stage involves intention to act on change behavior in the very near future. The action stage involves overt behavior that is aimed at directly or indirectly addressing the perceived problem (Prochaska et al., 1992). Prochaska et al. (1992) stated that persons who are considered to be in the action stage have initiated change behavior within a range of one day to six months. As the action stage ends at approximately six months post–behavior change, the maintenance stage begins and continues indefinitely, depending on the type of behavior that has been changed (Prochaska et al., 1992). Principally, the maintenance stage involves behaviors that are aimed at preventing recurrence of the previous problem and continuation of the new behavioral approach that has been developed by the person engaging in change (Prochaska et al., 1992).

When counselors work with clients of various backgrounds, it is essential to remember that at times, recovery is a non-linear process. Many people may engage in some preparation and attempt to make steps to change their behaviors before experiencing a major trigger that compels them to resume substance use. These incidents from the perspective of MI are opportunities for growth and learning (DuPont et al., 2017). When clients are in the pre-contemplative stage of change, it is important for counselors to conceptualize such individuals as being at the earliest stage of recovery as opposed to being viewed as 'resistant' to change or recovery.

There are various specific skills that are used to resolve ambivalence and help enhance an individual's commitment to change within the stages of change model. It is common for individuals who are receiving co-occurring disorders treatment to be justice linked and mandated for treatment (Surmon-Böhr et al., 2020). As these individuals are mandated for treatment, they may become frustrated with the process of treatment, experience irritability about exploring the benefits of recovery, and stay in the pre-contemplative stage of change as they feel powerless (Di Bartolomeo et al., 2021). To manage these instances, it is recommended that counselors engage

Skill	Definition	Client Statement	Counselor Response
Simple Reflection	Validates client's statement to elicit an opposing response.	"I don't have plans to quit drinking any time soon."	"You feel that sobriety isn't an option right now."
Double Sided Reflection	Acknowledging client's statement while using their past statements to build discrepancy.	"You want me to quit smoking weed but I am not going to do it."	"You have identified how using marijuana has caused problems in the past and you're not at the point of quitting."
Shifting Focus	Diffuse client frustration by adjusting the focus of discussion.	"I won't stop drinking when all of my friends meet up after work."	"Let's back up a bit; we were talking about your desire to find a different job. Let's pick up on this."
Agreement with a Twist	Adjusting discussion propelling change talk.	"You and my family are focused on my drinking. You would drink too if they were your family."	"You make a good point. Blaming you may not really address the bigger problem. This can be connected to the entire family dynamic."
Amplified Reflection	To reflect in an exaggerated way while still validating the client.	"I don't know why people care about my drinking."	"So they are worried about nothing?"
Reframing	Offering a positive view of a negative situation while still validating the client.	"My wife always calls me an alcoholic. It really bugs me."	"It sounds like she cares about you although she may not express it in the best way."

Figure 14.6 Rolling with Resistance Examples

Source: Satre et al. (2016)

in the skills of rolling with resistance. These are skills by which a counselor can validate a client's concerns while reconnecting to their commitment to change. Engaging in these skills also helps the individual identify their own motivating factors for considering change. Figure 14.6 outlines these skills.

Motivational Interviewing as a Psychotherapeutic Intervention

Origin of MI and Interface With the Stages of Change

Miller (1983) is credited with the initial conceptualization of motivational interviewing (MI) as a therapeutic intervention tool. Throughout the development of MI, the stages of change were incorporated into the therapeutic intervention, with the primary goal of MI being to elicit change talk by the client and facilitate positive movement throughout the stages of change. Communication between the counselor and the client is based on the principles of person-centered therapy, wherein the counselor connects with the client through a non-judgmental stance and a position of unconditional positive regard (Doweiko, 2009). To enhance discussions about the individual's substance use, counselors are advised to use the basic core counseling skills of open-ended questions, affirmations, reflective listening, and summarizing (OARS) to develop and enhance the therapeutic rapport, to clarify presenting information, and to move the session in a direction to consider the benefits of change. MI has been found to be an effective therapy tool in an array of health-care domains, especially in addiction treatment. The following content will explore some of the effectiveness of MI and highlight the utility of the intervention for persons with co-occurring substance use and mental health disorders.

Readiness to Change and Efficacy of MI

One of the most important aspects of the efficacy of MI and the stages of change is related to how 'ready' a client is to make changes, 'ready' being operationally defined as further along the stages of change. Krebs et al. (2018) conducted a meta-analysis of 76 studies related to therapeutic outcomes and the stages of change. The study involved over 25,000 participants and confirmed a link between the pre-treatment stage of change and the overall outcome of the process of behavioral health treatment. Essentially, the further along the individual was in the stage of change, the more promising the treatment outcome (Krebs et al., 2018). MI aims to facilitate movement in the stages of change, maximizing the moderating effect of stage of change on treatment outcome found by Krebs et al. (2018). Recent literature has continued to confirm that MI is successful in this approach, especially with clients who have co-occurring disorders.

The Efficacy of MI for Treating Co-occurring Disorders

Multiple research studies have confirmed the effectiveness of MI for persons with co-occurring disorders. Bagøien et al. (2013) conducted a longitudinal study involving 135 patients admitted for psychiatric care for whom substance use influenced the initial admission to treatment. The researchers measured self-reported substance use at various intervals for up to two years. Participants in the intervention group were given only two sessions of MI during the course of treatment. At the two-year interval, the MI intervention group reported significantly fewer days of substance use than the control group. The study by Bagøien et al. (2013) demonstrates that even the inclusion of only two sessions of MI for persons with co-occurring disorders can substantially affect long-term treatment outcomes. Along with Bagøien et al. (2013), Graham et al. (2016) measured the effectiveness of brief MI sessions conducted with persons admitted into psychiatric care who also had co-occurring substance use conditions. Graham et al. (2016) found that brief MI combined with treatment as usual resulted in greater overall treatment engagement when compared to the group of patients who received only treatment as usual.

Brown et al. (2015) conducted a similar study to that of Graham et al. (2016), with the exception that all the participants were adolescents. Brown et al. (2015) found that combining MI with treatment as usual resulted in a longer period of time before initiation of substance use post-discharge from hospitalization for adolescents with co-occurring disorders. Moreover, the researchers found that the MI intervention group reported less substance use for six months post-treatment than the treatment-as-usual group. Thus, research seems to point to MI improving overall treatment outcomes and engagement in treatment as a whole. Furthermore, MI is often combined with other modalities of treatment, similar to what was done in the Graham et al. (2016) study. One treatment intervention that is often coupled with MI is cognitive behavioral therapy (CBT), a substantially efficacious treatment on its own.

Riper et al. (2014) highlight the efficacy of MI when combined with cognitive behavioral therapy (CBT) for persons with alcohol use disorder (AUD) and co-occurring major depressive disorder (MDD). The study involved a meta-analysis of 12 articles and over 1,700 participants. Results indicated that combining MI and CBT for persons with AUD and MDD is significantly more effective than treatment as usual. In essence, the Riper et al. (2014) study provides insight into the overall clinical effectiveness of combining MI and CBT when treating persons with co-occurring mood and substance use disorders. Thus, the effectiveness of MI as both a stand-alone intervention and a combined therapy tool is evidenced in the literature (Bagøien et al., 2013; Riper et al., 2014).

In summary, the efficacy of MI for treating persons with co-occurring disorders is prevalent within the overall body of scholarly literature. The use of MI as a stand-alone intervention or combining it with CBT or other forms of treatment in a psychiatric treatment setting has demonstrated efficacy in research and practice. Despite the presence of multiple studies highlighting the effectiveness of MI for co-occurring disorders, considerable research is still needed to validate the differing effects of MI on multiple condition pairings. For example, how do the effects of MI differ for persons with co-occurring MDD and AUD and persons with co-occurring PTSD and cocaine use disorder? Or how do the effects of MI differ for persons with co-occurring mood, substance use, and personality disorders across the range of possible combined diagnoses? Along with the need for continued research into the efficacy of MI for specific conditions, there are some general limitations and challenges that are present with MI and the underlying stages of change model. These limitations and challenges are explored in the next section. Additionally, a discussion of cultural considerations regarding the stages of change is included.

Limitations and Challenges of Motivational Interviewing and the Stages of Change Model

A Reductionist View of Behavior Change

Throughout its development and application, the stages of change model has received criticism related to challenges and limitations within the model itself. Critical views of the model have been presented on a continuum, ranging from a foundational disregard for the model to general guidelines for cultural and diversity considerations related to the model's application in treatment and recovery (Krebs et al., 2018; West, 2005, 2006). West (2005) published perhaps one of the most critical reviews of the stages of change model. Specifically, West (2005) called for health-care practitioners to abandon use of the stages of change model. West (2005) indicated that one of the primary flaws of the stages of change model is that 'This approach fails to take account of the strong situational determinants of behavior. Behavior change can arise from a response to a trigger even in apparently unmotivated individuals' (p. 1038). Moreover, West (2006) implies that behavior itself is significantly more complex than the stages of change model purports it to be.

Essentially, West (2005) indicates that the stages of change model appears to be overly simplistic or reductionist with regard to conceptualizing the unique components of change. It must be noted, however, that multiple studies related to the predictive nature of the stages of change upon outcome of treatment have been published since the articles submitted by West (Krebs et al., 2018). However, some recent research studies have found that the stages of change essentially have mixed results with regard to overall efficacy (Dupont et al., 2017). Additional limitations to the stages of change model have recently been proposed by some of the original authors of the model itself.

Cultural Considerations

Krebs et al. (2018) discuss that of the hundreds of studies that exist related to the stages of change and psychotherapy, the overwhelming majority have been conducted with the utilization of participants who are white and live either in a European country or in North America (p. 1976). The researchers highlight that the stages of change model places inherent value on the act of change itself, which is rooted in the beliefs and values of Western culture (Krebs et al., 2018). Krebs et al. (2018) go on to point out that various cultures do not have as strong a belief in the concept 'that change represents progression, individually or culturally' (p. 1976). Ultimately, considerable research is needed to establish the generalizability of the stages of change model across cultures, especially with regard to persons with co-occurring disorders as well.

Resources for Motivational Interviewing and the Stages of Change

SAMHSA provides the following free resources:
https://store.samhsa.gov/sites/default/files/SAMHSA_Digital_Download/PEP20-02-02-014.pdf
https://store.samhsa.gov/sites/default/files/d7/priv/tip35_final_508_compliant_-_022520
20_0.pdf
Additional tools can be found at the following sites:
www.therapistaid.com/therapy-guide/motivational-interviewing
https://health.mo.gov/living/healthcondiseases/chronic/wisewoman/pdf/MIRollingwith
Resistance.pdf

Conclusion

In this chapter, there has been a thorough introduction to the development of recovery programming that occurred in the early twentieth century and how it developed from self-help to evidence-based therapeutic programs to assist those with substance use disorders and co-occurring mental disorders manage and recover from their disorders. In current times, there are 12-step programs and anonymous self-help community support for alcohol, cocaine, narcotics, overeating, and any number of other issues that people have developed. These community support programs have assisted millions of people. Motivational interviewing techniques help addiction counselors meet clients 'where they are' and help them overcome ambivalence toward change through a person-centered approach that empowers self-reflection on what one can do to help themselves. The MI approach has helped even the most resistant client see options for healing and personal growth. Cognitive behavioral therapy developed systematic and evidenced-based approaches to teach clients how to examine their own thoughts and core beliefs that are not in congruence with their life goals and aspirations. Over the decades, advances have been made that enhance and, in some cases, improve these approaches as neuropsychology, positive psychology, and further understanding of the body/mind/spirit approach to healing and recovery have developed new evidence-based practices.

Questions for Consideration

1. Thousands of self-help groups are held across the United States daily. List three ways that self-help is different from clinical treatment.
2. The stages of change can reflect various areas in which a client is motivated to work on goals. What skills are necessary to help an individual move through the stages of change?
3. Cognitive behavioral therapy has various components that are all necessary to engage in appropriate the CBT modality. Describe the feedback loop of the CBT model.
4. When a client does not adhere to treatment recommendations and continues to use substances, how is this experience conceptualized through motivational interviewing?

Case Study

Sean is a 42-year-old Caucasian married male attending treatment at the behest of his wife. During the last several months, he has experienced a lack of enjoyment in activities and reports that he has ongoing instances of sadness throughout the week. This has caused him to have instances in which he is irritable when interacting with his wife and two children. When asked to discuss his experience, Sean reports feeling that he is stuck in a dead-end job with no opportunity for advancement. He also reports feeling that he doesn't have the resources or the drive to engage in any changes in his job or career. Sean has reported that he has struggled with these thoughts for the last year, but this was exacerbated by a failed account at his job six months ago. Since then, Sean has increased his alcohol use from three beers on weekends to roughly four beers daily. He does not feel he has a problem with his drinking, although he has identified that his alcohol use has exacerbated problems with his wife and children. Sean reports feeling that he has no opportunities to improve the quality of his life and that alcohol is one of the only things that make him feel better.

Questions About Case Study

1. What are some potential cognitive distortions Sean is experiencing?
2. What stage of change is Sean currently in?
3. What are some ways to roll with resistance with Sean?

References

Allen, B. (2018). Implementing Trauma-Focused Cognitive-Behavioral Therapy (TF-CBT) with preteen children displaying problematic sexual behavior. *Cognitive and Behavioral Practice, 25*(2), 240–249.

American Counseling Association. (2014). *ACA code of ethics.* Author.

Arthur, N., & Collins, S. (2011). Infusing culture in career counseling. *Journal of Employment Counseling, 48*(4), 147–153.

Bagøien, G., Bjørngaard, J. H., Østensen, C., Reitan, S. K., Romundstad, P., & Morken, G. (2013). The effects of motivational interviewing on patients with comorbid substance use admitted to a psychiatric emergency unit: A randomised controlled trial with two-year follow-up. *BMC Psychiatry, 13*, 93. https://doi.org/10.1186/1471-244X-13-93

Bakos, D., & Kristensen, C. (2013). Supervising cognitive behavioral therapy practitioners in urban Brazil. *Journal of Cognitive Psychotherapy, 27*(1), 42–50.

Beck, J. (2011). *Cognitive behavior therapy: Basics and beyond* (2nd ed.). The Guilford Press.

Brown, R. A., Abrantes, A. M., Minami, H., Prince, M. A., Bloom, E. L., Apodaca, T. R., . . . Hunt, J. I. (2015). Motivational interviewing to reduce substance use in adolescents with psychiatric comorbidity. *Journal of Substance Abuse Treatment, 59*, 20–29. doi:10.1016/j.jsat.2015.06.016

Carpenter, J., Andrews, L., Witcraft, S., Powers, M., Smits, J., & Hofmann, S. (2018). Cognitive behavioral therapy for anxiety and related disorders: A meta-analysis of randomized placebo-controlled trials. *Depression & Anxiety, 35*(6), 502–514.

Cohen, J., Deblinger, E., & Mannarino, A. (2016). Trauma-focused cognitive behavioral therapy for children and families. *Psychotherapy Research, 28*(1), 47–57.

Corey, G. (2018). *Theory and practice of counseling and psychotherapy* (10th ed.). Cengage Learning. ISBN: 978-1305263727

Cuijpers, P., Cristea, I. A., Karyotaki, E., Reijnders, M., & Huibers, M. J. (2016). How effective are cognitive behavior therapies for major depression and anxiety disorders? A meta-analytic update of the evidence. *World Psychiatry, 15*(3), 245–258. doi:10.1002/wps.20346

David, D., Cotet, C., Matu, S., Mogoase, C., & Stefan, S. (2018a). 50 years of rational-emotive and cognitive-behavioral therapy: A systematic review and meta-analysis. *Journal of Clinical Psychology, 74*(3), 304–318.

David, D., Cristie, I., & Hofmann, S. (2018b). Why cognitive behavioral therapy is the current gold standard of psychotherapy. *Frontiers in Psychiatry, 9*(4). doi:10.3389/fpsyt.2018.00004

Di Bartolomeo, A. A., Shukla, S., Westra, H. A., Shekarak Ghashghaei, N., & Olson, D. A. (2021). Rolling with resistance: A client language analysis of deliberate practice in continuing education for psychotherapists. *Counseling & Psychotherapy Research, 21*(2), 434–442. https://doi.org/10.1002/capr.12335

Dobkin, R., Mann, S., Gara, M., Interian, A., Rodriguez, K., & Menza, M. (2020). Telephone-based cognitive behavioral therapy for depression in Parkinson disease: A randomized controlled trial. *Neurology, 94*(16). https://doi.org/10.1212/WNL.0000000000009292

Dodes, L., & Dodes, Z. (2014). *The sober truth: Debunking the bad science behind 12-step programs and the rehab industry*. Beacon Press.

Doweiko, H. (2009). *Concepts of chemical dependency* (7th ed.). Pearson Publishing.

Duncan, B., Miller, S., Sparks, J., Claud, D., Reynolds, R., Brown, J., & Johnson, L. (2003). The session rating scale: Preliminary psychometric properties of a "working" alliance measure. *Journal of Brief Therapy*, *3*(1), 3–12.

Dupont, H. B., Candel, M. J. J. M., Lemmens, P., Kaplan, C. D., van de Mheen, D., & De Vries, N. K. (2017). Stages of change model has limited value in explaining the change in use of cannabis among adolescent participants in an efficacious motivational interviewing intervention. *Journal of Psychoactive Drugs*, *49*(5), 363–372. https://doi.org/10.1080/02791072.2017.1325030

Easton, C., Crane, C., & Mandel, D. (2018). A randomized controlled trial assessing the efficacy of cognitive behavioral therapy for substance-dependent domestic violence offenders: An integrated substance abuse-domestic violence treatment approach (SADV). *Journal of Marital and Family Therapy*, *44*(3), 483–498.

Graham, H. L., Copello, A., Griffith, E., Freemantle, N., McCrone, P., Clarke, L., . . . Birchwood, M. (2016). Pilot randomised trial of a brief intervention for comorbid substance misuse in psychiatric in-patient settings. *Acta Psychiatrica Scandinavica*, *133*(4), 298–309. https://doi.org/10.1111/acps.12530

Hayes, S. C., & Hofmann, S. G. (2017). The third wave of CBT and the rise of process-based care. *World Psychiatry*, *16*, 245–246. doi:10.102/wps.20442

Karpiak, C., Norcross, J., & Wedding, D. (2016). Evolution of theory in clinical psychology. In J. Norcross, G. VandenBos, D. Freedheim & B. Olatunji (Eds.), *APA handbook of clinical psychology: Vol. 2. Theory and research* (pp. 3–17). American Psychological Association.

Kelly, J. F. (2017). Is alcoholics anonymous religious, spiritual, neither? Findings from 25 years of mechanisms of behavior change research. *Addiction*, *112*, 929–936. doi:10.1111/add.13590

Krebs, P., Norcross, J. C., Nicholson, J. M., & Prochaska, J. O. (2018). Stages of change and psychotherapy outcomes: A review and meta-analysis. *Journal of Clinical Psychology*, *74*(11), 1964–1979. https://doi.org/10.1002/jclp.22683

Krebs, P., Norcross, J. C., Nicholson, J. M., & Prochaska, J. O. (2019). Stages of change. In J. C. Norcross & B. E. Wampold (Eds.), *Psychotherapy relationships that work: Evidence-based therapist responsiveness* (pp. 296–328). Oxford University Press. https://doi.org/10.1093/med-psych/9780190843960.003.0010

Lee, S. A., & Edget, D. (2012). *Cognitive behavioral therapy: Applications, methods, and outcomes*. Nova Science Publishers, ISBN: 9781619426559

Leichsenring, F., Salzer, S., Beutel, M., Herpertz, S., Hiller, W., Hoyer, J., . . . Leibing, E. (2013). Psychodynamic therapy and cognitive-behavioral therapy in social anxiety disorder: A multicenter randomized controlled trial. *American Journal of Psychiatry*, *170*, 759–767.

Linehan, M. (1993). *Cognitive-behavioral treatment of borderline personality disorder*. Guilford Press.

Mehr, K., LaDany, N., & Caskie, G. (2010). Trainee nondisclosure in supervision: What are they not telling you? *Counseling and Psychotherapy Research*, *10*(2), 103–113.

Mendola, A., & Gibson, R. L. (2016). Addiction, 12-Step programs, and evidentiary standards for ethically and clinically sound treatment recommendations: What should clinicians do? *AMA Journal of Ethics*, *18*(6), 646–655. doi:10.1001/journalofethics.2016.18.6.sect1-1606

Miller, W. R. (1983). Motivational interviewing with problem drinkers. *Behavioral and Cognitive Psychotherapy*, *11*, 147–172. Retrieved from www.cambridge.org/core/journals/behavioural-and-cognitive-psycho therapy/article/motivational-interviewing-and-decisional-balance-contrasting-responses-to-client-ambivalence/74496E66A2D5625296F9B2EEE805B359

Prochaska, J. O., DiClemente, C. C., & Norcross, J. C. (1992). In search of how people change: Applications to addictive behaviors. *American Psychologist*, *47*(9), 1102–1114. https://doi.org/10.1037/0003-066X.47.9.1102

Reiser, R., & Milne, L. (2013). Cognitive behavioral therapy supervision in a university-based training clinic: A case study in bridging the gap between rigor and relevance. *Journal of Cognitive Psychotherapy*, *27*(1), 30–41.

Riper, H., Andersson, G., Hunter, S. B., Wit, J., Berking, M., & Cuijpers, P. (2014). Treatment of comorbid alcohol use disorders and depression with cognitive-behavioural therapy and motivational interviewing: A meta-analysis. *Addiction*, *109*(3), 394–406. https://doi.org/10.1111/add.12441

Roberts, N. P., Roberts, P. A., Jones, N., & Bisson, J. (2015). Psychological interventions for post- traumatic stress disorder and comorbid substance use disorder: A systematic review and meta-analysis. *Clinical Psychology Review, 38*, 25–38. doi:10.1016/j.cpr.2015.02.007

Roychowdhury, D. (2016). Mindfulness based CBT for treatment of PTSD. *Journal of Psychology and Clinical Psychiatry, 7*(2). doi:10.15406/jpcpy.2017.07.00429

Satre, D. D., Leibowitz, A., Sterling, S. A., Lu, Y., Travis, A., & Weisner, C. (2016). A randomized clinical trial of motivational interviewing to reduce alcohol and drug use among patients with depression. *Journal of Consulting and Clinical Psychology, 84*(7), 571–579. https://doi.org/10.1037/ccp0000096

Sisemore, T. (2007). Culturally responsive cognitive-behavioral therapy: Assessment, practice, and supervision. *Journal of Psychology and Christianity, 26*(2), 180–181.

Smith, R. H., & Wilson, B. (1939). *Alcoholics anonymous: The story of how more than one hundred men have recovered from alcoholism.* Works Publishing.

Surmon-Böhr, F., Alison, L., Christiansen, P., & Alison, E. (2020). The right to silence and the permission to talk: Motivational interviewing and high-value detainees. *American Psychologist, 75*(7), 1011–1021. https://doi.org/10.1037/amp0000588

Suveg, C., Jones, A., Davis, M., Jacob, M., Morelen, D., Thomassin, K., & Whitehead, M. (2018). Emotion-focused cognitive-behavioral therapy for youth with anxiety disorders: A randomized trial. *Journal of Abnormal Child Psychology, 46*, 569–580. https://doi.org/10.1007/s10802-017-0319-0

Vujanovic, A., Smith, L., Green, C., Lane, S., & Schmitz, J. (2018). Development of a novel, integrated cognitive-behavioral therapy for co-occurring posttraumatic stress and substance use disorders: A pilot randomized clinical trial. *Contemporary Clinical Trials, 65*, 123–129.

Warfield, J. (2013). Supervising culturally informed modified trauma-focused cognitive behavioral therapy. *Journal of Cognitive Psychotherapy, 27*(1), 51–60.

West, R. (2005). Time for a change: Putting the Transtheoretical (stages of change) model to rest. *Addiction, 100*(8), 1036–1039. https://doi.org/10.1111/j.1360-0443.2005.01139.x

West, R. (2006). The transtheoretical model of behavior change and the scientific method. *Addiction, 101*(6), 774–778. https://doi.org/10.1111/j.1360-0443.2006.01502.x

Wilson, B. (1981/1952). *Twelve steps and twelve traditions.* Alcoholics Anonymous World Services, Inc.

15 Biological Approaches

Pharmacotherapy, MAT, Orthomolecular Psychiatry, and Nutrition

Tricia L. Chandler, Mary C. Hoke, Tara G. Matthews, and Elizabeth Reyes-Fournier

Introduction

Pharmaceutical and non-pharmaceutical interventions can be used in conjunction with other therapies or as stand-alone treatments. After WWII, the pharmaceutical companies turned their efforts toward developing psychotropic medication for the treatment of mental health disorders, which have become mainstream over the past 70-plus years. Yet prior to WWII and after, there was another biological approach being researched for efficacy in treating brain chemistry deficiencies resulting in mental health disorders called orthomolecular psychiatry. Nutrition has been ignored for decades in the correlation between brain chemistry deficiencies and the onset of mental health disorders. In this chapter, we will review medically-assisted treatment (MAT) and explore orthomolecular psychiatry and the role of nutrition in the treatment of co-occurring disorders. Specialized training, certifications, and/or referrals to other health-care providers are needed for these interventions, but their efficacy makes them critical to integrative treatment. The history and use of pharmacotherapy, orthomolecular psychiatry, and nutrition are described, followed by case examples and recommended reading.

Learning Objectives

- Examine pharmacotherapy as a treatment for co-occurring disorders
- Describe orthomolecular psychiatry as a supplemental treatment for co-occurring disorders
- Recognize the link between nutrition and mental health

Key Terms

Chronic Brain Impairment: Scientific evidence presented that long-term use of psychotropic medications will create the same type of impairment in brain chemistry as use of illicit substances that becomes worse the longer these pharmaceutical substances are used.

Epigenetics: Emerging epigenetics research is demonstrating that stressors endured in the present can modify genes and potentially be passed from one generation to the next.

Medically Assisted Treatment: Medication-assisted treatment (MAT) is the use of medications, in combination with counseling and behavioral therapies, to provide a 'whole-patient' approach to the treatment of substance use disorders.

Orthomolecular Medicine/Psychiatry: Orthomolecular psychiatry attempts to establish a cause of individual symptoms through looking at vitamin and amino acids deficiencies and administering the exact amount of a substance (e.g., a vitamin or mineral) that will balance the brain chemistry of the patient.

Pharmacodynamics: The study of uptake, movement, binding, and interactions of pharmacologically active molecules at their tissue site(s) of action.

DOI: 10.4324/9781003220916-18

Pharmacokinetics: The study of the bodily absorption, distribution, metabolism, and excretion of drugs. The characteristic interactions of a drug and the body in terms of its absorption, distribution, metabolism, and excretion.

Medically Assisted Treatment

A use disorder is defined as a 'chronic, relapsing disorder characterized by compulsive drug seeking and use despite adverse consequences' (National Institute of Drug Addiction [NIDA], 2014). It is a disorder of the brain. The etiology of use disorders is directly related to a disruption in the brain that affects the thoughts and behaviors of the individual. As a result, it makes sense that there would be some form of medical protocol or medication to assist an individual with this serious medical condition. Medically assisted treatment (MAT) is a form of pharmacotherapy in line with other psychoactive medications used to treat mental disorders. Whether MAT is used to reduce cravings, mitigate withdrawal symptoms, curb use, or prevent relapse, the use of medications for the treatment of use disorders is an important resource for treatment planning (Lee et al., 2015).

Medically Assisted Treatment Defined

MAT is the use of psychoactive medication to mitigate withdrawal symptoms, cravings, and effects of drugs or alcohol. The most common forms of MAT are ones used to treat opiate, nicotine, and alcohol use disorders. The medications used are all approved by the Food and Drug Administration (FDA). The use of MAT in combination with medical counseling (i.e., education as to the importance of medication compliance) has been shown to be an effective form of use disorder treatment (Pettinati et al., 2006). MAT used in conjunction with behavioral counseling therapies has also been shown to be effective economically while reducing mortality and criminal activity (Saxon & McCarty, 2005).

For a physician to be able to prescribe these medications, they must receive permission and waivers from the Department Enforcement Agency (SAMHSA, n.d.a). With the increase likelihood of co-occurring mental health diagnosis and substance use disorder, it is critical that the medical professional assess the individual for possible mental disorders. Undiagnosed co-occurring disorders will seriously impede any therapeutic progress and can interfere with the individual's ability to comply with their MAT (Center for Substance Abuse Treatment, 2009). MAT is used as relapse prevention, withdrawal symptom reduction, harm reduction, and sobriety maintenance (Lee et al., 2015). A few of the more commonly prescribed medications are described herein. However, it is important to note, as a non-prescribing counseling professional, medication alone is not a 'cure' for co-occurring disorders. Medication can be used to supplement other therapies to improve the quality of the life of the persons living with co-occurring disorders, but it is not intended to replace the therapeutic work that needs to be done to effectively treat identified mental health and substance use disorders.

Methadone

Methadone is a synthetic opiate used in detoxification and treatment of opiate use disorders. Methadone is a mu agonist at the opioid receptor (Lee et al., 2015). Methadone is considered a weak narcotic with a long half-life that decreases the symptoms of opiate withdrawal but does not produce the typical narcotic euphoria (Kheradmand et al., 2010). The use of methadone has proven to be effective in treating opioid use disorders in addition to assisting the individual to reintegrate into their communities by attaining employment and reducing risk behaviors that lead to criminality and sexually transmitted diseases (Fernandez Miranda, 2005).

Buprenorphine

Buprenorphine is prescribed for the detoxification and treatment of opiate use disorder. Buprenorphine is a semi-synthetic opiate that is created from an alkaloid found in the poppy flower (Jasinski et al., 1978). Buprenorphine was created as an analgesic but has proven to be an effective medication for the treatment of opiate use disorder. Unlike methadone, buprenorphine is a partial agonist that is less toxic even in high doses and does not produce suppression of the respiratory system or sedation but still controls withdrawal symptoms (Welsh & Valadez-Meltzer, 2005). Studies show that buprenorphine is as effective as methadone for the treatment of withdrawal symptoms (Gowing et al., 2017). Buprenorphine is considered as effective as methadone for both detoxification and sobriety maintenance and has been shown to work better than a placebo for maintenance (Krook et al., 2002). High doses of buprenorphine have been shown to be effective in maintaining sobriety, especially for individuals with a history of multiple relapses (Johnson et al., 2000).

Buprenorphine-Naloxone

Buprenorphine-Naloxone, sold under the brand name Suboxone, is a partial opioid agonist that is the most commonly prescribed MAT for opioid use disorder (Connery, 2015). Suboxone is not as effective at long-term sobriety maintenance as methadone; however, there is little to no chance of an individual overdosing with this medication, and it is still considered a better choice for those at high risk of relapse and/or those with health issues (Srivastava et al., 2017). Unlike methadone, which is dispensed directly by the medical provider one dose at a time, suboxone is dispensed by prescription. This poses the issue that the individual is not required to attend any form of behavioral counseling services, which are still considered to be the most effective treatment (Connery, 2015).

Naltrexone

Naltrexone is an opioid antagonist used in the treatment of opioid use disorders. Despite its pharmacological qualities, it is also approved to be used as a treatment for alcohol use disorder. Naltrexone has been shown to block opioid receptors, reduce or eliminate the euphoric sensations of opiates and alcohol, and diminish cravings (Lee et al., 2015). Naltrexone, given intramuscularly in a long-acting formulation, is used to eliminate cravings and prevent relapse for individuals with alcohol and/or opiate use disorders (Aboujaoude & Salame, 2016).

Of all the medication approved for MAT, Naltrexone has been shown to be effective in a variety of uses. Naltrexone has also been found to be an effective pain reliever in low doses in cases of fibromyalgia (Younger & Mackey, 2009). Naltrexone is also effective in treating process and use disorders, such as nicotine and stimulant use disorders, trichotillomania, kleptomania, and gambling addiction. In fact, the specific pathophysiology of Naltrexone and its efficacy as a use and process disorder treatment have lent further evidence to the theory that most, if not all, use disorders are founded in the endogenous opioid system that moderates the dopaminergic reward pathways (Aboujaoude & Salame, 2016).

Disulfiram

Disulfiram is one of the more common drugs used to treat alcohol use disorder and the first medication approved by the US Food and Drug Administration (FDA). It works by inhibiting aldehyde dehydrogenase – a key enzyme involved in the breakdown of ethyl alcohol (Schatzberg & Nemeroff, 2013). It is considered most effective for individuals who have completed detoxification and are in the initial stage of abstinence. There are some common unpleasant side effects that can occur as soon as ten minutes after drinking even a small amount of alcohol and can last one or more hours. These side effects include nausea, headache, vomiting, chest pains, and difficulty breathing. The half-life of Disulfiram is 60 to 120 hours. It is contraindicated if an individual has been diagnosed with cardiovascular disease or a psychosis (Stahl, 2017).

Acamprosate

Acamprosate is prescribed for alcohol dependence treatment: namely, the maintenance of alcohol abstinence. Acamprosate works by reducing excitatory glutamate neurotransmission and increases inhibitory gamma-aminobutyric acid (GABA) neurotransmission. Because alcohol withdrawal can lead to excessive glutamate activity and deficient GABA activity, Acamprosate can act as an 'artificial alcohol' to mitigate these effects (Stahl, 2017). Side effects, though uncommon, can include nausea, anxiety, and depression. Acamprosate has been found to be effective primarily when used to decrease cravings for alcohol following detoxification (Schatzberg & Nemeroff, 2013).

GABAergic Medications – Baclofen, Tiagabine, Topiramate – The Anti-Craving Agents

Baclofen is a gamma-aminobutyric acid (GABA) agonist primarily used as a skeletal muscle relaxant for the relief of painful and uncomfortable muscle spasms caused by a variety of conditions. Baclofen has more recently been studied for the management of alcohol withdrawal; however, a conclusion has not been made regarding Baclofen efficacy for this condition. The pharmacodynamics of Baclofen with GABA-B receptor activation produce neurological effects, including anti-inflammatory properties of interest in addiction treatment. Studies have shown that GABA-B receptors have roles in memory storage and retrieval, reward, motivation, mood, and anxiety. Neuroimaging studies in humans indicate that Baclofen produces region-specific alterations in brain activity. Because Baclofen is partially metabolized in the liver, patients with impaired liver function should be regularly monitored with liver function tests. Baclofen is excreted mainly by the kidney as an unchanged drug. The half-life is 5.5 hours (Fu et al., 2012).

Tiagabine is an anti-convulsive medication primarily used in the treatment of panic disorder. Although the exact mechanism by which Tiagabine exerts its effect on the human body is unknown, it does appear to operate as a selective GABA reuptake inhibitor, enhancing the activity of gamma aminobutyric acid (GABA), the major inhibitory neurotransmitter in the central nervous system. Tiagabine binds to recognition sites, permitting more GABA to be available for receptor binding on the surfaces of post-synaptic cells. Tiagabine has shown efficacy in modifying cocaine-using behavior and reducing opiate withdrawal symptoms, including reducing aggressive behavior (Gowin et al., 2011).

Topiramate was originally developed for the treatment of epilepsy; however, it is now used to treat alcohol and cocaine addiction. Its use for the treatment of alcohol and cocaine addiction is considered 'off label' (Schatzberg & Nemeroff, 2013). Topiramate is known for having several mechanisms of action, including voltage-dependent sodium channels, and increases the activity of GABA. Side effects can include sedation; appetite loss; kidney stones; and, rarely, suicidal ideation. Topiramate has a half-life of 21 hours, and it is excreted in the urine.

Nicotine-Replacement Therapies (NRT) – Bupropion SR and Varenicline

Bupropion SR is commonly prescribed for nicotine addiction (Stahl, 2017). It works by boosting neurotransmitters norepinephrine, noradrenaline, and dopamine. The therapeutic action is usually not immediate but often delayed from two to four weeks. Bupropion, which was originally developed for use as an anti-depressant, is a non-nicotine pharmacotherapy that reduces the craving for nicotine (Schatzberg & Nemeroff, 2013).

Varenicline, developed in 2006, is a newer medication available for smoking cessation. It relieves symptoms of nicotine withdrawal. Varenicline works by causing the sustained release of small amounts of dopamine (Stahl, 2017).

The FDA issued a warning in 2009, noting that both Bupropion SR and Varenicline can increase suicidal behavior. Thus, the FDA recommended those individuals being treated with these medications be closely monitored for changes in behavior (Schatzberg & Nemeroff, 2013).

The Efficacy of MAT and Counseling

Medication-assisted treatment (MAT) is the use of medications with counseling and behavioral therapies to treat substance use disorders. This combination provides a 'whole-patient' approach to the treatment of substance use disorders. Research shows that a combination of medication and therapy can successfully treat these disorders and, for some people struggling with addiction, can help sustain recovery (SAMSHA, 2019).

According to Dugosh et al. (2016), counseling (individual and/or group) and other behavioral therapies are critical components of effective treatment for addiction. In therapy, patients are able to address issues of motivation, build skills to resist drug use, replace drug-using activities with constructive and rewarding non-drug-using activities, and improve problem-solving abilities. Behavioral therapy also facilitates interpersonal relationships and the individual's ability to function in the family and community (Dutra et al., 2008). The most recent comprehensive systematic review of findings on the role of counseling interventions in MAT (Dugosh et al., 2016) concluded that the efficacy of providing counseling interventions in combination with medications is generally supported. This 2016 systematic review by Dugosh et al. included 27 more recent studies that represented a range of psychosocial interventions, such as behavioral drug and HIV risk counseling, contingency management, general supportive counseling, CBT, web-based behavioral interventions, motivational interviewing, acceptance and commitment therapy (ACT), community reinforcement and family therapy, intensive role induction, and telephonic patient support.

A limiting factor in studies evaluating the effectiveness of counseling interventions is the quality of the intervention and the skill of the providers. In research and in clinical practice, the success of a psychosocial intervention may hinge on the provider's therapeutic knowledge and training, as well as their ability to convey empathy, warmth, and unconditional positive regard (Weiss et al., 2011; Moore et al., 2012).

Orthomolecular Psychiatry: Prevention and Treatment of SUDs and Co-occurring Disorders

Orthomolecular medicine and psychiatry are terms coined by Linus Pauling (1901–1994) in 1968 to suggest that what is needed to treat both physiological and psychiatric illnesses is an optimum molecular environment of endogenous and naturally occurring vitamins, amino acids, and mineral supplements in mega doses (Weiss, 2017; Zell, 2012). Pauling developed his interest in researching vitamin deficiencies and vitamin treatment of mental health and medical issues after becoming aware of the work of Dr. Abram Hoffer and Dr. Humphry Osmond, Canadian psychiatrists known for their work using nutrition to treat schizophrenia and cancer from the early 1950s throughout his life. Hoffer and Osmond were treating those with schizophrenia with mega doses of niacin that were 1,000 times the recommended dosage with success and no toxicity. Pauling maintained that diseases can be prevented or treated through an individual's balancing nutritional intake through proper supplements (Hawkins & Pauling, 1973; Hoffer, 1973; Hoffer & Prousky, 2008; Hoffer & Saul, 2009: Pauling, 1977; Pauling, 1995). Pauling discovered that brain chemistry is tied to having sufficient doses of vitamins, amino acids, and mineral supplements to maintain balance and that urine, blood, or hair analysis can effectively provide detailed information of deficiencies in these needed supplements. He believed in and spent his life researching the use of mega doses of vitamins, amino acids, and minerals to treat such diseases as cancer and mental disorders such as schizophrenia, bipolar disorder, and depression, combining his research efforts with noted psychiatrists in the 1970s (Hawkins & Pauling, 1973). Pauling received the Nobel Peace Prize in 1963 for this contribution to science, and orthomolecular physicians have, over the decades, focused on physiological and psychiatric disorders that they could trace to specific biochemical imbalances (Robinson & Pauling, 1974). Abram Hoffer is considered the founding father of orthomolecular psychiatry.

Pauling initially discovered that hemoglobin molecules caused sickle cell anemia when defective. From this discovery, he began exploring the role of molecular deficiencies in physical and mental disorders (Zell, 2012). Essentially, both doctors and nutritionists agree that vitamins, minerals, and amino acids are essential for good health, as well as proteins, carbohydrates, and fats. However, the controversy that has occurred in recent times is about the doses of these needed nutrients that are advantageous, with the FDA minimizing the need for these supplements while orthomolecular physicians state mega doses are needed to reverse deficiencies (Pauling, 1995, 2006). While this struggle has continued for decades, research has been ongoing, with the advantages of the orthomolecular medicine approach including better treatment through less intrusive means; less expensive and time-consuming treatment; less stigmatization from mental disorder diagnoses; no adverse side effects like those from psychotropic medications; and more objective, accurate, and easily obtained diagnoses (Lall, 1976; Pauling, 2006).

From the 1950s through the 1970s, the use of psychopharmacology was not as entrenched as the only treatment for mental illness, and many doctors were considering the nutritional treatment of mental disorders, addiction, and medical disorders. These nutritionally oriented doctors found that mental disorders such as depression, bipolar disorder, schizophrenia, obsessive-compulsive disorder, learning disorders, attention deficit hyperactive disorder, and antisocial disorders have the common issue of deficits of nutrients in the brain and that the best treatment for these issues is mega dosing of the needed nutrients by way of supplements (Saul, 2005). Blood tests and urine or hair analysis are the methods to determine what vitamins, amino acids, and minerals are deficient in one's diet.

This form of natural supplement can be given orally, in shots, or in intravenous cocktails that have been customized to the individual by a physician or psychiatrist. Oral supplements take longer to effect change in neurotransmitters as they must go through the digestive track before being absorbed into the bloodstream and crossing the blood-brain barrier. The reason for this is the psychokinetics and psychodynamics of dosing (Pinel, 2011; Schatzberg & Nemeroff, 2013). Psychokinetics and psychodynamics have to do with how substances act on the body and how they are absorbed. Bypassing the digestive system, intravenous solutions move quickly past the blood-brain barrier, providing direct and immediate access to brain chemistry (Pinel, 2011).

The development of treatment for schizophrenia was of great interest to Pauling and several psychiatrists he collaborated with in the 1970s. Treatment with high doses of niacin and vitamin C were used initially (Hawkins & Pauling, 1973). More recently, ecologic studies rekindled that interest in whether prenatal nutrition has some connection to the development of schizophrenia (Brown & Patterson, 2011). Focus has been on both genetic and epigenetic pathways that nutritional deficits might influence the risk of schizophrenia. A number of studies noted that famine – specifically, the one called the Dutch Hunger Winter in 1944–1945 – led to approximately 40,000 individuals being exposed to famine conditions during pregnancy, and researchers determined that women pregnant at the time had significantly greater risk of giving birth to a child who would at some point develop schizophrenia. These types of studies have noted that nutritional deficiencies can result in mutations in genes critical for brain development (Brown & Patterson, 2011).

Even Bill Wilson, co-founder of Alcoholics Anonymous (AA), promoted niacin therapy as early as the 1930s. He complained to his friend Dr. Smith of having depressive symptoms upon achieving sobriety and was told that he should be taking 10,000 units of niacin B3 per day to boost serotonin levels (Altschul et al., 1955). Upon following Dr. Smith's advice, Wilson recovered from the depressive symptoms he suffered and maintained his sobriety from alcohol. A study done by Rimland (1978) looked at B6 as a possible cure for autism. While only half the participants improved with the supplement, the fact that there were individuals who did improve with this supplement alone would suggest that more studies should be done that look at nutrition and nutritional support in the way of supplements to assist those with mental disorders. Nutritional doctors who prescribe to treat disorders first from the orthomolecular medicine approach suggest that supplements are far safer than psychotropic medications and restore health with natural support from what we eat and drink. Vitamins, amino acids, and minerals are capable of improving a nutritional deficiency while psychotropic medications mask symptoms and, if used long term, can lead to chronic brain impairment (Breggin, 2011). Considering the high cost of psychopharmaceuticals and the lack of cure involved with their use, looking into the concept of nutrition to improve mental and physical health is important to successfully treating the whole person.

Although dietary supplements, particularly at high doses as a part of the treatment of substance use disorders (SUDs), have been controversial, evidence does suggest that they can play a significant role in treatment. In addition, vitamins C and E, coenzyme Q10, alpha-lipoic acid, chromium, L-carnitine, and quercetin have demonstrated protective factors from oxygen free-radical damage, inflammation, and glycation (Janson, 2006). Research studies have evidenced that SUDs can affect the heart and cardiovascular system, including increasing risk for hypertension. Studies also demonstrate that SUDs increase the risk for type II diabetes (Snow et al., 2019).

Prevention of Co-occurring Physical Disorders

Vitamin C

Vitamin C has demonstrated benefits for a wide range of metabolic functions, including lowering blood pressure and pulse rate for individuals with nicotine addiction (Fotherby et al., 2000).

Vitamin E

Vitamin E has been shown to enhance immune system function and support functions that aid in maintaining homeostasis (Hathcock et al., 2005). Although some studies suggest that high doses of vitamin E may increase the risk of cardiovascular mortality, the conclusions of these studies have been found to be unreliable (Hathcock et al., 2005).

Coenzyme Q10

Coenzyme Q10 (CoQ10) is manufactured in the body, but individuals diagnosed with substance use disorders have inadequate levels for optimum health. Supplemental doses of CoQ10 have evidenced benefits in protecting the brain, in addition to its essential role in supporting healthy heart muscle (Schults et al., 2002).

Alpha Lipoic Acid

Alpha lipoic acid serves as a detoxifying agent in the body, as well as providing a protective mechanism for brain tissue (Hahm et al., 2004).

Chromium

Although chromium is a trace mineral, it has been shown to regulate blood sugar as well as lipid levels (Anderson, 1997). Chromium supplements have been shown to significantly reduce blood sugar levels and enhance high-density lipoprotein, thus protecting against the enhanced risk of individuals with SUDs developing type II diabetes.

L-Carnitine

L-carnitine is essential for the transport of free fatty acids across the mitochondrial membrane. Supplemental doses of L-carnitine have been shown to reduce the risk of heart disease in individuals with SUDs (Gomez et al., 2012).

Quercetin

Quercetin is a flavonoid that helps control allergy symptoms, particularly those of rhinitis and sinusitis. Individuals with SUDs who inhale drugs can develop – even with a single inhalation – a swelling of the inner linings of the nose, lung infections, and nasal blockages (Cornish et al., 2002).

Treatment of SUDs and Psychiatric Disorders

In treating the chemical imbalances that are both a cause of substance abuse and a result of long-term substance addiction, nutritional therapy has been shown to be helpful in restoring the proper biochemical balance in the brain (Blum et al., 2001). Proper nutrition can also help heal damage to the body caused by the depletion of nutrients commonly experienced with SUDs. The addition of appropriate amino acids serves as a building block for neurotransmitters in the brain and is an important use of nutrition in recovery and relapse prevention in SUDs. These amino acids help restore deficiencies that spur cravings (Blum et al., 2001).

D-Phenylalanine/DL-Phenylalanine

Supplementation has been shown to restore endorphins and reduce the desire for heroin, alcohol, marijuana, and tobacco. It also decreases depression and other mood disorders.

L-Tyrosine

Supplementation has been shown to restore norepinephrine and dopamine, leading to increased energy, improved attention in individuals diagnosed with attention deficit disorder, improved sleep, and a reduction in depression.

L-Tryptophan

Supplementation has been shown to restore serotonin and reduce irritability, obsessive/compulsive behaviors, and cravings for alcohol, ecstasy, marijuana, and tobacco.

Gamma-Amino Butyric Acid

Supplementation has been shown to restore GABA, promote calmness, and decrease cravings for valium, alcohol, marijuana, and tobacco.

L-Glutamine

Supplementation has been shown to enhance GABA, reduce mood swings, and reduce cravings for alcohol.

It is important to note that to assist in amino-acid nutritional therapy, the use of a multi-vitamin/mineral formula is recommended because vitamins and minerals have been evidenced to serve as co-factors in neurotransmitter synthesis (Blum et al., 2001).

Nutritional Psychiatry

Nutritional psychiatry is a growing discipline that focuses on the use of food and supplements to provide essential nutrients as part of an integrated treatment for mental health disorders (Marx et al., 2017). Case studies have shown that magnesium can help support recovery in patients with depression (Lakhan & Vieira, 2008), and supplementation with certain B vitamins has also been linked to a decrease in symptoms of depression (Lewis et al., 2013).

Research by Lakhan and Vieira (2008) determined that the trace mineral vanadium may be a causal factor in bipolar disorder. This study reported that vitamin C protected the body from the damage caused by excess vanadium, and supplementation with vitamin C could be useful in decreasing manic symptoms. They further reported that supplementation with certain B vitamins could help support treatment, noting that 80% of individuals with bipolar disorder have vitamin B deficiencies.

As an adjunct to anti-psychotic medication in the treatment of schizophrenia, Arroll et al. (2014) describe findings related to vitamin B9 (folate). Their research found that individuals diagnosed with schizophrenia have significantly lower levels of folate, and these low folate levels may be linked to a genetic susceptibility.

Lakhan and Vieira (2008) found that a deficiency in omega-3 fatty acids is one of the most common nutritional deficiencies found in patients with mental health disorders and that population studies have linked high fish consumption to a lower incidence of mental health disorders. A study that evaluated research data from 1980 to 2015 assessed the efficacy of omega-3 fatty acids in the treatment of various mental health disorders, including schizophrenia, bipolar mood disorders, anxiety disorders, and obsessive-compulsive disorder (Bozzatello et al., 2016).

The study found that, in patients with schizophrenia, postmortem brain cell samples often show low levels of EPA and DHA. The researchers go on to state that, in individuals with schizophrenia or related psychotic disorders, certain omega-3 fatty acid levels are reduced compared with healthy control samples. Medications and supplements are not the only way to treat and seek relief from symptoms of mental health and substance use disorders.

Food as an Agent to Treat Mental Health Disorders

Zehring (2016) cites the importance of dietary changes in the balancing of mood, enhancing brain function, and improving overall mental health. He suggests a correlation between mental health disorders and diet, leading to his recommendation of using food as an augmenting agent to medication and psychotherapy. In fact, the connection between mental health and nutrition has been made throughout history. Connections between scurvy, mental illness, and alcoholism in 1753; poor nutrition connected to depression in 1926; and, more recently, links between vitamin D and depression (Raju, 2017) have been made.

People living with co-occurring disorders can make nutritional choices that can aid in their recovery, reduce cravings, and improve their overall mood. Researchers in the field of epigenetics, the study of gene expression as a result non-genetic influence, continue to postulate that deficiencies of certain micro and macro nutrients are linked to depression, fatigue, schizophrenia, and other neuropsychiatric disorders (Stevens et al., 2018). We are a combination of our biological makeup and the choices we make. Poor diet can lead to the activation of otherwise dormant genes (Stevens et al., 2018), such as those involved in physical and mental health disorders. The food we consume can be a trigger for addictive cravings or supportive to our mental health.

Nutritional changes include reducing sugar and caffeine intake, bringing nutrition into the treatment process, and possibly making a referral to a nutrition expert. At the very least, treatment programs need to become aware of the impact of offering sugary, caffeine-filled snacks and drinks may have on the client's recovery. Ahmed (2012) suggested that sugar is as addictive to the brain as cocaine. GABA, serotonin, and dopamine neurotransmitters are linked to mood regulation. These neurotransmitters are essential to the body's ability to manage anxiety and depression. In fact, poor nutritional choices have an impact on the dopamine system and can lead to overeating, obesity, and depression (Wang et al., 2012). Sugar and caffeine are particularly potent and have a negative impact on our gut and our mental health.

We are holistic beings. This means that our social, behavioral, cognitive, physical, and spiritual well-being are being fed with every breath we take, every stress we experience, and everything we consume. In a world of malnutrition, obesity, addiction, and mental health issues, it is essential to explore the role of nutrition on the body and brain. Many people do not make the connection between what we put in our body and how our brain functions. Nutrition, for our purposes, is the intake of food, liquid, and other substances that we consume. All products consumed have an impact on our body and brain and, therefore, our overall functioning. This is especially true when mental health and addiction issues are present. Medication and psychotherapy are common interventions for co-occurring disorders. However, medications with exploration of gut health can increase efficacy (Lian et al., 2018).

Exploring the connection between nutrition and the brain is an evolving field of study (Raju, 2017) that continues to create opportunities for addiction professionals to reinforce opportunities to improve the overall health of each client. You do not need to be a nutritionist to open the conversation about caffeine, sugar, or eating habits. You do not need to be an expert to explore gut health; you just need to open the discussion. Treatment for co-occurring disorders is complex, and getting back to basics – 'What are you eating and drinking?' – is a great place to start. Make referrals as necessary.

Current treatment professionals are more receptive to being educated in nutritional therapies. The American Psychological Association (APA) has approved certain programs. These programs are designed to provide information on how to ethically, safely, and legally use nutritional psychology to inform the clinical practice of behavioral health-care specialists, as well as when and how to refer to other integrative medicine professionals. Making the brain-gut connection allows the counselor to explore nutrition as a supplemental treatment for co-occurring disorders.

Conclusion

Pharmaceutical and non-pharmaceutical interventions are supplemental treatments that can help people struggling with addiction and mental health, while nutrition can improve brain chemistry from both a preventative and an intervention approach. Counselors in the mental health and substance use treatment need to develop understanding of the place of nutrition and supplementing vitamins, amino acids, and minerals in the overall treatment of those with co-occurring disorders, even when clients are also taking some form of psychotropic or MAT approach as well. The least intrusive approach to treating children, adolescents, and adults with co-occurring disorders is to begin with nutritional and orthomolecular approaches to see if these forms of nutritional therapy will improve brain chemistry and overall functioning. Interventions introduced in this chapter require referrals, prescribing treatment professionals, and specialized training. Working with a treatment team of diverse professionals can provide the optimal individualized treatment plan for holistic healing.

Questions for Consideration

1. Why should medically assisted therapy be considered appropriate in the treatment of substance use disorders?
2. What are the risks of medically assisted therapy being used long term for clients?
3. What are the benefits of using nutritional supplements in mega doses to improve brain chemistry?
4. Why has orthomolecular psychiatry been relegated to alternative treatment and not explored and researched in the treatment of mental and addiction disorders?
5. How can clean nutrition improve outcomes for both mental illness and addiction disorders?

Case Study

Michael is a 37-year-old male who just entered treatment due to his alcohol use disorder and depression. He has been drinking since his teens and reports consuming more than 18 beers each time he drinks. He has been alcohol-free for 12 days. However, Michael shares that his mood swings have been significant, and his lows feel really low. Michael has been taking his antidepressant as prescribed by his psychiatrist but shares 'Sometimes, I just feel like I am riding the wave and waiting to crash'. Exploring what precipitates the 'wave and crash', you uncover that Michael's diet is high in sugar and caffeine. He reports that at every meeting, he eats sugary treats and drinks several cups of coffee with sugar. He also reports craving ice cream each night before he goes to bed.

Questions

1. Michael is taking a prescription for depression; what other factors might contribute to his ongoing symptoms despite medication compliance?
2. What nutritional shift may be happening since he stopped drinking?
3. What referrals or recommendation might be important for Michael's sobriety and mood?

Recommended Reading

Hoffer, A., & Saul, A. W. (2008). *Orthomolecular medicine for everyone: Megavitamin therapeutics for families and physicians*. Basic Health Publications, Inc.
Korn, L. (2016). *Nutrition essentials for mental health: A complete guide to the food-mood connection*. W.W. Norton & Company.
Walsh, W. J. (2014). *Nutrient power: Heal your biochemistry and heal your brain*. Skyhorse Publishing, Inc.

References

Aboujaoude, E., & Salame, W. O. (2016). Naltrexone: A pan-addiction treatment? *CNS Drugs*, *30*(8), 719–733. http://dx.doi.org/10.1007/s40263-016-0373-0
Ahmed, S. H. (2012). Is sugar as addictive as cocaine? In M. S. Gold & K. D. Brownell (Eds.), *Food and addiction: A comprehensive handbook* (1st ed., pp. 231–237). Oxford University Press.
Altschul, R., Hoffer, A., & Stephen, J. D. (1955). Influence of nicotinic acid on serum cholesterol in man. *Archives of Biochemistry and Biophysics*, *54*(2), 558–559.
Anderson, R. (1997). Nutritional factors influencing the glucose/insulin system: Chromium. *Journal of the American College of Nutrition*, *16*, 404–410.

Arroll, M., Wilder, L., & Neil, J. (2014). Nutritional interventions for the adjunctive treatment of schizophrenia: A brief review. *The Journal of Nutrition*, *16*, 13–91.

Blum, K., Ross, J., Reuben, C., Gastelu, D., & Miller, D. (2001, January/February). Nutritional gene therapy: Natural healing in recovery. *Counselor Magazine*.

Bozzatello, P., Brignolo, E., DeGrandi, E., & Bellino, S. (2016). Supplementation with omega-3 fatty acids in psychiatric disorders: A review of literature data. *Journal of Clinical Medicine*, *5*(8), 67.

Breggin, P. R. (2011). Psychiatric drug-induced Chronic Brain Impairment (CBI): Implications for long-term treatment with psychiatric medication. *Journal of Risk & Safety in Medicine*, *23*(4), 193–200.

Brown, A. S., & Patterson, P. H. (2011). *The origins of schizophrenia*. Columbia University Press.

Center for Substance Abuse Treatment. (2009). *Incorporating alcohol pharmacotherapies into medical practice*. Treatment Improvement Protocol (TIP) Series 49. HHS Publication No. (SMA) 09–4380. Substance Abuse and Mental Health Services Administration.

Connery, H. S. (2015). Medication-assisted treatment of opioid use disorder. *Harvard Review of Psychiatry*, *23*(2), 63–75. doi:10.1097/hrp.0000000000000075

Cornish, K., Williamson, G., & Sanderson, J. (2002). Quercetin metabolism in the lens: Role in inhibition of hydrogen peroxide induced cataract. *Free Radical Biology and Medicine*, *33*, 63–70.

Dugosh, K., Abraham, A., Seymour, B., McLoyd, K., Chalk, M., & Festinger, D. (2016). A systematic review on the use of psychosocial interventions in conjunction with medications for the treatment of opioid addiction. *Journal of Addiction Medicine*, *10*(2), 91–101.

Dutra, L., Stathopoulou, G., Basden, S., Leyro, T., Powers, M., & Otto, M. (2008). A meta-analytic review of psychosocial interventions for substance use disorders. *American Journal of Psychiatry*, *165*(2), 179–187.

Fernandez Miranda, J. J. (2005). Methadone maintenance treatment effectiveness. *Adicciones*, *17*(2). Retrieved from https://search.proquest.com/docview/1609142603?accountid=35796

Fotherby, M., Williams, J., Forster, L., Craner, P., & Ferns, G. (2000). Effect of vitamin C o ambulatory blood pressure and plasma lipids in older persons. *Journal of Hypertension*, *18*(4), 411–415.

Freinkel, S. (2005, May). Vitamin cure: Can common nutrients curb violent tendencies and dispel clinical depression? *Discover Magazine*.

Fu, Z., Yang, H., Xiao, Y., Zhao, G., & Huang, H. (2012). The Gamma-Aminobutyric Acid Type B (GABAB) receptor agonist baclofen inhibits morphine sensitization by decreasing the dopamine level in rat nucleus accumbens. *Behavioral and Brain Functions*, *10*, 8–20. doi:10.1186/1744-9081.8.20

Gomez, L., Heath, S., & Hagen, T. (2012). Acetyl-L-carnitine supplementation reverses the age- related decline in Carnitine Palmitoyltransferase 1 (CPT1) activity in interfibrillar mitochondria without changing the L-carnitine content in the rat heart. *Mechanisms of Ageing and Development*, *133*(2–3), 99–106.

Gowin, J., Green, C., Alcorn, J., Swann, A., Moeller, F., & Lane, S. (2011). Chronic tiagabine administration and aggressive responding in individuals with a history of substance abuse and antisocial behavior. *Journal of Psychopharmacology*. doi:https://doi.org/10.1177/026988111408962

Gowing, L., Ali, R., White, J. M., & Mbewe, D. (2017). Buprenorphine for managing opioid withdrawal. *The Cochrane Database of Systematic Reviews*, *2*(2), CD002025. doi:10.1002/14651858.CD002025.pub5

Hahm, J., Kim, B., & Kim, K. (2004). Clinical experience with thioctacid (thioctic acid [lipoic acid] in the treatment of distal symmetric polyneuropathy in Korean diabetic patients. *Journal of Diabetes Complications*, *18*, 79–85.

Hathcock, J., Azzi, A., & Blumberg, J. (2005). Vitamins E and C are safe across a broad range of intakes. *American Journal of Clinical Nutrition*, *81*, 736–745.

Hawkins, D. R., & Pauling, L. (1973). *Orthomolecular psychiatry: Treatment of schizophrenia*. San W. H. Freeman.

Hoffer, A. (1973). Orthomolecular treatment of schizophrenia. *Canadian Journal of Psychiatric Nursing*, *14*(2), 11–14.

Hoffer, A., & Prousky, J. (2008). Successful treatment of schizophrenia requires optimal daily doses of vitamin B3. *Alternative Medicine Review*, *13*(4), 287–291.

Hoffer, A., & Saul, A. W. (2009). *The vitamin cure for alcoholism: Orthomolecular treatment of addictions*. Basic Health Publications.

Howard, A. L., Robinson, M., Smith, G. J., Ambrosini, G. L., Piek, J. P., & Oddy, W. H. (2010). ADHD is associated with a "western" dietary pattern in adolescents. *Journal of Attention Disorders*, *15*(5), 403–411. https://doi.org/10.1177/1087054710365990

Janson, M. (2006). Orthomolecular medicine: The therapeutic use of dietary supplements for anti-aging. *Clinical Interventions in Aging, 1*(3), 261–265.

Jasinski, D. R., Pevnik, J. S., & Griffith, J. D. (1978). Human pharmacology and abuse potential of the analgesic buprenorphine. *Archives of General Psychiatry, 35*(4), 501. doi:10.1001/archpsyc.1978.01770280111012

Johnson, R. E., Chutuape, M. A., Strain, E. C., Walsh, S. L., Stitzer, M. L., & Bigelow, G. E. (2000). A comparison of Levomethadyl Acetate, Buprenorphine, and Methadone for Opioid dependence. *New England Journal of Medicine, 343*(18), 1290–1297. doi:10.1056/nejm200011023431802

Kheradmand, A., Banazadeh, N., & Abedi, H. (2010). Physical effects of methadone maintenance treatment from the standpoint of clients. *Addiction & Health, 2*(3–4), 66–73.

Krook, A. L., Brørs, O., Dahlberg, J., Grouff, K., Magnus, P., Røysamb, E., & Waal, H. (2002). A placebo-controlled study of high dose buprenorphine in opiate dependents waiting for medication-assisted rehabilitation in Oslo, Norway. *Addiction, 97*(5), 533–542. doi:10.1046/j.1360-0443.2002.00090.x

Lakhan, S., & Vieira, K. (2008). Nutritional therapies for mental disorders. *Journal of Nutrition, 7*, 2–14.

Lall, G. R. (1976). *Orthomolecular approach to the treatment of schizophrenia, childhood psychoses, and allied disorders such as: Hyperactivity, autism, hypoglycemia, and sub clinical pellagra* (pp. 1–15). Andrews University.

Lee, J., Kresina, T. F., Campopiano, M., Lubran, R., & Westley Clark, H. (2015). Use of pharmacotherapies in the treatment of alcohol use disorders and opioid dependence in primary care. *BioMed Research International*. http://dx.doi.org/10.1155/2015/137020

Lewis, C., Ripke, S., & Wray, N. (2013). A mega-analysis of genome-wide association studies for major depressive disorder. *Molecular Psychiatry, 18*, 497–511.

Lian, S., Wu, X., Hu, X., Wang, T., & Jin, F. (2018). Recognizing depression from the microbiota – gut – brain axis. *International Journal of Molecular Sciences, 19*(6), 1592. https://doi-org.libauth.purdueglobal.edu/10.3390/ijms19061592

Marx, W., Moseley, G., Berk, M., & Jacka, F. (2017). Nutritional psychiatry: The present state of the evidence. *The Proceedings of the Nutrition Society, 76*(4), 427–436.

Moore, B., Barry, D., Sullivan, L., O'Connor, P., Cutter, C., Schottenfeld, R., & Fiellin, D. (2012). Counseling and directly observed medication for primary care buprenorphine maintenance: A pilot study. *Journal of Addiction Medicine, 6*(3), 205–211.

National Institute of Drug Addiction [NIDA]. (2014). *Drugs, brains, and behavior: The science of addiction.* Retrieved from www.drugabuse.gov/publications/drugs-brains-behavior-science-addiction/drug-misuse-addiction#footnote

Pauling, L. (1977). Vitamin homeostasis in the brain and megavitamin therapy. *English Journal of Medicine, 297*(14), 790–791.

Pauling, L. (1995). Orthomolecular psychiatry: Varying the concentrations of substances normally present in the human body main control mental illness. *Journal of Nutritional & Environmental Medicine, 5*(2).

Pauling, L. (2006). *How to live longer and feel better* (Illustrated ed.). Oregon State University Press.

Pettinati, H. M., Anton, R. F., & Willenbring, M. L. (2006). The COMBINE study-: An overview of the largest pharmacotherapy study to date for treating alcohol dependence. *Psychiatry, 3*(10), 36–39.

Pinel, J. P. J. (2011). *Biopsychology* (8th ed.). Allyn & Bacon.

Pogue, J. M. (2014). Salt sugar fat: How the food giants hooked us by Michael Moss. *Baylor University Medical Center Proceedings, 27*(3), 283–284.

Raju, M. S. V. K. (2017). Medical nutrition in mental health and disorders. *Indian Journal of Psychiatry, 59*(2), 143–148. https://doi.org/10.4103/psychiatry.IndianJPsychiatry_193_17

Rieckmann, T., Muench, J., McBurnie, M. A., Leo, M. C., Crawford, P., Ford, D., . . . Nelson, C. (2016). Medication-assisted treatment for substance use disorders within a national community health center research network. *Substance Abuse, 37*(4), 625–634. https://doi.org/10.1080/08897077.2016.1189477

Rimland, B. (1978). Vitamin B6 helps autistic children. *Science News, 113*(19), 308–309.

Robinson, A. B., & Pauling, L. (1974). Techniques of orthomolecular diagnosis. *Clinical Chemistry, 20*(8), 961–965.

Saul, A. W. (2005). Mental health treatment that works. *Orthomolecular Medicine News Service*. Retrieved from www.orthomolecular.org

Saul, A. W. (Ed.). (2014). *Orthomolecular treatment of chronic disease: 65 experts on therapeutic and preventive nutrition.* Basic Health Publications, Inc.

Saxon, A., & McCarty, D. (2005). Challenges in the adoption of new pharmacotherapeutics for addiction to alcohol and other drugs. *Pharmacology and Therapeutics*, *108*(1), 119–128.

Schatzberg, A., & Nemeroff, C. (2013). *Essentials of clinical psychopharmacology*. American Psychiatric Publishing.

Schults, C., Oakes, D., & Kieburtz, K. (2002). Parkinson study group effects of coenzyme q10 in early Parkinson disease: Evidence of slowing of the functional decline. *Archives of Neurology*, *59*, 1541–1550.

Snow, S., Fonarow, G., Ladapo, J., Washington, D., Hoggatt, K., & Ziaeian, B. (2019). National rate of tobacco and substance use disorders among hospitalized heart failure patients. *The American Journal of Medicine*, *132*(4), 478–488.

Srivastava, M., Kahan, M., & Nader, A. (2017). Primary care management of opioid use disorders: Abstinence, methadone or buprenorphine-naloxone? *Canadian Family Physician*, *63*(3), 200–205.

Stahl, S. (2017). *Prescriber's guide*. Cambridge University Press.

Substance Abuse Mental Health Services Administration (SAMHSA). (n.d.a). *Apply for a practitioner waiver*. Retrieved from www.samhsa.gov/medication-assisted-treatment/training-materials-resources/apply-for-practitioner-waiver

Substance Abuse Mental Health Services Administration (SAMHSA). (n.d.b). *Medication and counseling treatment*. Retrieved from www.samhsa.gov/medication-assisted-treatment/programs/medication-and-counseling-treatment

Wang, G., Volkow, N. D., & Fowler, J. S. (2012). Dopamine deficiency, eating, and body weight. In M. S. Gold & K. D. Brownell (Eds.), *Food and addiction: A comprehensive handbook* (1st ed., pp. 185–193). Oxford University Press.

Weiss, K. J. (2017). Linus Pauling, Ph.D. (1901–1994): From chemical bond to civilization. *American Journal of Psychiatry*, *174*(6), 518–519.

Weiss, R., Potter, J., Fiellin, D., Byrne, M., Conner, H., Dickinson, W., . . . Ling, W. (2011). Adjunctive counseling during brief and extended buprenorphine-naloxone treatment for prescription opioid dependence: A 2-phase randomized controlled trial. *Archives of General Psychiatry*, *68*(12), 1238–1246.

Welsh, C., & Valadez-Meltzer, A. (2005). Buprenorphine: A (relatively) new treatment for opioid dependence. *Psychiatry*, *2*(12), 29–39.

Younger, J. W., & Mackey, S. C. (2009). Fibromyalgia symptoms are reduced by low-dose naltrexone: A pilot study. *Pain Medicine*, *10*(4), 663–672. doi:10.1111/j.1526-4637.2009.00613.x.

Zehring, B. (2016). *Psychiatric medications: Uses and implications for eating disorder recovery and optimizing registered dietician and psychologist teamwork* [Webinar]. Eating Disorder Registered Dietitians and Professionals (EDRDPRO). Retrieved from https://edrdpro.com/project/brad-zehring

Zell, M., & Grundmann, O. (2012, Fall). An orthomolecular approach to the prevention and treatment of psychiatric disorders. *Advances in Mind-Body Medicine*, *26*(2), 14–28.

16 Consciousness

Spirituality, Mindfulness, Meditation, and Mindfulness-Based Therapies

Tricia L. Chandler, Tara G. Matthews, Karlene Barrett, and M. A. Lawless Coker

Introduction

In early therapeutic approaches to addiction treatment, there was an understanding of how a personal spiritual practice can aid in the recovery process of substance use disorders within the AA and 12-step programs. However, spirituality was not an accepted part of mental health treatment. Consciousness work was initially part of the psychodynamic approach found in psychoanalysis, primarily through hypnosis, which bypasses the conscious mind to bring up emotional content found in the unconscious mind. The body, mind, spirit paradigm began making headway in the 1990s, with the endorsement of a wellness model of psychology by Martin Seligman when he was the president of the American Psychology Association (2002). With the mandate to use positive psychology approaches to develop a strength- or wellness-based approach to treatment, the door flew open to a biopsychosocial approach to assessment that included asking clients about their spiritual or religious needs for recovery, which also led to the development of the third wave of behavioral therapies like acceptance and commitment therapy (ACT) and dialectic behavior therapies (DBT) that include strategies of accepting thoughts as transient rather than attempting to refute irrational beliefs in traditional cognitive behavioral therapy (CBT). Additionally, Buddhist meditation and mindfulness techniques have become more widely accepted as approaches that soothe the mind, helping to relieve impulsivity, emotional dysregulation, at-risk behaviors, and triggers to behaviors that defeat the purpose of recovery.

Learning Objectives

- Develop an understanding of spirituality as a personal practice of increasing consciousness
- Understand how mindfulness, meditation, and mindfulness-based therapies have evolved in the therapeutic field for co-occurring disorders
- Understand how these approaches have demonstrated efficacy as part of the treatment protocols for those with co-occurring disorders

Key Terms

Consciousness: The state of being awake, aware of self, and aware of the world around the individual.

Hypnosis: A human state of consciousness in which an individual has reduced awareness outside themselves, can feel somewhat disconnected to consciousness, and is more likely to adhere to suggestions.

Meditation: The practice of training the mind to focus on one object, thought, or activity, helping an individual think clearly and feel calm.

Mindfulness: The practice of being focused on the present moment through connection to senses while acknowledging and accepting one's feelings and thoughts.

DOI: 10.4324/9781003220916-19

Religion: A particular system of faith and worship including rituals, holidays, and expected norms.

Spirituality: Being focused on aspects of concerns related to the soul as opposed to focused on worldly concerns. Often connected to an individual's core beliefs and sense of 'right and wrong'.

Subconscious: Concerning the part of the mind that is taking in and processing information, although the individual is not fully aware.

Consciousness

Consciousness has been viewed from many perspectives but can be broadly defined as awareness of one's subjective and objective experience, perceived through one's sensations, feelings, and thoughts. Farthing (1992) linked consciousness with aspects of awareness, attention, and memory. Pekala (1991) described the quality of consciousness as being inclusive of all perceptions, memory, mental images of imagery, alertness, self-awareness, positive and negative affect, body image, sense of time, and internal dialog.

Jungian theory states that the conscious mind maintains a relationship to the ego while the unconscious mind retains information not available to the ego. At the same time, the personal unconscious holds repressed memories, and the collective unconscious contains the dreams, visions, religious experiences, and myths of all cultures throughout the ages (Jones, 1999). These conscious and unconscious aspects of our minds can be equated with the duality of our minds. Jung suggested that the unconscious is inaccessible to the observing consciousness while another perspective asserts that the unconscious mind possesses infinite wisdom, power, and supply that are available to the conscious mind when it is open and receptive to it (Murphy, 1963). Murphy suggested that the unconscious or subjective mind works according to the law of belief and that all behavioral actions are the result of conscious reactions to one's thoughts (Murphy, 1963, p. 22). These are familiar spiritual concepts that are present in metaphysics, spiritism, and Eastern philosophy and may explain why some people are able to experience spontaneous and/or miraculous healings from terminal illnesses (Dossey, 1993; Page, 2003; Shealy & Myss, 1988; Shealy, 1999).

When considering consciousness and unconsciousness from the standpoint of early childhood trauma and neurobiology and neuropsychology, the unconscious mind becomes the automatic-pilot stream of consciousness that continually tells the individual self-sabotaging comments from core beliefs they have accepted from those familial relationships and cultural myths. When an individual has sufficient trauma to activate the mesolimbic brain and executive cognitive functioning is deemed secondary to survival, the automatic pilot of conditioned unconscious thoughts continues non-stop, reducing the individual's ability to make clear conscious decisions and to act rather than react to what is presented in their day-to-day life (Hawkins, 1995; Lipton, 2016). When the individual is stuck in the mesolimbic survival brain response, the rational mind is not easily accessed, and any amount of talk therapy will not be as effective as when the individual is consciously acting on their own behalf.

As positive psychology introduced the wellness- or strength-based approaches to counseling within the biopsychosocial approach, there developed an interest in using mindfulness approaches within counseling methods. These methods became the third wave of cognitive-behavioral therapies (CBT) and include dialectic behavioral therapy (DBT), acceptance and commitment therapy (ACT), and meditation-based stress reduction (MBSR), which include a mindfulness or meditation component. The concept of mindfulness is that rather than attempting to eradicate irrational thoughts, as is the concept in CBT, the Buddhist philosophy of understanding that thoughts are transient, and most are not truth, but automatic negative self-thoughts can allow them to pass by without causing emotional dysregulation to occur.

Hypnotherapy

> You use hypnosis not as a cure but as a means of establishing a favorable climate in which to learn.
> – Milton Erickson

Hypnosis predates Wundt's laboratory and any mention of psychology in the annals of history. However, hypnosis is inextricably connected to talk therapy. Hypnosis, hypnotherapy, and self-hypnosis are all forms of altered states of consciousness that allow the individual to develop insights and access memories without resistance. To explain hypnosis, not as a parlor trick or entertainment but as a viable and efficacious treatment for a myriad of psychological and intra-personal issues, this chapter will present a brief history of hypnosis as well as the neurobiology of this state. The chapter will also discuss the use of hypnosis as a treatment modality for both mental and use disorders.

Defining Hypnosis

The definition of hypnosis usually includes several factors. There is always mention of some form of susceptibility by the client, induction by a practitioner, a trance state that resembles deep relaxation, and suggestibility (Vickers et al., 2001). It can be argued that hypnosis, like most psychological phenomena, is a construct that is only understood as a syndrome in context. Therefore, hypnosis can be defined as a form of altered attention in which the individual is able to temporarily dissociate from conscious reality so they can access memories or thoughts that, during regular conscious activity, they attempt to deny, obfuscate, and generally pretend not to know. In this trance state, the individual also lets go of resistance and is open to direct and indirect suggestion (Zeig, 2008). In other words, hypnosis used in psychological treatment is simply a modality that allows the client to access information by bypassing resistance and lets them accept new information, whether in the form of counseling, metaphor, or direct suggestion, as in the restructuring of cognitive irrationalities.

Brief History of Hypnosis

Most historians would trace the roots of hypnosis to early shamanic and religious rituals. Whether through breath manipulation or use of substances to achieve an altered state, the use of trance to connect to something deeper and detach from reality is seen throughout the history of man. The first documented use of induction (one person speaking to induce a trance state in another individual) was done by Egyptians, who used rhythmic chants, incantations, and even having the individual fixate on something outside themselves (Edmonston, 1986).

Perhaps the beginning of questioning the efficacy or veracity of hypnosis was a byproduct of having the practice attached to historic individuals like Franz Anton Mesmer. Mesmer's use of hypnosis in the late 1700s and early 1800s was equally lauded and criticized. His theory of fluid magnetics and flair for the dramatic opened him to criticism by real scientists. Even though he would help people with his Mesmeric cure, he was seen as a charlatan by physicians and scientists (Hammond, 2013).

Dr. Ambroise-August Liebeault (1823–1904) was one of the first physicians to use a form of hypnosis to get his patients to relax and sleep. He also used affirmations and other suggestions to perform 'ego strengthening and symptom amelioration' (Hammond, 2013, p. 185). Jean-Martin Charcot (1825–1893), a neurologist, began using hypnosis to treat hysteria. But it was Janet (1859–1947) who first introduced the idea that hypnosis allows the individual a glimpse between the conscious and unconscious mind. In fact, Freud credits Janet with the terms related to consciousness, as well as the term 'psychological analysis' (Hammond, 2013). However, Freud's contributions to hypnosis are few since, by his own admission, he was not good at it and instead developed free association, which also worked to access the subconscious. Despite crediting hypnosis and practitioners for his foundational understanding of psychoanalysis, Freud felt that hypnosis was effective but relied too heavily on transference (Bachner-Melman & Lichtenberg, 2001).

Ultimately, it was the work of Milton H. Erickson that defined the use of hypnosis in a psychotherapeutic setting. His work with his clients, his scripts, and his historic work in *The February Man* (1989) focused the work of the practitioner and moved the work of hypnosis from a technique to a process. The use of hypnosis to address psychological issues was refocused in the process of 'building rapport, assessing client responsivity, focusing attention, framing client responses in a way that promotes therapeutic outcome, indirect suggestion, and utilizing more of a client's attitudes, understandings, and abilities on behalf of his or her desires and well-being' (Teleska & Roffman, 2004, p. 104). Ultimately, how is this different from psychotherapy in any form? Erickson is credited with creating 'brief therapy' as well as 'strategic therapy' with his use of hypnosis (Zeig, 2007, 2008).

Neurological Basis of Hypnosis

The neuroscience of hypnosis begins with a similarity to sleep and trance states. EEGs show slow theta waves, which are associated with cortical inhibition. This inhibition can explain the hypnosis side effects like a lack of thought and body dissociation (Holroyd, 2003). Theta waves are also associated with high susceptibility to hypnosis (Chandler, 2012). EEGs have shown that, during hypnosis, high-frequency slow waves are generated in the hippocampal-septal region, which produce slow waves in the frontal lobe. The hippocampal-septal region is also associated with the limbic system, which is connected to the frontal cortex, which is key in the formation and retrieval of semantic memories while also being connected to the hypothalamus and pituitary glands, which regulate the neurotransmitters that control sleep-wake cycles as well as analgesic affects (Reyes-Fournier, 2013).

Hypnotherapy as a Treatment Modality

Hypnosis as a treatment modality for use disorders is not common except for smoking cessation (Ahijevych et al., 2000). The efficacy of this modality for smoking cessation after treatment has been found to be 81%, with a one-year follow up of 48% who reported being smoke-free (Elkins & Rajab, 2004). Research using hypnotherapy for the treatment of alcohol use disorders has shown that 77% maintained sobriety after a one-year follow up (Potter, 2004). However, the data in this area is muddled since the effects of the modality cannot be extricated from the relaxing and/or meditative states that are created in the treatment (Stoil, 1989; Jenson et al., 2017).

Hypnosis can take several forms in the treatment of use disorders. It can be used specifically to create a relaxed state in which the individual can be more receptive to direct suggestion (e.g., 'You are smoke-free'), or the practitioner can employ suggestion, metaphor, and imagery while the client is induced (e.g., 'You have maggots in your right hand and cocaine in your left hand. You smash them together, and from now on, when you see cocaine, you will see maggots') (Vickers et al., 2001). Hypnotherapy, however, uses the trance state to conduct psychotherapy, therefore bypassing resistance and facilitating change (Dowd, 2012). Simply put, the practitioner performs a hypnotic induction, and, in that state, they can perform different therapies, including cognitive behavioral therapy (Balon, 2009), group therapy (Dickson-Spillmann et al., 2012), solution-focused therapy (Mahlberg & Sjoblom, 2004), and motivational interviewing (Patterson, 2010).

214 Chandler, Matthews, Barrett, Lawless Coker

Using hypnosis as an adjunct therapy or, at the very least, theories and techniques associated with the practice is quite common. Utilization sobriety, a brief treatment modality that purports to create gestalt in the individual by creating a state in which the needs met by the substance are met with other mental states, employs ideomotor questioning, which reportedly taps into the individual's subconscious and unconscious thoughts while they are engaged in counselling (Walsh, 2003). Much like a counselor will observe a client's body language, the counselor and client first agree to a hand gesture that means 'yes' or 'no' so that during a session, the client can be speaking or listening and responding idiosyncratically through these gestures, which would be 'truer' indications of their feelings.

Using Hypnosis for Posttraumatic Stress Disorder

Trauma and substance abuse go hand in hand. Research has shown that individuals diagnosed with SUD also have a co-occurring disorder of posttraumatic stress disorder. In fact, it has been estimated that individuals with SUD are seven times more likely to also meet criteria for PTSD (Mills et al., 2006). One of the hallmarks of PTSD is the resistance to reliving the experience and the reluctance of counselors to address this in a meaningful way for fear of an abreaction or further traumatizing the client (Lotzin et al., 2019).

However, with hypnotherapy, a client can access resource states (i.e., ego-strengthened areas created by affirmation or even spiritual connectivity), engage their dissociative tendencies, and access memories while being disengaged from the emotional volatility of the experience. One approach to using hypnosis as a treatment modality is the urges approach, which was created to treat PTSD and SUD simultaneously (Barbieri, 2008). This theory posits that trauma creates a split ego that creates two distinct ego states (child trauma state and addict ego state) and uses substances to induce a trance state to dissociate further from the emotions and memories associated with the trauma. This method analyzes the triggers for cravings and urges of the client to identify the initial trauma. Using concepts of hypno-behavioral therapy, eye movement desensitization regulation, and synergy psychology, the counselor uses these states to navigate the pockets of trauma and resolve the underlying conflict, pain, and emotional ambivalence found in most trauma, especially if created by a loved one (e.g., parent, caretaker, trusted adult).

Using Hypnotherapy for Depression and Anxiety

According to the World Health Organization, depression is the leading cause of all disability in the world, while anxiety disorders are ranked as sixth. The use of hypnosis to treat depressive disorders was avoided for a time for fear of triggering suicidal ideation (Alladin, 2009). However, with the use of hypnosis in conjunction with established approaches, such as cognitive behavioral therapy, cognitive hypnotherapy has become a viable therapy to address the needs of individuals with depressive disorders (Alladin, 2012). By using the byproducts of hypnosis, such as relaxation, awareness, ease of insight, and a general sense of positivity, an effective means of interrupting ruminations to be able to address the irrationalities underlying those beliefs is achieved, efficiently creating a quicker relief of symptoms for the client.

Most would focus on the relaxing component of hypnosis; however, the curative nature of hypnosis as it pertains to anxiety is the ability to focus and concentrate. The combination of CBT and hypnosis appears to be highly effective in the treatment of anxiety (Kirsch et al., 1995). Also, teaching the individual self-hypnosis is an effective method of treating anxiety with surprising lasting effects equal to CBT and even more than teaching a client relaxation techniques (O'Neill et al., 1999). Even when compared to CBT, hypnosis has long-lasting effects similar to the well-established therapy on stress- and anxiety-based disorders (Bryant et al., 2003).

Hypnotherapy and Use Disorders

The use of hypnosis in treatment has been limited, especially in the United States. However, the effectiveness of this modality in the treatment of use disorders has been shown repeatedly. One such study comparing the efficacy of nicotine replacement to hypnosis showed not only that hypnosis is a more effective form of treatment but also that the relapse rates are significantly lower for clients, and it's a healthier choice for individuals who are being forced to stop smoking due to medical issues (Hasan et al., 2014). Another recent study showed that despite the fact that hypnosis does not significantly affect the rate of success for individuals with opiate use disorders, hypnosis proved to provide significant relief for withdrawal symptoms, cravings, and relapse (Golabadi et al., 2012).

Regardless of the obvious benefits of hypnosis and those of conjunctive therapies, this is not a common modality in use disorder treatments. Combining hypnosis, with its obvious effects of relaxation, attention, and dissociation from emotional lability associated with individuals who have experienced trauma, with well-established treatment methods like CBT, motivational interviewing, and other brief therapies seems to be a worthwhile endeavor. The addition of hypnosis to treatment can significantly address issues of cravings and relapse, which plague the sustained sobriety of the individual (Molina, 2001). For individuals with co-occurring disorders, the use of this modality may afford them a respite from the stress of treatment and a tool to deal with future stresses in life.

Dialectic Behavioral Therapy – Neurobiological, Psychotherapeutic, and Mindfulness Focus

Dialectical behavior therapy (DBT) is a multifaceted approach that has been used to treat women diagnosed with borderline personality disorder who had suicidal ideation and lack of acceptance of treatment approaches initially (Chapman, 2006; O'Connell, 2014). It was developed by Dr. Marsha Linehan in the early 1990s, with the distinct purpose of developing an evidence-based practice that would help populations with co-occurring disorders who were at high risk for suicide (Linehan, 1993). DBT proposes that reality consists of two opposing forces, and when synthesis occurs between these forces, a new reality emerges that also has two opposing forces in a continual process of change (Baer, 2003). The central dialectic in DBT is the relationship between acceptance and change.

DBT has four components that include skills training in a group setting, individual psychotherapy, telephone consultation, and the use of a therapist consultation team (Linehan, 1993, 2015; May et al., 2016; McCauley et al., 2018). The program is highly structured in the same way as CBT, with group therapy, individual therapy, and homework assignments to continually follow through with the structural components of the therapy, which include four specific behavioral skills: mindfulness training, interpersonal effectiveness, emotional regulation, and distress tolerance. Mindfulness skills taught to clients include non-judgmental observation of thoughts, emotions, sensations, and environmental stimuli and acceptance of personal histories and current situations while working to change behaviors and environments that support building a better life (Baer, 2003; Linehan, 1993, 2015). Mindfulness exercises, rather than stressing meditation, are ideally taught in a six-month-long weekly skills group. In addition, the group is taught interpersonal effectiveness, emotional regulation, and distress tolerance skills using a workbook approach to exercises that are practiced within the group, worked on as homework assignments at home, and discussed in individual sessions with the counselor to apply the skills to the clients' daily lives (Linehan, 2015). Linehan Institute has compiled a list of randomized-controlled studies since 1981 that have demonstrated the efficacy of DBT with populations with trichotillomania, bipolar disorder, attention-deficit hyperactivity disorder, eating disorders, adolescent behavioral disorders, and posttraumatic stress disorder, as well as those with co-occurring substance use disorders, as these disorders share diagnostic criteria with BPD that include labile mood, impulsivity, interpersonal difficulties, suicidal behaviors, and engagement in risky behaviors (Linehan, 2014, 2015; May et al., 2016). A randomized clinical trial using DBT for adolescents at high risk for suicide concluded that DBT is an empirically supported treatment that is well established to reduce self-harm and suicide attempts in youth (McCauley et al., 2018).

Acceptance and Commitment Therapy (ACT) – Neurological, Psychotherapeutic, and Mindfulness Focus

More recent theoretical models that have emerged from positive psychology include acceptance and commitment theory (ACT) as a mindfulness-based theory. ACT is a branch of cognitive-behavioral therapy that was developed in 1982 by Stephen Hayes and uses acceptance and mindfulness strategies without stressing the use of meditation, together with commitment and behavior-change strategies to increase psychological flexibility (Baer, 2003; Hayes & Shenk, 2004). It differs from traditional CBT in that, instead of teaching individuals to control their thoughts, feelings, sensations, memories, and events, ACT teaches them to notice, accept, and embrace those events by contacting their transcendent sense of self. They are encouraged to observe or detach from any belief that they are their thoughts, feelings, sensations, memories, and events. ACT also contributes to helping a client define their values in order to use that knowledge to guide, inspire, and motivate the client to make appropriate lifestyle changes.

The six core principles of ACT are:

- *Connection* with the present moment allows for more openness, interest, and receptivity;
- *Cognitive diffusion* teaches that thoughts, images, emotions, and memories are not what they appear to be;
- *Acceptance* allows room to experience painful feelings and sensations;
- *Observing the self* from a transcendent sense of self is separate from the thinking self;
- Identifying *values* helps one discover what has the most meaning to the true self; and
- *Committed action* involves taking action guided by personal values, regardless of the discomfort or difficulty in accomplishing it.

(Hayes et al., 1999; Hayes & Shenk, 2004; Hayes et al., 2012; Robb, 2007)

Research into the effectiveness of ACT has demonstrated positive outcomes in treating anxiety and depression (A-Tjak et al., 2015; Forman et al., 2007; Zettle, 1989), chronic pain (Baranoff et al., 2016; Hayes et al., 1999; McCracken et al., 2005), addiction and craving (A-Tjak et al., 2015; Hayes et al., 2004; Saedym et al., 2018), somatic health issues (A-Tjak et al., 2015), and borderline personality disorder (Gratz & Gunderson, 2006) and has shown to be more effective than traditional CBT with incarcerated women with anxiety and substance use disorders (Lanza et al., 2014). Spidel et al. (2017) found efficacy in using ACT in an adult group context for those with psychological trauma and psychotic disorders. ACT has similar principles to what can be found in the 12-step literature and specifically notes the similarity between the Prayer of Serenity and the concepts of accepting what one cannot change, committing to changing what one can, and having the wisdom to know the difference. One such connection was made in research that used both the 12-step literature and ACT with opiate use disorder clients with success (Hayes et al., 2004) and a comparison study between ACT and the 12-step Narcotics Anonymous in the rehabilitative process found acceptance and commitment therapy enhanced positive emotions and well-being in those with substance use disorders who sought treatment in a randomized-controlled study (Azkhosh, 2016). ACT curriculum was introduced in a group context on an adolescent inpatient psychiatric unit in Canada and demonstrated that youth participation in group activities and parental response to the program was improved through the ACT protocols while the youth noted improved coping skills; acceptance of thoughts; improved focusing on the present; and improved mindfulness, emotional regulation, and stress reduction techniques while also improving ability to express emotions (Makki et al., 2018).

ACT also utilizes strategies that are similar to mindfulness-based therapies while using different language to describe how they work. Mindfulness skills are taught to clients to assist them in creating a richer and more meaningful life while effectively handling the pain and stress that occurs in any life. Mindfulness-based stress reduction (MBSR) is a group program that uses mindfulness meditation to alleviate suffering associated with physical, psychosomatic, and psychiatric disorders. Research studies into the effectiveness of MBSR have demonstrated effectiveness in the treatment of anxiety and panic (Kabat-Zinn et al., 1992; Miller et al., 1995), while a meta-analysis of 20 empirical studies suggests that MBSR may also help a wide range of individuals cope with depression, anxiety, pain, cancer, and heart disease (Grossman et al., 2004). Both ACT and MBSR show promise as therapies that help treat underlying emotional and anxiety-ridden thoughts. ACT combines mindfulness with cognitive-behavioral approaches to therapy and is part of the third wave of behavior therapy, along with dialectical behavior therapy (DBT), which has demonstrated sensitivity to the context and functions of psychological phenomena and tends to emphasize contextual and experiential change strategies in addition to more direct and didactic ones (Baer, 2003; Hayes & Shenk, 2004).

All three of these mindful and meditation-based behavioral therapies have demonstrated efficacy in helping populations with co-occurring disorders begin to understand how to work with managing emotional regulation, reduce reactivity to negative thoughts, and reduce impulsivity and risky behaviors while learning to manage their lives better.

Meditation and Mindfulness With Co-occurring Disorders

There is a plethora of research available about the utility of integrating mindfulness and meditation practices into the context of recovery-focused treatment (Alterman et al., 2004; Appel & Kim-Appel, 2009; Britton et al., 2010; Chiesa & Serretti, 2014; Shorey et al., 2014; Esmaeili et al., 2018). Thinking about the process of reclaiming oneself and one's relationship in the midst of substance abuse treatment may seem unlikely, although this is part of the rationale behind using these practices (i.e., to be able to do so calmly and with commitment). Meditation can be likened to another state of consciousness and a form of dissociation. Dissociation is something that can be a useful life skill, especially in a client's efforts to focus on their own healing process. The dissociated state that happens with meditation is a deliberate effort to disconnect (or dissociate) from what is troubling to the person in recovery treatment. This is one among many skills that the recovering client can benefit from practicing on a daily basis.

Indeed, mindfulness can be shown to have far-reaching effects on the recovering person's long-term well-being. A study done by Brewer et al. (2010) considered how mindfulness training might be effective with individuals with substance use disorders (SUDs) and co-occurring major depressive disorder (MDD). These researchers learned that mindfulness practices facilitated the recovering individual's capacity to tolerate unpleasant withdrawal and emotional states. These mindfulness-based efforts are hopeful and would be quite useful to potentially short-circuit the relapse process. In considering how to extend this work to implement it within the substance abuse field of treatment, the review conducted by Wilson and colleagues (2017) of many research studies focused on addiction and mindfulness interventions found positive results with regard to the various diagnoses and contexts for treatment. This is a hopeful position to be in, such that mindfulness skills are teachable.

Religion, Spirituality, and Co-occurring Disorders

Research indicates that spirituality and/or religion plays an important part in the lives of most people in general (Gallop Report, 2019) and among those experiencing co-occurring disorders (Fallot & Hickman, 2005). More than 76% of Americans identify with a religious group (Pew Research Center, 2015). In every religious group, there are positives and negatives, adherents who follow and integrate good and healthy practices and those who do not. In some cases, there are fringe extremists who misinterpret the tenets of the belief system to an extreme with devastating personal, familial, or global consequences. However, healthy religious and spiritual practices have been positively correlated to good mental and physical health (Newport, 2019; Plante, 2020; Wachholtz & Pargament, 2005). In other words, research indicates that people who embrace and integrate a religious/spiritual-based approach to life are happier and healthier and have a longer life expectancy and better social supports than people who do not (Plante, 2009).

Dacher (2014) discusses the history of the departure of mind-body connection in modern medicine and the value of this perspective in order to optimize human health and well-being. Research consistently supports the positive role of faith-based practices in mental and physical health both in the US and globally (Grim & Grim, 2019; Koenig, 2018) and in the treatment of/recovery from substance use disorders (Lyons et al., 2010). The National Center on Addiction and Substance Abuse (CASA, 2001) found that substance abuse was lower among adults whose religious practices are important to them and that faith had a buffering impact for adolescents (e.g., teens who did not consider religious beliefs important were eight times more likely to smoke marijuana and five times more likely to binge on alcohol). Similar results were found by Ford and Hill (2012). Captari et al. (2018), in their meta-analysis of 97 outcome studies (combined N = 7,181), found that psychotherapies that incorporated religious/spiritual values were significantly more effective than those that did not in improving mental health and spiritual functioning. In summary, the research demonstrates that people who integrate faith positively into their mental health/ substance abuse treatment have significantly improved outcomes over those who do not.

The substance abuse treatment community has had a long history with religious/spirituality-based intervention, primarily in the work of 12-step support groups and church-based organizations. Grim and Grim (2019) found that the financial and social value of the contributions of individuals and ministry/religious organizations was significant and very effective in addressing and preventing substance abuse. For example, they state that 'Volunteer addiction recovery support groups meeting in congregations around the USA contribute up to $316.6 billion in benefit to the US economy every year *at no cost to tax payers*' (Grim & Grim, 2019, para. 69).

Mental health professionals sometimes operate under the misconception that clients do not want to integrate their religious preferences or belief systems into their treatment or that they should not. Contrary to this belief, since most people consider religion important, it is prudent to at least explore clients' preferences in addressing or incorporating their beliefs into treatment. In fact, research indicates that most people would like to discuss their religious or spiritual beliefs with a therapist but may be afraid to do so (Plante, 2020). Because there is little or no emphasis incorporating a religious or spirituality component in most graduate training programs, students often feel unprepared or ill equipped to address these issues, which are germane to the lives of many clients (Plante, 2020).

The other perspective is that since clinicians are primarily mental health experts and not religious experts, then to include religious matters in treatment would be unethical. To practice outside one's training, skills, or competence is, indeed, unethical, but opening the door for a discussion of a client's preferences is good clinical practice and incorporates the core ethical values of respect and dignity. For some clients, religion or spirituality is part of their cultural identity, so a considered incorporation of their beliefs is also a matter of cultural competence. It should be noted here that not all individuals have had a positive experience within their religious/spiritual practices, and sensitivity to this is important, as well as to clients who do not practice their religion in ways that are healthy.

Opening the door for discussion means a client can have an opportunity to express preferences, and a clinician can identify their limitations and facilitate consultations with, or referrals to, others who are more competent to address spiritual or religious matters (Plante, 2020). In the same manner clinicians refer to a medical doctor for physical health concerns or to a social worker, employment counselor, attorney, or other professional, a referral to a spiritual or religious expert would be appropriate. Perhaps the client does not need or require a referral, but by being open to acknowledging their beliefs, rapport and trust can be enhanced. Also, if the client is engaging in unhealthy religious or spiritual practices, there will be an opportunity to explore this more fully if the door to this discussion and consultation is opened.

Best Practices

While it is not possible or necessary to know about every religion or spiritual practice in depth, it is good practice to know about, and respect, the beliefs and practices of members of the communities in which clinicians' practice and whom they are likely to treat. Grim and Grim (2019) indicate that a lack of familiarity with religion sets a dangerous precedent, ignoring the fiscal contribution to the economy of faith-based groups and organizations and their long-term impact on mental, physical, and social well-being.

Having a non-judgmental approach is not only a recommendation of the ethics code of mental health organizations (e.g., American Psychological Association, 2017; National Association of Alcohol and Drug Abuse Counselors, 2016), it is essential to developing trust and demonstrating respect. Practitioners who may be unaware of or have a bias against religion or spirituality may benefit from a review of the history of the relationship between religion and psychology and current trends (Dacher, 2014; Grim & Grim, 2019; Koenig, 2018).

Plante (2020) asserts that within communities of faith, there is diversity along cultural, ethnic, and language lines that requires multicultural as well as religious/spiritual competency. Further, there is diversity within religious groups and traditions, in which some members may be more conservative, traditional, liberal, or orthodox. Obtaining additional education from a multicultural and diversity perspective may be an appropriate option for some practitioners. For others, especially those who are themselves people of religious/spiritual beliefs, the possibility of advanced training in the integration of religion and spirituality may be a consideration. Professionals should be aware of personal bias in working with clients who identify as religious or spiritual and would like to incorporate their beliefs into therapy (Plante, 2020). They are free to engage in and practice their religion or spirituality privately but should not impose these on others, just as they do not impose other values. They should not use the broad terms of religion or spirituality to engage a client without a clear understanding of what they mean to the client. It is also necessary to be aware that some religious/spiritual beliefs are incorporated into popular culture and language in subtle ways, and it would be unethical to present these to clients in treatment without acknowledging their roots. For example, while meditation is common to many religions, specific practices that incorporate mindfulness, yoga, chanting, memorization, etc. are particular to specific religions.

Consultation with religious experts and leaders in the community can be an effective way to develop relationships that benefit clients and clinicians in the long term (Plante, 2020). Collaboration, mutual education, and coordination of care are only some of the benefits identified by Plante that derive from consultation. Plante further points out that there are several resources developed by the psychological and religious communities that provide guidance in collaboration and consultation.

There are also many evidence-based approaches and programs that already integrate religious, spiritual, or faith-based practices. Interested practitioners may obtain training in a similar manner that they would for any other evidence-based treatment. There are also a small number of graduate schools that offer programs to prepare clinicians to integrate faith and psychology in professional practice.

Religion and spirituality are important aspects of the lives of the majority of the US population, and many clients indicate an interest in having these as available elements in their treatment. For those with co-occurring disorders, this is also an important consideration, and clinicians should be open to inviting clients to talk about this need and implement best practices in working with them. Clinicians do not have to be experts themselves in integrating religious/spiritual practices but should be aware of resources and be willing to refer clients or consult with experts.

Conclusion

From the perspective of the body-mind-spirit continuum in working with the whole person to recover from co-occurring disorders, there are helpful spiritual practices that can be a part of the whole-treatment approach. While hypnosis was used after World War I and World War II to treat veterans with traumatic stress, the advent of positive psychology opened the door for counselors to include a spiritual and/or religious perspective in treating those with co-occurring disorders, along with a holistic and integrative approach to recovery regimens. Buddhist meditation techniques led to the development of mindfulness-based therapies that have demonstrated efficacy across populations of those with co-occurring disorders and have enhanced the body-mind-spirit approach to working with the whole person. Used in combination with other integrative practices, these modalities of care can help clients regain a sense of life purpose that supports recovery.

Questions for Consideration

1. What evidenced-based value can you identify that merits the use of consciousness interventions and discussions with clients in recovery from co-occurring disorders?
2. What disadvantages to the client exist if consciousness is not addressed in the treatment process?
3. What resources could you provide a client who wanted to integrate more of a spiritual approach to their treatment?

Case Study

Sarah is a 39-year-old married Caucasian women with three children. She is sick and tired of feeling sick all the time. She struggles to get out of bed, and when she does, she drinks. Sarah tells you that her home life is awful and that her husband has been abusing her for years. She has finally got the courage to leave him but knows that if she does not get her drinking and depression under control, he will try to take the kids away. Sarah's lawyer confirmed this and has advised her to seek treatment so she can share custody of the children. She was raised Catholic, and since her pending divorce is becoming public knowledge, she is feeling rejected from her church community. This social rejection is adding to her feelings of depression and increasing her drinking.

Questions

1. Sarah is using words like 'depression' and 'drinking', but she has never been diagnosed with any mental health or substance use disorders. What clinical information would you need to identify her diagnosis and determine the appropriate level of care?

2. What role does her Catholic background play into her current situation? What role does it need to play in her treatment?

3. Using the whole-person approach, it will be important to address spirituality with Sarah. Is spirituality the same as religion in her life? What healing may be needed here?

4. What resources, recommendations, or suggestions do you have for Sarah with regard to consciousness?

References

Ahijevych, K., Yerardl, R., & Nedilsky, N. (2000). Descriptive outcomes of the American Lung Association of Ohio hypnotherapy smoking cessation program. *International Journal of Clinical and Experimental Hypnosis, 48*(4), 374–387. doi:10.1080/00207140008410367

Alladin, A. (2009). Evidence-based cognitive hypnotherapy for depression. *Contemporary Hypnosis, 26,* 245–262.

Alladin, A. (2012). Cognitive hypnotherapy for major depressive disorder. *American Journal of Clinical Hypnosis, 54*(4), 275–93. Retrieved from https://search.proquest.com/docview/1015724975?accountid=35796

Alterman, A. I., Koppenhaver, J. M., Ladden, L. J., & Baime, M. J. (2004). Pilot trial of effectiveness of mindfulness meditation in substance abuse patients. *Journal of Substance Use, 9*(6), 259–268.

American Psychological Association. (2017). *Ethical principles of psychologists and code of conduct* (2002, Amended June 1, 2010 and January 1, 2017). Retrieved from www.apa.org/ethics/code/index.aspx

Appel, J., & Kim-Appel, D. (2009). Mindfulness: Implications for substance abuse and addiction. *International Journal of Mental Health & Addiction, 7*(4), 506–512.

A-Tjak, J. G. L., Davis, M. L., Morina, N., Powers, M. B., Smits, J. A. J., & Emmelkamp, P. M. G. (2015). A meta-analysis of the efficacy of acceptance and commitment therapy for clinically relevant mental and physical health problems. *Psychotherapy & Psychosomatics, 84*(1), 30–36.

Azkhosh, M., Farhoudianm, A., Saadati, H., Shoaee, F., & Lashani, L. (2016). Comparing acceptance and commitment group therapy and 12-steps narcotics anonymous in addict's rehabilitation process: A randomized controlled trial. *Iranian Journal of Psychiatry, 11*(4), 244–249.

Bachner-Melman, R., & Lichtenberg, P. (2001). Freud's relevance to hypnosis: A reevaluation. *American Journal of Clinical Hypnosis, 44*(1), 37–50. doi:10.1080/00029157.2001.10403454

Baer, R. A. (2003). Mindfulness training as a clinical intervention: A conceptual and empirical review. *Clinical Psychology: Science and Practice, 10*(2), 125–143.

Balon, R. (2009). Cognitive-behavioral therapy, psychotherapy and psychosocial interventions in the medically ill. *Psychotherapy and Psychosomatics, 78*(5), 261–264. Retrieved from https://search.proquest.com/docview/235477339?accountid=35796

Baranoff, J., Hanrahan, S., Burke, A., & Connor, J. (2016). Changes in acceptance in a low intensity, group-based Acceptance and Commitment Therapy (ACT) chronic pain intervention. *International Journal of Behavioral Medicine, 23*(1), 30–38.

Brewer, J. A., Bowen, S., Smith, J. T., Marlatt, G. A., & Potenza, M. N. (2010). Mindfulness-based treatments for co-occurring depression and substance use disorders: What can we learn from the brain? *Addiction, 105*(10), 1698–1706.

Britton, W. B., Bootzin, R. R., Cousins, J. C., Hasler, B. P., Peck, T., & Shapiro, S. L. (2010). The contribution of mindfulness practice to a multicomponent behavioral sleep intervention following substance abuse treatment in adolescents: A treatment-development study. *Substance Abuse, 30*(2), 86–97.

Bryant, R. A., Moulds, M. L., & Nixon, R. V. (2003). Cognitive behaviour therapy of acute stress disorder: A four-year follow-up. *Behaviour Research and Therapy, 41*(4), 489–494. doi:10.1016/s0005-7967(02)00179-1

Captari, L. E., Hook, J. N., Hoyt, W., Davis, D. E., McElroy-Heltzel, S. E., & Worthington, E. L., Jr. (2018). Integrating clients' religion and spirituality within psychotherapy: A comprehensive meta-analysis. *Journal of Clinical Psychology, 74*(11), 1938–1951. doi:10.1002/jclp.22681.

Cardena, E. (2000). Hypnosis in the treatment of trauma: A promising, but not fully supported, efficacious intervention. *International Journal of Clinical and Experimental Hypnosis, 48*(2), 225–238. doi:10.1080/00207140008410049

Chandler, T. (2012). Hypnosis. In R. W. Rieber (Eds.), *Encyclopedia of the history of psychological theories*. Springer Publishing.

Chapman, A. L. (2006). Dialectical behavior therapy: Current indications and unique elements. *Psychiatry*, *3*(9), 62–68.

Chiesa, A., & Serretti, A. (2014). Are mindfulness-based interventions effective for substance use disorders? A systematic review of the evidence. *Substance Use & Misuse*, *49*(5), 492–512.

Dacher, E. S. (2014). A brief history of mind–body medicine. *International Journal of Transpersonal Studies*, *33*(1), 148–157. doi:10.24972/ijts.2014.33.1.148

Dickson-Spillmann, M., Kraemer, T., Rust, K., & Schaub, M. (2012). Group hypnotherapy versus group relaxation for smoking cessation: An RCT study protocol. *BMC Public Health*, *12*, 271. http://dx.doi.org/10.1186/1471-2458-12-271

Dossey, L. (1993). *Healing words: The power of prayer and the practice of medicine*. HarperCollins.

Dowd, E. T. (2012). Cognitive therapy and hypnotherapy: A cognitive-developmental approach. *Journal of Cognitive and Behavioral Psychotherapies*, *12*(1), 103–119. Retrieved from https://search.proquest.com/docview/1010384513?accountid=35796

Edmonston, W. E. (1986). *The induction of hypnosis*. Wiley.

Elkins, G. R., & Rajab, M. H. (2004). Clinical hypnosis for smoking cessation: Preliminary results of a three-session intervention. *The International Journal of Clinical and Experimental Hypnosis*, *52*(1), 73–81. Retrieved from http://search.ebscohost.com/login.aspx?direct=true&db=mdc&AN=14768970&site=ehost-live

Erickson, M. H., & Rossi, E. L. (1989). *The February man: Evolving consciousness and identity in hypnotherapy* (1st ed.). Routledge.

Esmaeili, A., Khodadadi, M., Norozi, E., & Miri, M. R. (2018). Effectiveness of mindfulness-based cognitive group therapy on cognitive emotion regulation of patients under treatment with methadone. *Journal of Substance Use*, *23*(1), 58–62.

Fallot, R. D., & Hickman, J. P. (2005). Religious/spiritual coping among women trauma survivors with mental health and substance use disorders. *Journal of Behavioral Health Sciences & Research*, *32*(2), 215–226.

Farthing, G. W. (1992). *The psychology of consciousness*. Prentice-Hall.

Ford, J. A., & Hill, T. D. (2012). Religiosity and adolescent substance use: Evidence from the national survey on drug use and health. *Substance Use and Misuse*, *47*(7), 787–798. doi:10.3109/10826084.2012.667489.

Forman, E. M., Herbert, J. D., Moltra, E., Yeomans, P. D., & Geller, P. A. (2007). A randomized controlled effectiveness trial of acceptance and commitment therapy and cognitive therapy for anxiety and depression. *Behavior Modification*, *31*(6), 772–799.

Gallop Report. (2019). *What is your religious preference . . .?* Retrieved from https://news.gallup.com/poll/1690/religion.aspx

Golabadi, M., M.D., Taban, H., M.D., Yaghouhi, M., M.Sc., & Gholamrezaei, A., M.D. (2012). Hypnotherapy in the treatment of opium addiction: A pilot study. *Integrative Medicine*, *11*(3), 19–23. Retrieved from https://search.proquest.com/docview/1030276821?accountid=35796

Gratz, K. L., & Gunderson, J. G. (2006). Preliminary data on an acceptance-based emotion regulation group intervention for deliberate self-harm among womenwith borderline personality disorder. *Behavior Therapy*, *37*(1), 25–35.

Grim, B. J., & Grim, M. E. (2019). Belief, behavior, and belonging: How faith is indispensable in preventing and recovering from substance abuse. *Journal of Religion and Health*, *58*(5), 1713–1750. doi:10.1007/s10943-019-00876-w

Grossman, P., Niemann, L., Schmidt, S., & Walach, H. (2004, July). Mindfulness-based stress reduction and health benefits: A meta-analysis. *Journal of Psychosomatic Research*, *57*(1), 35–43.

Hammond, D. C. (2013). A review of the history of hypnosis through the late 19th century. *American Journal of Clinical Hypnosis*, *56*(2), 174–191. Retrieved from https://search.proquest.com/docview/1562028174?accountid=35796

Hasan, F. M., Zagarins, S. E., Pischke, K. M., Saiyed, S., Bettencourt, A. M., Beal, L., . . . McCleary, N. (2014). Hypnotherapy is more effective than nicotine replacement therapy for smoking cessation: Results of a randomized controlled trial. *Complementary Therapies in Medicine*, *22*(1), 1–8. http://dx.doi.org/10.1016/j.ctim.2013.12.012

Hawkins, D. R. (1995). *Power vs. force: An anatomy of consciousness: The hidden determinants of human behavior*. Hay House, Inc.

Hayes, S. C., Bissett, R., Korn, Z., Zettle, R. D., Rosenfarb, I., Cooper, L., & Grundt, A. (1999). The impact of acceptance versus control rationales on pain tolerance. *The Psychological Record, 49*, 33–47. Retrieved November 17, 2008, from www.contextualpsychology.org

Hayes, S. C., & Shenk, C. (2004). Operationalizing mindfulness without unnecessary attachments. *Clinical Psychology: Science and Practice, 11*(3), 249–254.

Hayes, S. C., Strosahl, K. D., & Wilson, K. G. (2012). *Acceptance and commitment therapy: The process and practice of mindful change* (2nd ed.). Guilford Press.

Hayes, S. C., Wilson, K. G., Gifford, E. V., Bissett, R., Piasecki, M., Batten, S. V., . . . Gregg, J. (2004). A preliminary trial of twelve-step facilitation and acceptance and commitment therapy with polysubstance-abusing methadone-maintained opiate addicts. *Behavior Therapy, 35*, 667–688.

Holroyd, J. (2003). The science of meditation and the state of hypnosis. *The American Journal of Clinical Hypnosis, 46*(2), 109–128. Retrieved from https://search.proquest.com/docview/71357988?accoun tid=35796

Kabat-Zinn, J., Massion, A. O., Kristeller, J., Peterson, L. G., Fletcher, K. E., Lenderking, W. R., & Santorelli, S. F. (1992). Effectiveness of a meditation-based stress reduction program in the treatment of anxiety disorders. *American Journal of Psychiatry, 149*, 936–943.

Kirsch, I., Montgomery, G., & Sapirstein, G. (1995). Hypnosis as an adjunct to cognitive behavioral psychotherapy: A meta-analysis. *Journal of Consulting and Clinical Psychology, 63*(2), 214–220. doi:10.1037//0022-006x.63.2.214

Koenig, H. G. (2018). *Religion and mental health: Research and clinical applications*. Academic Press.

Lanza, P. V., Garcia, P. F., Lamelas, F. R., & Gonzalez-Menendez, A. (2014). Acceptance and commitment therapy versus cognitive behavioral therapy in the treatment of substance use disorder with incarcerated women. *Journal of Clinical Psychology, 70*(7), 644–657.

Linehan, M. M. (1993). *Cognitive-behavioral treatment of borderline personality disorder*. Guilford Press.

Linehan, M. M. (2015). *DBT skills training manual* (2nd ed.). Guilford Press.

Linehan, M. M., Dimeff, L., Koerner, K., & Miga, E. M. (2014). *Research on dialectical behavior therapy: Summary of the data to date*. Retrieved from http://behavioraltech.org/downloads/research-on-dbt_summary-of-data-to-date.pdf

Lipton, B. (2016). *The biology of belief: Unleashing the power of consciousness, matter & miracles*. Hay House Publishing.

Lotzin, A., Buth, S., Sehner, S., Hiller, P., Pawils, S., Metzner, F., . . . Schäfer, I. (2019). Reducing barriers to trauma inquiry in substance use disorder treatment: A cluster-randomized controlled trial. *Substance Abuse Treatment, Prevention, and Policy, 14*(23), 1–11. https://doi.org/10.1186/s13011-019-0211-8

Lyons, G. C. B., Deane, F. P., & Kelly, P. J. (2010). Forgiveness and purpose in life as spiritual mechanisms of recovery from substance use disorders. *Addiction Research & Theory, 18*(5), 528–543. doi:10.3109/16066351003660619

Mahlberg, K., & Sjoblom, M. (2004). *Solution-focused education*. Mahlberg & Sjoblom. (Swedish edition Stockholm: Mareld 2002).

Makki, M., Hill, J. F., Bounds, D. T., McCammon, S., McFall-Johnsen, M., & Delaney, K. R. (2018). Implementation of an ACT curriculum on an adolescent inpatient psychiatric unit: A quality improvement project. *Journal of Child & Family Studies, 27*(9), 2918–2924.

May, J. M., Richardi, T. M., & Barth, K. S. (2016). Dialectical behavior therapy as treatment for borderline personality disorder. *Mental Health Clinician, 6*(2), 62–67.

McCauley, E., Berk, M. S., Asarnow, J. R., Adrian, M., Cohen, J., Korslund, K., . . . Linehan, M. M. (2018). Efficacy of dialectic behavior therapy for adolescents at high risk for suicide: A randomized clinical trial. *JAMA Psychiatry, 75*(8), 777–785.

McCracken, L. M., Vowles, K. E., & Eccleston, C. (2005). Acceptance-based treatment for persons with complex, long standing chronic pain: A preliminary analysis of treatment outcome in comparison to a waiting phase. *Behavior Research and Therapy, 43*, 1335–1346.

Miller, J. J., Fletcher, K., & Kabat-Zinn, J. (May, 1999). Three-year follow up and clinical implications of a mindfulness meditation-based stress reduction intervention in the treatment of anxiety disorders. *General Hospital Psychiatry, 17*(3), 192–200.

Mills, K., Teeson, M., Ross, J., & Peters, L. (2006). Trauma, PTSD, and substance use disorders: Findings from the Australian national survey of mental health and well-being. *American Journal of Psychiatry, 163*(4), 652. doi:10.1176/appi.ajp.163.4.652

Molina, D. P. (2001). Hypnosis in the cognitive-behavioral therapy: Applications in the field of addictions. *Adicciones, 13*(1). Retrieved from https://search.proquest.com/docview/1609163457?accountid=35796

Murphy, J. (1963). *The power of your subconscious mind.* Prentice-Hall.

National Association of Alcohol and Drug Abuse Counselors. (2016). *Code of ethics.* Retrieved from www.naadac.org/code-of-ethics

National Center on Addiction and Substance Abuse. (2001). *So help me God: Substance abuse, religion, and spirituality.* Retrieved from www.centeronaddiction.org/addiction-research/reports/so-help-me-god-substance-abuse-religion-and-spirituality

Newport, F. (2019, August 12). Religion and drinking alcohol in the U.S. *Polling Matters.* Retrieved from https://news.gallup.com/opinion/polling-matters/264713/religion-drinking-alcohol.aspx

O'Connell, B. (2014). Dialectical Behavioral Therapy (DBT) in the treatment of borderline personality disorder. *Psychiatric and Mental Health Nursing, 21*(6), 477–571.

O'Neill, L. M., Barnier, A. J., & McConkey, K. (1999). Treating anxiety with self-hypnosis and relaxation. *Contemporary Hypnosis, 16*(2), 68–80. doi:10.1002/ch.154

Page, C. (2003). *Spiritual alchemy.* C. W. Daniel.

Patterson, D. R. (2010). Motivational interviewing. In *Clinical hypnosis for pain control* (pp. 185–209). American Psychological Association. https://doi.org/10.1037/12128-008

Pekala, R. J. (1991). Development, reliability, and validity of the phenomenology of consciousness questionnaire. In *Quantifying consciousness. Emotions, personality, and psychotherapy.* Springer. https://doi.org/10.1007/978-1-4899-0629-8_6

Pew Research Center. (2015). *Religious landscape study: America's changing religious landscape: Christians decline sharply as share of population; unaffiliated and other faiths continue to grow.* Pew Research Center. Retrieved from www.pewresearch.org

Plante, T. G. (2009). *Spiritual practices in psychotherapy: Thirteen tools for enhancing psychological health.* American Psychological Association. http://dx.doi.org/10.1037/11872-001

Plante, T. G. (2020). Consultation with religious professionals and institutions. In C. A. Falender & E. P. Shafranske (Eds.), *Consultation in psychology: A competency-based approach* (pp. 221–237). American Psychological Association. http://dx.doi.org/10.1037/0000153-013

Reyes-Fournier, E. (2013). Neurological and behavioral effects of trance states. *Journal of Heart-Centered Therapies, 16*(1), 53–69.

Robb, H. (2007). Values as leading principles in acceptance and commitment therapy. *International Journal of Behavioral Consultation and Therapy, 3*(1), 118–123.

Saedym, N., Rezaei Ardani, A., Kooshki, S., Firouzabadi, M. J., Emamipour, S., Darabi Mahboub, L., & Mojahedi, M. (2018). Effectiveness of acceptance-commitment therapy on craving beliefs in patients on methadone maintenance therapy: A pilot study. *Journal of Rational-Emotive & Cognitive-Behavior Therapy, 36*(3), 288–302.

Seligman, M. E. P. (2002). *Authentic happiness: Using the new positive psychology to realize your potential for lasting fulfillment.* Free Press.

Shealy, C. N. (1999). *Sacred healing: The curing power of energy and spirituality.* Element Books.

Shealy, C. N., & Myss, C. M. (1988). *The creation of health: The emotional, psychological, and spiritual responses that promote health and healing.* Stillpoint.

Shorey, R. C., Brasfield, H., Anderson, S., & Stuart, G. L. (2014). Mindfulness deficits in a sample of substance abuse treatment seeking adults: A descriptive investigation. *Journal of Substance Use, 19*(1/2), 194–198.

Spidel, A., Lecomte, T., Kealy, D., & Daigneault, I. (2017). Acceptance and commitment therapy for psychosis and trauma: Improvement in psychiatric symptoms, emotion regulation, and treatment compliance following a brief group intervention. *Psychology and Psychotherapy, 91*(2), 248–261.

Stoil, M. J. (1989). Problems in the evaluation of hypnosis in the treatment of alcoholism. *Journal of Substance Abuse Treatment, 6*(1), 31–35.

Teleska, J., & Roffman, A. (2004). A continuum of hypnotherapeutic interactions: From formal hypnosis to hypnotic conversation. *American Journal of Clinical Hypnosis, 47*(2), 103–15. Retrieved from https://search.proquest.com/docview/218789072?accountid=35796

Vickers, A., Zollman, C., & Payne, D. K. (2001). Hypnosis and relaxation therapies. *The Western Journal of Medicine*, *175*(4), 269. Retrieved from https://search.proquest.com/docview/1781980395?accountid=35796

Wachholtz, A. B., & Pargament, K. I. (2005). Is spirituality a critical ingredient of meditation? Comparing the effects of spiritual meditation, secular meditation, and relaxation on spiritual, psychological, cardiac, and pain outcomes. *Journal of Behavioral Medicine*, *28*(4), 369–384.

Walsh, B. J. (2003). Utilization sobriety: Brief, individualized substance abuse treatment employing ideomotor questioning. *American Journal of Clinical Hypnosis*, *45*(3), 217–224. Retrieved from https://search.proquest.com/docview/218781449?accountid=35796

Wilson, A. D., Roos, C. R., Robinson, C. S., Stein, E. R., Manuel, J. A., Enkema, M. C., . . . Witkiewitz, K. (2017). Mindfulness-based interventions for addictive behaviors: Implementation issues on the road ahead. *Psychology of Addictive Behaviors*, *31*(8), 888–896.

Wilson, K. G., Hayes, S. C., & Byrd, M. R. (2000). Exploring compatibilities between acceptance and commitment therapy and 12-step treatment for substance abuse. *Journal of Rational-Emotive and Cognitive-Behavior Therapy*, *18*(4), 209–234.

World Health Organization [WHO]. (2017). *Depression and other common mental disorders: Global health estimates (CC BY-NC-SA 3.0 IGO)*. Retrieved from World Health Organization website https://apps.who.int/iris/bitstream/handle/10665/254610/WHO-MSD-MER-2017.2-eng.pdf?sequence=1

Zeig, J. K. (2007). A tribute to Jay Haley 1923–2007. *American Journal of Clinical Hypnosis*, *50*(1), 5–9. Retrieved from https://search.proquest.com/docview/218781270?accountid=35796

Zeig, J. K. (2008). An Ericksonian approach to hypnosis: The phenomenological model of hypnosis; the nature of hypnotic "states"; Multilevel communication and indirection; and why all hypnosis is not self-hypnosis. *Australian Journal of Clinical and Experimental Hypnosis*, *36*(2), 99–114. Retrieved from https://search.proquest.com/docview/211029158?accountid=35796

Zettle, R. D. (2005). The evolution of a contextual approach to therapy: From comprehensive distancing to ACT. *International Journal of Behavioral Consultation and Therapy*, *1*(2), 77–89.

17 Creative Arts and Somatic Therapies

Psychodrama, Eye Movement Desensitization Regulation, and Body/Mind Therapies

Tricia L. Chandler, Roberta Shoemaker-Beal and M. A. Lawless Coker

Introduction

In our postmodern era, with the advanced research of neuropsychology and neurophysiology, it has become evident that there is relevance to the body-emotions-mind-spirit paradigm. Research on consciousness and creativity is ongoing and remains a broad and often controversial subject when viewed empirically (Shoemaker-Beal, 1995). Recent studies into the nature of resiliency have found that creativity is one of the central attributes for success in psychotherapy (Flach, 1990, Chandler, 2010). The use of dance, music, and imagery from expressive art making moves a clinical session beyond mental and verbal interventions while demonstrating an ability to access various and more foundational levels of consciousness and emotional content to assist in the healing process. The creative aspects of these therapeutic modalities have been explored and researched in both medical and mental health settings with increasing success, and findings within these studies provide evidence that there are healing powers within the expressive arts for all levels of well-being, from levels of consciousness to psychological and psycho-neuro-immunological health (Penebaker, 1995; Richards, 2000, 2001). The research of Dr. Peter Levine (1997, 2010) expanded understanding of the neurobiology of how the limbic brain becomes stuck due to trauma, and his development of somatic expression as a form of whole-brain healing has substantiated decades of the therapeutic use of creative arts and somatic therapies for whole-brain healing and integration of trauma memories and supports the findings of Dr. Bessel van der Kolk concerning healing trauma (1994). This chapter provides a thorough history of the development of creative arts therapies to treat those with trauma histories, mental health challenges, and substance use disorders, along with best practices for using these modalities in a variety of settings.

Learning Objectives

* Learn how creativity leads to whole-brain integration
* Understand the way somatic therapies use the whole brain and soothe the limbic brain
* Understand the way preverbal arts therapies tap into the whole brain, to access and soothe the limbic brain
* Understand how all the arts – music, movement, and visual therapies, along with other combined preverbal and verbally focused therapies – contribute to whole-brain healing
* Understand an evolutionary and neurologically developmental brain map that aligns with the use of eye movement desensitization regulation, psychodrama, and other emerging multidimensional therapeutic approaches that research shows soothe limbic brain responses, which align holistically with the arts therapies
* Understand how whole-brain functioning aligns with the body-emotions-mind-spirit therapies for an inclusive holistic approach to therapeutic interventions

DOI: 10.4324/9781003220916-20

Key Terms

Creative Arts Therapies: The creative arts therapies (CATs) are those therapeutic interventions using arts making. CATs can tap into the preverbally based primal and foundational neuro-structures for a holistic approach to therapeutic interventions.

Eye Movement Desensitization Regulation: EMDR is a body/mind approach to decreasing emotional triggers activated due to trauma by using a 'set up memory of the trauma' with synchronized eye movements that move the focus from one brain hemisphere to the other while helping soothe the limbic brain. The hand movements of EMDR align kinesthetically with 'the scribbling out' of hand-drawn visual imagery that an individual may wish to 'erase from their visual memory'.

Psychodrama: Psychodrama is a creative approach to improving communication skills in family and group interactions. Recent psychodrama approaches, especially forms of 'constellation therapy', can be specifically designed for an individual's family dynamics in a closely guided and supportive group therapy setting.

Somatic Therapies: Somatic means 'of the body' as somatic therapies use body/mind approaches that are psychotherapeutic and holistic. Kinesthetic approaches can be accessed through dance-movement therapy, which has been a foundation of somatic approaches.

History of Creative Art Therapies and Somatic Therapies

Creativity has been a central dynamic of the preverbal art therapies, such as music therapy, dance-movement therapy, and art therapy, since their pioneering decades (Shoemaker, 1978; Shoemaker-Beal, 1995). Dr. Carl Jung explored dream interpretation, encouraging creative expression in his clients using his analytical psychology approach (Jung, 1961). Jung went on to do in-depth study of the human psyche, beyond the personal unconsciousness, when he identified a deeper level of potential meaning as an archetype realm of global imagery in the mostly unconscious contents of human consciousness, which could be actively resourced as the creative unconscious. Thus, Jung suggested a map of the human psyche that recognized the preverbal and symbolic psyche, naming the 'transcendent function', which may have been his strongest divergence from Freud's theories. Jung trusted his creative unconscious and went on to paint his own dreams by exploring his extensive creative life and the values of spiritual experience, as seen in his recently released *Red Book* (Jung et al., 2009). As Jung was developing his analytical psychological approach, he developed an approach to processing dream images by finding relevant meanings, called active imagination. This approach to a personal processing of a self-expression of hidden aspects of a human story from dreams strongly aligns with the processing of self-expressive artwork found in in-depth art therapy work. Jungian studies, especially his honoring of human creative potential, have guided many art therapists, especially career art therapists in private practice, several of whom have gone on to become Jungian analysts, such as art therapists Dr. Sondra Geller and Dr. Nora Swan Foster, author of *Jungian Art Therapy* (Swan-Foster, 2017). Jung's autobiography, *Memories, Dreams, Reflections*, is a very useful reference to 'the visual creative life' of a highly productive and significant life well lived (Jung, 1961).

Many clinicians, theoreticians, and researchers on creativity, the creative expressive arts therapies, and other therapies like the somatic therapies and psychodrama have successfully laid the foundation for a whole-brain approach to offering therapeutic services that are more pervasive, transformational, and long lasting. A whole-brain approach can both enhance personal growth and improve the functioning of people's troubled lives, as well as literally being able to 'rewire the neuro-structures' of traumatized brains. Clinical discoveries about the creative arts therapies have shown that interventions utilizing arts experiences have proven successful in treating special-needs populations, people with traumatized brain functioning, and those with co-occurring disorders based on research in designing the best practices for therapeutic interventions that can affect whole-life restoration and fuller functioning for a satisfying, creative, productive, and meaningful life design (Shoemaker-Beal, 1979/1993).

The earliest uses of the preverbal therapies were in music therapy after WW I, with the earliest uses of art therapy in the US being developed in the 1940s to assist psychiatrists and psychoanalysts in working verbally with clients (Miller, 2005; Rubin, 1984, 1988). The professional organizations for art and dance therapy gained momentum in the open-minded and socially expressive decade of the 1960s. In the 1970s, arts therapists worked where the main focus in psychiatric treatment was Neo-Freudian, recognizing and defining pathology and ameliorating symptoms of human despair, mostly using talk therapy, medications, and, when necessary, hospitalization when serious harm threatened a person's life. The creative arts therapies grew and were introduced into visionary and acceptant psychiatric hospitals like the premier training psychiatric hospitals of the Menninger Foundation, then in Topeka, Kansas and the Sheppard and Enoch Pratt Hospital (Sheppard), which was affiliated with Johns Hopkins Hospital in Baltimore, Maryland. At Menninger's and Sheppard, art and dance therapy were incorporated into treatment protocols by the senior training psychiatrists, so the creative arts therapies could 'redirect patient's efforts into creative expressive outlets', especially those in extreme distress, who needed readmission even though they had had years of verbal therapy (Shoemaker, 1978). At Sheppard, a special treatment protocol guided referrals for self-destructive patients, especially cutters, who may have been receiving verbal therapy for years, to be admitted into art and dance therapy sessions as soon as possible (Bergland, 1992). That therapeutic focus on creative potential, an echo of the openness of the 1960s, seemed to offer places for safe emotional release, as well as to access creative, active problem-solving skills that tapped a deeper level of human expression that goes beyond words (Shoemaker, 1978).

Art therapists at Sheppard were challenged to explain how and why their treatment sessions were so effective. In 1977, an evolutionary brain map for the preverbal art therapies was funded by the Sheppard research department as the CONED: a continuum for neurological and evolutionary development. The CONED offered a theoretical guide to understanding how challenging 'people puzzles', for whom verbal cognition and verbal communication were absent, would find therapeutic benefit in art and dance therapy sessions. The darkest and most disturbing 'hidden secrets of a tormented and dysfunctional life' are allowed to be channeled through creative visual avenues of self-expression that 'safely stay on the drawing page', without any risky, dangerous acting out (Shoemaker, 1978).

When children are afforded early-learning experiences with guidance to learn, move, and act at these preverbal and formative experiential levels of behavior and neurophysiology, cognitive perceptions can be dependable, socially communicative, and functional. Conversely, if a person has genetic mutations, such as birth injury, poor nutrition, undependable nurturance, or abusive parenting, the synaptic highway of their neurology is poorly formed and idiosyncratic, possibly in a pathological way. Hence, the CONED, as a continuum brain map for neurological and evolutionary development, emerged as a theoretical guide to understanding how challenging 'people puzzles' needed the experience of creative arts therapies such as music, dance, or image making to access the deeper and older neuro-structures that form the foundational neurological imprint for reliable language development and the storytelling of hidden and unspeakable stories of traumatic proportions. Through the preverbal arts therapies, creative self-expression can be developed into conscious problem solving in the supportive group exchanges, speaking safely among others, guided by trained professionals who know how to access and process idiosyncratic preverbal messages.

Neurological research was pioneered, at a time when little was known about what was going on 'inside the brain', at the Johns Hopkins Medical School, Adolph Meyer Psychiatric Institute and Department of Neurology. Based on the pioneering work of neurologist Dr. Solomon Snyder, his doctoral student Candace Pert's psychopharmacological research identified neurotransmitters as the molecules of emotion that communicate along the synaptic highways of the human brain' at the molecular level was being understood as significant transforming molecules in human behavior. For change to happen, the emotions must be involved (Pert, 1999).

Slowly, over the decades, the creative arts therapies have been invited into more psychiatric settings, special-needs educational centers, and a variety of mental health, treatment, and reha-bilitation centers as psychiatry and psychology began to shift away from a focus on pathology toward a focus on creative interventions for more effective treatment (Rubin, 1988). Creativity is not only part of the 1990s' emergence of energy psychology; it is also a part of the somatic therapy approaches that use both hemispheres. All neuro-structures of the brain utilized intercon-nectedly, with movement experiences for the body in the creation process, help integrate trauma, soothe the limbic brain, and begin the healing process (Levine, 1997; van der Kolk, 1994; van der Kolk et al., 1996). During the 1990s, Dr. Don Campbell wrote *The Mozart Effect*, which identi-fied the neurological foundations and best practices for music therapy for a variety of people, in a variety of settings (Campbell, 1997).

Peter Levine's work, documented in *Waking the Tiger: Healing Trauma* (1997), developed around studying animals' responses to shaking off trauma after surviving a fight, flight, freeze state. Levine created an approach called somatic expression, which uses the body and all areas of the brain for a human equivalent of the violent shaking an animal does to reset its brain after surviving a traumatic event. It might be good to think of a deer that escaped a lion as an example of this approach. Levine found that animals violently shake to reset the limbic brain as an obser-vation of why trauma gets stuck in the limbic brain in humans. Levine believes humans tend to repress emotions rather than reset the brain (Levine, 1997, 2010). Any form of creative process that includes preverbal somatic responses, combined with logic and intuition, helps the brain heal from trauma as a more whole-brain intervention.

Art and Other Creative Tools: Neurological and Whole-Brain Factors

Art, journaling, dancing, and other creative forms of expression are whole-brain activities increas-ingly being used in psychiatric and recovery settings to assist in releasing emotional pain, allow-ing the limbic brain to be soothed while also using all areas of the brain that facilitate healing the trauma brain (Levine, 1997, 2010; van der Kolk, 1994; van der Kolk et al., 1996). Express-ing emotions and our deep-body feelings requires opening up to oneself and one's experiences, letting down defenses, and dissolving numbness. The artistic process cuts through intellectual defenses by accessing the unconscious mind and, especially, the creative unconscious. Creative expressive art processes can be an effective assessment tool in the therapeutic alliance. In the safety of a therapeutic session, sharing the idiosyncratic creative process of any individual allows a safe place to let the dark contents of the psyche emerge in a safe manner while letting down defenses to allow insight and understanding to emerge (Edwards, 2000). The creative art–making process does not have to involve specific artistic talent (Richards, 2007a, 2007b); the approach is useful in any art therapy milieu. People of all ages and without perceived talent can tap into the creative process simply by selecting a color from any medium and allowing it to begin to access emotional content (Wadeson, 1987). Art has continued to be proven therapeutic just in the pro-cess of producing it and can be used with other, more traditional psychotherapeutic techniques to aid in the exploration of difficult emotional content and in addiction recovery programming (Matto et al., 2003). In working with the co-occurring disordered population who have had sus-tained trauma in life, the therapist becomes the witness while providing a safe container for the client where the experience can bring forth deeper understanding of the unconscious content of fears, anger, pain, and emotional disturbance in the creative work being created (Allen, 1995; Edwards, 2000).

Psychological Factors

The creative arts therapies are effective in helping clients express their emotions while looking for patterns of cognitive distortion and destructive behaviors. Each image in a piece of self-expressive artwork has a story to share. Art therapy sessions follow a sequenced format, from an initial orientation, moving into a chosen arts process, with the resulting self-expressive art product as an enduring record and as a basis for an art-based assessment of the person's silent story to be unfolded across time. The person, along with their developmental states, the process of creative capabilities and blocks demonstrated in observable behaviors, and self-expressing visual symbolism of the product, is both self-reflection and a permanent record of one's self-perceptions and provides conscious awareness that is explored in the verbal processing in the therapeutic session.

Certain creative arts therapy methods of treatment are often used as an adjunctive therapy in the healing process with mental health and addiction treatment, with a range of symptoms of illnesses, across the lifespan, from children to adolescents to adults and when eldercare is needed (Chandler, 1994, 2010, 2013; Shoemaker-Beal, 2006). Catharsis of emotional distress and bringing to consciousness unconsciously held memories and information while offering a vital form of observable assessment of traumatic life histories can assist in integrating whole-brain healing. Clinical observations of clients creating art can facilitate the healing of the wounded inner child within clients, as seen in groups like the Adult Children of Alcoholics (ACOA), who are particularly drawn to expressing themselves through artistic means. These people report that they seem to find answers and hope in their own ability to overcome their pain in a manner they had never expected (Capacchione, 1991).

Art Therapy

To a trained art therapist, self-expressive artwork may contain visual indicators of trauma and abuse, even for those abused people who do not have the conscious assessment tools to have accessed the preverbal levels of human experience and memory, often bringing to conscious awareness psychological distress and memories of trauma. Formal art-based assessment processes incorporate psychological testing approaches like house, tree, person; the draw a clock test, and Bender gestalt drawings for brain damage have lent credibility to arts-based assessments and to the significance of verbally processing self-expressive artwork, and inventories of these assessments are available for trained art therapists (Brooke, 2004). The Mandala Art Research Instrument (MARI) was developed by Joan Kellogg and has demonstrated the drawing of a circle (mandala) as an effective arts assessment that has been used with children, adolescents, and adults (Fincher, 1991; Kellogg et al., 1977; Kellogg, 1978; Rubin, 1984, 1988).

Mandalas represent the whole and offering a simple circle while providing the client an array of media to use can provide an opening to allow unconscious emotions and content to emerge organically for the artist. The process can be illuminating for the artist, as well as be an opening for therapeutic exploration. Figure 17.1 shows an image created by Tricia L. Chandler as an example of how this process emerges. The image, entitled *Thoughts*, began with random colors being used and forms being identified as the picture emerged. It could be an internal or preverbal form of introspection, allowing internal content to emerge from the unconscious.

One art-based assessment format, the Rainbow Phenomenon (Shoemaker-Beal, 1993), was used in a research project with clients with schizophrenia to study any correlation between reported traumas, stressors and illness by examining the random selection of colors for each client's personal signature rainbow drawing (Chandler, 1994). The results of the pilot study showed the use of color as a psychophysiological indicator, demonstrating a correlation for clients between self-reported somatic distress and the alignment in a color diagram of physical energy

Figure 17.1 Thoughts

Source: Chandler, 2001. Unpublished original art.

systems, known as chakras in Eastern yogic traditions, that align with the endocrine system of the body. Shoemaker-Beal has talked about the 'rainbow brain' as an alignment of the evolution of human energy psychophysiology along with the evolution of neurological development (Shoemaker-Beal, 2009). Her clinical observations suggest that engaging in creative activities appears to neurologically light up the whole brain, helping heal trauma by rewiring the synaptic highways among all neuro-structures with a flood of neurotransmitters that sustains and energizes a creative person who can work with an authentic creative flow process. Shoemaker-Beal has continued to work with the CONED Brain Map to further develop the Quatrune Brain Map, which can be used as a continuum checklist of four levels of neurological and developmental behaviors that trauma can freeze and detour from a fully functioning, healthy, and productive skill set for life challenges.

For example, profound therapeutic shifts can be recorded when any of clients troubling self-views that have been transformed from a pathological perception to a healthier self-view. Those self-views, which art therapists and their clients can identify as self-limiting, can be transformed, once expressed visually, and identified into self-enhancing views for future growth. Self-views can include, but are not limited to, body image distortions; self-identity views as being incompetent; social self-view as a failure; and worldviews, environmental views, and/or cosmic views that contribute to maladaptive coping mechanisms and pathological patterns (Shoemaker-Beal, 2006). Art therapists are trained to guide perceptual shifts of self-views. For example, when working with people suffering with the extreme thinness of anorexia nervosa, it is often observed that their body image drawings contain extreme body distortions, as one woman drew herself as 'a fat pig', despite her body actually being dangerously thin. Anorexia nervosa has elements that are related to body dysmorphic disorder, which makes successful treatment more difficult to obtain (American Psychiatric Association, 2013). Through the use of whole-brain creative therapies, clients can begin to let go of their unhealthy obsession with internal images of the body dysmorphic concepts.

The Creative Rainbow Brain

VII. Holistic Center ✳
   integration and wonderment

VI. Conscious Thought Center
   verbal and executive brain ✳

V. Conscious Motor Center
   voluntary movements ✳

IV. Sensory Awareness
   Center ✳

III. Visual Center ✳
   the threshold of CNS

II. Reactive Center ✳
   movement response

I. Primal Survival Center ✳
   passive pulsing cycle
   social being beginning *in uteri*

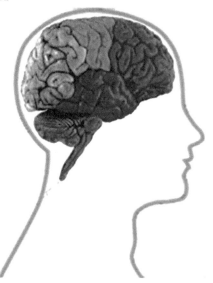

Figure 17.2 The Creative Rainbow Brain Illustration

Source: Shoemaker-Beal (1993)

Music Therapy (MT) and Music-Based Interventions (MBI)

A mega analysis of the literature done by Hohmann et al. (2017) found 34 quantitative and six qualitative studies that demonstrated efficacy in using either music therapy (MT) or music-based interventions (MBI) in substance use treatment. While this does not indicate robust results from these forms of creative therapies, the qualitative studies found that MT revealed themes of improvement in areas that improved quality of life through skill development and group interactions and in emotional expression (Hohmann et al., 2017). By using MT, clients with mental health and substance use disorders have shown improvement in mood, stress, self-esteem, motivation, emotional expression, and social cohesion while, specifically in women and adolescents, MT improved anxiety and internal locus of control (Malchiodi, 2005; Shuman, et al., 2016; Pelletier, 2004; Ross et al., 2008; Baker et al., 2007; Gold et al., 2013; Gardstrom & Diestelkamp, 2013; James, 1988).

The musical brain is the foundational level of holistic and preverbal therapies in that even in the womb, fetuses regulate and are calmed by soothing music, and this is most primal developmentally and is located at the top of the spinal cord, the brain stem, the medulla oblongata, and the limbic system. Music has been used since the dawn of human experience to celebrate within communities in rituals and chanting and is written about as the cognitive origins of art, religion, and science by Dr. Steven Mithen (1999), who wrote *The Prehistory of the Human Mind*. Best practices for music therapy can be developed for deep emotional recognition and processing simply by listening to and playing music. The act of composing music uses whole-brain processing, contributing to healing the limbic brain when it is stuck in the fight, flight, freeze survival response to traumatic memories, utilizing the concept elicited in the Quatrune Brain Map. The trained music therapist has innate music ability combined with professional counseling skills to work with clients.

Dance-Movement Therapy (DMT)

Within the development of the dance-movement brain, there is a connection to a kinesthetic reaction that provides the ability to access action and movement in the face of threats of danger within the brain. Dance-movement therapy, as the next level of formation for creative arts expression and whole-brain integration, has developed quantitative and qualitative research to demonstrate that movement and dance therapies have positive effects on well-being, increasing body awareness, social skills, and empathy while improving quality of life and decreasing symptoms of depression and anxiety and also reducing attachment trauma (Brauninger, 2012; Kiepe et al., 2012; Koch et al., 2014; Mala et al., 2012; Wagner, 2015). What has been demonstrated in these studies is that while continued research is needed, music and dance therapy are part of the pioneering creative and somatic therapies that help soothe the limbic brain and provide whole-brain integration, through which the executive cognitive functioning of the brain can take control again (Levine, 1997, 2010). Considering the formation of our cerebellum to coordinate movement, along with its extensive neuro-connections to our sensory brain functions, we can understand how, deep in our species' ancestral history, movement shapes every creative capability in our lives. Graduate-level professional training of dance-movement therapists includes anatomy, knowledge of sensory receptors, and gross and fine motor movement in a repertoire of choreographic and musical selections that can offer a wide range of therapeutic interventions for trauma and developmental disabilities that need remediation.

Best Practices for Dance-Movement and the Somatic Therapies

Dance therapy and the creative somatic therapies have shown efficacy with adolescents and adults in individual and group therapy in rehabilitation, inpatient, and outpatient settings. These practices help cut through cognitive defenses to access deep emotional issues that may be beneath the surface of consciousness and, therefore, verbal expression. Dance-movement therapy can be used in an integrative treatment setting to help to rewire the synapses and heal the broken, stunted, and blocked neurological connections between the cerebellum and the various synaptic highways that interconnect the primal-ness of movement with corresponding neuro-structures to soothe the limbic brain, help clients integrate adverse situations into their schema of personal growth, and form a deeper resiliency for day-to-day life events. Any of the movement therapies can be used as an adjunct to other recovery strategies for those dealing with the results of trauma and co-occurring disorders.

Eye Movement Desensitization Regulation (EMDR) – Neurological and Psychological Factors

Eye movement desensitization regulation (EMDR) was developed by psychologist Dr. Francine Shapiro in 1989 to address the brain trauma that occurs due to adverse life experiences. Dr. Shapiro developed this eight-stage approach to achieve rapid positive therapeutic outcomes without the client having to really relive the psychological trauma event through verbally focused therapy approaches (Shapiro, 2002). This approach has shown in several studies that EMDR therapy was more effective than trauma-focused, verbal cognitive behavioral therapy (TF-CBT) and decreased negative emotions and disturbing images, often experienced as nightmares and troublesome flashbacks by traumatized people, and other memory effects of psychological trauma (Shapiro, 2002). The efficacy of EMDR therapy is due to the rapid decrease of distressing symptoms of posttraumatic stress disorder (PTSD), with standard EMDR being completed in 8 therapeutic sessions while TF-CBT can take up to 50 sessions to effect even close to the same level of emotional regulation and mediation of trauma symptoms (van der Kolk, 1994; van der Kolk et al., 1996; van der Kolk, 2006a).

Best Practices

EMDR therapy has eight phases to it that include:

* History taking
* Preparation of clients for EMDR process
* Assessment of aspects of memory
* Desensitization
* Installation of connections to positive cognitive networks
* A body scan to complete processing
* Closure

(Shapiro, 2002)

In using these steps, the emotional charge, physiological sensations, and any negative beliefs are released as the target memory becomes more adaptive to conscious integration (Shapiro, 2002). The use of EMDR has been supported by the ACEs study done by Kaiser Permanente (Felitti et al., 1998) for treating a variety of trauma and abuse symptoms along with exposure to stressful events in children, adolescents, and adults, and the American Psychiatric Association, the Department of Defense, and the World Health Organization recommend it as effective treatment for trauma victims (American Psychiatric Association, 2004; Veterans Health Administration, 2010; World Health Organization, 2013).

Psychodrama – Neurological, Psychological, and Biological Factors

As early as the 1960s, psychodrama was called a body/mind therapy approach that incorporated creativity, somatic experience, and creative consciousness using the drama in the human condition to gain insight into perspectives that assist in healing wounded family systems. Psychotherapy sessions are guided by trained counselors and are considered part of somatic and creative self-expression as well. Psychodrama creatively utilizes the emotional motivation of dealing with the pain of the drama of a family dysfunction with somatic expression via physical movement, as well as visualizing, as a form of 'acting out the family issue' to be creatively resolved in the societal support psychodrama session (Blomkvist et al., 2000).

The development of psychodrama by the Morenos was followed by creative adaptions as a healing methodology that uses somatic movement, along with assuming and acting out the roles of others to explore the dynamics of familial, relational, and interpersonal issues. In the 1970s, Dr. Fritz Perls created gestalt therapy using sensitivity groups, sometimes staged with an 'empty chair' placed in the center of a group for a person of focus at any given session (Perls, 1973). Psychodrama was also later developed to increase communication skills in family therapy by Dr. Virginia Satir, who developed a form of 'family sculpting' and re-sculpting sessions (Satir,

1988). More recently, psychodrama approaches, especially forms of 'constellation therapy', were also specifically designed for an individual's family dynamics in a closely guided and supportive group run by non-licensed psychiatric practitioners trained in the constellations systems approach (Wolynn, 2021).

Psychodrama is considered a 'deep action' means to explore clients' unspoken reactions by trying out novel approaches to the problems happening in their lives (Garcia & Buchanan, 2000). This process can be quite appealing for the newly recovering addict who wants to do more than 'sit and talk', which is what they will verbally process following the action-oriented psychodrama session. Involving the action of somatic movement appears to assist with realigning problem-solving skills. This is a useful modality for those with addiction issues and to help resolve interpersonal concerns. Although there is a cognitive process happening for most of us when we are not standing or moving, the cognitions seem to shift in different ways as we change our physical position and connect with our body's somatic memory. As a whole-brain therapeutic approach, psychodrama may be the most holistic as a whole-brain engagement in sessions actively taps into every level of Quatrune brain functioning. Each psychodrama session includes the sounds of, perhaps, triggering verbal interchanges based on the emotional issues addressed experientially. The rhythms and intensity of the movements of participating group members, with suggested and personally challenging expressive choreography, can finally be more extroverted 'performances', which will have visual memories activated in the corrective recapitulation of an acting out, perhaps of past trauma. These 'acting-out sessions' are surrounded by the supportive psychodrama audience, who will also be affected by the acting-out performance and become a part of the verbal sharing for follow-up session processing.

This shift is true when we try to understand something new – like the recovery mindset – and see it as a locomotive experience. Konopik and Cheung (2012) relate that the methods used in psychodrama are focused on improving a client's outlook on life. As an individual with a substance use disorder, some of the things that may need to happen include being still and moving less. This is one reason that psychodrama is attractive to substance abusers – i.e., they can move around and get to practice seeing things from other perspectives than just their own. This is also the 'magic' that happens in psychodrama, in that a changing perspective is a real commodity in the recovery world. Furthermore, Ramseur and Wiener (2003) delineate that, by dramatically enacting roles of others in their lives, insights can be found, and clients can create healthier alternatives in expressing themselves with others and for their own improved understanding of those in their lives. Psychodrama is often done as a group experience, which is how this will be detailed to look at what happens.

Psychodrama Processes and Parts

Clients can change in their outlook and attitudes over the course of implementing psychodrama, which is indicative of healing. The techniques used might include rehearsals for life in sobriety, which will take some time to identify and then practice using. Another of the usual methods in psychodrama is to enact a significant scene from the addict's life; this involves bringing something from the past – an event that could be labeled as 'there and then' – and bringing it into the 'here and now'. Dushman and Bressler (1991) describe how, within psychodrama, the client 'protagonist' makes the choice in the drama event as to how greater closure can be gained through changes in behavior in the here and now.

This process incorporates recognition of specific aspects of the individual's life – this person is the main actor or 'protagonist'. Anyone else who supports the work of the protagonist is known as an 'auxiliary'; this can be specific persons in the protagonist's life, people who are resources for the protagonist, or people who can be helpful in some way in the enactment (or drama). Finally, the audience is anyone who's not in the drama. The three parts of a psychodrama are the warm-up, the enactment, and the sharing. The warm-up is what happens in getting ready for the action of the drama; this might be after other action has happened. The enactment is the drama or the main event, which takes up the majority of the time. Afterward, everyone shares their personal reactions to the protagonist's work; this is done with the protagonist, who may just listen and should not respond.

One of the more usual exercises or psychodrama action methods is the role play, which is an activity that many who are not involved in psychodrama are familiar with. This involves deciding who will be the main actor or protagonist and then training auxiliaries for their role or part in a dialogue. In the treatment of substance abuse issues, these auxiliaries can be the person's sponsor, someone in the protagonist's family, or maybe a friend or coworker. The director facilitates the training for the auxiliary and sets up the scene in which the protagonist and the auxiliary will have their dialogue. This is a powerful therapeutic approach to use with both adolescents and adults in working through troubling family dynamics and interpersonal concerns.

Another activity involves the warm-up, which some may think of as 'icebreakers'. These are directed exercises that facilitate individuals getting ready for more action – usually in the drama. Movement exercises consist of any other activities that we might do in psychodrama. One of these might be a feelings walk, which is usually a favorite in groups of substance abusers. Everyone in the group gets in a line facing in the same direction. The director identifies specific feelings for all the members to show as they walk across the room.

Tian Dayton (2003) details that psychodrama is 'an action method' that fosters changes in addicts 'through exploratory, healing role play and role training or practicing more functional behaviors. It offers a living laboratory' for addicts to see themselves by 'comparing and contrasting differing sets of behaviors, separating the past from the present and making conscious choices as to what may work' well in the process of recovery.

Best Practices for Psychodrama

Psychodrama is a useful strategy in group therapy or family therapy that can be used with adolescents or adults in rehabilitation, inpatient, or outpatient therapy settings. Often memories emerge, and insights are gained from reenacting family dynamics through role play. This is an extraordinary process to work through childhood issues involving family dynamics, as well as practicing strategies to improve communication with family members while releasing body memories as well.

Conclusion

The creative arts therapies, somatic therapies, EMDR, and psychodrama have been well researched within the body-emotion-mind-spirit and psychodynamic paradigm for decades. As adjunctive therapies within holistic and inclusive therapeutic approaches as far back as the talk therapies of Freud's and Jung's works, the unconscious memories that people hold deeply in their bodies and their unconscious due to past trauma, abuse, and physiological distress have been recognized. These therapies using the whole-person body-emotion-mind-spirit approach in more recent times have been shown effective in reducing the survival mechanism in the limbic brain to allow executive cognitive functioning to increase while anxiety-producing triggers and cravings are reduced. Using a whole-brain approach, such as the Quatrune Brain Map, like EMDR, can soothe initial trauma responses and, with all the creative arts therapies, can be effectively used with adolescents and adults with co-occurring mental illness and substance use disorders in conjunction with other practices to assist with recovery and healing of any individual, group, and family therapy modalities along with a variety of safe therapeutic milieus. To become proficient in using these therapeutic techniques, additional training will be required, but these approaches are used in many mental health milieus that treat co-occurring disorders.

Questions for Consideration

1. How does using both hemispheres of the brain along with somatic movement help soothe the limbic brain?
2. How can creative arts be incorporated into addiction treatment to aid with recovery programming?
3. How does EMDR help reset the brain through eye movements that soothes the limbic response to trauma?
4. When would using psychodrama in a group format be helpful in the recovery process?
5. What are some of the ways psychodrama can be used with adolescents?

Case Study

Tom is a 20-year-old Caucasian male who has been admitted to the behavioral health psychiatric/detoxification unit of a hospital after throwing himself out a three-story window in another psychiatric ward and breaking both his legs. He is the only child of two corporate professionals, who provided him with most of the luxuries of life except for their time and nurturing. As a teen, Tom began smoking cannabis and drinking, but over the last six months, he has been engaging in using heroin. Once detoxed, he also received a diagnosis of bipolar I disorder, as well as polysubstance use disorders. Tom has struggled with learning about his diagnoses and has been resistant to beginning treatment. During an art therapy group, he was asked to use an art medium to get in touch with his emotions around how he views his diagnoses and disorders. This is one picture Tom created that expresses his anger at his substance use disorder and his grief around the interpersonal and mental health problems created by both the SUD and the mood disorder. In creating this image, Tom began to soften his defense mechanisms to engaging in the treatment process.

Figure 17.3 Client Art Therapy Picture Showing Grief and Loss Due to Co-occurring Disorder Diagnosis

Source: Client art (Chandler, 1993), unpublished

Questions to Consider

1.   How do creative therapies offer a unique view into Tom's reality?
2.   Can creative therapies work to help Tom reach his treatment goals?
3.   Using an integrative approach, what treatments may be most effective when working with Tom?

References

American Psychological Association. (2004). *Practice guideline for the treatment of patients with acute stress disorder and posttraumatic stress disorder*. American Psychiatric Association.

American Psychiatric Association. (2013). *Diagnostic and statistical manual of mental disorders* (5th ed.). Authors.

Baker, F. A., Gleadhill, L. M., & Dingle, G. A. (2007). Music therapy and emotional exploration: Exposing substance abuse clients to the experiences of non-drug-induced emotions. *Arts Psychotherapy, 34,* 321–330.

Bergland, R. C. (1992, July). Treatment choices: Rehabilitation choices used by patients with multiple personality disorders. *American Journal of Occupational Therapy, 46*(7).

Blomkvist, L. D., Moreno, Z., & Rutzel, T. (2000). *Psychodrama, surplus reality and the art of healing* (1st ed.). Routledge.

Brauninger, I. (2012). The efficacy of dance movement therapy group on improvement of quality of life: A randomized controlled trial. *The Arts in Psychotherapy, 39*(4), 296–303.

Brooke, S. L. (2004). *Tools of the trade: A therapist's guide to art therapy assessments*. Charles C. Thomas Publishing, LTD.

Campbell, D. (1997). *The Mozart effect: Tapping the power of music to heal the body, strengthen the mind, and unlock the creative spirit*. Avon Books.

Capacchione, L. (1991). *Recovery of your inner child: The highly acclaimed method for liberating your inner self*. Simon & Schuster.

Chandler, P. (2010). *Resiliency in healing from childhood sexual abuse*. Dissertation that partially fulfills the requirements for the Degree of Doctor of Philosophy (Psychology). ProQuest Dissertations.

Chandler, T. (1994). *The body, emotions, mind, and spirit paradigm: How the use of color and mandala reflect in artwork*. Thesis submitted in partial satisfaction of Master of Arts in Transpersonal Counseling Psychology & Art Therapy, Naropa University.

Chandler, T. (2013). Integrative treatment pilot study: An extended care holistic treatment facility for women with co-occurring disorders. *Annals of Psychotherapy & Integrative Health, 16*(3), 62–73.

Dayton, T. (2003). Addictions and women. In J. Gershoni (Ed.), *Psychodrama in the 21st century: Clinical and educational applications*. Springer.

Dushman, R. D., & Bressler, M. J. (1991). Psychodrama in an adolescent chemically dependent treatment program. *Individual Psychologist: Journal of Adlerian Theory, Research and Practice, 47,* 515–520.

Edwards, C. G. (2000). Creative writing as a spiritual practice: Two paths. In M. E. Miller & S. R. Cook-Greuter (Eds.), *Creativity, spirituality, and transcendence: Paths to integrity and wisdom in the mature self* (pp. 3–23). Albex Publishing Corporation.

Felitti, V. J., Anda, R. F., Nordenberg, D., Williamson, D. F., Spitz, A. M., Edwards, V., . . . Marks, J. S. (1998). Relationship of childhood abuse and household dysfunction to many of the leading causes of death in adults: The Adverse Childhood Experiences (ACE) study. *American Journal of Prevention Medicine, 14*(4), 245–258.

Fincher, S. (1991, 2020 revised). *Creating mandalas: For insight, healing, and self-expression*. Shambhala Publications.

Flach, F. (1990). Disorders of the pathways involved in the creative process. In M. A. Runco & R. Richards (Eds.), *Eminent creativity, everyday creativity, and health* (pp. 179–190). Ablex.

Freeman, L. W. (2004). *Mosby's complementary and alternative medicine: A research-based approach* (2nd ed.). Mosby.

Freeman, L. W. (2006). Imagery as a group therapy for cancer survivors. Retrieved November 17, 2008, from www.saybrook.edu

Garcia, A., & Buchanan, D. R. (2000). Psychodrama. In P. Lewis & D. R. Johnson (Eds.), *Current approaches in drama therapy*. Charles C. Thomas Publishing, LTD.

Gardstrom, S. C., & Diestelkamp, W. S. (2013). Women with addictions report reduced anxiety after music therapy: A quasi-experimental study. *Voices World Forum Music Therapy, 13.*

Gold, C., Mossler, K., Grocke, D., Heldal, T. O., Tjemsland, L. Aarre, T., et al. (2013). Individual music therapy for mental health clients with low therapy motivation: Multicentre randomized controlled trial. *Psychotherapy Psychometrics, 82,* 319–331.

Hohmann, L., Bradt, J., Stegemann, T., & Koelsch, S. (2017). Effects of music therapy and music-based interventions in the treatment of substance use disorders: A systematic review. *PLoS One, 12*(11).

Kellogg, J. (1978). *Mandala: The path of beauty.* The Mandala Assessment Research Institute.

Kellogg, J., Mac Rae, M., Bonny, H. L., & di Leo, F. (1977). The use of the mandala in psychological evaluation and treatment. *American Journal of Art Therapy, 16*(4), 123–134.

Kiepe, M., Stockgit, B., & Keil, T. (2012). Effects of dance therapy and ballroom dances on physical and mental illnesses: A systematic review. *The Arts in Psychotherapy, 39*(5), 404–411.

Koch, S., Kunz, T., Lykou, S., & Cruz, R. F. (2014). Effects of dance movement therapy and dance on health-related psychological outcomes: A meta-analysis. *The Arts in Psychotherapy, 41*(1), 46–64.

Konopik, D. A., & Cheung, M. (2013/2012). Psychodrama as a social work modality. *Social Work, 58*(1), 9–20.

James, M. R. (1988). Music therapy values clarification: A positive influence on perceived locus of control. *Journal of Music Therapy, 25,* 206–215.

Jung, C. G. (1961). *Man and his symbols.* Doubleday.

Jung, C. G. (2009). *The red book (Philemon)* (S. Shamdasani, Ed. & Trans., M. Kyburz & J. Peck, Trans.). W. W. Norton & Company.

Levine, P. A. (1997). *Waking the tiger: Healing trauma.* North Atlantic Books.

Levine, P. A. (2010). *In an unspoken voice: How the body releases trauma and restores goodness.* North Atlantic Press.

Mala, A., Karkou, V., & Meekums, B. (2012). Dance/Movement Therapy (DMT) for depression: A scoping review. *The Arts in Psychotherapy, 39,* 287–295.

Malchiodi, C. A. (2005). Expressive therapies: History, theory, and practice. In C. A. Malchiodi (Ed.), *Expressive therapies* (pp. 1–15). Guilford Press.

Matto, H., Cocoran, J., & Fassler, A. (2003). Integrating solution-focused and art therapies for substance abuse treatment: Guidelines for practice. *The Arts in Psychotherapy, 30*(1), 265–272. doi:10.1016/j.aip.2003.08.003

Miller, D. (2005). Mandala symbolism in psychotherapy: The potential utility of the Lowenfeld Mosaic Technique for enhancing the individuation process. *Journal of Transpersonal Psychology, 37*(2).

Mithen, S. (1999). *The prehistory of the mind: The cognitive origins of art, religion, and science.* Thames & Hudson.

Nicosia, G., Minewiser, L., & Freger, A. (2019). World Trade Center: A longitudinal case study for treating post traumatic stress disorder with emotional freedom technique and eye movement desensitization regulation. *Work, 63*(2), 199–204.

Pelletier, C. L. (2004). The effect of music on decreasing arousal due to stress: A meta-analysis. *Journal of Music Therapy, 41,* 192–214.

Penebaker, J. W. (Ed.). (1995). *Emotions, disclosure, and health.* American Psychological Association.

Perls, F. (1973). *The gestalt approach and eye witness to therapy.* Science and Behavior Books.

Pert, C. B. (1999). *Molecules of emotion: The science behind mind-body medicine.* Simon and Schuster.

Peterson, C. (2006). *A primer in positive psychology.* Oxford University Press.

Ramseur, C. A., & Wiener, D. J. (2003). Rehearsals for growth applied to substance abuse groups. In D. J. Weiner & L. K. Oxford (Eds.), *Action therapy with families and groups: Using creative arts improvisation in clinical practice.* American Psychological Association.

Richards, R. (2000–2001). Millennium as opportunity: Chaos, creativity, and Guilford's structure of intellect model. *Creativity Research Journal, 13*(3 & 4), 249–265.

Richards, R. (2007a). Everyday creativity: Our hidden potential. In R. Richards (Ed.), *Everyday creativity and new views of human nature: Psychological, social, and spiritual perspectives* (pp. 25–54). Brunner/Mazel.

Richards, R. (2007b). Everyday creativity and the arts. *World Futures, 63,* 500–525.

Riley, D. (2004). The creative mind. *Art Therapy: Journal of American Art Therapy Association, 21*(4), 184–190.

Ross, S., Cidambi, I., Dermatis, H., Weinstein, J., Ziedonis, D., & Roth, S., et al. (2008). Music therapy: A novel motivational approach for dually diagnosed patients. *Journal of Addictive Diseases, 27*, 41–53.

Rubin, J. A. (1984). *The art of art therapy.* Brunner/Mazel.

Rubin, J. A. (1988). *Approaches to art therapy.* Brunner/Mazel.

Satir, V. (1988). *The new people making.* Science and Behavior Books, Inc.

Schmanke, L. (2017). *Art therapy and substance abuse.* Jessica Kingsley Publishers.

Shapiro, F. (2002). *EMDR as an integrative psychotherapy: Experts of diverse orientations explore the paradigm prism.* American Psychological Press.

Shoemaker, R. (1978). *The significance of the first picture in art therapy.* Chapter proceedings of the 1977 annual conference of the American Art Therapy Association. Co-editors: Roberta Shoemaker and Susan Gonick-Barris, AATA Publisher.

Shoemaker-Beal, R. (1979/1993). *The rainbow booklet: A guidebook for rainbow assessment workshops, a psychophysiological theory of color usage for research.* White Chapel Press. (Self-published).

Shoemaker-Beal, R. (1995). *An experiential taxonomy for the study of subtle energies in a wholistic model.* White Chapel Press.

Shoemaker-Beal, R. (2006). *Art therapy across the lifespan: An orientation and organizational manual.* White Chapel Press.

Shoemaker-Beal, R. (2009). *The Quatrune brain research grant proposal.* Prepared for the International Neuroscience and Consciousness Studies, Inc., Austin, Texas.

Shuman, J., Kennedy, H., Dewitt, P., Edelblute, A., & Wamboldt, M. Z. (2016). Group music therapy impacts mood stated of adolescents in a psychiatric hospital setting. *Arts Psychotherapy, 49*, 50–56.

Swan-Foster, N. (2017). *Jungian art therapy: Images, dreams, and analytical psychology* (1st ed.). Routledge.

van der Kolk, B. A. (1994). The body keeps the score: Memory and the evolving psychobiology of post-traumatic stress. *Harvard Review of Psychiatry, 1*, 253–265.

van der Kolk, B. A. (2006a). Clinical implications of neuroscience research in PTSD. [Electronic version]. *Annuals of the New York Academy of Sciences, 17*(1), 277–293. Retrieved March 3, 2008, from ProQuest database.

van der Kolk, B. A. (2006b). Developmental trauma disorder: A new, rational diagnosis for children with complex trauma histories. [Electronic version]. *Psychiatric Annals, 200X*, 2–8. Retrieved March 3, 2008, from ProQuest database.

van der Kolk, B. A., McFarlane, A. C., & Weisaeth, L. (1996). *Traumatic stress: The effects of overwhelming experience on mind, body, and society.* Guilford Press.

Wadeson, H. (1987). *The dynamics of art psychotherapy.* Wiley & Sons.

Wagner, D. (2015). Polyvagal theory and peek-a-boo: How the therapeutic pas de deux heals attachment trauma. *Body, Movement and Dance in Psychotherapy, 10*(4), 256–265. https://doi.org/10.1080/174329 79.2015.1069762

Wolynn, M. (2021, May). *Information gained by personal communication via the Internet.*

18 How East Met West

The Emergence of Energy Psychology as a Body/Mind Treatment Approach

Tricia L. Chandler

Introduction

Eastern energy healing, medicine, and psychology techniques began to be embraced by holistic psychologists, psychiatrists, and medical doctors in the US in the 1960s. The use of acupuncture for pain relief and healing was introduced in the US when it became known that acupuncture was successfully used as pain treatment by a journalist in China post-surgery, following an emergency appendectomy in 1970. The interest in the body-mind connection was being explored by many researchers in multidisciplinary fields. Drs. Elmer and Alyce Greene were researching the effect of biofeedback and later bio-neurofeedback as effective brain-wave mapping by measuring deeper stages of relaxation at the research division of the psychiatric treatment and training center of the Menninger Foundation in Kansas. Dr. Patricia Norris explored the use of biofeedback with guided visualization to effectively treat what were previously considered untreatable neurological disorders, co-authoring, with her patient, a book *Why Me?* (1985) on his healing process. Dr. Jeanne Achterberg started researching guided visualization while working in a burn clinic in Dallas, Texas, in connection with her doctoral research in the 1960s and wrote *Imagery in Healing: Shamanism and Modern Medicine* (1985), discussing how guided visualization taps into the ability to influence the course of a disease and cope with pain. Dr. George Goodwin and Dr. David Hawkins, among other psychiatrists and psychologists, were studying the use of kinesiology to explore the way the body can tell the mind what is needed and what is going on in the body with a simple technique. This amazingly creative time with research exploring the understanding of how to work with the whole person emerged into the Holistic American Medical Association created by Dr. C. Norman Shealy in 1978, which is still active today in researching and advocating for the use of holistic and integrative medicine by all licensed health-care providers (Porter and Norris 1985; Achterberg, 1985).

The decades of research into the efficacy of energy medicine (Oschman, 2000) and energy techniques for healing physiological and psychological disorders have been explored for issues developed due to trauma (Levine, 1997, 2010; van der Kolk et al., 1996; van der Kolk, 2014). These modalities of treatment combine somatic therapies, cognitive therapies, energy medicine, and consciousness/creativity approaches to bring the body and mind back into balance. This chapter acknowledges the historical use of acupuncture that has developed and been accepted to treat triggers and cravings for those with substance use disorders and pain syndromes. It explores kinesiology and how it has been used in exploring the body/mind concerns a person may be experiencing and acupressure as the beginning processes that have led to thought field therapy and emotional freedom technique. These therapeutic approaches have demonstrated evidence-based outcomes for releasing emotional dysregulation due to intense trauma memories that maintain activation in the limbic (survival) brain while reducing emotional dysregulation, depression, anxiety symptoms, and triggers. By reducing the activation of the limbic brain through a combination of integrative approaches, clients with co-occurring disorders are able to access higher executive

DOI: 10.4324/9781003220916-21

cognitive functioning, resulting in other therapeutic approaches having better outcomes (Levine, 1997, 2010).

Learning Objectives

- Understand how energy psychology techniques are soothing to the amygdala and hippocampus and how this leads to increased executive cognitive functioning
- Learn the background of acupressure, kinesiology, and using somatic and cognitive memory reconsolidation approaches reduce trauma responses
- Learn about the EP approach of the emotional freedom technique.

Key Terms

- **Epigenetics:** The study of changes within the human genome as a result of behavioral and environmental factors. Unlike genetic changes, epigenetic changes are reversible and do not change the DNA sequence, but they can change how the body reads a DNA sequence.
- **Emotional Freedom Technique:** A somatic and cognitive (body/mind) exposure technique for psychological trauma in which acupuncture points that are linked to specific internal organs or emotions are tapped with the fingers. EFT was developed after TFT and uses tapping with set-up statements to rebalance the body's energy system and reduce emotional dysregulation around traumatic memories.
- **Heart Rate Variability:** HRV is a measure of the naturally occurring beat-to-beat changes in heart rate/heart rhythms.
- **Kinesiology:** The study of the anatomy, physiology, and mechanics of body movement, especially in humans. The application of the principles of kinesiology to the evaluation and treatment of muscular imbalance or derangement.
- **Limbic Brain:** A set of brain structures located on both sides of the thalamus, immediately beneath the medial temporal lobe of the cerebrum, primarily in the forebrain, also known as the survival brain.
- **Meridians:** Various sets of pathways in the body along which vital energy is said to flow. There are 12 such pathways associated with specific organs.
- **Polyvagal Theory:** Describes the process in which neural circuits read cues of danger in our environment as neuroception and send messages from the body back to the limbic brain through the brain stem.
- **Somatic Therapy:** Somatic means 'of the body', as somatic therapies use body/mind approaches that are psychotherapeutic and holistic. A kinesthetic approach can be accessed through dance-movement therapy, which has been the foundation of somatic approaches.
- **Thought Field Therapy:** A mind-body self-treatment combining modern psychotherapy and Eastern tradition, it draws heavily on ancient Chinese medical practices, including acupressure, which emphasize the presence of an internal energy system.

History of Kinesiology, Acupuncture, and Acupressure as Energy Medicine Tools

Kinesiology

Kinesiology is an energy approach that uses one's own (somatic) body wisdom to answer questions posed about any perceived health concern. The increased understanding of the innate wisdom of the body led to researching ways this approach could be used to effect change in the body/mind. Applied kinesiology was developed by Dr. George Goodheart after exploring how a physical stimulus could either increase strength or weakness in muscles (Gin et al., 1997; Hawkins,

1995). Dr. Goodheart found that below ordinary consciousness and through the technique of muscle testing, the body knew what was 'good' or 'bad' for it. Dr. Diamond refined the discipline into behavioral kinesiology when he found that the indicated muscles became weak or strong based upon either positive or negative intellectual or physical stimuli (Diamond, 1985, 1997; Hawkins, 1995). This has been found to be an effective technique that can bring up information that the body holds, from food preferences and allergies to trauma memories held in different areas of the body.

Steps to Perform Kinesiology (Requires Two People)

- The subject stands erect, right arm relaxed at their side, left arm held out parallel to the floor, elbow straight.
- Face the subject and place your left hand on their right shoulder to steady the subject. Then place your right hand on the subject's extend left arm above the wrist.
- Tell the subject you are going to try to push their arm down as they resist with all their strength.
- Push down on the subject's arm quickly, firmly, and evenly. This is just to test the spring of the arm.
- Have the subject think of a known fact (like their name) to demonstrate that the arm will stay firm when being pushed on. Then think of a defeating thought, and when pushed, the arm will go slack.

Applied kinesiology has been used by practitioners in a variety of settings since the 1970s, including being used by psychiatrists and psychologists (Hawkins, 1995). Consistently, it has been found that test subjects did not need to have any conscious knowledge of a subject, but as they are put through the kinesiology approach, if questions were asked with yes/no responses, the subjects' bodies knew the correct answers as if there was cellular access to knowledge. This research has continued to demonstrate that humans are part of a universal energy field, and all knowledge is available through that universal energy field, which corresponds to discoveries in quantum physics, consciousness, and long-distance healing (Achterberg et al., 2005; Hawkins, 1995; Oschman, 2000). Additionally, studying kinesiology led to further developments by Goodheart and his colleagues, Dr. Diamond and Dr. Callahan, that started considering the way acupuncture was used to stimulate meridians in the body and how these could improve psychological functioning.

Acupuncture

Acupuncture is an energy medicine approach that came into use more than 4,000 years ago in China and was codified by 100 BCE (Kaptchuk, 2000). Acupuncture became known in the United States in the early 1970s, when a reporter from *The New York Times* described how amazed he was by the way that acupuncture relieved his pain following an emergency appendectomy in China. Acupuncture analgesia has been linked to activation of endogenous opioid peptides in the central nervous system and is just one of its many uses (Freeman, 2004). Additionally, studies done by a neurosurgeon in Hong Kong in 1972 found that the analgesic properties of acupuncture could be helpful in the treatment of opiate addiction (Margolin et al., 1993).

The National Institutes of Health (NIH) Consensus Development Panel on Acupuncture (1998) published findings that acupuncture demonstrated effectiveness in treating postoperative pain, chemotherapy nausea, and vomiting and that acupuncture has demonstrated some usefulness in the treatment of stroke rehabilitation and headache, along with pain issues like menstrual cramps, tennis elbow, fibromyalgia, myofascial pain, osteoarthritis, low back pain, carpal tunnel syndrome, and health challenges like asthma. The NIH panel suggested that evidenced-based efficacy studies should be designed to examine acupuncture as used in clinical practice and that research showed sufficient evidence of acupuncture's potential value to encourage further studies and expand its use in conventional medicine, which has since been done using fMRI to show how acupuncture stimulates the limbic system (Hui et al., 2000; Hui et al., 2005; NIH Consensus Development Panel on Acupuncture, 1998). Since that time, numerous studies have concluded that acupuncture is beneficial in treating opiate and alcohol dependence, along with cravings associated with these substance use disorders and the trauma associated with early-childhood sexual abuse (Pradhan, 2010). Acupuncture can be used as an adjunct treatment in addiction recovery programs but can also be used medically to treat pain in children, adolescents, and adults in a non-intrusive approach.

The National Acupuncture Detoxification Association (NADA) was developed in the 1970s when it was discovered that a five-needle protocol in the ear was effective in reducing tremors, shakes, and both physical and mental agitation in heroin addicts while in detoxification units (Huff, 2007). Although the results of clinical studies have been mixed on demonstrated effectiveness of addiction treatment using the NADA protocols, more than 1,500 clinical sites around the world currently use these protocols. The NADA protocols began to be used with traumatized populations in New York after the September 11, 2001, attacks. The group Acupuncturists without Borders has been going to natural disaster sites since then to provide trauma relief using NADA and acupuncture protocols (Hollifield et al., 2007; Huff, 2007).

Combining Acupressure Tapping and the Emergence of Thought Field Therapy

Acupressure uses the same meridians that are energy centers corresponding to organs in the body in acupuncture but uses tapping (acupoint) on these meridians rather than using needles to activate a response. When Dr. Diamond was developing his understanding of applied kinesiology through muscle testing, he joined Dr. Goodheart's team, leading to speculation that these techniques connected to acupuncture and meridians would be useful in working with emotional and psychiatric issues in clients (Diamond, 1997; Hawkins, 1995; Mollon, 2007). Dr. Roger Callahan, a clinical psychologist who was one of the pioneers of cognitive therapy, began working with Dr. Diamond and experimented with muscle testing with a client who had a long-standing phobia about water. He determined that the issue of the phobia was associated with the meridian of the stomach and had the client tap on one end of the meridian (under the eye). After a few minutes of tapping on the spot, the client jumped into a swimming pool, exclaiming that the anxiety was completely gone (Callahan, 1985). With continued research, Callahan called the technique thought field therapy (TFT), due to determining that a person's thoughts are part of an information energy field that can be accessed through the traditional acupuncture meridians, which was the beginning of specific energy psychology techniques that use tapping (Callahan, 1985). TFT consists of tapping on specific meridian points in a specific pattern that has been found to provide long-lasting resolution of psychological and emotional disturbances by successfully neutralizing emotional reaction to trauma memories (Hawk, 1999).

A basic assumption is that TFT challenges what a negative emotion is, the role of suffering in one's life, what constitutes treatment in healing, and the time required for positive change in one's healing journey. When trauma occurs, whether that is a single incident, chronic trauma issues, or a major trauma, the memory is what activates emotional disturbance that can disrupt the limbic brain. In TFT, the trained clinician does not need to know what the trauma is specifically but does need to determine the subjective level of distress (SUDs) rating from 0 to 10 when one brings the memory to mind. Hawk stated in 1999 that treating trauma with this method had a 70% success rate when the procedure was done correctly by a trained clinical professional. TFT has specific tapping algorithms that have been used for trauma, complex trauma, simple

Tapping Points

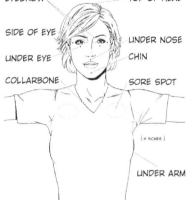

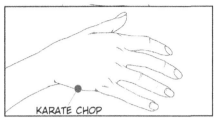

Courtesy of www.ThrivingNow.com & www.Joy-Connection.com
Visit us for free reprint information and energy tapping tips
© 2009 - Reprint information and links must remain with the image

Figure 18.1 Acutapping Points Illustration
Source: Wilkes, 2021

and specific phobias, addictive urges, obsession, anger, guilt, rage, depression, simple anxiety or stress, jealousy, fatigue, physical pain, and even nasal congestion (Hawk, 1999).

A set of studies that began in 2009 as a pilot was done using TFT to treat the long-term chronic trauma in orphaned children who had survived genocide decades earlier in Rwanda (Stone et al., 2009). The response was so powerful in helping the children that the team went back in 2010 to work with the staff of the orphanage. The success of these two research studies prompted Drs. Sakai, Connelly, et al. to return to Rwanda several times over the years to successfully treat child survivors with PTSD due to the genocide (2010). Dr. Sakai presented findings from her trips to Rwanda at the Association for Comprehensive Energy Psychology (2019), describing that TFT had been so successful in reducing trauma symptoms that it was even being taught to people who were incarcerated due to issues that happened at the time of the genocide that destroyed families.

The Emergence of the Emotional Freedom Technique

In 1995, exploration of these techniques led to another tapping technique being developed by Gary Craig: an easier form of TFT that he called the emotional freedom technique (EFT). Craig used a basic recipe of tapping on acupoints but added in phrases that were identified by the client that touched on sensations of fear, anxiety, trauma, and phobias while tapping on the acupressure points as well as using the client's comments of discomfort to focus on the emotion attached to the discomfort. It has been determined that TFT and EFT have strong similarities to eye movement desensitization regulation (EMDR) but use tapping on meridians instead of just using eye movements while thinking of a traumatic event, which has been shown effective in working with those with PTSD symptoms (Mollon, 2005; Nelms, 2017; Shapiro, 2002). In 1998, The Association for Comprehensive Energy Psychology was formed to promote research, training, and ethical principles at the international level for those who use these techniques clinically (Mollon, 2007).

The history of how emotional freedom technique and thought field therapy approaches developed combines an understanding the body's own internal wisdom using kinesiology and acupressure tapping on specific meridians while focusing first on a small segment of a memory or an event of trauma or anxiety, then using set-up statements that acknowledge the level of emotional distress while also providing unconditional acceptance of the self (Church et al., 2018; Feinstein, 2018). The clinically trained practitioner provides trauma-informed care when the client follows the directed set-up statements that have been determined from the practitioner assessment of the subjective units of distress the client is feeling when thinking of a short (two-to-three-minute) memory. The practitioner directs the client to tap on the meridian points, restating some of the initial set-up statements, until the emotional charge is released from the memory acknowledged by the client in lower units of subjective distress as the physiology is calmed. There are several protocols used to maintain the safety of the situation by helping the client maintain a place of tolerance for any discomfort in accessing where the sensation is on the body. Dr. David Feinstein noted seven targeted outcomes for acupoint tapping from a practitioner survey that include eliminating unwanted physiological or emotional responses to a trauma memory, specified triggers, a maladaptive self- or world belief, a maladaptive habit, and emotional obstacles to reaching a preferred goal, along with shifting an affective state and establishing and reinforcing beliefs or behaviors that support positive change toward problems or goals (2019).

What Is the Heart/Brain Connection in TFT and EFT?

Heart-rate variability (HRV) is the method that has been used in many studies to monitor and study how psychological functioning affects the coherence of the heart rhythm, and when there is a great deal of anxiety, impatience, frustration, and fear, they are reflected in the heart rhythm and lead to incoherent rhythm, which is what Callahan speculated was being changed in the TFT procedures he was studying in the 1980s (Callahan, 2001a, 2001b). Researchers have continued to study the connection between HRV and tapping on acupoints, with Pignotti and Steinberg (2001) researching clinical applications of TFT in behavioral medicine utilization in HMO services, along with Bair (2008).

Research suggesting the heart/brain controls the body and brain through neural pathways that start with the polyvagal nerve in the gut sending messages of safety or lack of safety to the brain in a bottom-up approach supports the concept that somatic modalities such as tapping decrease the heart rate, increase coherence between body and mind, and need to be considered in integrative treatment approaches to work with the whole person is ongoing in many multidisciplinary areas. In a study (2019) Bach, Groesbeck, Stapleton, Sims, Blickheuser, and Church used EFT on 203 participants over a four-day workshop looking at CNS, heart rate variability (HRV) and heart coherence, resting heart rate (RHR), and blood pressure (BP). Results demonstrated reduction in anxiety (−40%), depression (−35%), PTSD (−32%), and cravings (−74%). Increase in RHR, cortisol, and systolic and diastolic BP indicated use of EFT resulted in positive health effects (Bach et al., 2019). When energy psychologists and practitioners become coherent with clients prior to beginning to use energy techniques, we are in a better position to help them become coherent in their own systems of body/brain, which again helps release the emotional dysregulation caused by trauma and pain, allowing for empowerment and self-healing (Church et al., 2012; Church et al., 2016; Diepold & Goldstein, 2009; Levine, 1997, 2010).

The findings of all these researchers have been studied from different fields of inquiry using a transtheoretical approach. However, similar constructs around developing resiliency through positive emotions which feeds back to the physical body with less stress levels found in HRV and heart coherence provides a loop of psychological resilience and emotional well-being that has also been found in the resiliency research (Fredrickson, 2001). These different forms of research are linking the body-brain-emotion-spirit in an energetic field that suggests body/mind approaches are needed to effectively reduce the emotional charge of trauma memories, mood incongruence, and triggers that stimulate the desire to numb pain (Ecker et al., 2012; Gilomen &

Lee, 2015; Nelms, 2017; Schwarz, 2012, 2014). While more research studies are needed to deter-mine the physiological effect of these techniques, there has been considerable research to dem-onstrate the efficacy and evidence base for thought field therapy (TFT) and emotional freedom technique (EFT) in reducing emotional disruption that maintains hyperarousal as a trauma-informed care approach, while reducing anxiety, depression, PTSD symptoms, and cravings for substances (Balha et al., 2020; Stapleton, 2019).

Psychological Factors Found in EFT and TFT

There have been over 115 studies done on energy psychology effectiveness since 2000, with 65 randomized controlled trials and over 50 pre-post outcomes studies establishing that protocols of EFT and TFT are evidence based (Feinstein, 2018; Mollon, 2007). These studies include benefi-cial outcomes for the treatment of anxiety, depression, PTSD, and food and substance cravings, along with studies on physiological effects of EFT, with three studies showing changes of DNA markers, cortisol changes, heart-rate variability, and blood pressure, along with immune system biomarkers (Nelms & Castel, 2016; Nelms, 2017; Stapleton, 2018). While more research will continue to demonstrate the efficacy of energy psychology in speeding up the individual's abil-ity to improve mental and physical health, reducing the emotional triggers in those with trauma backgrounds and PTSD, the efficacy of these techniques has been recognized by the Veterans Administration and have been accepted in the United Kingdom's National Health Service from preliminary evidence that EFT should be of the highest priority to research for the treatment of PTSD (Feinstein, 2018; Sebastian & Nelms, 2017).

Energy Psychology Neurobiological Factors

What would be the reason to use an approach like the emotional freedom technique with those who are struggling with childhood trauma, PTSD, and co-occurring disorders? Through the advances in neurobiology and neuropsychology, we have learned that trauma activates the mesolimbic brain, and executive cognitive functioning takes a back seat, letting the limbic brain maintain neurological functions. This discovery alone indicates that talk therapies like cognitive behavioral therapy (CBT) that suggest reasoning can overcome irrational thoughts will not work effectively until the amygdala within the limbic brain is soothed sufficiently for survival instincts to go into a neutral setting (Levine, 1997, 2010; van der Kolk, 1994; van der Kolk et al., 1996, 2014). Not only does addiction hijack the brain by flooding the reward system (Harvard Mental Health, 2011), trauma can also take over the brain, both resulting in the inability to access higher cognitive functioning. Trauma and fear memories, when initially formed, are considered labile but become fixed in the amygdala and neural pathways of the brain; this has been considered extraordinarily difficult to extinguish or to successfully reconstruct by any methods used prior to the development of somatic therapies and energy psychology techniques (Argen et al., 2012; Schwarz, 2012).

TFT and EFT come from a combination of CBT's exposure response prevention (ERP) ther-apy and tapping on acupoints, incorporating a somatic/cognitive/energy approach (Diamond, 1985, 1997; Hawkins, 1995). While ERP therapy works for individuals over time, EMDR and EP techniques can work with only a small segment of the traumatic memory within a fraction of the time of ERP to soothe the hippocampus in the limbic brain through introducing new proteins in the amygdala, allowing for reconsolidation of fear memories and release of the emotional charge to the trauma memories (Argen et al., 2012; Nelms, 2017; Shapiro, 2002). These findings are in line with the findings of a ten-year research study at Harvard Medical School that found that the stimulation of certain acupoints generates deactivation in the amygdala and other areas of the limbic brain (Hui et al., 2005). When the limbic brain is soothed, the higher cognitive functioning of the prefrontal cortex comes back online, and other therapies can be used with greater success in treating co-occurring disorders (Levine, 1997, 2010).

Protocols for Using EFT

It is important to understand that, due to EFT developing outside the psychology field initially, there are self-help techniques that may be called palliative that can be used with processes of EFT, and there are comprehensive therapeutic methods in EFT that require additional training and certification as a trauma-informed therapist (Schwarz, 2002, 2012). The process of setting up the procedures for using the emotional freedom technique with self or a client begins with attuning to an emotion or feeling about the target problem, which tends to quickly bring up effects of trauma or emotional wounds and physiological sensations tied to those trauma memories. This approach helps with understanding the issue from the client's perspective, and the therapist stays in current moment while doing this in the therapeutic relationship. Exploring the roots of the problem and any related symbolism leads the client to a sense of enhanced emotional safety and self-acceptance while tapping on the meridians (Feinstein, 2012, 2015, 2019).

Basic Procedures

- Recall an incident that brings up feelings of trauma, anxiety, or fear and focus on only two or three minutes of the memory that note emotional and body distress.
- Determine the level of discomfort from 0 to 10 in a subjective unit of distress (SUDs).
- Using the subjective words defined by the client, the therapist taps with the client, beginning with tapping on the side of the hand (karate chop) while making a set-up statement: 'Even though [the terrible thing] happened, I deeply and completely accept myself'.
- Continue to explore the root of the problem using the client's words of distress while tapping on the meridians: Top of the head, between the eyebrows, side of temple, under the eye, below the nose, and on the chin. Then, with both hands, tap on the collar bone and under the arm.
- Check back in with the client to see if the SUDs number dropped, which indicates emotional distress has decreased while thinking about the traumatic event.
- Repeat this process until the initial score of discomfort drops to 0.

This process is used with a variety of EFT clinical set-up approaches that help keep the client feeling safe within the margin of emotional control while reducing emotional dysregulation in the clinical setting. The process typically takes considerably fewer sessions than ERP and is less intrusive, with evidence that procedures do not tend to retraumatize the client while the process is occurring due to only having to remember a small segment of the traumatic memory, rather than repeating the whole traumatic event in each session. While ERP can take 20 or more sessions to be effective, it also requires exposing the client to the trauma over and over again to reduce the reconsolidation of the fear memory. In one research trial with military veterans with PTSD after the use of the CBT and extinction approach, as many as two-thirds of the participants still had PTSD at the end of the trial (Steenkamp et al., 2015). In the real world, many people drop out of that type of treatment due to the retraumatizing effects of the approach. EFT or TFT can effectively reduce the trauma memory in fewer sessions without retraumatizing the client in most instances, and has shown efficacy in treating veterans with PTSD, depression, and anxiety to help reconsolidate memories without the emotional charge from trauma with the additional benefit of retention in treatment (Church et al., 2013; Church et al., 2018; Nelms, 2017; Nelms & Castel, 2016; Nicosia et al., 2019). This approach can be adapted for young children and has been used successfully with children, adolescents, and adults.

When using clinical EFT with clients who have co-occurring disorders, the approach can be used specifically to reduce the emotional dysregulation and hyperarousal of trauma memories; relieve cravings and those maladaptive responses to triggers; address the underlying emotional concerns that contribute to substance misuse; and increase client skills and self-efficacy for managing cravings, anxiety, stress, and pain while developing increased self-acceptance and confidence (Feinstein, in press). When counselors address the trauma symptoms that have the client stuck in the survival brain first in an integrative approach that uses an energy psychology approach like EFT or TFT, the result is that the client will find it easier to engage in treatment with higher cognitive functioning. Like the concepts of CBT or DBT that teach the client to use skills learned to enhance the treatment and to manage their own symptoms, EFT and TFT can become processes that are used for self-help, once learned, whenever anxiety, stress, or pain presents itself in daily life.

Conclusion

Energy psychology has developed over the past few decades from the understanding that the physical body has innate intelligence and that body and brain work together to manage all physical, mental, and emotional systems through the meridians associated with energy centers in the body along with the limbic brain and brain stem. Being vibrational energy as humans, our thoughts, emotions, spirit, and physical systems work together for maximum health. By tapping into this innate intelligence, our body can and will tell us what is needed at any given time. Emotional freedom technique and thought field therapy are but two of many energy psychology techniques that have proven effective for soothing the limbic brain, specifically the amygdala and hippocampus, which allows executive cognitive functioning to be regained in those who have gotten stuck in their survival brain. Using this whole body-mind-emotion-spirit approach, an individual can calm triggers, cravings, and impulsivity while becoming more receptive to insight therapies.

The energy psychology techniques of TFT and EFT have evolved from the Eastern energy medicine approaches of acupuncture, acupressure, and kinesiology and have combined approaches found in CBT's use of ERP therapy while tapping on acupressure points and, like CBT, can be taught to children, adolescents, and adult clients to use as self-help measures once the practice has been learned to manage anxiety during the recovery process and afterward when life is chaotic. Working with a clinically trained TFT or EFT practitioner has been demonstrated to be effective for decreasing or eliminating the emotional charge associated with trauma memories quickly by soothing the limbic brain through regulating the heart-rate variation while soothing the CNS to the brain stem and limbic brain due to feeling safe. Each of these approaches is part of the integrative model for working with those who have co-occurring disorders and can be learned for clinical use as a trauma-informed approach through ACEP.

Questions for Consideration

1. How might tapping on the meridians calm the polyvagal nerve and heart-rate variability?
2. What is the basic premise of using the emotional freedom technique as a trauma-informed approach to treatment?
3. How did EFT evolve from TFT?
4. Why is soothing the limbic brain an important therapeutic approach for reducing trauma?
5. How can energy psychology techniques improve the recovery from co-occurring disorders?
6. Why is it important for counselors to learn additional therapeutic skills related to trauma-informed care to work with those with co-occurring disorders?

Case Study

Ginny, a 29-year-old woman, was in a car crash six months ago when she was stopped at a red light. The driver behind her did not slow down and hit her from behind. She saw the car coming toward her, and with nowhere to go, she braced herself for the crash. She suffered a concussion and a pinched nerve in her shoulder and developed an intense fear of driving that was impacting her ability to function in her daily life. She had surgery on her shoulder and had been seeing both an acupuncturist and a chiropractor to work with the neck issues that continued to affect her, but nothing she tried had reduced the extreme anxiety she had every time she got in her car. The anxiety began pouring into all aspects of her life, and she went to her doctor for a prescription for anti-anxiety medication. After six months, her anxiety had not decreased, and her medication was not enough. When she returned to her doctor, she was told she could not get another refill for her anti-anxiety medication and would need to find a therapist to work with her.

She sought out a therapist trained in clinical EFT, and the healing process began. The therapist had her imagine just those seconds of anticipation when she was watching the car speeding toward her and her realization she was stuck. Her initial subjective unit of distress (SUD) was 10, but after a few rounds of tapping, using both the basic and nine gambit protocols, Ginny stated her SUD rating was at 0. After a few more sessions, Ginny had worked through the whole traumatic event and reported she had no anxiety around driving, and no fearful memories were resurfacing.

1. What has the study of kinesiology done to promote the understanding of the body/mind communication? Would it be appropriate to use initially in the session with Ginny? Why or why not?
2. What will tapping on acupoints do to subdue Ginny's trauma response to the car accident?
3. If Ginny had not found the therapist trained in EFT, what progression might her mental health and substance use taken?
4. Her doctor could have sent her to a substance abuse therapist or a mental health therapist for her use of pills or her anxiety. If Ginny came to your clinic, based on your current training, how would you approach her treatment?
5. What resources are available in your area? How can you identify and locate them or train to be able to offer this powerful technique?

Additional Resources

Association for Comprehensive Energy Psychology. www.energypsych.org
EFT International. https://eftinternational.org
EFT Universe. https://eftuniverse.org
National Acupuncture Detoxification Association (NADA). www.acudetox.com

References

Achterberg, J. (1985). *Imagery in healing: Shamanism and modern medicine*. Shambala.
Achterberg, J., Cooke, K., Richards, T., Standish, L. J., Kozak, L., & Lake, J. (2005). Evidence for correlations between distant intentionality and brain function in recipients: A functional magnetic resonance imaging analysis. *The Journal of Alternative and Complementary Medicine, 11*(6), 965–972.
American Psychological Association. (2004). *Practice guideline for the treatment of patients with acute stress disorder and posttraumatic stress disorder*. American Psychiatric Association.
Argen, T., Engman, J., Frick, A., Bjorkstrand, J., Larsen, E., Fumark, T., & Fredrikson, M. (2012). Disruption of reconsolidation erases a fear memory trace in the human amygdala. *Science, 337*, 1550–1552.

Bach, D., Groesbeck, G., Stapleton, P., Sims, R., Blickheuser, K., & Church, D. (2019). Clinical EFT (Emotional Freedom Techniques) improves multiple physiological markers of health. *Journal of Evidence-Based Integrative Medicine, 24.*

Bair, C. C. (2008). The heart field effect: Synchronization of healer-subject heart rates in energy therapy. *Advanced Mind Body Medicine, 23*(4), 10–19.

Balha, S. M., Abo-Baker, O., & Mahmoud, S. (2020). Effect of emotional freedom techniques on psychological symptoms and cravings among patients with substance related disorders. *International Journal of Novel Research in Healthcare and Nursing, 7*(2), 30–45.

Briere, J., & Richards, S. (2007). Self-awareness, affect regulation, and relatedness: Differential sequels of childhood versus adult victimization experiences. *The Chicago Journal of Nervous and Mental Disease, 19*(6), 497–508.

Callahan, R. J. (1985). *Five minute phobia cure: Dr. Callahan's treatment for fears, phobias, and self-sabotage.* Enterprise Publishing.

Callahan, R. J..(2001a). The impact of thought field therapy on heart rate variability. *Journal of Clinical Psychology, 57*(10), 1153–1170.

Callahan, R. J. (2001b). Raising and lowering of heart rate variability: Some clinical findings of thought field therapy. *Journal of Clinical Psychology, 57*(10), 1175–1186.

Centers for Disease Control and Prevention, Kaiser Permanente. (1995–1997). *Adverse childhood experiences.* Retrieved from www.cdc.gov/violenceprevention/childabuseandneglect/acestudy/about.html

Cho, Z. H., Chung, S. C., Jones, J. P., Park, J. B., Park, H. J., Lee, H. J., . . . Min, B. I. (1998). New findings of the correlation between acupoints and corresponding brain cortices using functional MRI. *Proceedings of National Academy of Sciences, 95,* 2670–2673.

Church, D., Hawk, C., Brooks, A., et al. (2013). Psychological trauma in veterans using EFT (Emotional Freedom Technique): A randomized controlled trial. *Nervous Mental Disorders, 201,* 153–160.

Church, D., Stapleton, P., Mollon, P., Feinstein, D., Boath, E., Mackay, D., & Sims, R. (2018). Guidelines for the treatment of PTSD using clinical EFT (Emotional Freedom Techniques). *Healthcare (Basal).*

Church, D., Yount, G., & Brooks, A. J. (2012). The effect of emotional freedom techniques on stress biochemistry: A randomized controlled trial. *Journal of Nervous Mental Disorders, 200,* 891–896.

Church, D., Yount, G., Rachlin, K., Fox, L., & Nelms, J. (2016). Epigenetic effects of PTSD remediation in veterans using clinical EFT (Emotional Freedom Techniques): A randomized controlled pilot study. *American Journal of Health Promotion, 32*(1), 112–122.

Connolly, S. M., & Sakai, C. E. (2012). Brief trauma symptom intervention with Rwandan genocide survivors using thought field therapy. *International Journal of Emergency Mental Health, 13*(3), 161–172.

Deegan, P. E. (2004). *Recovery and the conspiracy of hope.* Paper presented at The Sixth Annual Mental Health Services Conference of Australia and New Zealand, Brisbane, Australia.

Department of Veterans Affairs, Department of Defense. (2010). *VA/DoD clinical practice guideline for management of post-traumatic stress.* Veterans Health Administration.

Diamond, J. (1985). *Live energy.* Paragon House.

Diamond, J. (1997). *Your body doesn't lie.* Eden Grove.

Diepold, J. H., & Goldstein, D. (2009). Thought field therapy and QEEG changes in treatment of trauma: A case study. *Traumatology, 15,* 85–93.

Ecker, B., Ticic, R., & Hulley, L. (2012). *Unlocking the emotional brain: Eliminating symptoms at their roots using memory reconsolidation.* Routledge.

Feinstein, D. (2012). Acupoint stimulation in treating psychological disorders: Evidence of efficacy. *Review of General Psychology, 16,* 364–380.

Feinstein, D. (2015). How energy psychology changes deep emotional learnings. *The Neuropsychotherapist, 10,* 39–49.

Feinstein, D. (2018). Energy psychology: Efficacy, speed, mechanisms. *Explore: The Journal of Science and Healing, 15*(5), 1–15.

Feinstein, D. (2019). Words to tap by: The use of language in Energy Psychology protocols. *Energy Psychology, 11*(1), 1–16.

Feinstein, D. (in press). Energy psychology in the treatment of substance use disorder. In R. Carroll (Ed.), *Complementary and integrative approaches to substance use disorders.* Nova Science Publishers.

Frankl, V. (1962). *Man's search for meaning.* Beacon Press.

Fredrickson, B. L. (2001). The role of positive emotions in positive psychology: The broaden-and-build theory of positive emotions. *American Psychologist, 56*(3).

Freeman, L. W. (2004). *Mosby's complementary and alternative medicine: A research based approach* (2nd ed.). Mosby.

Gilomen, S. A., & Lee, C. W. (2015). The efficacy of acupoint stimulation in the treatment of psychological distress: A meta-analysis. *Journal of Behavior Therapy and Experimental Psychiatry, 48*, 140–148.

Gin, R. H., Green, B. N., & Goodheart, G. J. (1997). A history of applied kinesiology. *Journal of Manipulative Physiology Therapy, 20*(5), 331–337.

Harvard Mental Health. (2011, July). How addiction hijacks the brain. *Harvard Health Publishing; Harvard Medical School*. Retrieved from www.health.harvard.edu/newsletter_article/how-addiction-hijacks-the-brain

Hawk, C. (1999). *Thought field therapy: A 21st century exploration of consciousness*. Intentionality and Consciousness, 9th Annual ISSEEEM Conference.

Hawkins, D. R. (1995). *Power vs. force: An anatomy of consciousness: The hidden determinants of human behavior*. Hay House, Inc.

Hollifield, M., Sinclair-Lian, N., Warner, T. D., & Hammerschlag, R. (2007). Acupuncture for posttraumatic stress disorder: A randomized controlled pilot trial. *Journal of Nervous and Mental Disorders, 195*(6), 504–513.

Huff, M. (2007, May). Montpelier acupuncturists hope to help Iraq vets with post-traumatic stress. [Vermont] *Times Argus*.

Hui, K. K. S., Liu, J., Makris, N., Gollub, R. W., Chen, A. J. W., Moore, C. I., . . . Kwong, K. K. (2000). Acupuncture modulates the limbic system and subcortical gray structures of the human brain: Evidence from fMRI studies in normal subjects. *Human Brain Mapping, 9*, 13–25.

Hui, K. K. S., Liu, J., Marina, O., Napadow, V., Ha-selgrove, C., Kwong, K. K., . . . Makris, N. (2005). The integrated response of the human cerebrocerebellar and limbic systems to acupuncture stimulation at ST 36 as evidence by fMRI. *NeuroImage, 27*, 479–496.

Kaptchuk, T. J. (2000). *The web that has no weaver: Understanding Chinese medicine*. McGraw-Hill.

Levine, P. A. (1997). *Waking the tiger: Healing trauma*. North Atlantic Books.

Levine, P. A. (2010). *In an unspoken voice: How the body releases trauma and restores goodness*. North Atlantic Books.

Liboff, A. R. (2004). Toward an electromagnetic paradigm for biology and medicine. *Journal of Alternative and Complementary Medicine, 10*(1), 41–47.

Lipton, B. (2016). *The biology of belief: Unleashing the power of consciousness, matter & miracles*. Hay House Publishing.

Lipton, B., McCraty, R., Stapleton, P., Jahnke, R., & Wahbeh, H. (2019). The science of energy healing 2. *Association for Comprehensive Energy Psychology*.

Margolin, A., Avants, S. K., Chang, P., & Kosten, T. R. (1993). Acupuncture for the treatment of cocaine dependence in methadone-maintained patients. *The American Journal on Addiction, 15*, 194–201.

McCraty, R. (2017). New frontiers in heart rate variability and social coherence research: Techniques, technologies, and implications for improving group dynamics and outcomes. *Frontiers in Public Health, 5*, 267.

McCraty, R., & Shaffer, F. (2015). Heart rate variability: New perspectives on physiological mechanisms, assessment of self-regulatory capacity, and health risk. *Global Advances in Health and Medicine: Improving Healthcare Outcomes Worldwide, 4*, 46–61.

Mollon, P. (2005). *EMDR and the energy therapies: Psychoanalytic perspectives*. Karnac.

Mollon, P. (2007). Thought field therapy and its derivatives: Rapid relief of mental health problems through tapping on the body. *Primary Care and Community Psychiatry, 12*(3–4), 123–127.

Nelms, J., & Castel, D. (2016). A systematic review and meta-analysis of randomized and non-randomized trials of Emotional Freedom Techniques (EFT) for the treatment of depression. *Explore: The Journal of Science and Healing, 12*(6), 416–426.

Nicosia, G., Minewiser, L., & Freger, A. (2019). World Trade Center: A longitudinal case study for treating post traumatic stress disorder with emotional freedom technique and eye movement desensitization regulation. *Work, 63*(2), 199–204.

National Institutes of Health (NIH) Consensus Development Panel on Acupuncture. (1998). Acupuncture: NIH consensus conference. *The Journal of the American Medical Association, 280*(17), 1518–1524.

Oschman, J. L. (2000). *Energy medicine: The scientific basis*. Churchill Livingston.

Pignotti, M., & Steinberg, M. (2001). Thought field therapy clinical applications: Utilization in an HMO in behavioral medicine and behavioral health services. *Journal of Clinical Psychology, 57*(10), 1229–1235.

Porges, S. W. (2001). The polyvagal theory: Phylogenetic substrates of a social nervous system. *International Journal of Psychophysiology, 42*, 123–146.

Porges, S. W. (2011). *The polyvagal theory: Neurophysiological foundations of emotions, attachment, communication, and self-regulation.* Norton.

Porter, G., & Norris, P. A. (1985). *Why me? Harnessing the healing power of the human spirit.* Stillpoint Publishing.

Pradhan, E. (2010). *Acupuncture and Meditation for Wellness (AMWELL): Targeted to female adult survivors of childhood sexual abuse.* University of Maryland School of Medicine.

Sakai, C., Connolly, S., & Oas, P. (2010). Treatment of PTSD in Rwanda child genocide survivors using thought field therapy. *International Journal of Emergency Mental Health, 12*(1), 41–50.

Sebastian, B., & Nelms, J. (2017). The effectiveness of Emotional Freedom Techniques in the treatment of posttraumatic stress disorder: A meta-analysis. *Explore: The Journal of Science and Healing, 13*, 16–25. https://doi.org/10.1016/j.explore.2016.10.001

Schwarz, R. (2002). *Tools for transforming trauma.* Brunner Routledge.

Schwarz, R. (2012, January/February). Enhancing traditional therapy with energy psychology interventions. *The National Psychologist.*

Schwarz, R. (2014). *Neuroscience and the effectiveness of energy psychology (Part 3 of 3).* Retrieved from https://youtube/LUQDINV8hM

Schwarz, R. (2018). *Energy psychology as a poly-vagal interventions for trauma in clinical applications of Polyvagal Theory* (S. Porges & D. Dana, Eds.). W.W. Norton.

Sebastian, B., & Nelms, J. (2017). The effectiveness of emotional freedom techniques in the treatment of posttraumatic stress disorder: A meta-analysis. *Explore: The Journal of Science and Healing, 13*, 16–25. https://doi.org/10.1016/j.explore.2016.10.001

Shapiro, F. (2002). *EMDR as an integrative psychotherapy: Experts of diverse orientations explore the paradigm prism.* American Psychological Press.

Stapleton, P. (2018, August). *Research spotlight: EFT, stress, and anxiety.* Retrieved from www.youtube.com/watch?v=KKr_egYXnhQ

Stapleton, P. (2019). *The science behind tapping: A proven stress management technique for the mind and body.* Hay House.

Steenkamp, M. M., Litz, B. T., Hoge, C. W., & Marmar, C. R. (2015). Psychotherapy for military related PTSD: A review of randomized trials. *Journal of the American Medical Association, 314*, 489–500.

Stone, B., Leyden, L., & Fellows, B. (2009). Energy psychology treatment for posttraumatic stress in genocide survivors in a Rwandan orphanage: A pilot investigation. *Energy Psychology: Theory, Research, & Treatment, 1*(1), 73–82.

Stone, B., Leyden, L., & Fellows, B. (2010). Energy psychology treatment for orphan heads of households in Rwanda: An observational study. *Energy Psychology: Theory, Research, & Treatment, 2*(2).

van der Kolk, B. A. (1994). The body keeps the score: Memory and the evolving psychobiology of posttraumatic stress. *Harvard Review of Psychiatry, 1*, 253–265.

van der Kolk, B. A. (2006a). Clinical implications of neuroscience research in PTSD. [Electronic version]. *Annuals of the New York Academy of Sciences, 17*(1), 277–293.

van der Kolk, B. A. (2006b). Developmental trauma disorder: A new, rational diagnosis for children with complex trauma histories. [Electronic version]. *Psychiatric Annals, 200X*, 2–8.

Van der Kolk, B. A. (2014). *The body keeps the score: Brain, mind, and body in the healing of trauma.* Penguin.

van der Kolk, B. A., McFarlane, A. C., & Weisaeth, L. (1996). *Traumatic stress: The effects of overwhelming experience on mind, body, and society.* Guilford Press.

World Health Organization. (2013). *Guidelines for the management of conditions specifically elated to stress.* World Health Organization.

19 Animal-Assisted Therapies

Tara G. Matthews and Dawn Yelvington

Introduction

Animals have been used in work with humans for thousands of years. Animal-assisted therapy (AAT) has many names and has evolved over the decades. There are several subsets of AAT. In the literature, AAT is an all-encompassing term that includes animals helping the vision impaired, companion animals, animals used in rehabilitation, animals visiting people in assisted-living facilities, and animals used in the therapeutic environment. As the evidence grows to support the use of animals in a professional therapeutic setting, it is important to differentiate between the non-professionally led and the professionally led therapies that incorporate animals into their treatment modalities. Professionally led interventions include both a trained animal and a trained therapist who work as a team to assist their clients. AAT is not intended to be a separate intervention, but rather a complimentary treatment to strengthen the therapeutic alliance (Monfort Montolio & Sancho-Pelluz, 2019). The need for a strong therapeutic alliance can be challenging with clients struggling with multiple diagnoses. Substance abuse treatment is complex and often rooted in unresolved trauma. This trauma can be exacerbated by substance use or can trigger underlying mental health conditions. Trained animals are non-judgmental, live in the here and now, and can be used as an asset in treatment. As the animals help facilitate the professionally trained therapist's work, they become a tool in the intervention tool belt. This is often called animal- assisted psychotherapy (AAP). This chapter will focus on the professionally led interventions of AAP that include canine-assisted therapies (CAP) and equine-facilitated psychotherapy (EFP).

Learning Objectives

*   Explore the role of animal assisted psychotherapy for co-occurring disorders
*   Identify key benefits and considerations when using trained dogs in therapeutic interventions
*   Identify key benefits and considerations when using trained horses in therapeutic interventions

Key Terms

Animal-Assisted Activities (AAA): The use of animals to enhance recreational needs for individuals with various abilities.

Animal-Assisted Psychotherapies (AAP): The use of animals to help obtain mental health outcomes through interactive behaviors between client and animal guided by a treatment provider.

Emotional Support Animal: A pet providing emotional support to individuals living with various mental health diagnoses. The emotional support animal is not a trained service animal and does not have the same rights and community access as a service animal.

Equine Therapy: Various treatment activities between client and horses to help obtain mental health–related goals.

DOI: 10.4324/9781003220916-22

Human-Animal Bond: A mutually beneficial experience for both humans and animals during AAA and AAP.

Pet Therapy: A broad conceptualization of using animals in various roles, including AAA and AAP. This is often a very general definition that requires more specification about the type of treatment provided.

Service Animal: A trained animal (may also live as a pet) required to accomplish specific tasks that enhance the quality of life of those living with disabilities.

Utilizing Animals for Integrated Treatment

Integrated treatment interventions for those living with co-occurring disorders can be pivotal in making connection, being present in the here and now, and lowering psychological blocks or resistance to other forms of treatment. Use of canines as an adjunct to traditional psychotherapy is showing promise in treatment of childhood trauma with children (Dravsnik et al., 2018), mental health treatment with adolescents (Jones et al., 2019), and trauma-informed care with incarcerated women (Holman et al., 2020). The body of research continues to grow supporting the use of canines to increase engagement in therapy, which can be particularly challenging when working with adolescents with co-occurring disorders (Trujillo et al., 2020). Canines can be used in individual or group sessions and may simply be a calming presence to facilitate an atmosphere of trust.

Horses can also be used to create an atmosphere of trust and unlock barriers to working through unresolved trauma. Equine-facilitated psychotherapy (EFP) is a flexible, complementary therapy that can be effectively coupled with evidence-based practices (EBP) to meet the unique needs of the client (Ratliffe & Sanekane, 2009; Schultz et al., 2006). EFP is readily adaptable to individual, group, and family therapy sessions, and activities are tailored to the client's unique treatment plan and goals (Ratliffe & Sanekane, 2009; Schultz et al., 2006; Trotter et al., 2008).

Counselors often struggle to find treatment modalities that motivate clients living with substance use disorders to remain in treatment for sufficient time to enable beneficial change in morbidity (Dalsbø et al., 2010). Animals may draw people to sessions and to remain in treatment longer. No matter the modality or the complexity of diagnosis, an individually tailored treatment approach is fundamental to healing. The key to a tailored individual approach is listening to the client, and who can do that better than a non-judgmental animal who does not interrupt or distract and who simply meets the client where they are emotionally. Trained animals connect emotionally, spiritually, and physically during the therapeutic encounter. This connection can enhance the therapeutic alliance between the counselor and client. The animal becomes a tool in the counselor's tool belt of interventions to connect and to create an atmosphere of healing.

A good therapeutic relationship is a strong predictor of successful treatment in addiction and other psychological illnesses (Kern-Godal et al., 2016). As part of a large mixed-method study of equine-assisted psychotherapy (EAP) in SUD treatment, semi-structured interviews were used to gather information about their experiences of EAP. Participants' own descriptions suggested that the horse(s) were facilitators of positive self-construct and provided important emotional support during treatment (Kern-Godal et al., 2016). This study further revealed that the relationship with the horse, emotional effect, and mastery were important and interconnected themes. This study offered results that are consistent with key addiction treatment theories and contributed to the understanding and impact of EAP on SUD treatment. An exploratory study using canines compared treatment engagement and outcomes between two groups of adolescents living with co-occurring disorders. Trujillo et al. (2020) found that participants who received treatment with AAT attended more therapy sessions in a 16-week period than those who did not participate in AAT. Additionally, the AAT group had a greater improvement in overall well-being than those who did not receive AAT. Both studies demonstrate that animals provide considerable benefit to therapeutic engagement.

Figure 19.1 Boy with Horse
Source: Yelvington, 2021

Lentini and Knox (2009) completed a review of 16 qualitative and quantitative equine-assisted activities and therapies (EAAT) articles. Participants were noted to have a range of emotional or behavioral difficulties including abuse, trauma, behavioral disorders, and mental illness. Research conclusions varied, although the authors generally identified EAAT as a beneficial intervention for individuals with mental health concerns. Participants demonstrated a decrease in anger, depression, aggressive behavior, and dissociation as well as an increase in self-confidence and self-esteem, locus of control, and overall functioning (Lentini & Knox, 2009).

Brief Overview of Theoretical Orientations Incorporating Animals as a Therapeutic Tool

Experiential Therapy

Central to the model of experiential therapy is the use of intentional experiential activities to assist clients in achieving an array of therapeutic goals (Russell & Gillis, 2008). Utilizing the senses in therapy allows for a whole-person approach. It is reasoned that the use of experiential therapy may be less limiting, carry less stigma, and more accurately capture how physical activity, creative arts, equine-assisted psychotherapy, adventure activities, and other forms of experience are used in the clinical setting to better understand the psychological and emotional issues underlying a client's need for treatment (Russell & Gillis, 2008). Incorporating horses for growth and learning in an experiential modality is one approach. Participants learn about themselves and others by participating in activities with the horses and then processing (or discussing) thoughts, beliefs, behaviors, and patterns (EAGALA, 2015). Throughout the experiential learning process, the client is actively engaged in posing questions, investigating, experimenting, being curious, solving problems, assuming responsibility, being creative, and constructing meaning (EAGALA, 2015). The client sees, smells, hears, and experiences the animal in the therapeutic process, engaging the whole person. The clinician's primary role in experiential therapy is to establish suitable experiences, posing problems, setting boundaries, supporting clients, ensuring physical and emotional safety, and facilitating the learning process (EAGALA, 2015). With both horses and canines, the sheer presence of the animal helps create an atmosphere of safety and trust. The animal is a living, breathing, here-and-now-orientated, fully present, non-judgmental support to both the client and the counselor, offering the client a place to fully be themselves.

Gestalt Therapy

Gestalt therapy emphasizes awareness of the self, including one's internal emotions, needs, and desires, in a relational context (Kirby, 2010; Brandt, 2013). Gestalt therapy is helpful for clients who struggle to accurately match body language with their emotions (Kirby, 2010; Schultz et al., 2006; Whitley, 2009; Brandt, 2013). Like CBT, gestalt therapy incorporates mindfulness techniques to encourage the use of, and further develop, non-verbal cues and body language (Brandt, 2013). This integration of mind and body allows the client to deal with unfinished business and express unresolved emotion. Interactions with animals can facilitate this awareness, and clients may feel more comfortable talking to an animal than directly to a counselor (Chandler et al., 2010). Both canines and horses serve an important role by listening and being fully present with the client. In EAP, the horse(s) respond(s) to the client authentically and without judgment, providing a safe space for the client to explore their emotions (Kirby, 2010; Brandt, 2013). Gestalt therapy underscores that all experiences are relationally interpreted. While participating in EAP, the client's relationship and interactions with the horse(s) provide opportunity for transference to be addressed and worked through (Kirby, 2010; Whitley, 2009; Brandt, 2013). In gestalt therapy, there is a need to use action-oriented techniques to intensify immediate experience to bring about awareness of current feelings (EAGALA manual, 2015). This can be facilitated by making up stories about the animal or by action-oriented activities with the animal (Chandler et al., 2010).

Person-Centered Therapy

Person-centered techniques focus on the healing power of safe, supportive, and non-judgmental relationships (Kirby, 2010; Chandler et al., 2010; Brandt, 2013). The client plays a key role in their own therapeutic process in person-centered therapy while working collaboratively with their therapist. A sociable animal, such as a trained therapy dog, could help facilitate the atmosphere of trust and safety (Chandler et al., 2010). The simple presence of the animal without any specific interaction can be a non-directive way to allow the client to experience the here and now. During EAP, the therapist often allows the client to work through the activity on their own, only providing support or suggestions when prompted. Similarly, horses provide the client with opportunities to assertively, yet respectfully, direct the activity. In doing so, clients gain confidence in their abilities and learn how to express their needs and emotions in a relationship (Chandler et al., 2010; Brandt, 2013). Person-centered therapy in conjunction with a therapy animal is non-invasive and allows the client to direct the amount of interaction they have directly with the animal.

Solution-Focused Therapy

Solution-focused therapy is a strengths-based approach, emphasizing the resources people invariably possess and how these can be applied to the change process (Corcoran & Pillai, 2009, p. 234). The assumption is that individuals have the necessary resources to resolve their own problems. The clinician works collaboratively with the client to build self-awareness of strengths, which are then assembled and applied to problem situations (Corcoran & Pillai, 2009, p. 235). EAGALA (2015) believes that, whether it is the relationship with the horse(s) or their relationship to people, places, things, or concepts in their lives, clients have their own best solutions if just given the opportunity to discover them. EAGALA model work re-creates these life situations through the work with the horse(s). In this therapeutic environment, clients have the opportunity to work through these struggles, problem solve, and practice new ways of living experientially (EAGALA, 2015). With the EAGALA approach, we do not focus on the task with horses, but rather, we focus on the process a client adopts for problem solving and the ability to overcome challenges and difficulties in life and relationships (EAGALA, 2015). The tools to solve their own problems are lifelong and will help clients no matter the situation.

Cognitive Behavioral Therapy (CBT)

CBT is a therapeutic technique that focuses on changing an individual's maladaptive or unhealthy thoughts, beliefs, and behaviors. This is accomplished through identifying and reframing distorted or unrealistic thoughts, as well as changing the affiliated maladaptive behaviors (Beck, 2011). CBT has repeatedly been found to effectively treat several mental health disorders as well as enhancing the outcome of equine-assisted psychotherapy (EAP) (Beck, 2011; Muñoz-Solomando et al., 2008; Brandt, 2013). EAP requires the client to participate in physical, psychological, and emotional exercises. As emotions arise due to interacting with or observing the horse(s), they can immediately be discussed (Rothe et al., 2005). The client must learn how to identify and regulate their emotions when working with the horses. If clients react too strongly or are emotionally incongruent with their verbal and non-verbal cues, the horse(s) will either physically remove themselves from the area or refuse to comply with the client's requests (Chandler et al., 2010; McCormick & McCormick, 1997; Brandt, 2013).

Reality Therapy

Reality therapy is a choice-based approach that focuses on meeting our fundamental needs, which include survival, love and belonging, self-worth, freedom, and fun (Wubbolding & Brickell, 1999). Finding a way to meet those needs without mood-altering substances can be challenging, particularly when mental health issues are also present. Choice, connection, and relationships are key to healing co-occurring disorders, but first the shame must be addressed. Shame shapes the choices that we make. Shame does not shape the choices that canines and horses make. They seek to meet their fundamental needs in a simple and direct way by living in the here and now.

We develop shame (both healthy and unhealthy) through relationships with others (Bradshaw, 1988). From infancy, we learn how to get our needs met through the reaction of those around us. Humans have basic needs. Shame allows us to recognize our limitations and find ways to get these needs met. How those we are in relationship with react to our needs will determine how our shame develops throughout our lifetime (Bradshaw, 1988). Our parents (or caregiver) are the first people to provide survival for us and develop our sense of shame. This process can result in shamed trauma or survival skills that will last a lifetime.

Animals offer an opportunity to explore total behavior (thoughts, feelings, and behaviors) and receive immediate feedback in a less threatening environment (Chandler et al., 2010). Animals allow clients to redefine themselves and open the psychological door to developing self-worth.

Getting unstuck and feeling a sense of worthiness are key to making different choices: Different choices that get those fundamental needs met, rather than the unhealthy, shame-based choices that have led to self-destructive behaviors and thought patterns. Treatment that includes animals can be fun, laying the foundation for getting the fun and enjoyment need met in a healthy way. Freedom and fun are connected to shame. Shame-based people may struggle to connect to others, remain stagnant, and are limited by their desire to escape their reality (Bradshaw, 1988). People with healthy shame are able to see the beauty in life and gain perspective on their experiences (Bradshaw, 1988). True freedom can be gained through a sense of perspective and self-worth. Animals call this joy.

Group Therapy Versus Individual Therapy Using Animals as a Therapeutic Tool

Animals can be used in both group and individual therapy as a therapeutic tool. Depending on the animal and the format of treatment, their uses can range from interactive activities to simply being present with the client. Yalom (1995) believes that a number of curative factors underlie change in a variety of group settings: The installation of hope, universality, imparting of information, altruism, the corrective recapitulation of the primary family group, development of socializing techniques, imitative behaviors, interpersonal learning, group cohesiveness, catharsis, and existential factors (Forsyth, 2010, p. 501). In therapy, group members can observe the actions of others and learn from those who model healthy ways of dealing with interpersonal situations. Members can also practice and receive feedback about their success in performing specific behaviors, so that with time and practice, they feel a sense of mastery (Forsyth, 2010, p. 505). Exchanges among members of a therapy group are viewed as instrumental in bringing about change. Group interaction provides a level of support, caring, confrontation, and other qualities not found in individual therapy (Corey & Corey, 1992). Some groups are constructed to include only members who are in a similar stage of readiness to change while other groups are mixed, with members at different levels of change readiness. Most groups will ultimately end up mixed, with participants in various stages each experiencing their own process (Velasquez et al., 2016).

There are advantages and disadvantages when using the group format with culturally diverse populations. Groups, by nature, include people of diverse ages, backgrounds, experiences, and perspectives. Many people gain a tremendous amount from group feedback, group support, the installation of hope by seeing others change, and the cultural context of group dynamics (Corey & Corey, 1992). The animal in the group environment becomes another member of the group, a participant whose engagement and reactions are based in the here and now. However, not all clients will thrive in group therapy due to a variety of factors.

A primary factor is reluctance. Some individuals may be reluctant to disclose in a group format. They may see it as shameful to have personal problems and even more shameful to talk about these problems in front of a group of 'strangers' (Corey & Corey, 1992). This may be a cultural or clinical consideration, but it may also just be a personal preference. Addressing these concerns directly with the client during the initial assessment is imperative to appropriate placement. Some advantages of individual animal-assisted psychotherapy are the ability for the client in tandem to build representations and complete activities independently of how others may view things. Individual sessions allow for more one-on-one time with the therapist and the animals. They also allow the client to address personal treatment goals without feedback from their peers in a group.

Effectiveness With Veteran Populations, PTSD, Trauma

Treating the effects of trauma is never easy. And in military culture, the challenge is even greater. The reality is that traditional psychotherapy can be stigmatizing and feel like 'just a lot of talk' among people who value doing and action. Service members are hands on. They trust their experience and the people with whom they serve. In order to engage them in their own healing process, the solutions offered need to respect who they are, respect their culture, and meet them squarely on their own terms (EAGALA military brochure). In a recent interview (Carey, 2017, p. 3), Dr. Dawn Yelvington shared, 'Clinical evidence and human experience show that horses have a special ability to help people work through emotional barriers without shame or stigma. This is especially true and valuable for people who suffer the effects of trauma'.

Craig (2020) completed a qualitative study that included observations and interviews with 11 adolescents with adverse childhood experiences (ACEs) and examined equine communication as a mechanism for client awareness and emotional regulation, the development of communication competencies, and the transference of communication competencies to other relational contexts. Findings suggest that adolescents learned to explore the world and not just react to it through their participation in equine-assisted psychotherapy (EAP). Craig (2020)

> states working with equines at liberty – without a lead or any type of physical tethering to the equine – was challenging and empowering. Adolescents projected good energy and requested movements from the equine which required intense focus, skillful communication, cooperation between horse and adolescents, belief in oneself, and the courage to communicate. In most cases, these adolescents were challenged with new tasks, communicating their wants and needs to others, and setting new goals in diverse contexts.

(p. 652)

Equine-facilitated therapy for complex trauma is a promising new model of equine-assisted psychotherapy. Recent research on traumatic stress and its treatment suggests that novel and nontraditional forms of therapy may be advantageous (Metcalf et al., 2016, p. 290). Three core components of intervention that target areas impacted by exposure to trauma are addressed to include safety, attachment, and regulation. A client who has suffered severe trauma can learn, using the same elements in his or her relationship with the horse, how to create safe and trusting relationships with humans involving safe and nurturing physical touch (Naste et al., 2018). Once effective communication between the client and the horse is established, then the client can learn to attend to the emotional world of the horse. The horse, in turn, begins to focus on the client and the client's interactions by developing trust and a deep attachment between them. The benefit of this experience is the development of new communication skills and the resulting attachment, which can then be generalized to human relationships (Naste et al., 2018). Lastly, bodily dysregulation is a common feature of complex trauma symptomatology, and thus, techniques to improve body awareness are often incorporated in treatments for this population (e.g., Ogden et al., 2006; Warner et al., 2013). As the clients learn how their gestures and postures impact the horse's responses, they can then generalize these lessons to communicate with friends and family (Naste et al., 2018).

Equine-assisted psychotherapy (EAP) is a relatively new treatment for trauma and PTSD. Staudt and Cherry (2017) completed a research review to examine the use of EAP with clients suffering from trauma and PTSD. A search of the relevant databases resulted in nine peer reviewed studies that met criteria. Four studies included youth (Goodkind et al., 2012; Kemp et al., 2014; McCullough et al., 2015; Yorke et al., 2013). Children who experienced sexual abuse or maltreatment showed improvement in PTSD, depression, anxiety, and internalizing/externalizing behaviors after participation in EAP. Of the five studies with samples of adults, one included veterans (Earles et al., 2015; Goodkind et al., 2012; Nevins et al., 2012; Schroderer & Stroud, 2015; Shambo et al., 2010). After participation in EAP, adult populations showed improvements in cultural identity, coping strategies, quality of life, social adjustment, PTSD symptoms, mindfulness, depression, dissociative symptoms, and anxiety. Staudt and Cherry conclude by stating that EAP is a relatively new modality of therapy but offers promise when treating trauma and PTSD (2017).

Romaniuk et al. (2018) completed a study that evaluated outcomes of an equine-assisted psychotherapy (EAP) program for Defense Force veterans and their partners (47 participants: 25 individuals and 22 couples) across the psychological domains of depression, anxiety, stress, posttraumatic stress, happiness, and quality of life, as well as comparing the outcomes of an individual and couples program. The study sought to expand on prior research and contribute to growing evidence of the effectiveness of equine-assisted therapy programs for veteran populations who identify as 'wounded, injured, or ill'. The results indicate that equine-assisted therapy might be useful in the reduction of depression, anxiety, stress, and PTSD symptoms and the improvement of quality of life. However, these gains may be short term unless partners are integrated into the interventions. While these findings demonstrate a promising trend, no conclusions regarding efficacy can be made, and a controlled trial with a larger sample size would help determine if equine-assisted therapy is an effective intervention for veteran populations (Romaniuk et al., 2018).

Yelvington, in an interview with Carey (2020), shared,

> An interesting aspect of equine assisted psychotherapy for those who have served in the military is that the herd dynamic that horses employ can help clients better understand the dynamics of their own family, military unit and community. Horses also offer an emotionally safe way to work through trauma and strengthen relationships. Equine assisted psychotherapy is ideal for individuals who may not flourish in a traditional therapy setting. Many clients, particularly those who are dealing with military trauma or addiction, find themselves able to interact with the horses and begin to problem solve in a way that they have not been able to do with other therapy methods.
>
> (p. A4)

Multicultural Considerations

When incorporating animal-assisted interventions into the therapy setting with a client, it is important that the clinician have background knowledge of the client's experience with animals. A client who has had experience with animals and has their own companion animal may feel comfortable with a therapy animal. In contrast, clients who have had negative experiences with animals may experience anxiety and fear in working with a therapy animal (Matuszek, 2010; Sheade & Chandler, 2012). When appropriately incorporated into treatment by a qualified mental health professional, equine-assisted psychotherapy can be an effective intervention for a diverse range of clients, including minority populations (Dell et al., 2008; Trotter et al., 2008; Brandt, 2013). People may differ greatly in their perceptions, beliefs, and attitudes toward animals across racial groups, geographical regions, genders, socioeconomic status groups, and levels of education (Sheade & Chandler, 2012). It is important that practitioners explore multicultural and diversity considerations as culture can greatly influence the effectiveness of treatments (Haubenhofer & Kirchengast, 2006; Sheade & Chandler, 2012).

Best Practices

Although animal-assisted therapy has been found to be beneficial, mental health professionals need to be mindful of cultural values and beliefs that may influence a client's receptivity of a specific therapeutic modality. Additionally, clinicians should follow best practice standards and provide treatment within their areas of competency (Cepeda, 2011). When appropriately incorporated into treatment by a qualified mental health professional, EAP can be an effective intervention for a diverse range of clients, including minority populations (Dell et al., 2008; Trotter et al., 2008). One reason for this may be related to the experiential nature of EAP. Experiential learning, particularly during EAP sessions, is frequently more active than traditional therapeutic techniques

(Stauffer, 2006). Consequently, animal-assisted therapy may reduce some of the stigma associated with talk therapy.

Both dogs and horses have demonstrated the ability to reduce stigma, strengthen the therapeutic alliance, and help clients reach their treatment goals. However, the counselor and the animal must be trained and carefully select their species-specific interventions. Carefully selecting animals and tending to the mental and physical health of the animals used in AAT are of utmost importance (Lerner, 2019; Fine et al., 2019). Licensed therapists who want to facilitate animal-assisted interventions in their work need to be trained themselves, as well as have the animal evaluated by a certified evaluator (Fine et al., 2019). An unlicensed professional and an untrained animal would be unethical and could result in a negative experience for all involved.

Conclusion

Animals allow us to transcend our human perspectives and grow beyond our narrow viewpoint (Randour, 2000). Although humans and animals have experienced a mutual beneficial experience for thousands of years, the manualization of AAT gained momentum through the end of the twentieth century into the twenty-first century. Various forms of AAT have been used to assist those living with co-occurring mental health and substance use diagnoses. Treatment can take the form of using animals via individual and group sessions. Skilled treatment providers and trained animals can create a strong therapeutic alliance that allows for healing to occur. Additionally, service animals and emotional support animals can be used to enhance the lived experiences of their caretakers, helping reinforce interpersonal and intrapersonal skills. The use of AAT should be made with verified professionals in accordance with a client's cultural perspectives and background. The utilization of AAT can enhance various aspects of recovery and treatment for those living with co-occurring disorders.

Recommended Resources

American Kennel Club (AKC) Recognized Therapy Dog Organization. www.akc.org/sports/title-recognition-program/therapy-dog-program/therapy-dog-organizations/
Certification Board for Equine Interaction Professionals. www.cbeip.org/
EAGALA. www.eagala.org/
Pet Partners (in development) with the Association of Animal-Assisted Intervention Specialists. https://petpartners.org/learn/aat-professionals/
Therapy Dogs International (TDI). www.tdi-dog.org/

Questions for Consideration

1. As you consider your future clients, what benefits could animal-assisted therapy offer them?
2. Considerable training and supervision are needed to facilitate animal-assisted therapies. Would you be interested in seeking the training? Why or why not? What do you think the first step in making that decision might be?
3. All treatment programs that offer animal-assisted therapies are not created equal. How could you identify, verify training, and make ethical recommendations to programs that offer animal assisted therapies?

Case Study

Aria is a 31-year-old female in group therapy for substance use disorders and anxiety. During a group therapy session, she had a panic attack when another client mentioned a traumatizing experience. Her panic attack escalated to hyperventilation and heart palpitations and required calling emergency services. Since there were two licensed therapists and a canine running the group therapy session, one therapist left the group to talk with Aria while awaiting emergency services. The therapist asked Aria to sit down and facilitated relaxation breaths. The therapist realized she would have to turn her attention to the phone to call for medical support. The canine was asked to help Aria and given the command for support. He simply walked over and placed his head on her lap and took over. Within minutes and before emergency services arrived, Aria's breathing and heart rate had returned to normal. She sat looking into the dog's eyes and patting his head. Her breathing regulated to his, and when emergency services arrived, they gave Aria the option to stay as no evidence of a panic attack was currently present. She was then able to return to the group and process her internal and external experience to the topic of trauma.

Questions

1. What was the animal able to do that a human therapist could not?
2. If Aria had to be taken to the emergency room, how would her therapeutic healing have been interrupted? Would she still have been able to work through the experience?
3. If there was only one therapist in the room, how could the canine have helped?

References

Beck, J. (2011). *Cognitive behavior therapy: Basics and beyond* (Kindle DX). The Guilford Press.

Bradshaw, J. (1988). *Healing the shame that binds you.* Health Communications. ISBN: 0932194869

Brandt, C. (2013). Equine-facilitated psychotherapy as a complementary treatment intervention. *Journal of Counseling and Professional Psychology, 2,* 23–42.

Burlingame, G. M., Fuhriman, A., McRoberts, C. H., Hoag, M. J., & Anderson, E. (1995, August). *The differential effectiveness of group psychotherapy: A meta-analytic review.* In A. Fuhriman (Chair.), Group Psychotherapy Efficacy: A Meta-Analytic Perspective, Symposium conducted at the 103rd Annual Convention of the American Psychological Association, New York, NY.

Carey, D. M. (2017, December, 7). EAGALA equine therapy offers unique interventions. *Hometown News.*

Carey, D. M. (2020, November, 4). Horses as Healers. *Hometown News.*

Cepeda, J. (2011). *Equine-assisted psychotherapy: A manual for therapists in private practice.* Doctoral dissertation. Retrieved from ProQuest. (UMI No. 3440790).

Chandler, C. K., Portrie-Bethke, T. L., Barrio Minton, C. A., Fernando, D. M., & O'Callaghan, D. M. (2010). Matching animal-assisted therapy techniques and intentions with counseling guiding theories. *Journal of Mental Health Counseling, 32*(4), 354–374. https://doi-org.libauth.purdueglobal.edu/10.17744/mehc.32.4.u72lt21740103538

Corcoran, J., & Pillai, V. (2009). A review of the research on solution-focused therapy. *British Journal of Social Work, 39,* 234–242.

Corey, M. S., & Corey, G. (1992). *Groups process and practice* (6th ed.). Brooks/Cole Publ.

Craig, E. A. (2020). Equine-assisted psychotherapy among adolescents with aces: Cultivating altercentrism, expressiveness, communication composure, and interaction management. *Child & Adolescent Social Work Journal, 36*(6), 643–656. https://doi-org.stetson.idm.oclc.org/10.1007/s10560-020-00694-0

Dalsbø, T. K., Hammerstrøm, K., Vist, G., Gjermo, H., Smedslund, G., & Steiro, A. (2010). Psychosocial interventions for retention in drug abuse treatment. *Cochrane Database of Systematic Reviews, 1.*

Dell, C., Chalmers, D., Dell, D., Sauve, E., & MacKinnon, T. (2008). Horse as healer: An examination of equine assisted learning in the healing of first nations youth from solvent abuse. *A Journal of Aboriginal and Indigenous Community Health, 6*(1), 81–106.

Dravsnik, J., Signal, T., & Canoy, D. (2018). Canine co-therapy: The potential of dogs to improve the acceptability of trauma-focused therapies for children. *Australian Journal of Psychology, 70*(3), 208–216. https://doi-org.libauth.purdueglobal.edu/10.1111/ajpy.12199

Earles, J. L., Vernon, L. L., & Yetz, J. P. (2015). Equine-assisted therapy for anxiety and posttraumatic stress symptoms. *Journal of Traumatic Stress, 28*(2), 149–152. https://doi.org/10.1002/jts.21990

Equine Assisted Growth and Learning Association (EAGALA). (2015). Fundamentals of the EAGALA model. In *Fundamentals of EAGALA model practice: Equine assisted psychotherapy certification program*. Author.

Fine, A. H., Beck, A. M., & Ng, Z. (2019). The state of animal-assisted interventions: Addressing the contemporary issues that will shape the future. *International Journal of Environmental Research and Public Health, 16*(20). https://doi.org/10.3390/ijerph16203997

Forsyth, D. R. (2010). Group processes and group psychotherapy: Social psychological foundations of change in therapeutic groups. In J. E. Maddux & J. P. Tangney (Eds.), *Social psychological foundations of clinical psychology* (pp. 497–513). The Guilford Press.

Forsyth, D. R., & Gorazzini, J. (2000). Groups as change agents. In C. R. Snyder & R. E. Ingram (Eds.), *Handbook of psychological change: Psychotherapy processes and practices for the 21st century* (pp. 309–336). Wiley.

Goodkind, J., LaNoue, M., Lee, C., Freund, R., & Freeland, L. (2012). Feasibility, acceptability, and initial findings from a community-based cultural mental health intervention for American Indian youth and their families. *Journal of Community Psychology, 40*(4), 381–405. https://doi.org/10.1002/jcop.20517

Haubenhofer, D., & Kirchengast, S. (2006). Austrian and American approaches to animal-based health care services. *Anthrozoös, 19*(4), 365–373. https://doi.org/10.2752/089279306785415484

Holman, L. F., Ellmo, F., Wilkerson, S., & Johnson, R. (2020). Quasi-experimental single-subject design: Comparing seeking safety and Canine-assisted therapy interventions among mentally ill female inmates. *Journal of Addictions & Offender Counseling, 41*(1), 35–51. https://doi-org.libauth.purdueglobal.edu/10.1002/jaoc.12074

Jones, M. G., Rice, S. M., & Cotton, S. M. (2019). Incorporating animal-assisted therapy in mental health treatments for adolescents: A systematic review of canine assisted psychotherapy. *PloS One, 14*(1), e0210761. https://doi.org/10.1371/journal.pone.0210761

Kemp, K., Signal, T., Botros, H., Taylor, N., & Prentice, K. (2014). Equine facilitated therapy with children and adolescents who have been sexually abused: A program evaluation study. *Journal of Child and Family Studies, 23*(3), 558–566. https://doi.org/10.1007/s10826-013-9718-1

Kern-Godal, A., Brenna, I. H., Kogstad, N., Arnevik, E. A., & Ravndal, E. (2016). Contribution of the patient-horse relationship to substance use disorder treatment: Patients' experiences. *International Journal of Qualitative Studies on Health and Well-Being, 11*. https://doi-org.stetson.idm.oclc.org/10.3402/qhw.v11.31636

Kirby, M. (2010). Gestalt equine psychotherapy. *Gestalt Journal of Australia and New Zealand, 6*(2), 60–68.

Lentini, J. A., & Knox, M. (2009). A qualitative and quantitative review of Equine Facilitated Psychotherapy (EFP) with children and adolescents. *The Open Complementary Medicine Journal, 1*, 51–57. https://doi.org/10.2174/1876391x00901010051

Lerner, H. (2019). A proposal for a comprehensive human-animal approach of evaluation for animal-assisted interventions. *International Journal of Environmental Research and Public Health, 16*(22). https://doi.org/10.3390/ijerph16224305

Matuszek, S. (2010). Animal-facilitated therapy in various patient populations: Systematic literature review. *Holistic Nursing Practice, 24*(4), 187–203. https://doi-org.libauth.purdueglobal.edu/10.1097/HNP.0b013e3181e90197

McCormick, A., & McCormick, M. (1997). *Horse sense and the human heart: What horses can teach us about trust, bonding, creativity and spirituality*. Health Communications.

McCullough, L., Risley-Curtiss, C., & Rorke, J. (2015). Equine facilitated psychotherapy: A pilot study of effect on posttraumatic stress symptoms in maltreated youth. *Journal of Infant, Child, and Adolescent Psychotherapy, 14*(2), 158–173. https://doi.org/10.1080/15289168.2015.1021658

Metcalf, O., Varker, T., Forbes, D., Phelps, A., Dell, L., DiBattista, A., Ralph, N., & O'Donnell, M. (2016). Efficacy of fifteen emerging interventions for the treatment of posttraumatic stress disorder: A systematic review. *Journal of Traumatic Stress, 29*(1), 88–92. https://doi.org/10.1002/jts.22070

Monfort Montolio, M., & Sancho-Pelluz, J. (2019). Animal-assisted therapy in the residential treatment of dual pathology. *International Journal of Environmental Research and Public Health, 17*(1). https://doi.org/10.3390/ijerph17010120

Muñoz-Solomando, A., Kendall, T., & Whittington, C. J. (2008). Cognitive behavioural therapy for children and adolescents. *Child and Adolescent Psychiatry, 21*, 331–337.

Naste, T. M., Price, M., Karol, J., Martin, L., Murphy, K., Miguel, J., & Spinazzola, J. (2018). Equine facilitated therapy for complex trauma (EFT-CT). *Journal of Child & Adolescent Trauma, 11*(3), 289–303. https://doi.org/10.1007/s40653-017-0187-3

Nevins, R., Finch, S., Hickling, E., & Barnett, S. (2012). The Saratoga WarHorse project: A case study of the treatment of psychological distress in a veteran of Operation Iraqi Freedom. *Advances in Mind-Body Medicine, 27*(4), 22–25.

Ogden, P., Pain, C., & Fisher, J. (2006). A sensorimotor approach to the treatment of trauma and dissociation. *Psychiatric Clinics of North America, 29*(1), 263–279. https://doi.org/10.1016/j.psc.2005.10.012

Randour, M. I. (2000). *Animal grace: Entering a spiritual relationship with our fellow creatures.* New World Library.

Ratliffe, K. T., & Sanekane, C. (2009). Equine-assisted therapies: Complementary medicine or not? *Australian Journal of Outdoor Education, 13*(2), 33–43.

Romaniuk, M., Evans, J., & Kidd, C. (2018). Evaluation of an equine-assisted therapy program for veterans who identify as 'wounded, injured or ill' and their partners. *PLoS ONE, 13*(9). https://doi-org.stetson.idm.oclc.org/10.1371/journal.pone.0203943

Rothe, E., Vega, B., Torres, R., Soler, S., & Pazos, R. (2005). From kids and horses: Equine facilitated psychotherapy for children. *International Journal of Clinical and Health Psychology, 5*(2), 373–383.

Russell, K. C., & Gillis, H. L. (2008). Experiential therapy in the mental health treatment of adolescents. *Journal of Therapeutic Schools and Programs, 3*, 47–74.

Schroeder, K., & Stroud, D. (2015). Equine-facilitated group work for women survivors of interpersonal violence. *The Journal for Specialists in Group Work, 40*(4), 365–386. https://doi.org/10.1080/01933922.2015.1082684

Schultz, P. N., Remick-Barlow, G. A., & Robbins, L. (2006). Equine-assisted psychotherapy: A mental health promotion/intervention modality for children who have experienced intra-family violence. *Health & Social Care in the Community, 15*(3), 265–271. https://doi.org/10.1111/j.1365-2524.2006.00684.x

Shambo, L., Seely, S., & Vonderfecht, H. (2010). A pilot study on equine-facilitated psychotherapy for trauma-related disorders. *Scientific and Educational Journal of Therapeutic Riding, 16*, 11–23.

Sheade, H., & Chandler, C. (2012, November 16). *Cultural diversity considerations in animal assisted counseling.* Paper based on a presentation at the 2012 Texas Counseling Association Conference, Article 76, 1–11.

Staudt, M., & Cherry, D. (2017). Equine facilitated therapy and trauma: Current knowledge future needs. *Advances in Social Work, 18*(1), 403–414.

Stauffer, C. (2006). *Leadership skills through equine-assisted learning: The participant's perspective* (Unpublished manuscript). Sienna Heights University, MI.

Trotter, K. S., Chandler, C. K., Goodwin-Bond, D., & Casey, J. (2008). A comparative study of the efficacy of group equine assisted counseling with at-risk children and adolescents. *Journal of Creativity in Mental Health, 3*(3), 254–284.

Trujillo, K. C., Kuo, G. T., Hull, M. L., Ingram, A. E., & Thurstone, C. C. (2020). Engaging adolescents: Animal assisted therapy for adolescents with psychiatric and substance use disorders. *Journal of Child & Family Studies, 29*(2), 307–314.

Velasquez, M., Crouch, C., Stephens, N., & DiClemente, C. (2016). *Group treatment for substance abuse: A stages-of-change therapy manual* (2nd ed.). The Guilford Press.

Warner, E., Koomar, J., Lary, B., & Cook, A. (2013). Can the body change the score? Application of sensory modulation principles in the treatment of traumatized adolescents in residential settings. *Journal of Family Violence, 28*(7), 729–738. https://doi.org/10.1007/s10896-013-9535-8

Whitley, R. (2009). *Therapeutic benefits of equine assisted psychotherapy for at-risk adolescents.* Retrieved from Pro Quest Dissertations and Theses. (UMI No. 3405795).

Wubbolding, R. E., & Brickell, J. (1999). *Counselling with reality therapy.* Speechmark Publishing.

Yalom, I. D. (1995). *The theory and practice of group psychotherapy* (4th ed.). Basic Books.

Yorke, J., Nugent, W., Strand, E., Bolen, R., New, J., & Davis, C. (2013). Equine-assisted therapy and its impact on cortisol levels of children and horses: A pilot study and meta-analysis. *Early Child Development and Care, 183*(7), 874–894. https://doi.org/10.1080/03004430.2012.693486

Conclusion

While this text is used to enhance the treatment provided by both mental health and substance use counselors, current and future research will continue to enhance these skills. Frontline counselors must be willing to share their experiences and knowledge by participating in ongoing research about clinical practice. Also, frontline counselors must be involved with their local, state, and national organizations to advocate for clients and to improve treatment protocols with multi-cultural sensitivity and an awareness of the complexity of co-occurring disorders. The National Association for Addictions Professionals (NAADAC) and the American Mental Health Counselors Association (AMHCA) are working together to provide enhanced education, training, and consultation for their respective members to assist in enhancing their treatment of individuals living with co-occurring disorders. The National Council for Mental Wellbeing has continued to advocate for those living with co-occurring disorders through community engagement and connecting with lawmakers to enact policy change. Additionally, the American Counseling Association (ACA) has also worked to provide ongoing support to counselor educators, vocational counselors, school counselors, and clinical counselors in the area of substance use training. To further enhance the counseling profession (substance use and mental health), it is strongly recommended that counselors join and participate in their national agencies to continue to improve integrated care. Information can be found at the following websites:

The National Association for Addictions Counselors (NAADAC). www.naadac.org
The American Mental Health Counselors Association (AMHCA). www.amhca.org
The National Council for Mental Wellbeing. www.thenationalcouncil.org
The American Counseling Association (ACA). www.counseling.org
The American Psychology Association (APA). www.apa.org

DOI: 10.4324/9781003220916-23

Index

12-steps 122, 177, 178

acceptance and commitment therapy (ACT) 25, 210, 211, 216
acupressure 242, 244, 245, 246, 249
acupuncture (NADA) 241, 242–250
acute pain 123
adolescents 18–23, 51, 52, 58, 62–64, 76, 112–119, 127
adverse childhood experiences (ACE) 6, 101, 104
affect 41, 42
Alcoholics Anonymous (AA) 83, 90, 177, 178, 179, 202
all or nothing thinking 181
ambivalence 177
American Mental Health Counseling Association (AMHCA) 20
American Society of Addiction Medicine (ASAM) 159, 166–169
amygdala 19, 242, 247, 249
androgyny 134
animal assisted activities (AAA) 245
animal assisted psychotherapies (AAP) 245
anxiety disorders 17, 18, 21, 23–26, 66, 67, 90–92, 100, 101, 114–116, 118, 124, 125, 127, 204, 214
arbitrary inferences 181
art therapy 227, 228
asexual 133–134
assessment 31, 61, 63, 72, 74, 93, 104, 110, 114, 120, 159–174
attention 102, 104, 106
attention deficit disorder (ADD) 60, 68, 203
attention deficit hyperactive disorder (ADHD) 58, 59, 61–68, 115, 116
audio hallucinations 29
automatic thoughts 177

baby boomer generation 123
Beck's Depression Inventory (BDI) 165
bias 24, 100, 106, 133, 143, 144, 147, 148, 149, 159, 219
biopsychosocial model 110, 162, 181
bipolar disorder/manic depression 18, 19, 20, 21, 22, 99, 100, 101, 201, 204

bipolar spectrum diagnostic scale (BSDS) 162, 166
bisexual 133
blaming 182
body dysmorphic disorder 41, 49
body mass index (BMI) 121

CAGE 165
catastrophizing 182
Centers for Disease Control and Prevention (CDC) 21
childhood sexual abuse/trauma 25, 26, 29, 30, 33, 34, 51, 66, 80, 109
chronic brain impairment 52, 196
chronic care model 124, 128
chronic pain 112, 162
cisgender 133
clinical interview (unstructured interview) 162
cognitive behavioral therapy (CBT) 36, 53, 54, 91, 130, 177, 179, 180–193
cognitive restructuring 177
concentration 101, 102, 103, 106
concurrent treatment 21, 29, 32
conduct disorder 102, 104, 107, 109, 110
consciousness 13, 29, 36, 59, 68, 69, 124, 210–213, 217, 219, 220, 221, 226, 227, 230, 233, 234, 241, 243
contemplation 188
continuum for neurological and evolutionary development (CONED) 228
co-occurring disorders 19, 21, 27, 29, 31, 33, 39, 40, 53, 54, 58, 59, 65, 70, 71, 73, 77, 78, 79, 81, 84, 89, 90, 91, 92, 93, 100, 101, 102, 104, 106, 110, 115, 121, 125, 128, 131, 132, 177, 205
core beliefs 81, 177
countertransference 77, 79, 87, 88, 89, 90, 91, 93, 112, 113
creative arts therapies (CATS) 25, 118, 226–237
cultural influence 52
culturally responsive treatment 143
culture 52, 79

dance therapy 32, 228, 233
delusions 60, 61, 62, 63, 64
depressive disorders 13, 17–21, 23–25, 30, 32, 33, 35, 43, 49, 62–65, 74, 76–78, 87, 91, 92,

99, 100, 101, 103, 114, 124, 161, 190, 214, 217
detoxification services 23, 159
dialectic behavioral therapy (DBT) 51, 210, 211, 215, 217
diathesis stress 17
dissociative reactions and disorder 33, 50

eating disorders 47, 121, 128, 129, 130, 133
eating disorder diagnostic scale (EDDS) 166
emotional freedom technique (EFT) 12, 25, 241, 242, 244–249
emotional reasoning 182
emotional support animal 254
energy psychology 229, 241, 242, 244, 245, 247, 249, 250
epigenetics 196, 201, 204, 242
equine assisted therapy (EAP) 261
ethnicity 94, 95, 98, 116, 143, 145, 146, 152
evidence based practice 33, 77, 78, 79, 91, 93, 113, 120, 130, 131, 177
executive functioning 102, 106, 114
exercise addiction 121, 129, 130, 133
eye movement desensitization regulation (EMDR) 25, 93, 227, 233, 234, 236, 237, 245, 247

failure to thrive 123
fallacy of fairness 182
family therapy 129
fetal alcohol syndrome 87
filtering 182
four-quadrant model approach 172

gamblers anonymous 122
gambling disorder 120, 121, 122, 125, 126, 127, 128, 129, 130, 131, 133
gay 133, 134, 137, 140
gender dysphoria 134, 135
gender fluid 134
gender nonconforming 134
gender responsive treatment 88–89
generalized anxiety disorder 7 item (GAD 7) 165
generativity 123
genetic addiction risk score (GARS®) 23, 24
gestalt therapy 234, 257
global appraisal of individual needs-initial (GAIN-I) 162, 165
group therapy 26, 80, 91, 112, 115, 129
guided visualization 241

heart rate variability 242, 246
hoarding disorder 41, 49
hospice care 124
human-animal bond 255
hyperactivity 47, 102, 106
hyperkinetic disease of infancy 103
hypnosis 210, 212–215
hysteroscopy 88

implicit bias 144
impulsivity/impulse control 67, 102, 103, 106, 109, 110
individual therapy 80, 91, 129
inpatient care 70, 160, 166, 170
insomnia 167
integrated care 3, 11, 12, 130, 171
internet addiction 120, 121, 126, 127, 128, 129, 130, 131, 132, 133
interpersonal abuse/problems 80
interpersonal partner violence 126
intersex 133, 134, 135

jumping to conclusions 182

kinesiology 241–246

lesbian 133, 134
levels of care 87
lifespan perspective 22
limbic brain 20, 31, 33, 51

magical thinking 113
maladaptive coping behaviors 40
males 29, 41, 42, 44, 48, 50, 51, 65, 82, 110, 111, 112, 113, 114, 115, 124, 125, 127, 128
Mandala 230
medication assisted treatment (MAT) 23, 196, 197–200, 205
meditation 210, 211, 215, 216, 217, 219, 220
megacognition 177
menses 41, 130
menopause 88
mental health disorders 19, 20, 28, 29, 32, 33, 43, 58, 59, 65, 70, 73, 74, 77, 78, 100, 101, 102, 104, 112, 114, 115, 120, 128, 164
mentalization-based therapy 92
meridians 242
microaggressions 134, 147
mindfulness 25, 51, 66, 90, 93, 118, 210, 211, 215–220, 257, 260
mindfulness-based behavioral therapies 25, 51, 66, 90, 93, 118, 210, 211, 215–220
minnesota multiphasic personality inventory 2 (MMPI-2) 165
molecules of emotion 229
mood disorders 39, 40, 41, 42, 50, 51, 52, 54, 63, 69, 114, 125, 129
morbid obesity 121, 129
motivation 177
motivational interviewing (MI) 131, 177, 189–192
Mozart Effect, The 229
multicultural competence 52
multidimensional family therapy (MDFT) 118
multidisciplinary treatment 59
music therapy 227

National Association for Alcoholism and Drug Abuse Counselors (NAADAC) 160
negative symptoms 25, 26, 50, 60, 61, 70, 72, 82, 85

neuroscience/neurobiology 21, 22, 42, 44, 50, 67
neurotransmitters 45, 52, 199, 204
nicotine replacement therapies (NRT) 199–200
non-suicidal self-injury (NSSI) 79, 85, 93
nutrition 52, 54, 67, 93, 129, 196, 201, 202–206

obesity 112, 121, 127, 128, 129
obsessive compulsive disorder 41, 49, 203
oniomania 122
oppositional defiant disorder 102, 104, 108, 109, 110
orthomolecular psychiatry 52, 196, 201
osteoporosis 88, 92
outpatient treatment 70, 71, 74, 89, 160
overgeneralizing 182
overweight 122, 128

palliative care 124
pap smear 88
paranoia 60, 65, 66, 82, 83
parental attachment 112, 180
personality clusters 60, 79, 81, 82, 83, 84, 85, 86, 87, 88, 89, 90
personality disorders 60, 77, 78, 79, 80, 81, 82, 83, 84, 85, 86, 87, 88, 89, 90, 91, 92, 93, 109, 111, 114, 125, 128, 129
personalization 182
person-centered therapy 189
pet therapy 255
pharmacodynamics 196, 201
pharmacokinetics 197, 201
pharmacology 25
polyvagal theory 242
positive and negative syndrome scale (PANSS) 165
positive symptoms 60, 61
posttraumatic stress disorder (PTSD) 21, 22, 28–31, 34, 42, 50, 51, 69, 124, 125, 126, 127
posttraumatic stress disorder (PCL-C, S, M) 162, 166
pre-contemplative 177, 187–188
process use disorders 40, 120, 121, 122, 123, 131, 132
PROMIS (Emotional Distress-Depression Short Form) 164
public health 22, 25
psychodrama 226, 227, 234–237
psychological decompensation 42
psychosis psychotic disorders 45, 46, 58, 59, 60, 61, 62, 63, 64, 65, 66, 67, 68, 69, 70, 71, 72, 73, 82
psychospiritual crisis 36
psychotropic medication 70, 71, 72, 74, 107, 113, 114, 115, 131, 197–200
puberty 112

quatrune brain map 231, 233, 235, 236
queer/questioning 133

race 5, 98, 144, 145, 152
rational emotive behavioral therapy (REBT) 180
reality therapy 258

recovery programming 90, 109, 170
reflective local practice 144
religion 129, 143, 146, 161, 211, 218, 219, 220, 221, 233
residential treatment 160, 166, 169, 170
resilience 4, 8, 246
reward center of the brain 24, 33, 45
Reward Deficiency Syndrome (RDS) 23, 24
rolling with resistance 177, 189

schema 178
schizophasia 60
schizophrenia disorders 60, 61, 62, 63, 64, 65, 67, 68, 78, 82, 84, 111, 201, 204
screening 31, 32, 160
self-evaluation 144, 148, 151–153
self-help groups 122, 178
self-help sponsor 178
self-report 32, 114, 163
semi-structured interview 163
service animal 254
severity index 164
sexual addiction 120, 121, 122, 123, 124, 131, 132
shopping addiction 120, 124, 125, 131
should statements 182
Socratic questioning 178
somatic expressive therapies 25
somatic therapies 119, 226, 227, 229, 231, 233, 235, 236, 237, 241, 242, 247
solution focused therapy 258
spiritual emergence 29, 30, 36
spirituality 30, 146, 161, 178, 179, 182, 185, 210, 211, 218, 219, 220, 221
stages of change model 187
stagnation 107, 124
stimulants 102, 113, 114, 116, 130
Strengthening Families Programs (SFP) 26, 226
structured interview 162, 163
subconscious 180, 181, 211, 213, 214
subjective level of distress (SUDs) 244
Substance Abuse and Mental Health Services Administration (SAMHSA) 29, 31, 160, 164, 172, 173, 200
Substance Abuse Subtle Screening Inventory 4 (SASSI-4) 165
substance use disorders 19–21, 25, 26, 29–33, 39, 40, 51, 53, 58, 59, 63, 65–67, 69–71, 73, 74, 77–81, 84, 85, 87–93, 100–102, 104, 106–109, 111–116, 120, 121, 123, 125, 131, 159–170, 200, 202
suicidal ideation, attempt, completion 33, 41, 47, 93, 109, 112, 168, 199

tardive dyskinesia 30
therapeutic boundaries 44, 48
thought field therapy 241, 242, 244, 245, 247, 249
transference 44, 49, 50, 52, 65, 66, 106, 137, 213, 257, 260
trauma 3–14, 17, 23, 24, 25, 27–34, 87, 88, 89, 90–94, 98, 99, 101, 104, 105, 112–119, 127,

129, 161, 162, 166, 168, 211, 214–216, 220,
226–230, 233–237, 241–250, 254–256,
258–263
trauma-informed perspective 89

violence 7, 8, 9, 62, 75, 88, 89, 90, 91, 101, 105,
108, 114, 116, 118
visual hallucinations 29, 30, 34, 39, 46, 47

WHO Disability Assessment Schedule 2
(WHODAS 2.0) 165
withdrawal management 54, 64, 123, 128, 131,
164, 166, 170, 197–199
women 29, 41, 42, 44, 47, 48, 50, 54, 65, 111, 112,
113, 114, 115, 125, 127, 128
World Health Organization (WHO) 22, 35

young mania rating scale 166

Made in the USA
Coppell, TX
25 March 2022

75535653R00162